Paola De Bernardi • Danny Azucar

Innovation in Food Ecosystems

Entrepreneurship for a Sustainable Future

Paola De Bernardi
Department of Management
University of Turin, School of
Management and Economics
Turin, Italy

Danny Azucar
Department of Management
University of Turin, School of
Management and Economics
Turin, Italy

ISSN 1431-1941 ISSN 2197-716X (electronic)
Contributions to Management Science
ISBN 978-3-030-33504-5 ISBN 978-3-030-33502-1 (eBook)
https://doi.org/10.1007/978-3-030-33502-1

© Springer Nature Switzerland AG 2020
This work is subject to copyright. All rights are reserved by the Publisher, whether the whole or part of the material is concerned, specifically the rights of translation, reprinting, reuse of illustrations, recitation, broadcasting, reproduction on microfilms or in any other physical way, and transmission or information storage and retrieval, electronic adaptation, computer software, or by similar or dissimilar methodology now known or hereafter developed.
The use of general descriptive names, registered names, trademarks, service marks, etc. in this publication does not imply, even in the absence of a specific statement, that such names are exempt from the relevant protective laws and regulations and therefore free for general use.
The publisher, the authors, and the editors are safe to assume that the advice and information in this book are believed to be true and accurate at the date of publication. Neither the publisher nor the authors or the editors give a warranty, expressed or implied, with respect to the material contained herein or for any errors or omissions that may have been made. The publisher remains neutral with regard to jurisdictional claims in published maps and institutional affiliations.

This Springer imprint is published by the registered company Springer Nature Switzerland AG.
The registered company address is: Gewerbestrasse 11, 6330 Cham, Switzerland

Foreword (1): The Future of Food Ecosystems

The food system encompasses a multitude of actors, elements, and processes that relate to the production, processing, distribution, preparation, consumption, and disposal of food. It includes the environment, people, businesses, infrastructure, institutions, and the effects of their activities on our society, economy, landscape, and climate.

It is a *complex* system made up of many interrelations—and it is *adaptive*—influenced by endogenous and exogenous factors.

Today's food systems are evolving to meet consumers' ever-changing demand for healthy and nutritious food that is accessible and affordable for all, ensuring high levels of food safety and traceability coherent with sustainable and resource-efficient business models, and aiming to conserve our planet's precious resources for future generations. People are becoming aware of the deep impact the current food system has had on the planet and society and are demanding a new way of producing and delivering food.

The global food system still faces many interlinked challenges: growing consumer demand for ever higher quality ingredients, locally grown products based on climate smart food systems adaptive to climate change, conservation of natural resources, and implementation of resource-efficient circular economy principles, all the while reducing the environmental footprint and safeguarding ecosystems which includes soil quality and pollination. At the same time, there remains the need to address hunger and malnutrition, reduce the incidence of non-communicable diet-related diseases, and help all citizens adopt sustainable and healthy diets for good health and well-being.

In this context, food systems are recognised as one of the main drivers of global environmental change and are now known to impact many socio-economic dimensions. Indeed, according to the UN (2019), food production around the world currently accounts for 40% of land use, 30% of greenhouse gas emissions, and 70% of freshwater consumption. What's more, the world population is expected to increase from 7 to 10 billion people by 2050, and global demand for food is expected to increase roughly 60% (UN, 2019). Meanwhile, the process of exponential urbanisation will cause a rise in the percentage of people living in urban areas from 50% to 80%. This process of urbanisation creates the negative effects of an increase in natural resource use in urban areas depending largely on imported resources, which in turn creates the need for longer supply chains resulting in increased greenhouse gas emissions and more food waste.

It is clear that food systems must be transformed through boosting innovation while empowering communities, industries, institutions, policymakers, and civil society to contribute to the solution of the grand challenges mentioned above.

As a result of the changes and the pertinent challenges, it is now imperative to treat these challenges together using a multidimensional and pluri-disciplinary approach, in order to manage interdependencies between key parts of the food system and avoiding the risks of overlooking trade-offs and synergies. That means thinking of the food system as a broad *innovation ecosystem* that leads to new business models and value-added products, goods, and services, meeting the needs, values, and expectations of society in a responsible and ethical way. Behavioural research on consumerism, new farming methods, new ingredients, and the adoption of digital technologies to food production and delivery processes shows that there are big opportunities for change.

The key levers for transforming the food system and delivering impact have been identified as innovative forward-thinking approaches that include growing entrepreneurial skills to develop the right innovations and bring them to market, as well as embracing digitalisation and data analytics to find new solutions which will feed the world, address health issues, and tackle the environmental crisis. In order to provide sustainability for, and 'future proof' our food ecosystems, food institutions and stakeholders must be able to encourage innovation, promote sustainable living, and include every member of the food ecosystem when proposing innovations or radical transformations.

These transformations will require unprecedented collaboration between stakeholders, and both radical and incremental innovation across the entire food value chain, including food production and processing side streams. In many cases, such innovations tend to arise in a 'bottom-up' fashion from small and medium-sized enterprises (SMEs) and emerging start-ups. Unfortunately, clear guidelines or 'blueprints' for identifying entrepreneurial individuals and recommendations on the best methods to support their business ventures are still scant from both literature and practice.

This book provides an essential synthesis of the nexus between innovation and entrepreneurship in food ecosystems and an in-depth discussion of the processes seen throughout the developmental cycle of start-ups: from the identification of entrepreneurial talent, identifying business opportunities, designing the business, funding business ventures, and the transition from individual entrepreneurship centres to promote innovation to the creation of multicentre and interdisciplinary innovation ecosystems.

It is an important piece for researchers and academics who wish to help drive sustainability in food ecosystems through innovation and entrepreneurship. It provides clear examples of real-world scenarios of food ecosystems that provide the reader with a window to the many possibilities for entrepreneurship and innovation in food ecosystems.

I wish you joy and insights from reading this important book.

EIT Food, Heverlee, Belgium

Andy Zynga

Foreword (2): 'Open Innovation in Food Ecosystems'

The European food system—from farmers and fishermen to consumers—is currently delivering ample and safe food to Europeans, who benefit from a historically unique and stable supply of high-quality and healthy food year-round based on the Mediterranean diet. The food system at large is providing jobs for millions of people and income for thousands of smaller companies and cooperatives (EU, 2019)[1]. Yet, the global food system still faces a range of challenges, including the triple burden of malnutrition (i.e. undernutrition, over-nutrition, and micronutrient deficiencies), biodiversity loss, climate change, resource scarcity, growing and ageing populations, urbanisation, food waste, and food poverty. This requires food systems' *transformation* with a shift towards more *sustainable* and *healthy* diets aiming to ensure food and nutrition security for all, in essence food that is good for you and good for the planet.

Innovative strategies and solutions that tackle systemic challenges, having high social, environmental, and economic impact, will play an essential role, becoming an unavoidable interplay of various parties who combine their knowledge, turning challenges into opportunities.

The idea that ad hoc interactions to provide solutions and business opportunities to challenges in food ecosystems is no longer the rule but the exception. Economies and industries have recently transitioned to a system of global innovations, where collaborations based on compatible and complementary differences must be sought.

Companies most likely to thrive in the emerging complex economies are, not surprisingly, those that are able to innovate effectively in collaborative environments. Effective innovations in the increasingly interconnected global environment will therefore depend on co-creation efforts that transcend individual company or organisational boundaries.

---

[1] Niels Halberg, Henk Westhoek, The added value of a Food Systems Approach in Research and Innovation, European Commission, July 2019.

In this context, food companies are looking beyond the walls of their own organisations, actively seeking knowledge, technology, and partners to implement a portion of the innovation process. They can orchestrate open innovation strategies, forming external networks to develop innovation processes among the partners they collaborate with (i.e. chain partners, knowledge institutions, governmental bodies, and even competitors), thus contributing to tackle food system's challenges in the whole ecosystem.

Open innovation ecosystem approach involves the sharing of knowledge between multiple stakeholders in order to gain, at the same time, sustainability and business goals, co-creating and co-sharing product and service innovation. Alliances, partnerships, and alignments in the food ecosystem, downstream, upstream, and side-stream, are paramount for cross-fertilisation and synergy, representing a paradigm shift towards accelerating co-development of sustainable innovation, with alignment of the entire value chain with a consumer-centric focus.

Successful food companies and emerging start-ups are usually those that are able to identify and exploit opportunities to co-create value by challenging the traditional 'closed' approaches to research and development and innovation. Adopting the notion of open innovation within food ecosystems involves embracing both internal and external resources and 'paths to markets'—and especially, moves food stakeholders away from the idea that successful innovation requires strict control, and stimulates towards a set of more organisation-wide 'open principles'.

This book provides an overview of entrepreneurship and innovation in food ecosystems, and a critical discussion of how 'open innovation' is currently adopted and implemented among food companies and emerging start-ups. Specifically, the authors provide a range of important examples and a case study representing a comprehensive synthesis of the emergence of open innovation strategies in food ecosystems. Furthermore, the book highlights the role of academia, food companies, and research institutions in creating successful ecosystems centred on a culture of open innovation. Finally, the authors present a summary of the main challenges in the creation of food ecosystems and highlight the possible implications for the future of open innovation in food ecosystems.

The authors harness this reality and discuss specific recommendations to facilitate this process and engage in open innovation in food ecosystems with the involvement of food companies, start-ups, and individual stakeholders in the so-called knowledge triangle.

The authors have clearly highlighted that successful open innovation culture requires slight transformations across the entire food value chain, presenting critical discussions, insights, and recommendations to make these transitions towards open innovation in food ecosystems successful.

Open Innovation Senior Manager,
Barilla Group
Parma, Italy

Giancarlo Riboldi

Preface

Recent experience has taught me that many students and scholars cultivate ideas that have the power to drive meaningful transformations in the food ecosystem but oftentimes lack knowledge and resources to turn them into viable business ventures.

Many authors suggest that a massive barrier to translate research and innovation into business ventures is the low level of essential business creation skills among academics and low levels of research expertise from business experts, e.g. significant amounts of funding are often lost when supporting new ventures that are not scientifically proven to work, and breakthrough scientific discoveries are seldom supported by business creation experts.

This gap in multidisciplinary knowledge and entrepreneurship mindset for business innovation is what ignited my motivation to write this book.

Entrepreneurship and innovation have become extremely relevant in the European Union especially since the passing and approval of the Sustainable Development Goals (SDGs).

With this book, we address the intersection of entrepreneurship, innovation, and sustainability in food ecosystems and critically discuss the importance of transforming food production and consumption in order to achieve worldwide sustainability goals.

This book is specifically written for aspiring entrepreneurs, students, food ecosystem stakeholders, and organisations seeking to create a new systemic approach for the 'future of food'. Today, food companies find themselves operating in a competitive and interconnected market that inevitably reduces the life cycle of products and services launched on the market, thus affecting margins and performances. In this scenario, it is easy to understand how it is no longer possible to confine innovation processes, but it is appropriate to open them to collaboration with an extensive network of external actors to find new ideas, leverage external resources, develop new products, and generate sustainability and value for the whole ecosystem. To do this, it is necessary to be able to generate and consolidate relationships with a wide range of players, interfacing not only with suppliers and customers along the food value chain but also including companies specialising in innovation, research centres and universities, and business incubators, accelerators, technology parks, and ecosystems of innovation that consider start-ups one of its founding elements.

The main contribution of this book is to provide a basis of support for stakeholder-led innovation and entrepreneurial endeavours. It describes how multi-actor approaches and multidisciplinary environments can co-create and co-share innovative and sustainable solutions that can tackle present and future challenges threatening our food ecosystems.

Turin, Italy

Paola De Bernardi

Contents

1 The Food System Grand Challenge: A Climate Smart and Sustainable Food System for a Healthy Europe 1
    1.1   Introducing Actual Food Systems: *From "Farm to Fork" to "Industry to Fork"* 2
        1.1.1   Grand Challenges Related to Actual Food Systems 2
        1.1.2   A Focus on the European Scenario 4
        1.1.3   Global Food Systems in a Networked Society 5
    1.2   Sustainable Development in Food Systems: Highlighting a Need for Transition 6
    1.3   Holistic Thinking and Sustainable Food Systems 8
        1.3.1   A Sustainable Food System Approach: The Food System Wheel 10
        1.3.2   The Food System Development Paradigm 11
    1.4   Addressing the Sustainability Paradigm in the European Union . . 12
        1.4.1   Safeguarding the Agricultural Sector and Food Consumers 13
        1.4.2   Managing Waste: The Waste Framework Directive and Other Network Policies 14
        1.4.3   Transitioning Toward a Circular Economy: The Circular Economy Action Plan 15
    1.5   From Food Systems to Food Ecosystems 15
        1.5.1   Innovation as a Driver in Food Ecosystems 17
        1.5.2   Sustainable Innovation in Food Ecosystems 18
    1.6   Entrepreneurship and Innovation as Key Elements for Sustainability 19
    1.7   Conclusion 20
    References 22

2 The Role of Universities in Harnessing Entrepreneurial Opportunities 27

2.1 Introduction: Entrepreneurs and Entrepreneurial Opportunities in Food Systems 27

2.2 It All Begins with an Opportunity 30

2.3 The Focus on Entrepreneurship 31

2.4 Entrepreneurial Opportunity 35

2.5 Opportunity Discovery and Creation in Food Systems 39

2.5.1 Opportunity Creation: Tangible Resources 41

2.5.2 Opportunity Recognition: Intangible Resources 41

2.6 Entrepreneurial Universities 42

2.7 Entrepreneurship Education 46

2.8 Entrepreneurship Centers 49

2.8.1 Technology Transfer Offices/Centers 52

2.8.2 Incubators 53

2.8.3 Accelerators 54

2.9 Triple-Helix Approaches 55

2.9.1 The Knowledge Triangle 56

2.10 Conclusion 58

References 60

3 Innovation and Entrepreneurial Ecosystems: Structure, Boundaries, and Dynamics 73

3.1 Introducing the Ecosystems Concept 74

3.2 Innovation Ecosystems 75

3.2.1 Differences Between Innovation Ecosystems and Other Cluster Approaches 76

3.2.2 An Innovation Ecosystems Mapping Effort: The Ecosystem Pie Model 76

3.3 Entrepreneurial Ecosystems 79

3.3.1 The Emergence of Entrepreneurial Ecosystems 81

3.3.2 Limitations and Further Developments of Current Studies 82

3.4 Structure of Innovation and Entrepreneurial Ecosystems 83

3.4.1 Similarities 83

3.4.2 Differences 85

3.4.3 Boundaries 86

3.4.4 Personal and Systemic 90

3.4.5 Dynamics 90

3.4.6 Change, Growth, and Performance 91

3.4.7 Drivers 95

3.4.8 Challenges 97

3.5 Food Systems 98

3.6 Conclusion 99

References 100

Contents

4 Innovation for Future Proofing the Food Ecosystem: Emerging Approaches ... 105
4.1	Introduction	105
4.2	Innovation in Food Ecosystems	107
4.3	Open Innovation in Food Ecosystems	108
4.4	Emerging Food Approaches	110
4.5	Vertical Farms	117
	4.5.1 Aeroponics	118
	4.5.2 Aquaponics	118
	4.5.3 Hydroponics	119
4.6	Short Food Supply Chains	120
4.7	Precision Agriculture	123
4.8	Bio-Fertilizers	125
4.9	Meat Alternatives	126
4.10	Waste Reduction	127
4.11	Health and Wellbeing	128
4.12	Conclusion	130
References		131

5 Entrepreneurial Food Ecosystem: Strategic Driver to Boost Resilience and Sustainability ... 135
5.1	Introduction	135
5.2	Beyond Linearity in Food Supply Chains: Systems Thinking	137
5.3	Resilience and Sustainability in Food Ecosystem	140
	5.3.1 Barriers to Resilience	141
5.4	Holistic Innovation and Entrepreneurship	143
5.5	Systems Thinking for Food System Transformation	145
5.6	Responsible Research and Innovation (RRI) and Food Systems	148
5.7	Multi-level Innovation and Entrepreneurship	152
5.8	Conclusions	153
References		156

6 Startups and Knowledge Sharing in Ecosystems: Incumbents and New Ventures ... 161
6.1	Introduction	162
6.2	Knowledge into Practice	165
6.3	Startups and High Growth Firms (HGFs)	166
6.4	Aligning Solutions to Consumer Needs	169
	6.4.1 Market Research	170
	6.4.2 Competitive Landscape	171
	6.4.3 SWOT Analysis	171
6.5	From Ideas to Business Models and Business Plans	173
	6.5.1 Writing a Business Plan	173
	6.5.2 Company Overview: 'About Us'	174
	6.5.3 Product or Service Offered	174

	6.5.4	Target Market, Customers, and Competition	174
	6.5.5	Sales and Marketing Strategies	175
	6.5.6	Operations	175
	6.5.7	The Startup Team	176
	6.5.8	The Financial Plan	176
6.6		Digitalization as a Driver for Entrepreneurial Ecosystems and Business Creation: Fact or Fiction	177
6.7		Startups and Innovation Ecosystems: Do They Work?	179
6.8		Your Startup, Your Brand	182
	6.8.1	Brand Positioning	183
	6.8.2	Sustainability and Brand Creation	183
6.9		Conclusion	184
References			185

7 Innovative and Sustainable Food Business Models

7.1	Introduction	190
7.2	Business Model	190
7.3	Business Model Innovation	192
7.4	Business Model Innovation for Sustainability	197
7.5	Circular Business Models	198
7.6	Business Modelling: Tools for Designing New Business Models	202
7.7	Business Models in the Food Sector: Where Are We Going?	207

	7.7.1	Food-Tech	208
	7.7.2	Agri-Tech	210
	7.7.3	Food Digital Platform	211
	7.7.4	Urban Food	212
	7.7.5	Food on Demand	213
7.8		Conclusion	214
References			215

7 Innovative and Sustainable Food Business Models 189

8 Funding Innovation and Entrepreneurship ... 223

8.1	Introduction	223
8.2	The Supply of Finance	226
8.3	Venture Capital	230

	8.3.1	Structure	233
	8.3.2	Investment Strategy	234
	8.3.3	Corporate Governance	236
	8.3.4	Alignment of Interest: Carried Interest	239
8.4		Corporate Venture Capital	239
8.5		Conclusions	242
References			243

9 A European Food Ecosystem: The EIT Food Case Study 245
   9.1 Introduction: The European Institute of Innovation
       and Technology (EIT) 246
       9.1.1 Knowledge and Innovation Communities (KICs) 249
   9.2 EIT Food: Pan-European Food Network 250
       9.2.1 EIT Food Co-location Centers 251
   9.3 EIT Food Vision, Mission, Strategy, Values and Goals 256
   9.4 EIT Food Strategic Pillars and Business Areas 261
       9.4.1 Innovation 262
       9.4.2 EIT Food's Innovation Programs 263
       9.4.3 Education 264
       9.4.4 Business Creation and Entrepreneurship 264
       9.4.5 Communication and Public Engagement 265
   9.5 EIT Food Growth Strategy 267
   9.6 EIT Food Organizational Structure 268
       9.6.1 EIT Food Organizational Governance Structure 268
   9.7 Multi-Annual Business Models 269
       9.7.1 Financial Sustainability 272
   9.8 EIT Community 272
       9.8.1 EIT Food Partnerships 272
       9.8.2 Partner Categories 273
   9.9 Start-Up Support 275
       9.9.1 Rising Food Stars 275
       9.9.2 EIT Food Sparks 276
   9.10 EIT Food Impact 276
       9.10.1 EIT Food Impact through Synergies 276
       9.10.2 Key Performance Indicators 277
   9.11 Conclusions 278
   References 279

List of Figures

Fig. 1.1	How food systems are connected with all the SDGs. Source: Azote for Stockholm Resilience Center, Stockholm University (2016)...	7
Fig. 1.2	The food system wheel. Source: FAO (2018)	11
Fig. 1.3	The food system development paradigm. Source: FAO (2018)....	12
Fig. 1.4	The CAP food system vision. Source: Recanati et al. (2018)	13
Fig. 3.1	The ecosystem pie model. Source: Talmar et al. (2018)	78
Fig. 3.2	Structural framework for entrepreneurial ecosystems. Source: Autio et al. (2018)	80
Fig. 5.1	Diagram of food system simplified. Source: Food 2030	139
Fig. 5.2	Holistic model of food ecosystems. Source: NourishLife.Org (2019)	147
Fig. 6.1	SWOT analysis grid output—food system example. Source: Author's elaboration	172
Fig. 7.1	Business model canvas. Source: Based on Osterwalder and Pigneur (2010)	203
Fig. 7.2	Lean business model canvas. Source: Based on Maurya (2012)	204
Fig. 7.3	Sustainable business model canvas. Source: Based on Joyce and Paquin (2016)	206
Fig. 7.4	Circular business model. Source: Planing (2015), adapted from Ellen MacArthur Foundation (2014) and Stahel and Reday-Mulvey (1981)	207
Fig. 8.1	The investment cycle. Source: Adapted from Cardullo (1999)	228
Fig. 8.2	Investment process. Source: Own elaboration	237
Fig. 8.3	The startup funding cone. Source: Own elaboration	238
Fig. 9.1	Knowledge and innovation communities. Source: EIT (2019c)	250
Fig. 9.2	Visual cloud of EIT food members. Source: EIT Food (2018)	256
Fig. 9.3	EIT food co-location centers. Source: EIT Food (2018)	257
Fig. 9.4	EIT food estimated budget. Source: EIT Food (2018)	258
Fig. 9.5	Four pillars of EIT food. Source: EIT Food (2019b)	261

Fig. 9.6	Smart entrepreneurial development model. Source: EIT Food (2018)	266
Fig. 9.7	EIT food organizational structure. Source: EIT Food (2018)	269
Fig. 9.8	Multi-annual business model. Source: EIT Food (2018)	273
Fig. 9.9	Projected impacts of EIT food. Source: EIT Food (2018)	278

List of Tables

Table 2.1	Triple-Helix approaches	55
Table 3.1	From clusters to innovation ecosystems	77
Table 3.2	Invariants of the ecosystem approach	87
Table 3.3	Conceptual overview of innovation and entrepreneurial ecosystems	92
Table 4.1	Inventory of possible R&I breakthroughs	112
Table 4.2	High tech indoor farming	120
Table 6.1	Business concepts 101	168
Table 6.2	Solo and partnered—what's in it for me?	168
Table 7.1	Definitions of a business model	193
Table 7.2	Business model innovation definitions	195
Table 7.3	Sustainable business model definitions	199
Table 7.4	Sustainable business model innovation definitions	201
Table 8.1	Life cycle phases and types of operation	231
Table 8.2	The corporate venture capital models	242
Table 9.1	List of member countries and partners by country	252
Table 9.2	Governance, management, and executive positions of EIT food	270
Table 9.3	EIT food core processes	271

xxi

Chapter 1
The Food System Grand Challenge: A Climate Smart and Sustainable Food System for a Healthy Europe

Abstract Current food systems rely on mass production processes that should be designed to provide people with nurturing and healthy food, and to ensure food access to every region around the world. However, unprecedented growing world populations, emerging production technologies, and diverging agendas from food system stakeholders have created a chasm in food systems. This chasm is evident in the alarming rate food production is straining environmental systems, as well as in the current rates of malnutrition and lack of food access. Indeed, evidence suggests that food production is one of the main contributors to climate change, biodiversity loss, freshwater use, and land systems change. Due to the threats posed by current, interconnected, global food systems to health and environmental degeneracy, attempts to transform them in a more sustainable way are increasingly emerging all-around the world. In particular, the trend is to shift from isolated and individualized agendas to collective and integrated strategies with combined and interdependent targets that can effectively support the actual transformation of food systems to be more sustainable. In this chapter, we discuss how this sustainable transition of current food production and consumption systems may be spurred across multiple scales. We begin with an analysis of the Sustainable Development Goals (SDGs) and discuss how they are all in some way related to multi-actor and trans-disciplinary food systems. We provide a synthesis of the current policies and strategies that most effectively drive toward a more holistic thinking of food systems. In this sense, the European scenario is particularly analysed, by introducing the concept of food ecosystems and how they help to address the sustainability paradigm. Finally, how the presence of an entrepreneurial mindset, skills, and opportunities can spur sustainable innovation is taken into consideration.

Keywords Food systems · Grand challenges · Sustainable development goals (SDGs) · Food ecosystems · Food sustainability

---

© Springer Nature Switzerland AG 2020
P. De Bernardi, D. Azucar, *Innovation in Food Ecosystems*, Contributions to Management Science, https://doi.org/10.1007/978-3-030-33502-1_1

1.1 Introducing Actual Food Systems: *From "Farm to Fork" to "Industry to Fork"*

Historical trends in human activity have been creating mounting pressures on Earth's ecosystems and its natural resource supplies. In this regard, traditional food systems, coupled with economic growth, are recognized as the most significant cause of global environmental change (Willett et al., 2019). The expression food system is commonly employed in discussions about nutrition, meal production and consumption, health, economic development, and agriculture. Food systems can be described as adaptive systems exhibiting complex dynamics and oriented to feed the world's growing population (Ingram, 2011; Jagustović et al., 2019), including both the inputs needed (e.g., natural resources) and outputs generated (e.g., innovations and sustainable solutions) within the food supply chain. Indeed, they comprise all the processes, infrastructures, and actors involved throughout each level in the agri-food chain, going from food production, aggregation, and processing that originate from agriculture, forestry or fisheries, to food distribution, consumption, and disposal (Muth et al., 2019).

Our current food system, which is often focused on mass production, is a result of the industrial revolution that fuelled large-scale industrialization and a mass labour market (Johnson, 1941). The industrial revolution witnessed a shift from self-relying people for food sources, to counting on bigger food organizations and productions, thereby slowly improving food security and diversity (Kamminga & Cunningham, 1995; Overton, 1996). These processes, however, inadvertently also led to a dramatic lengthening of the food supply chains, thereby intensifying the need for resources and energy and the emission output of global food industries. So, in its attempts to provide greater food access for the world's populations, the food industry slowly transitioned from a system of "farm to fork" to "industry to fork".

1.1.1 Grand Challenges Related to Actual Food Systems

Those fundamental shifts in agricultural production have undoubtedly exacerbated the human impact on the so-called grand challenges, environmental, and societal problems that need to be addressed in a few decades or will lead to disruptive global consequences (Robertson & Swinton, 2005; Rounsevell et al., 2012). Examples of grand challenges related to current food production methods are the extensive use of fertile land and freshwater, ocean acidification, high levels of greenhouse gas (GHG) emissions, the disruption of nitrogen and phosphorus cycles, and the contribution to biodiversity loss (Hoekstra & Wiedmann, 2014; Rockström et al., 2009; Steffen et al., 2015; Whitmee et al., 2015). Therefore, actual food systems have led to a more significant impact of the ecological footprint of human activities, which increased its demand from requiring less than one 'Earth' worth of natural resources for healthy living in 1961 to needing two Earths by 2030 (Global Footprint Network, 2019).

According to recent estimates of the Food and Agriculture Organization (FAO) of the United Nations, for example, around 40% of global land is used for agricultural purposes (Foley et al., 2005). Moreover, as a result of the emergence of productivity-enhancing technologies and significant increases in natural resources employment for farming, agricultural production more than tripled between 1960 and 2015 (FAO, 2017). The burden that food systems place on the environment is also evident in marine systems. Oceans appear overexploited for about 90% with 60% of world fish stocks full and more than 30% overfished (Willett et al., 2019). As a consequence, food production is responsible for about 30% of GHG emissions (Vermeulen, Campbell, & Ingram, 2012) and 70% of freshwater use (Steffen et al., 2015), while global marine fisheries have experienced a steady decline in catch throughout the past couple of decades (Food and Agriculture UN, 2016).

Krijin J. Poppe, chair of the independent Food 2030 European Commission expert group defined the food system as a system far from being resilient. "It has too many negative effects on the environment and on our health. The system delivers more affordable food at larger quantities than ever, but this goes at the expense of future generations. This is an important insight for the direction in which we have to innovate the food system. At a global level this has been recognised by the adoption of the Sustainable Development Goals (SDGs) and the signing of the Paris' Agreement on climate change (COP21)" (European Commission, 2018d, p. 3).

Given the above, it is clear that, in efforts to ensure food availability to a significant number of people, traditional food production approaches have progressively compromised the world's capability to fulfil its future food and nutritional needs (De Bernardi, Bertello, & Venuti, 2019; De Bernardi, Bertello, Venuti, & Zardini, 2019). This has sharply highlighted the necessity of addressing grand challenges through a transition towards more sustainable systems, adjusting actual food production practices for ensuring they become suitable to the evolving availability of resources in the global environment. Some experts predict that if food production and consumption patterns continue in line with the traditionally adopted Western models, these environmental pressures will only intensify in occurrence and magnitude and steady increases in population growth could further aggravate them (Davis et al., 2016; Jalava, Kummu, Porkka, Siebert, & Varis, 2014; Springmann, Godfray, Rayner, & Scarborough, 2016; Tilman & Clark, 2014). In 2010 the global population was estimated at 6.8 billion people, and this number is projected to reach between 8.5 and 10 billion people by the year 2050, a 34% increase (Samir & Lutz, 2017). Most of the population increases are expected to occur in the world's developing countries and urban areas, with an expected growth of more than 70% of the global urban population. Therefore, urbanization will bring additional changes in food production and consumption behaviours within cities. Providing healthy and nutritious food for such an increased number of world inhabitants signifies that the subsequent food demand will directly amplify the existing environmental pressure exerted by food production on the planet. Especially, it is projected that by 2050 the global food production, in quantity terms, would have to increase by 60% in order to meet the expected food demand (Alexandratos & Bruinsma, 2012; Tilman, Balzer, Hill, & Befort, 2011).

Besides representing one of the most significant environmental challenges of current ages, food also poses itself as one of the major health challenges of the twenty-first century. Throughout the past decades, as previously stated, societies have shaped global food production and consumption patterns based on a quantitative model. This attention to improving production practices and increasing their related outputs, on one hand, has had positive impacts in reducing hunger, improving life expectancy, lowering child mortalities, and decreasing global poverty (Steffen et al., 2015; Whitmee et al., 2015). On the other, driven by trends in rapid urbanization and increasing incomes, these health enhancements have been offset by global changes toward detrimental consumption behaviours and dietary preferences (Willett et al., 2019). Food overconsumption, unbalanced high-calorie diets, and consumption of high quantities of heavily processed and animal source foods can be listed among the others. As a consequence, in recent years, steady increases in overweight and obesity rates have been registered around the world. According to the World Health Organization (2018), over 650 million adults resulted in being obese (13% out of the world population) and more than 1.9 billion adults overweight (39% out of the world population) in 2016, leading to almost triple the global obesity rate since 1975.

Nevertheless, one relevant aspect to note is that despite the prominent increases in food production and the complex evolution of supply chains, persistent starvation and poor nutrition still represent significant threats that are diffused all over the world. In particular, inadequate food production and availability remain the primary cause of food insecurity in Sub-Saharan Africa, where 23% of people remain undernourished (Conceição, Levine, Lipton, & Warren-Rodríguez, 2016; FAO, 2017). Conversely, in Southern Asia and South America, the prevalence of undernourishment increased, respectively, from 9.4% to 11.5% and from 5% to 5.6% in the biennium 2015–2016 (FAO, 2017).

1.1.2 A Focus on the European Scenario

For what concerns the European Union (EU), specifically, since countless actors take part in the production, refining, transportation, marketing, and selling of food, the food sector represents one of the main contributors to employment and gross domestic product (GDP). However, it is estimated that approximately one-fourth of the European population (around 119 million people) were exposed to poverty or were socially marginalized in 2015, while about 42.5 million people were unable to have access to a high-quality meal every other day (Eurostat, 2019). Furthermore, much like at the global scale, the European food system also employs many natural resources, such as freshwater, land, and energy, additionally contributing to their depletion and GHG emissions production. For example, agriculture alone is responsible for 70% of European freshwater consumption, whereas industrial activities related to food systems require approximately 26% of Europe's energy demand (Willett et al., 2019). Additionally, it is appraised that around 87 million tons of food are wasted in the EU every year, with associated costs estimated at 143 billion Euros. More generally, current estimates report that around one-third of all produced food perishes before reaching consumer markets or is thrown away in households (Springmann et al., 2018). Subsequently, if compared to countries, wasting food would be the third in the world in regards to GHG emissions (FAO, 2017; Gustavsson, Cederberg, Sonesson, van Otterdijk, & Meybeck, 2011).

Innovation and research are the key drivers that can help to boost up sustainable, diversified, inclusive and resilient processes coping with the complex social and ecological effects of increased urbanisation, population growth, changing demographics, climate change and resource scarcity. Indeed, the European Commission's FOOD 2030 initiative, defined a clear strategy for the European food system based on four priorities: (i) nutrition for sustainable and healthy diets; (ii) climate smart and environmentally sustainable business models; (iii) circular and resource efficiency-based food systems; (iv) innovation and empowerment of communities.

1.1.3 Global Food Systems in a Networked Society

Considering Europe is the world's largest exporter and importer of agricultural and food products (European Commission, 2018a), these environmental impacts are not limited to its boundaries but affect other countries as well. Indeed, every global food system can be seen as an assortment of sub-systems (e.g., farming, waste management, marketing, and distribution) that directly and continuously interact with each other and other global systems (e.g., energy, technology, and health systems). These intertwined interactions and their interdependencies imply that direct changes in one system or sub-system may potentially exacerbate or alleviate issues in others. Additionally, and even more importantly, global food systems are influenced by the broader social, political, economic, and environmental elements characterizing the contexts in which they are embedded. As a consequence, structural changes in food systems do not necessarily originate from within the specific system itself but may also come from alterations in other systems. For example, a local policy that bans the use of plastic could drive changes for alternative packaging options, or consumers may drive production trends in producing specific food products that match their expectations (e.g., low fat, organic, vegan). For these reasons, as well as evolving in parallel to societal demands, food systems necessarily require human capital, research, innovation, and education (Ericksen, 2008; Wilkins & Eames-Sheavly, 2011). Indeed, an improved comprehension of the interplays between the different actors and elements constituting the current food systems may accelerate the required transition toward sustainability. In this sense, communication technologies, and especially the Internet, have paved the way in recent years, also facilitating connections between diverse global systems.

The increasing interconnected challenges that limit natural resource availability and population growth, together with their resulting consequences on European and global food systems, have catapulted sustainable production and security of food as an urgent objective in a rapidly changing world (De Bernardi, Bertello, & Venuti, 2020). The emergence of globally networked societies has marked a transition from the industrial society to the networked society, that has emerged as a network of networks (Tataj, 2015). In conclusion, the complexity of food systems and their mutual interdependence with other global systems thus requires a holistic and coordinated approach that can tackle not only the challenges related to the prompt availability of food for populations but also the increased demand on global resources. Many of the current food security and sustainability challenges are complex. As a result, their proposed solutions usually transcend disciplinary, cultural, and institutional boundaries.

1.2 Sustainable Development in Food Systems: Highlighting a Need for Transition

For investigating the state of global ecosystems and assessing the consequences of their changes on human well-being, the Millennium Ecosystem Assessment (MEA) project was founded from 2001 to 2005 (Millennium Ecosystem Assessment, 2005). What resulted from the MEA analysis was that more than 60% of the investigated ecosystems were in a state of degradation or not being used sustainably (FAO, 2009). The predictions for future environmental ecosystems and the prospects of the Earth's natural resources bring up the issue if the projected food demand can be satisfied while achieving sustainability and if so, how?

The belief that we are currently living in an environmentally turbulent world and need nothing less than a transformation towards a sustainable future is internationally widespread across many industries and disciplines. As a consequence, in September 2015, this belief culminated in the adoption of the United Nations (UN) 2030 Agenda for Sustainable Development and its 17 related targets (United Nations, 2015). These targets, the Sustainable Development Goals (SDGs), can be described as a call to action for each of the 196 signatory countries, from developing countries to high-income ones, "to promote prosperity while protecting the planet".[1] They address the grand challenges human populations currently face, including poverty, climate change, inequality, and justice. Moreover, they recognize that strategies for improving human life must be interconnected with strategies able to leverage economic development and fulfil a multitude of social needs such as instruction, social welfare coverage, and employability. In essence, the SDGs provide a blueprint to accomplish a better and more sustainable future for everyone, which can be considered both a tremendous opportunity and monumental obligation for humanity (Rockström & Sukhdev, 2016). For a full list of the SDGs, please visit—https://sustainabledevelopment.un.org/?menu=1300.

Specifically, within the agreement of the SDGs and their objectives, lies the humanitarian consensus to eradicate hunger, improve food security and nutrition,

---

[1] https://www.un.org/sustainabledevelopment/

1.2 Sustainable Development in Food Systems: Highlighting a Need for Transition

and promote sustainable agriculture and food production by 2030 (Goal 2). Notably, the 2030 Agenda acknowledges that the way food production and consumption are effectively managed and sustainable agriculture supported directly impact on progress toward achieving several of the other SDGs. Examples can be the eradication of poverty (Goal 1), the response to climate change (Goal 13), and the sustainable use of ecosystems, both marine and terrestrial (Goals 14 and 15). Rockström and Sukhdev, CEO of the EAT Advisory Board and CEO of the Green Indian States Trust Advisory, respectively, have further confirmed this conclusion during their keynote speech at the Stockholm EAT Food Forum in 2016. Indeed, they discussed an innovative way of viewing the economic, social, and ecological aspects of the SDGs, highlighting that all those targets are directly or indirectly connected to sustainable food production and consumption (Fig. 1.1).

Progress toward SDG 2 is strictly connected with addressing diverse factors that drive other SDGs and vice-versa. Subsequently, for effectively achieving sustainable food production and consumption, all the possible interactions between them, both in a synergic or balancing way, should be considered. For this reason, the UN 2030 Agenda for Sustainable Development encourages countries to explicitly pursue political unity toward sustainability and establish enabling environments for sustainable development at all levels and by all actors (SDG 17). However, despite the proposal of these international and collaborative frameworks for sustainable

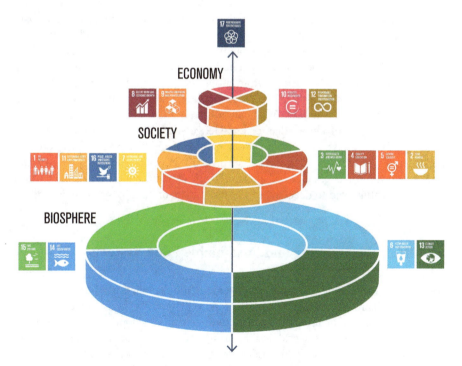

Fig. 1.1 How food systems are connected with all the SDGs. Source: Azote for Stockholm Resilience Center, Stockholm University (2016)

developments, clear strategies for achieving sustainable food production and consumption remain scant, and national action plans and political involvement in this topic vary (Wezel et al., 2018).

With this in mind, the international community has also recognized and begun to address the grand challenges associated with accomplishing the SDGs' objectives. A significant challenge in adopting sustainable practices is that attempts to increase sustainability in one industry, such as the food industry, may often lead to the degradation of other systems. Further evidence suggests that existing endeavours to achieve sustainability in food production and consumption will not be enough to meet SDG 2 and eradicate hunger by 2030 (FAO, 2017). This is troublesome since food security has been a pressing global issue for a long time, and as outlined in the SDGs, transformation toward a sustainable global food industry necessitates harmonious progress on economic, social, and environmental avenues. The well-documented and long-standing effects of the current food industry on natural resource depletion, exhaustion of freshwater reserves, forest and biodiversity loss, and erosion serve as precise indicators of this challenge. Given the many scenarios regarding the mutuality between food and sustainability, it is safe to say that the ability to provide food for health and poverty alleviation are crucial characteristics in a successful transition to achieving the SDGs; a transition that must occur at a rapid pace. Specifically, research also encourages a continued movement toward sustainability that is inclusive of innovation, and challenges stakeholders to engage in a paradigm shift of truly seeing planet Earth as non-negotiable, while simultaneously not viewing this fact as a limitation for prosperity, transformation, and success.

Solving the challenges with sustainability and food systems requires all stakeholders, including both private and public institutions, to act in a synergistic way within food systems at all levels, from global to local ones, and across multiple avenues including agriculture, commerce, policy, public health, education, and infrastructure to name a few. What authors and field experts recommend is a synergetic merging of knowledge, or knowledge sharing, rather than a destructive clashing of progressive ideas from various industries and disciplines. Therefore, the present food scenario is in desperate need of investments, both of monetary and intellectual value to curve the food industry's impact on the environment and create a more sustainable dyad to decelerate the present rates of natural resource decline.

1.3 Holistic Thinking and Sustainable Food Systems

Research points out that the imminent increase in food demand will be the combined result of the increasing world population, especially in urban areas, and their related incomes, as well as of the gradual food saturation in developing countries (FAO, 2009). For decades, the world has been slowly heading toward unhealthy and unsustainable patterns of food production and consumption. These patterns not only pose numerous challenges to sustainability efforts, but they also serve as reminders that current resource-intensive food production practices do not represent

1.3 Holistic Thinking and Sustainable Food Systems

adequate vehicles for achieving sustainable agriculture and food production. The industrial era was brought about by the availability of natural resources, new methods to quantitatively improve food production, and access to networks of power and decision making. However, the newly emerging and interconnected global society is conditioned by the availability of knowledge, resources, and connectivity to multiple other global resources, production, and service systems (Tataj, 2015). As extensively evidenced in the literature, food systems face complex and systematic challenges that cannot be tackled by single subjects, and thus require stakeholders at every level, from local actors to large corporations and institutions, to collectively contribute to tackling these challenges (FAO, 2018).

In this regard, the idea of systematically thinking about food systems must be appraised in the context of co-occurring environmental elements, rapid population growth and urbanization processes, income increases, evolving consumer behaviours, natural resources depletion, and the interdependencies afforded by globalization (Nguyen, 2018). An improved comprehension of the diversity of food systems and the interconnected actions of their actors are crucial to minimizing their negative contributions, especially those related to the environment, and maximizing their beneficial impacts. For these reasons, food systems thinking seems particularly proper. Food systems thinking does not segregate single actors (e.g., farmers, producers, distributors, retailers) (Rezaei, Papakonstantinou, Tavasszy, Pesch, & Kana, 2019), sub-systems (e.g., food marketing, production), or disciplines, but instead enhances the illustration and understanding of sustainability challenges in the food sector as an intricate and interacting web of member activities and feedback (FAO, 2018).

The notion of food systems as interconnected organisms is fostered by increased global connectivity and has led to the concept of sustainable food systems, namely systems providing individuals reliable access to sufficient and nourishing amounts of food while not compromising the necessary resources for achieving the same result in the future (FAO, 2018). The concept of building sustainable food systems is at the core of the UN 2030 Agenda, which demands disruptive shifts in both agriculture and food systems for ending hunger and achieving both food security and nutrition through the SDGs. In order to reach the SDGs, global food systems will need to be revised to become not only more sustainable, but also more efficient, embracing towards all its members, resilient, and capable of delivering health-giving food to everyone. Following this idea, during the SDG-Conference "Towards Zero Hunger: Partnerships for Impact" held at the Wageningen University and Research Centre on August 2018, the food systems approach emerged as a major buzzword and a viable solution to address sustainability challenges. Van Berkum, Dengerink, and Ruben (2018) expressly defined the food systems approach as analysing "the relationship between different parts of the food system and the outcomes of activities within the system in socio-economic and environmental/climate terms". Therefore, speakers, panellists, and other field experts not only agreed that food systems need a transition, but they also recognized the food systems approach as a crucial takeaway concept for achieving a successful sustainability development.

A food systems approach takes into consideration the element of interconnectedness amongst system members, assesses the food system in its entirety, and considers all the food system components, their relationships, and resulting consequences. Therefore, it helps to overcome the existing constraints of many conventional production and consumption approaches to achieve food security, which are usually segmented with narrow objectives that are either handled by single institutions or apply systemic thinking to specific sub-systems' challenges. Promoting systems thinking amongst all members results in increased multi-actor collaborations and policy actions that promote a harmonious interaction of resource input and value output to address future sustainability challenges.

1.3.1 A Sustainable Food System Approach: The Food System Wheel

Merging the agendas of the varied selection of food system stakeholders will, of course, provide both challenges (e.g., conflicting priorities of food sub-systems, adherence to SDGs) and opportunities (e.g., knowledge sharing, increased communication and collaboration amongst members) to accomplish multiple objectives. A well-adopted framework proposed by the FAO (2018) to illustrate systems thinking in food is the "food system wheel" (Fig. 1.2), which provides a sort of guideline for assessing the performance of a system in achieving the FAO's primary goals of reducing poverty and achieving food security and nutrition. These goals are reported at the centre of the wheel.

Furthermore, this framework posits that achieving overall system goals depends on the conduct of stakeholders within the whole food chain. Particularly, it includes layers of both production and consumption behaviours and of services that condone them. These behaviours are themselves embedded and affected by the more significant social context, which includes existing policies, laws, and regulations, as well as social norms and existing infrastructures, all of which depend on natural resources. In this sense, the food system wheel posits the idea that the development of food systems must address sustainability threefold. First, economically, by providing benefits for each of the involved stakeholders and guaranteeing profits of fiscal viability throughout. Second, socially, by assuring widespread and equally distributed benefits to people, especially considering vulnerable groups, and advancing essential socio-cultural factors (e.g., food nutrition and security, health, and welfare). Third, environmentally, not harming the planet, by ensuring that the involved stakeholders' activities impact on natural resources positively or at worst neutrally. In fact, the three dimensions of sustainability in food systems highlight that any proposed innovation to address sustainability challenges must be holistically appraised to ensure there is minimal to no risk for unwanted consequences on other sustainability dimensions. This holistic vision of food systems allows for the exploitation of emerging synergies to reveal eventually hidden trade-offs, ensuring that both the targeted result of specific policies or activities and their overall net impact remain positive for the entire food system.

1.3 Holistic Thinking and Sustainable Food Systems

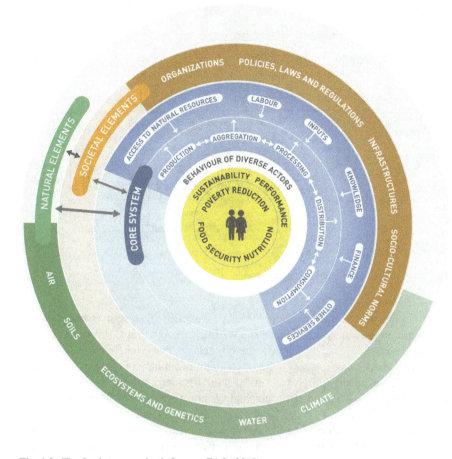

Fig. 1.2 The food system wheel. Source: FAO (2018)

1.3.2 The Food System Development Paradigm

With a specific focus on the economic dimension of sustainability, the FAO has further developed its "food system development paradigm" (Fig. 1.3). As mentioned above, economic sustainability is respected if the benefits for each of the involved stakeholders are guaranteed. So, the FAO (2018) has identified five main components that have to be encompassed: (i) returns to asset owners, mainly referring to profits for entrepreneurs; (ii) salaries to employees; (iii) benefits to consumers, with particular attention on food supplies, respecting both food security and nutrition; (iv) fiscal incomes to governments and public institutions; (v) a positive, or at least neutral, impact on the socio-cultural and natural environment. Moreover, according to the FAO, the value added by respecting the economic dimension of the sustainability paradigm is what catalyses the four feedback loops

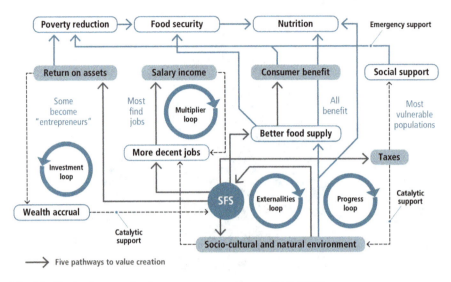

Fig. 1.3 The food system development paradigm. Source: FAO (2018)

shown in Fig. 1.3, which are referred to as: (i) the economic resources reinvested by companies in the food system, in the shape of savings and profits (investment loop); (ii) the increased level of wealth generated by salaries that workers spend (multiplier loop); (iii) the positive impact on the socio-cultural and natural environment, driven by public investments (progress loop); (iv) the broader impact of food systems on other economic, social, and environmental systems (externalities loop). That said, it is clear that the four feedback loops are broadly related to each of the three dimensions of sustainability (economic, social, and environmental) and could boost the sustainable shift of food systems if effectively used. Indeed, these feedback loops could foster and guide a transformational change of food systems by helping to change behaviours and countries to address the SDGs.

1.4 Addressing the Sustainability Paradigm in the European Union

In the European Union, policies and legislation that aim at protecting plants, animals, and human health, as well as their host environment, have long been employed. For example, in full compliance with the UN 2030 Agenda and the Paris Climate Agreement, signed during the COP 21 in 2016, the European Union plays a significant role in helping the world to transition toward resource-efficient economies. Furthermore, some of the policies that have been developed to foster transitions toward a sustainable future will be briefly presented in the following sub-paragraphs.

1.4.1 Safeguarding the Agricultural Sector and Food Consumers

One of the first policies ever instituted was the Common Agriculture Policy (CAP) in 1962, which poses itself as a partnership between the EU and both its farmers and citizens. This policy, renewed in 2018 through the presentation of a legislative proposal regarding the CAP beyond 2020, aims at supporting farmers, assuring them better conditions to conduct a reasonable living, improving agricultural productivity, and ensuring stable supplies of affordable food (European Commission, 2018b). Moreover, it helps to promote employability in the agricultural and other related sectors, address climate change, avoid the depletion of natural resources, and preserve territories and landscapes across Europe. Recanati, Maughan, Pedrotti, Dembska, and Antonelli (2018) provided a visual abstract (Fig. 1.4) of the current food system under the CAP and the way it simultaneously drives a transition toward more sustainable food production and consumption models and supports European farmers for the competitivity of food systems.

Conversely, for what concerns protecting consumers' interest more specifically, the Regulation on Food Information to Consumers (European Commission, 2019a) was launched in 2011. The Regulation takes into special consideration health and ethical behaviours, asking food manufacturers and retailers to provide food information and labels readily to consumers, thus empowering them to make informed decisions regarding the safety and effects of food. Current practices to label food dates (e.g., use by, best before, or sell before) in the food system also contribute a significant impact on food waste (Wilson, Rickard, Saputo, & Ho, 2017). In 2018, for example, the European Commission published a study that explored date marking practices, reporting how 10% of the total amount of food waste that is annually produced in the EU is linked to them (European Commission, 2018c).

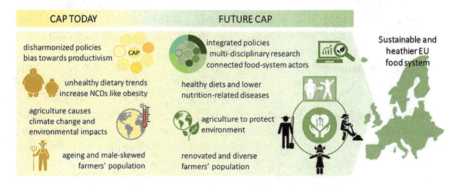

Fig. 1.4 The CAP food system vision. Source: Recanati et al. (2018)

1.4.2 Managing Waste: The Waste Framework Directive and Other Network Policies

The European Commission is an active player also in tackling the issue of food waste, recognizing that it has significant implications for reducing food systems' resource over-exploitation. For example, European Waste Framework Directive (WFD) was initially introduced in 1975 and successively amended in 1991, 2006, and 2018 in which three new targets related to the municipal waste management were introduced. Particularly, these targets are to prepare to recycle or re-use at least 55% of waste by weight by 2025, leveraging this rate to 60% by 2030, and 65% by 2035, where preparing refers to all the activities that are necessary to make products ready for being recycled or re-used (e.g., being sorted, checked, cleaned or repaired). Indeed, the main function of the WFD is to turn Europeans into a recycling society, establishing the main concepts and rules regarding waste management and requiring member states to decrease their outputs of food waste at every stage of the food supply chain. In this sense, the WFD illustrates how to distinguish between real waste and products that can be recovered, living a second life or becoming raw materials, or that can be recycled. The directive also individuates what substances are considered harmful and must be removed from products, as well as how to manage waste without harming human health or the planet.

Tackling the ever-present issues of food waste however requires the coordinated actions between key players in the food chain (e.g., farmers, manufacturers, retailers, policymakers, and consumers themselves) to better identify, understand, and find possible solutions. Therefore, some policies oriented to build multi-actor networks have also been instituted. For example, in 2016 the EU "Platform on Food Losses and Food Waste" (FLW) was founded to accelerate the progress toward achieving the SDG 12.3, namely reducing food losses along the food production and supply chains (European Commission, 2019b). To do so, the FLW launched an open call to actively engage institutions and field experts from both public and private sectors to define how food losses and waste can be avoided, share their best practices, and assess the advancements made in that regard (European Commission, 2019b). Furthermore, for addressing SDG 12.3, a digital network for improving collaborations and information exchanges amongst field experts from 12 European countries and China was established in 2017. The objective of this network, called "Resource Efficient Food and dRink for the Entire Supply cHain" (REFRESH), is to pose a scientific base to understand the food waste problem better. In this sense, REFRESH was born as an international research project finalised at: (i) supporting policymakers to develop informed legislations and frameworks regarding food waste; (ii) improving the decision-making process of relevant food systems' stakeholders; and (iii) developing new processes and technology-based solutions for reducing food waste and enhancing its valorisation (European Commission REFRESH, 2019).

1.4.3 Transitioning Toward a Circular Economy: The Circular Economy Action Plan

The European Commission has long acknowledged the need to work on sustainable transitions relating to food and particularly toward circular economy models as evidenced by the Circular Economy Action Plan (CEAP) adopted in 2015 (European Commission, 2019d). Indeed, the European Commission further argues that the traditional linear model of economic growth (i.e., take-make-dispose), and especially its usage of natural resources, is no longer sustainable for the environment. Furthermore, the European Commission acknowledges the need for progress in scaling up circular economies and highlights five key requirements to achieve this objective: (i) continued support and investments for research to develop and demonstrate innovative solutions; (ii) address the challenges related to the circular use of natural resources; (iii) support new circular business models and consumption production patterns; (iv) enhance circular and sustainable water use; and (v) develop appropriate indicators and governance systems to measure the progress and accelerate the transition to circular economy. The concept of the circular economy provides an opportunity to balance environmental, social, and economic goals while simultaneously guiding human activities to a path toward sustainability. Beyond the creation of new knowledge, innovation, company-wide solutions, and industrial transformations, implementing a circular economy agenda will also require significant changes in the way people behave toward, and perceive food.

Notably, the CEAP calls for revisions to waste legislation, and proposes pioneering recycling targets, i.e., the first European strategy for plastics in the circular economy and its proposed actions on single-use plastics, and a revision on fertilizers regulation that focuses on waste-based products (European Commission, 2019d). Moreover, it also sets out 54 actions to close the loop of product and material life cycles through improved eco-friendly designs, increased recycling, and greater re-use of materials; currently, all 54 actions have been or are being implemented. This Action Plan has been considered a model for smart policymaking at the international level in the efforts to transition to a circular economy. Indeed, the European Commission won the World Economic Forum's Circular Economy prize for it.

1.5 From Food Systems to Food Ecosystems

Re-defining the food system and its practices is necessary in order to tackle current and future barriers for achieving sustainability. For example, traditional vertically operating food industries offer standardized food access and employment opportunities but do not usually include an ongoing concern for smaller stakeholders or the environmental effects of the recent lengthening of food supply chains. This can be the case of small farmers who might not have adequate resources for marketing their locally grown products and as a result lose consumers in favour of bigger industries. One way to address this apprehension toward sustainability is by making the food industry itself more efficient, resilient, and inclusive of stakeholders at every level. However, due to the known complexities that persist in coordinating multiple members of the food supply chain, many of the efforts for improved sustainability have been undertaken by single actors and have thus yielded impacts that are less than remarkable. In light of this realization, to achieve increased sustainability in food production and consumption behaviours, a handful of industry stakeholders have begun coordinated inter-disciplinary and inter-country collaborations, designed to consolidate individual efforts into a consortium of actors for increased effectiveness in sustainable endeavours.

Food systems are often uncertain, and this uncertainty is determined by compound multilevel environmental, societal, and technological trends. The accompanying uncertainty and complexity in tackling grand global challenges, especially in their relation to food systems, requires more than innovative technology-driven paradigms; technology is fundamental of course, but not enough to solve the cross-societal and pressing global issues. Sustainability and its complex interactions with different systems and resources is a longitudinal and multidisciplinary endeavour that requires the involvement of a wide range of stakeholders. This transition toward an approach where actors, knowledge, techniques, institutions, and the entirety of members interact within systems has been regarded as the creation of an ecosystem. Ecosystems have been adopted as the concept that describes the *"evolutionary features of the interactions between individuals, their relationships with innovative activities, and their relations with the environment in which they operate"* (Mercan & Goktas, 2011, p. 103). Whereas systems are composed of components interacting with each other according to pre-defined rules, ecosystems can be described as the associations that are formed between, and within, communities of living beings and their environment. The components within an ecosystem develop a specific network for the exchange of resources (i.e., tangible and intangible) and the maintenance and development of their own activities.

Given these conceptualizations of ecosystems, food ecosystems can be described as composed of industries, farmers, retailers, academia, research institutions, startups, Small and Medium sized Enterprises (SMEs), and consumers, to name a few. The ecosystem approach to food systems has been harnessed as an integral component to tackling the elaborate challenges for food systems, primarily since it facilitates the consideration of the dynamic interactions that occur within different sections of the food production system and value chains at various levels. This view of food ecosystems, therefore, implies that a natural, and continuous, exchange of knowledge between different members of the ecosystem is essential. For example, "Forward Fooding" is a global network of entrepreneurs that involves both large and small actors, from institutions and established food companies to farmers and other individual food system members. In this way, it seeks to provide appropriate and timely support systems for enabling collaborations and partnerships between subjects who seek to create innovative solutions and products through startups (Forward Fooding, 2019). A similar initiative is "Future Food", which is an exclusive network and inspirational platform designed to drive positive transitions in the global food system. At the core of their operations lie the principles of excellence for food intelligence, and a training platform for change makers, climate shapers, and future leaders in food innovation (Future Food Network, 2019). Finally, in view of the 2015 Expo "Feeding the Planet, Energy for Life", the Municipality of Milan launched its "Urban Food Policy Pact", a voluntary action pact which has been signed by mayors of more than 199 cities from all over the world, comprising over 450 million inhabitants. The purpose of the Urban Food Policy Pact is to use their inter and trans-disciplinary network of inhabitants and professionals to provide strategies to member cities to help them achieve more sustainable food systems (Milan Urban Food Policy Pact, 2015).

1.5.1 Innovation as a Driver in Food Ecosystems

The natural structure of food ecosystems generates relationships amongst its members that, in turn, influence their behaviour and capabilities. Members of food ecosystems are interdependent and can themselves impact one another's incentives and capacities to drive change. The recent guidelines that offer insight toward creating and measuring food systems' performance in terms of sustainability, for example, are a result of these intertwined connections between members of the food ecosystem. Governments, companies, farms, consumers, and every other stakeholder have the power to influence the overall performances of the system, initiating or inspiring change and shaping the conduct of every other member. Therefore, an evolutionary process always defines the ecosystem structure (FAO, 2018).

According to Durst and Ståhle (2013), like open innovation (discussed in Chap. 5), food ecosystems depend on the knowledge shared among interdisciplinary system members, which results in facilitated collaboration and co-creation. This view is in line with the ideas expressed by Laursen and Salter (2014), who argue that companies need to learn from a large number of subjects, co-creating and sharing knowledge with them if they want to innovate effectively. Both ideas proposed by the scholars mentioned above confirm that innovation appears as an ever-present, self-perpetuating system of information exchange and knowledge sharing. Thus, in the era of rapid dissemination of information and communication, innovation becomes a collective distributed open learning process and an essential component of the capacity to transform in a continually changing world (Tataj, 2015). Furthermore, Tataj (2015) defines innovation as a social process of knowledge production and dissemination, during which human creativity leads to a translation of knowledge into shared and enriched capacities, she then goes on to state that innovation can be either low-cost and non-technological yet entrepreneurial and meaningful. Innovation in the food ecosystem may range from food technologies, food biochemistry, to agricultural processes, and production strategies. Furthermore, innovation has been evidenced as an essential element to facilitate the food ecosystems' transition to achieve sustainability. According to Jonker (2018), CEO of EIT Digital, "The future of innovation is ecosystems, bringing together stakeholders working towards the same goals, and having both economic and societal impact".

1.5.2 Sustainable Innovation in Food Ecosystems

As stated by Hirsch-Kreinsen (2008), in slow-growing industries innovation mainly comes from the industry's existing knowledge base, usually implying small improvements to existing products and services or companies' processes, namely defined as incremental innovations. Conversely, the characteristics of the interplays between individual actors and their relations with both innovation activities and the environment in which they take part are capably described by the ecosystem concept (Mercan & Goktas, 2011). Therefore, innovations toward sustainability in the food industry, which has up until recently been considered a slow-growing sector, tend to depend on individual member contribution, the interactions between them, and their existing collective knowledge that is distributed through exchanges in formal and informal networks. Actually, what can be called a food ecosystem.

The recently attributed importance to sustainability and the food industry's outstanding role in the future of natural resources, has fostered the transitions from a focus of simply improving food availability through more complex supply chains and higher production, to a focus on creating ecosystems designed to promote knowledge sharing in order to develop solutions for food sustainability through entrepreneurship and innovation. There has never been a better moment to redefine how we produce, distribute, and consume our food. If the necessary steps toward sustainability in food ecosystems are taken, agriculture, forestry, and fisheries would be able to provide nutritious food for all populations, while preserving the environment. A remarkable transformation in the current food ecosystem is needed in order to sustain the 815 million people who suffer from hunger today, and the additional two billion people expected to be undernourished by 2050 (FAO, 2017).

The theories that guide the onset of innovation are perfectly suited in the context of knowledge sharing within food ecosystems. Holding the idea that the subjects taking part in ecosystems do not seek innovation for themselves but aim to co-create it in collaboration with other members of their ecosystem, innovation processes necessarily require interactions between them and can be defined as systemic in nature (Bayona-Saez, Cruz-Cázares, García-Marco, & Sánchez García, 2017). This definition is also in line with the idea of innovation systems, introduced by Freeman in 1987 through analysis of networks established between institutions of both the public and private sectors (Freeman, 1987). Therefore, the invaluable combination of the food ecosystem concept and collaborative innovation approaches has the potential to help design innovation-oriented policies and support a sustainable transition of multi-actor and interdisciplinary innovation communities (Pigford, Hickey, & Klerkx, 2018).

However, one major challenge with innovations toward greater sustainability in food ecosystems is that only a small portion of the innovative products and services reaching the market are able to provide the necessary disruptive changes. Winger and Gavin (2006) for example, report that 75% of all new products in the food industry are considered failures, and when they compared the food industry to others, they found lower levels of engagement in research and development. In this direction, according to Bayona-Saez et al. (2017), the food industry is progressively implementing open innovation changes, but new frameworks are needed to guide the newly emerging relationships between actors at diverse levels of the industry and increase their innovative output.

1.6 Entrepreneurship and Innovation as Key Elements for Sustainability

The key issue for sustainable economic development regards not only what is produced in food systems, but also how. The "how" regarding food production, however, is a complex web of never-ending interactions that still have to be clearly studied and defined. Therefore, to effectively tackle the challenges in our current turbulent food ecosystems we must adopt the notion of a knowledge-driven economy, where innovation and entrepreneurship, and their advanced networks and nature of knowledge sharing, are critical drivers for growth (Tataj, 2015). Entrepreneurship has been widely regarded as one of the most significant contributors to innovation and economic development. The concepts of innovation and entrepreneurship are usually considered as overlapping. Entrepreneurs are risk-takers and adventurers by nature since they like exploring unconventional practices and unknown areas (Knudson, Wysocki, Champagne, & Peterson, 2004), to the extent that they have often been defined as individuals that carry out activities all related to innovation (Wee, Lim, & Lee, 1994). Specifically, entrepreneurs of the food ecosystem are no exception. Over the past decades, the changes in economic and environmental scenarios have placed unsustainable pressures on global food supplies and security. Thus, novel practices regarding food are ever emerging due to the current uncertainty within the food ecosystem, which has fostered several important innovations regarding its processes and procedures (e.g., sustainable packaging and substitutes for unsustainable food products, discussed further in Chap. 7).

According to Liang (2018), there are three pillars for establishing a successful venture: (i) having the appropriate mindset and attributes; (ii) possessing entrepreneurial knowledge and skill; (iii) and taking the right opportunities. Food ecosystems involve resources, decisions, actions, and outcomes that include every phase of the supply chain, which face significant challenges that give appealing opportunities to entrepreneurs that want to actively develop innovative solutions to existing problems. In current competitive and dynamic food ecosystems, limitless chances for providing entrepreneurial skill and opportunities exist, therefore individuals and organizations must adopt an entrepreneurial strategy for acquiring competitive advantages through continually seeking innovation. In particular, scholars (Short, Ketchen Jr, Shook, & Ireland, 2010) suggest four factors that could drive changes in future food ecosystems: (i) consumer demand, (ii) changes in resources, (iii) information exchanges, and (iv) external market changes. The first, consumer demand, creates opportunities for entrepreneurs to cater to newly emerging market needs. For example, increasing consumer awareness of healthy and sustainable food or locally sourced produce might drive changes in market expectations, and entrepreneurs could benefit from addressing these emerging demands. Secondly, changes in resources, such as limited natural resources or development of new flavour or packaging products, offer entrepreneurs opportunities to remodel their value chains. The third driver, information exchanges, may provide more opportunities for those entrepreneurs that possess the right skill and resources to address them. Fourth, external market changes are positioned to present the most comprehensive opportunities, such as companies seeking alternatives to single-use plastics after the European policies that have banned them (Watts, 2019).

However, entrepreneurs seeking to disrupt current food ecosystems should consider developing concepts based on feedback from the entire food value chain. Importantly, the idea of entrepreneurship should not be limited to only financial returns; whatever the value, social and economic entrepreneurship is inherently linked to innovation, where social entrepreneurship can be defined as a specific kind of entrepreneurial activity designed to bring impact rather than generate profit that fosters a new model for growth (Tataj, 2015). First, because innovation needs entrepreneurs to take it to the market and society, and secondly because entrepreneurship requires innovation since entrepreneurs reallocate resources in a more competitive manner (Tataj, 2015). As innovations happen in different dimensions, entrepreneurship does not necessarily have to adopt a for-profit agenda, thus introducing the concept of social entrepreneurship (Tataj, 2015). Through social entrepreneurship, companies are assisted in redesigning their value chains and business model innovations, in integrating social metrics with financial criteria, and in adopting social capital as a new asset class. Nowadays, many entrepreneurs recognize that current food production and consumption patterns are a severe problem in the modern world. For this reason, they have started being increasingly engaged in knowledge exchanges and interdisciplinary efforts to address the SDGs. Entrepreneurship has long been a critical driver in the design and development of innovative food strategies at local, national, and regional levels. As a consequence, policymakers have acknowledged that an immense amount of entrepreneurial and innovative potential is hidden in the food industry. Following this idea, in 2008 the EU founded the European Institute of Innovation and Technology (EIT), which later established a specific Knowledge and Innovation Community (KIC) aimed at empowering all the relevant stakeholders to cultivate innovative solutions for improving current food ecosystems (Kuckertz, Hinderer, & Röhm, 2019). Name of this pan-European consortium is EIT Food, deeply examined in Chap. 9.

1.7 Conclusion

The European food industry is still in need of a systems approach to foster transformations toward sustainable practices. Specifically, a better understanding of the critical interactions between the abundant networks of members is crucial for an effective change (Gill et al., 2018). The adoption and integration of open innovation, knowledge sharing, and collaboration amongst multiple partners from the industry place the future of sustainability within the food industry not on a single actor or institution, but concedes responsibility to the collective ecosystems and its networks (Bayona-Saez et al., 2017; Kühne, Vanhonacker, Gellynck, & Verbeke, 2010).

For what regards research streams, the European Commission recommends prioritizing and integrating research and innovation on four key areas that are considered necessary elements for EU food ecosystems to become sustainable, resilient, responsible, competitive, diverse, and inclusive (European Commission, 2019c). These key areas are (i) nutrition, (ii) climate, (iii) circularity, and (iv) innovation. However, even though sustainability research has skyrocketed in recent years (Fischer et al., 2015), research alone is not enough. Successful transitions also require the translation of research into practice and should not be thought of as an optional undertaking, but as a collective responsibility that is shaped by the behaviour of every member of the food ecosystem (Tataj, 2015). Therefore, action from stakeholders is needed now more than ever to effectively change consumer behaviour patterns and deliver social impact (Willett et al., 2019); this is also believed to depend on a certain degree of openness from the members of the ecosystem themselves (Bayona-Saez et al., 2017).

Current food ecosystems require innovation that protects and improves the available natural resource supplies while simultaneously improving investments, productivity, skills, and infrastructures (Parfitt, Barthel, & Macnaughton, 2010). Technological enhancements, along with substantial reductions in economy-wide and food ecosystem natural resource use, would also help reduce future negative impacts that affect all of the Earth's ecosystems and diurnal aspects of human life. A recent report by the FAO concludes that massive efforts are necessary for transforming global food ecosystems to achieve environmental sustainability and food security by 2050 (FAO, 2017). It is now that radical transitions are needed towards a safe operating space that promotes resilience and sustainability in food ecosystems. Fundamentally, food ecosystem sustainability requires a shift towards a new paradigm that reconnects food production and consumption strategies to the biosphere as a pathway for healthy and sustainable diets for the future (Springmann et al., 2018). From the literature, two overarching conditions emerge as essential for achieving these objectives. The first is to invest more in research and development for guaranteeing advancements in productivity rates, infrastructures, policy-making, and resource management and preservation. The second is to adopt policies that ensure access to nutritious food, with particular attention on the most vulnerable populations and social groups. Due to recent shifts toward food ecosystems and the necessity of innovative frameworks (Traitler, Watzke, & Saguy, 2011), the food industry seems a great avenue to explore.

The purpose of this book is to provide a critical review of the trends and challenges that limit food ecosystems' sustainability, and the technological and innovative solutions proposed by entrepreneurs and other stakeholders. We discuss the role that innovation and entrepreneurial ecosystems play within food ecosystems for sustainability. Specifically, we dive into the topic of entrepreneurship and innovation in food ecosystems, and their role in ameliorating sustainability issues and tackling sustainability challenges in food production and consumption at the local community, state, and national levels. Further, we discuss the potential impact of specific innovations that drive major transformations toward sustainability in food ecosystems. Finally, we discuss the best strategies and practices to foster the development of innovation in food ecosystems through entrepreneurial thinking from a diverse range of fields and backgrounds and present a case study of one of Europe's most innovative and cutting edge food ecosystems, the EIT Food.

References

Alexandratos, N., & Bruinsma, J. (2012). *World agriculture towards 2030/2050: The 2012.* Rome: FAO.

Azote for Stockholm Resilience Center, Stockholm University. (2016). Stockholm EAT Forum. Retrieved from https://www.stockholmresilience.org/research/research-news/2017-02-28-con tributions-to-agenda-2030.html

Bayona-Saez, C., Cruz-Cázares, C., García-Marco, T., & Sánchez García, M. (2017). Open innovation in the food and beverage industry. *Management Decision, 55*(3), 526–546.

Conceição, P., Levine, S., Lipton, M., & Warren-Rodríguez, A. (2016). Toward a food secure future: Ensuring food security for sustainable human development in Sub-Saharan Africa. *Food Policy, 60*, 1–9.

Davis, K. F., Gephart, J. A., Emery, K. A., Leach, A. M., Galloway, J. N., & D'Odorico, P. (2016). Meeting future food demand with current agricultural resources. *Global Environmental Change, 39*, 125–132.

De Bernardi, P., Bertello, A., & Venuti, F. (2019). Online and on-site interactions within alternative food networks: Sustainability impact of knowledge-sharing practices. *Sustainability, 11*(5), 1437.

De Bernardi, P., Bertello, A., & Venuti, F. (2020). Community-oriented motivations and knowledge sharing as drivers of success within food assemblies. In *Exploring digital ecosystems* (pp. 443–457). Cham: Springer.

De Bernardi, P., Bertello, A., Venuti, F., & Zardini, A. (2019). Knowledge transfer driving community-based business models towards sustainable food-related behaviours: A commons perspective. *Knowledge Management Research & Practice,* 1–8. https://doi.org/10.1080/14778238.2019.1664271

Durst, S., & Ståhle, P. (2013). Success factors of open innovation – A literature review. *International Journal of Business Research and Management, 4*(4), 111–131.

Ericksen, P. J. (2008). Conceptualizing food systems for global environmental change research. *Global Environmental Change, 18*(1), 234–245.

European Commission. (2018a). *Remarks on world food day 2018.* Retrieved from https://ec.europa.eu/commission/commissioners/2014-2019/hogan/announcements/remarks-world-food-day-2018_en

European Commission. (2018b). *The common agriculture policy at a glance.* Retrieved from https://ec.europa.eu/info/food-farming-fisheries/key-policies/common-agricultural-policy/cap-glance_en

European Commission. (2018c). *Date marking and food waste.* Retrieved from https://ec.europa.eu/food/safety/food_waste/eu_actions/date_marking_en

European Commission. (2018d). Executive summary. In *Recipe for change: An agenda for a climate-smart and sustainable food system for a healthy Europe.* EC FOOD 2030 Expert Group.

References

European Commission. (2019a). *Food information to consumers – Legislation*. Retrieved from https://ec.europa.eu/food/safety/labelling_nutrition/labelling_legislation_en

European Commission. (2019b). *EU platform on food losses and food waste*. Retrieved from https://ec.europa.eu/food/safety/food_waste/eu_actions/eu-platform_en

European Commission. (2019c). *Food 2030: Empowering cities as agents of food system transformation*. Retrieved from https://ec.europa.eu/info/funding-tenders/opportunities/portal/screen/opportunities/topic-details/ce-fnr-07-2020

European Commission. (2019d). *Innovative action on circular economy wins WEF award*. Retrieved from https://ec.europa.eu/environment/efe/themes/economics-strategy-and-information/innovative-action-circular-economy-wins-wef-award_en

European Commission REFRESH. (2019). *EU platform on food losses and food waste: REFRESH*. Retrieved from https://ec.europa.eu/food/sites/food/files/safety/docs/fw_eu-platform_20190506_flw_pres-07.pdf

Eurostat. (2019). *People at risk of poverty or social exclusion*. Retrieved from https://ec.europa.eu/eurostat/statistics-explained/index.php/People_at_risk_of_poverty_or_social_exclusion

FAO. (2009). *How to feed the world in 2050*. Retrieved from http://www.fao.org/fileadmin/templates/wsfs/docs/expert_paper/How_to_Feed_the_World_in_2050.pdf

FAO. (2017). *The future of food and agriculture: Trends and challenges*. Retrieved from http://www.fao.org/3/a-i6583e.pdf

FAO. (2018). *Sustainable food systems: Concept and framework*. Retrieved from http://www.fao.org/3/ca2079en/CA2079EN.pdf

Fischer, J., Gardner, T. A., Bennett, E. M., Balvanera, P., Biggs, R., Carpenter, S., . . . Tenhunen, J. (2015). Advancing sustainability through mainstreaming a social – Ecological systems perspective. *Current Opinion in Environmental Sustainability, 14*, 144–149.

Foley, J. A., DeFries, R., Asner, G. P., Barford, C., Bonan, G., Carpenter, S. R., . . . Snyder, P. K. (2005). Global consequences of land use. *Science, 309*(5734), 570–574.

Food and Agriculture UN. (2016) *Is the planet approaching "peak fish"? Not so fat, study says*. Retrieved from http://www.fao.org/news/story/en/item/1144274/icode/

Forward Fooding. (2019). *Forward fooding: Powering the food revolution*. Retrieved from https://forwardfooding.com/

Freeman, C. (1987). *Technology policy and economic performance: Lessons from Japan*. London: Pinter.

Future Food Network. (2019). *Future food institute*. Retrieved from https://futurefood.network/institute/

Gill, M., Den Boer, A. C. L., Kok, K. P., Cahill, J., Callenius, C., Caron, P., . . . Lappiere, A. (2018). *A systems approach to research and innovation for food system transformation*. FIT4FOOD2030.

Global Footprint Network. (2019). *Global Footprint Network promotes real-world solutions that #MoveTheDate, accelerating the transition to one-planet prosperity*. Retrieved from https://www.footprintnetwork.org/2019/07/23/press-release-july-2019/

Gustavsson, J., Cederberg, C., Sonesson, U., van Otterdijk, R., & Meybeck, A. (2011). *Global food losses and food waste: Extent, causes and prevention*. Rome: FAO. Retrieved from http://www.fao.org/3/a-i2697e.pdf

Hirsch-Kreinsen, H. (2008). "Low-tech" innovations. *Industry and Innovation, 15*(1), 19–43.

Hoekstra, A. Y., & Wiedmann, T. O. (2014). Humanity's unsustainable environmental footprint. *Science, 344*(6188), 1114–1117.

Ingram, J. (2011). A food systems approach to researching food security and its interactions with global environmental change. *Food Security, 3*(4), 417–431.

Jagustović, R., Zougmoré, R. B., Kessler, A., Ritsema, C. J., Keesstra, S., & Reynolds, M. (2019). Contribution of systems thinking and complex adaptive system attributes to sustainable food production: Example from a climate-smart village. *Agricultural Systems, 171*, 65–75.

Jalava, M., Kummu, M., Porkka, M., Siebert, S., & Varis, O. (2014). Diet change—A solution to reduce water use? *Environmental Research Letters, 9*(7), 074016.

Johnson, E. A. J. (1941). New tools for the economic historian. *The Journal of Economic History, 1*(S1), 30–38.

Jonker, W. (2018). Tech Talk with Anu – Anu Deshpande/Willem Jonker, CEO of EIT Digital – Episode 5 [Video file]. Retrieved from https://www.youtube.com/watch?v=tmSYsza2uXo

Kamminga, H., & Cunningham, A. (1995). *The science and culture of nutrition, 1840–1940*. Broll Rodopi.

Knudson, W., Wysocki, A., Champagne, J., & Peterson, H. C. (2004). Entrepreneurship and innovation in the agri-food system. *American Journal of Agricultural Economics, 86*(5), 1330–1336.

Kuckertz, A., Hinderer, S., & Röhm, P. (2019). Entrepreneurship and entrepreneurial opportunities in the food value chain. *NPJ Science of Food, 3*(1), 6.

Kühne, B., Vanhonacker, F., Gellynck, X., & Verbeke, W. (2010). Innovation in traditional food products in Europe: Do sector innovation activities match consumers' acceptance? *Food Quality and Preference, 21*(6), 629–638.

Laursen, K., & Salter, A. J. (2014). The paradox of openness: Appropriability, external search and collaboration. *Research Policy, 43*(5), 867–878.

Liang, K. (2018). Theme overview: The linkages between entrepreneurship and sustainable regional food networks. *Choices, 33*(2), 1–3.

Mercan, B., & Goktas, D. (2011). Components of innovation ecosystems: A cross-country study. *International Research Journal of Finance and Economics, 76*, 102–112.

Milan Urban Food Policy Pact. (2015). *Milan urban food policy pact, text*. Retrieved from http://www.milanurbanfoodpolicypact.org/text/

Millennium Ecosystem Assessment. (2005). *Ecosystems and human well-being: Synthesis*. Washington, DC: Island Press. Retrieved from https://www.millenniumassessment.org/documents/document.356.aspx.pdf

Muth, M. K., Birney, C., Cuéllar, A., Finn, S. M., Freeman, M., Galloway, J. N., . . . Zoubek, S. (2019). A systems approach to assessing environmental and economic effects of food loss and waste interventions in the United States. *Science of the Total Environment, 685*, 1240–1254.

Nguyen, T. (2018). CEO incentives and corporate innovation. *The Financial Review, 53*(2), 255–300.

Overton, M. (1996). Agricultural revolution in England: The transformation of the agrarian economy 1500–1850. In *Cambridge studies in historical geography*, Cambridge: Cambridge University Press.

Parfitt, J., Barthel, M., & Macnaughton, S. (2010). Food waste within food supply chains: Quantification and potential for change to 2050. *Philosophical Transactions of the Royal Society B: Biological Sciences, 365*(1554), 3065–3081.

Pigford, A. A. E., Hickey, G. M., & Klerkx, L. (2018). Beyond agricultural innovation systems? Exploring an agricultural innovation ecosystems approach for niche design and development in sustainability transitions. *Agricultural Systems, 164*, 116–121.

Recanati, F., Maughan, C., Pedrotti, M., Dembska, K., & Antonelli, M. (2018). Assessing the role of CAP for more sustainable and healthier food systems in Europe: A literature review. *Science of the Total Environment, 653*, 908–919.

Rezaei, J., Papakonstantinou, A., Tavasszy, L., Pesch, U., & Kana, A. (2019). Sustainable product-package design in a food supply chain: A multi-criteria life cycle approach. *Packaging Technology and Science, 32*(2), 85–101.

Robertson, G. P., & Swinton, S. M. (2005). Reconciling agricultural productivity and environmental integrity: A grand challenge for agriculture. *Frontiers in Ecology and the Environment, 3*(1), 38–46.

Rockström, J., Steffen, W., Noone, K., Persson, Å., Chapin, F. S., III, Lambin, E., . . . Foley, J. A. (2009). A safe operating space for humanity. *Nature, 461*, 472.

Rockström, J., & Sukhdev, P. (2016). Keynote speech: Prof. Johan Rockström & CEO Pavan Sukhdev [Video file]. Retrieved from https://www.youtube.com/watch?v=tah8QlhQLeQ

Rounsevell, M. D. A., Pedroli, B., Erb, K.-H., Gramberger, M., Busck, A. G., Haberl, H., . . . Wolfslehner, B. (2012). Challenges for land system science. *Land Use Policy, 29*(4), 899–910.

References

Samir, K. C., & Lutz, W. (2017). The human core of the shared socioeconomic pathways: Population scenarios by age, sex and level of education for all countries to 2100. *Global Environmental Change, 42*, 181–192.

Short, J. C., Ketchen, D. J., Jr., Shook, C. L., & Ireland, R. D. (2010). The concept of "Opportunity" in entrepreneurship research: Past accomplishments and future challenges. *Journal of Management, 36*(1), 40–65.

Springmann, M., Clark, M., Mason-D'Croz, D., Wiebe, K., Bodirsky, B. L., Lassaletta, L., . . . Jonell, M. (2018). Options for keeping the food system within environmental limits. *Nature, 562*, 519–525.

Springmann, M., Godfray, H. C. J., Rayner, M., & Scarborough, P. (2016). Analysis and valuation of the health and climate change cobenefits of dietary change. *Proceedings of the National Academy of Sciences, 113*(15), 4146–4151.

Steffen, W., Richardson, K., Rockström, J., Cornell, S. E., Fetzer, I., Bennett, E. M., . . . Sörlin, S. (2015). Planetary boundaries: Guiding human development on a changing planet. *Science, 347*(6223), 1259855.

Tataj, D. (2015). *Innovation and entrepreneurship. A growth model for Europe beyond the crisis.* New York: Tataj Innovation Library.

Tilman, D., Balzer, C., Hill, J., & Befort, B. L. (2011). Global food demand and the sustainable intensification of agriculture. *Proceedings of the National Academy of Sciences, 108*(50), 20260–20264.

Tilman, D., & Clark, M. (2014). Global diets link environmental sustainability and human health. *Nature, 515*, 518–522.

Traitler, H., Watzke, H. J., & Saguy, I. S. (2011). Reinventing R&D in an open innovation ecosystem. *Journal of Food Science, 76*(2), R62–R68.

United Nations. (2015). *About the sustainable development goals.* Retrieved from https://www.un.org/sustainabledevelopment/sustainable-development-goals/

Van Berkum, S., Dengerink, J., & Ruben, R. (2018). *The food systems approach: Sustainable solutions for a sufficient supply of healthy food.* The Hague: Wageningen Economic Research.

Vermeulen, S. J., Campbell, B. M., & Ingram, J. S. (2012). Climate change and food systems. *Annual Review of Environment and Resources, 37*, 195–222.

Watts, J. (2019). *Business ideas for 2019: Plastic alternatives.* Retrieved from https://startups.co.uk/business-ideas-plastic-alternatives/

Wee, C. H., Lim, W. S., & Lee, R. (1994). Entrepreneurship: A review with implications for further research. *Journal of Small Business & Entrepreneurship, 11*(4), 25–49.

Wezel, A., Goette, J., Lagneaux, E., Passuello, G., Reisman, E., Rodier, C., & Turpin, G. (2018). Agroecology in Europe: Research, education, collective action networks, and alternative food systems. *Sustainability, 10*(4), 1214.

Whitmee, S., Haines, A., Beyrer, C., Boltz, F., Capon, A. G., de Souza Dias, B. F., . . . Yack, D. (2015). Safeguarding human health in the Anthropocene epoch: Report of The Rockefeller Foundation–Lancet Commission on planetary health. *The Lancet, 386*(10007), 1973–2028.

Wilkins, J., & Eames-Sheavly, M. (2011). *A primer on community food systems: Linking food, nutrition and agriculture.* Retrieved from https://www.farmlandinfo.org/sites/default/files/Primer_1.pdf

Willett, W., Rockström, J., Loken, B., Springmann, M., Lang, T., Vermeulen, S., . . . Jonell, M. (2019). Food in the anthropocene: The EAT–Lancet Commission on healthy diets from sustainable food systems. *The Lancet, 393*(10170), 447–492.

Wilson, N. L., Rickard, B. J., Saputo, R., & Ho, S. T. (2017). Food waste: The role of date labels, package size, and product category. *Food Quality and Preference, 55*, 35–44.

Winger, R., & Gavin, W. (2006). *Food product innovation: A background paper.* Rome: Food and Agriculture Organization of the United Nations.

World Health Organization. (2018). *Obesity and overweight.* Retrieved from https://www.who.int/en/news-room/fact-sheets/detail/obesity-and-overweight

Chapter 2
The Role of Universities in Harnessing Entrepreneurial Opportunities

Abstract Universities have been documented as key influencers in the performance of agri-food innovation and entrepreneurial activities, and have been evidenced as significant contributors to building the competencies of food system members. Their role in promoting sustainable transitions in food systems through knowledge creation and human capital development cannot be ignored. The current food systems provide an array of entrepreneurial opportunities for its institutions and invidual members who seek to create value while simultaneously ameliorating the present challenges that threaten natural resources. However, it has been noted that individual entrepreneurial skills are not enough to fully assess the presence of opportunities in the complex food system. Universities are therefore seen as key elements to provide further practical education that includes social and interaction techniques, education for business creation, and provide access to diverse networks and viable markets in order to boost opportunity recognition capacities for aspiring entrepreneurs. In this chapter we provide a review of the main drivers of the university's role in promoting research, innovation, and entrepreneurship through their entrepreneurial strategies and programmes.

Keywords Entrepreneurial university · Knowledge spillover · Entrepreneurship · Entrepreneurial education · Entrepreneurial opportunity

2.1 Introduction: Entrepreneurs and Entrepreneurial Opportunities in Food Systems

It is widely accepted that organizations and individuals seeking to create or capture value through entrepreneurial initiatives and innovations in order to tackle sustainability challenges cannot act in isolation. Our current global environment is rapidly changing, and specifically, the increases in food production, consumption, and waste due to a growing population, combined with rapidly evolving dietary behaviors pose serious challenges to the global food system (Lindgren et al., 2018). One important question that professionals from interdisciplinary backgrounds seek to answer is

© Springer Nature Switzerland AG 2020

P. De Bernardi, D. Azucar, *Innovation in Food Ecosystems*, Contributions to Management Science, https://doi.org/10.1007/978-3-030-33502-1_2

how to meet the increasing food demand while simultaneously providing healthy and high quality food for present and future generations, without compromising the Earth's natural resources and without trespassing the planetary boundaries (Godfray et al., 2010; Steffen et al., 2015). The Food and Agriculture Organization (FAO) (FAO, 2014, 2016) recommends that agriculture systems and food supply chains transition from the dominant industrial system designed for abundant production, sufficiency, and affordability (Prost et al., 2017), to a system concerned with sustainable agri-food business models that conserve land, water, and other natural resources, and that are not socially or environmentally oppressive but economically viable and culturally acceptable (FAO, 1989).

To date however, little attention has been paid to the critical components of food systems that ignite these sustainable transitions to begin with, i.e. entrepreneurs. An evident example of this is the Global Entrepreneurship Monitor, an international study that annually compares entrepreneurial activities for a number of economies, which surprisingly does not provide any information regarding entrepreneurship in the food industry (Global Entrepreneurship Monitor, 2019). Furthermore, GEM categorizes entrepreneurs as either necessity (e.g., pushed into an endeavor) or opportunity-driven (e.g., pulled into an endeavor). This fact is of particular interest since global food systems, with their complexity and desperate need for transitions, provide a quintessential environment for entrepreneurial opportunities based on both need and desire.

The relationship between food systems and entrepreneurs has only recently gained marked recognition by European policy makers, and the appreciation of this dyad is one of the major elements that led to the creation of the Food Knowledge and Innovation Community within the European Institute of Innovation and Technology, i.e. EIT Food, that aims to empower entrepreneurs and others to provide novel solutions to the most relevant challenges with our food systems (EIT Food, 2019).

Furthermore, researchers and field experts highlight that the food system's industrial approach to the use of natural resources has lost its ability to produce satisfactory results, thus giving rise to the knowledge economy as a possible solution to the planetary challenges affecting our lifestyles today (Carayannis & Rakhmatullin, 2014; Di Nauta, Merola, Caputo, & Evangelista, 2018). Food systems are experiencing a shift in productivity and growth practices, in which they are becoming more dependent on human resources in terms of social capital (e.g., knowledge and relationships) than on the availability of physical resources, which outlines the importance for effective interactions between universities, societies, private industrial sectors, and governments.

The emergence of the knowledge economy as a main driver for sustainable transitions has been accompanied by an interest in the role of universities as conduits for economic development within regions, and as nodes for entrepreneurial development (Guerrero, Granados, & González, 2014). In addition, in the knowledge economy, universities are encouraged to actively seek close interactions with private industry and government entities in order to achieve socio-economic development.

2.1 Introduction: Entrepreneurs and Entrepreneurial Opportunities in Food Systems

This involves interweaving universities, industries, and governments in a pattern of linkages to advance economic and social development through innovation strategies (Etzkowitz, Schuler, & Gulbrandsen, 2000). The knowledge economy by nature signifies a rejection of the traditional organizational, cultural, and normative processes that have segmented these entities at the cost of economic competitiveness and technological progress (Etzkowitz & Leydesdorff, 2000).

Europe, along with most regions of the world (e.g., USA, China, and Brazil), has experienced a gradual transition toward a knowledge-based economy, which has not only served as an important driver for the emergence of entrepreneurial activities, but has also introduced knowledge and innovative ideas as substitutes for physical capital and as sources of competitive advantage (Thurik, Stam, & Audretsch, 2013).

Universities are viewed as essential actors with a key role in regional development, and as catalysts for entrepreneurship since they supply the regional entrepreneurial ecosystem with a skilled labor force by developing new knowledge and technologies and by making resources readily available for organizations and individuals, and have been recognized for their role in cultivating human capital and fostering an environment that is supportive of entrepreneurship (Abreu & Grinevich, 2013; De Bernardi, Bertello, & Forliano, 2019; Etzkowitz & Dzisah, 2008; Grimaldi, Kenney, Siegel, & Wright, 2011; Lindqvist, Ketels, & Sölvell, 2013; Miller, Alexander, Cunningham, & Albats, 2018).

Increasingly, more universities around the world have begun to implement entrepreneurial activities and mechanisms to support entrepreneurship within their institutions (Gür, Oylumlu, & Kunday, 2017). This has resulted in a transition in university research from a model of isolated knowledge hubs to engaging in partnerships with business entities and governmental organizations (Zhang, MacKenzie, Jones-Evans, & Huggins, 2016). However, a 'uniform' method to guide how universities should engage in collaboration with businesses and governments remains absent, and manifestations of these collaborations vary.

Universities are also considered key players in promoting and stimulating knowledge sharing (Theodoraki, Messeghem, & Rice, 2018). For instance, the creation of startups using knowledge cultivated by universities is considered an important source of knowledge spillover for regional economic development (Belitski & Heron, 2017).

Due to the aforementioned characteristics of universities, their strategic positioning within ecosystems and communities, and their role in knowledge spillovers and trans-disciplinarity ignited by the knowledge economy, we believe that exploring the leading role of universities as key players to drive and promote the identification and eventual exploitation of entrepreneurial opportunities, where the entrepreneurship process begins, is essential. We further posit that the successful identification and exploitation of entrepreneurial opportunities for food system development that involves business sectors, policy makers, and universities as nodes that connect these stakeholders to community members is the starting point, and a driving force for transformations toward sustainable food systems.

2.2 It All Begins with an Opportunity

Entrepreneurial opportunity is essential to the entrepreneurial process, and opportunities present themselves in food systems in four different ways, as outlined by economic theory (Alvarez & Busenitz, 2001). The first is through consumer demands, which provide opportunities for entrepreneurs to envision and create products and services that satisfy consumers; these demands can arise from increased customer knowledge about healthy or sustainable products that drive new market expectations. A second opportunity comes from changes in supply chains such as new products or new processes, which allow entrepreneurs to remodel existing value chains. Third, entrepreneurial opportunities may arise from new information outlets that expose sectors in need of improvements; these information outlets may include platforms for information sharing between food consumers and producers about production processes, food risks, food transparency and traceability, and food waste. Finally, opportunities for entrepreneurs in food systems may be due to outside shocks to the market; for example, policy changes such as the European Union's (EU) initiative to ban single-use plastics and promote a circular economy, which prompts entrepreneurs to invent sustainable alternatives (European Commission, 2018a).

In a recent study, Kuckertz, Hinderer, and Röhm (2019) investigated the presence of entrepreneurial opportunities in food systems by identifying where startup investors allocated their investments, specifically, in the categories of 'agriculture and forestry' and 'food and beverage'. They categorized investments into a five-step conceptualization of the food value chain: (i) agriculture, (ii) transforming, (iii) converting and packaging, (iv) shipping & selling, and (v) consuming. They conclude that most investments (63%) were allotted to (iii) converting and packaging, which is where products are composed from ingredients and packaged ready for transportation (Kuckertz et al., 2019). For their study, they employed the Dow Jones VentureSource database (a comprehensive database tracking the behavior of startup investors in Europe and the U.S.) for the period of 2013–2017 and focused on investments in food startups. Overall the authors report an increase in investment activity in the food value chain, with arise from 443 investment deals in 2013 to 747 in 2017, thus evidencing a growing interest in food startups (Kuckertz et al., 2019) and highlighting the rising potential for entrepreneurship and innovation in food systems.

As heavily discussed in the literature, entrepreneurs in food systems, as like many other systems, are the drivers of innovations, which if properly supported and educated can succesfully develop sustainable solutions to challenges in achieving the SDG's in relation to food systems.

It is mainly through an exploration of the mechanisms that drive entrepreneurial opportunities that researchers can best describe the ways to promote entrepreneurial activity, and implement the appropriate training and education methods to stimulate food system members to create value and sustainable initiatives through innovation. Recently, the increased attention to sustainable development and the emergence of entrepreneurial talents in many industries have found an important commonality, i.e. the interest of using entrepreneurship as an instrument for sustainable development in food systems. This new synergy translates to an increased demand for improved knowledge, information, and technologies, which have been traditionally mostly generated by universities (Opolot, Isubikalu, Obaa, & Ebanyat, 2018); universities by nature connect and interact with a wide range of public and private organizations and institutions and are in a central position to act as advocates for entrepreneurship (O'Connor & Reed, 2018). Furthermore, the Organization for Economic Cooperation and Development (OECD) and the European Commission have focused on how future developments will depend on a large part on how well universities adapt to unpredictable global environments, therefore they run different schemes to stimulate entrepreneurial development in European universities (Gibb, Haskins, & Robertson, 2013).

2.3 The Focus on Entrepreneurship

Entrepreneurs are oftentimes considered national assets that may be cultivated, stimulated, and rewarded to a great extent. They drive changes in populations' lifestyles and work behaviors, and when successful, oftentimes introduce innovations that improve quality of life, create wealth through their business ventures, and generate the necessary conditions for a prosperous and sustainable society. Entrepreneurs are people, the actors or members of ecosystems who are unafraid to take risks and are adept at identifying entrepreneurial opportunities where most people do not. Entrepreneurs are considered open-minded individuals with a focus on driving change in situations where they may not be satisfied with the status quo. This active involvement in driving change and creating value through innovation is known as entrepreneurship, i.e., what entrepreneurs do. Entrepreneurship is a process of designing, launching, and running a business, which oftentimes begins as a startup, small business, or service.

In simple terms, entrepreneurs are people and entrepreneurship is a process, entrepreneurs are organizers while entrepreneurship is an organization, entrepreneurs are the inventors or innovators while entrepreneurship is the resulting innovation.

Entrepreneurship can be defined as a project-oriented process where an entrepreneur, or team of entrepreneurs, re-allocates limited resources to areas where they can achieve higher productivity in order to create superior value (Tataj, 2015). Entrepreneurship is also defined as an activity that involves the discovery, evaluation, and exploitation of opportunities to introduce new goods and services, ways of organizing markets, processes, and raw materials through efforts that previously had not existed (Shane, 2003). Cogliser and Stambaugh further expand on this definition and split the entrepreneurial process into three phases—(i) variation (i.e., opportunity discovery), (ii) selection (i.e., opportunity evaluation), and (iii) retention (Cogliser & Stambaugh, 2008). They argue that at each of these phases, the probability of success depends on environmental uncertainty, organization of the local ecosystem, and cognitive qualities of the entrepreneur. Furthermore, entrepreneurship has also been conceptualized as the ability to integrate a set of elements into a relationship in order to achieve a goal, or a project that can create value by evolving into a profitable business, improving a new institution, or enhancing human health or innovativeness of a region (European Commission, 2018b). Another popular conceptualization of entrepreneurship is the academic entrepreneur, who is defined by commercializing outcomes of academic research (Grimaldi et al., 2011).

The value created through entrepreneurship can be tangible, intangible, economic, and social (Tataj, 2015). Economic value creation is manifested as new jobs, economic prosperity, societal stability, and equal opportunities, while social value can be a reduction in poverty, increasing the well-being of communities, and better working conditions. Entrepreneurship can be thought of as a means to satisfy the needs of users and customers, bring innovations to underserved communities, and most importantly a means to tackle the current challenges associated with global sustainability of resources.

Entrepreneurship has also been described as a powerful attitude and a discipline that's transversal to the areas of knowledge, science, and organizations (Brito, 2018). In a broader sense, entrepreneurship is a transversal phenomenon that can be well defined in a number of different settings including the non-profit and public sectors. For the purpose of this book, we adopt the definition of entrepreneur as proposed by Schumpeter, in which all of the entrepreneur's activities are related to innovation (Wee, Lim, & Lee, 1994).

Transforming an industry is an important element in describing entrepreneurs, and as stated by Isenberg (2011), entrepreneurs are individuals who continuously seek to create economic value through growth—implying that they are often unsatisfied with the status quo (Isenberg, 2011). Ahmad and Seymour (2008) provide further elaborations and describe entrepreneurs as those who seek to generate value by creating or expanding economic activity and by identifying and exploiting opportunities to create new products, processes, or markets (Ahmad & Seymour, 2008; Kuckertz et al., 2019). These conceptualizations of entrepreneurs, and their goals specifically, illustrate the reasons why they should be supported; through their many activities and initiatives they have the potential to contribute to achieving SDG's and sustainable food systems specifically.

Given the existing conceptualizations of entrepreneurship and entrepreneurs, it is evident that the promotion of entrepreneurship plays an essential role in improving the emergence and competitiveness of SMEs and in enhancing economic opportunities (Ramana, Prasad, & Guda, 2018). Furthermore, knowledge emerges as the most important aspect of entrepreneurs, and is considered the result of a collaborative approach between different members of economic activities that link innovation, learning, and entrepreneurship (Brito, 2018; Ratten, Marques, & Braga, 2018). As noted by Abreu and Grinevich (2013), entrepreneurship involves several activities that go beyond the simple commercialization of goods and services. These activities can involve innovatively combining resources to cultivate new ways of organizing offerings, or establishing new processes to deliver them, and organized efforts put into exploiting opportunities.

The university is one of the most essential institutions to promote entrepreneurship and innovation since its members, i.e., academics, can engage in a wide range of activities which are deemed to be entrepreneurial such as facilitating networks with industry or providing experienced faculty to offer consultancy to aspiring entrepreneurs, which are important steps to reaping academic and commercial rewards, not only for the academic engaging in these activities but for the university; so long as effective knowledge management processes are in place (Miller et al., 2018).

In efforts to provide further insight into the role of universities in fostering entrepreneurship, O'Connor & Reed provide a framework that identifies five specific roles universities play in contributing to regional entrepreneurial development (O'Connor & Reed, 2018).

1. **Human capital development**: Supports the idea of educating highly skilled graduates. This also supports the idea of a broad entrepreneurial education across the diverse disciplines in universities.
2. **Intellectual Resource**: Provides conduits for knowledge sharing across academic members from diverse disciplines, and as a hub that can create system wide collaborations with private and public sectors.
3. **Regional Governance**: Includes long-term commitment, strategy development, providing leadership, being an operational informant, and self-regulated to maximize community resource efficiencies. The long-term commitment stems from the idea that developing an entrepreneurial ecosystem will take time, and the history of longevity in the university system raises expectations that universities are well positioned to 'stay the course' and provide a steady hand (as neither government nor industry are positioned to fulfill this role).
4. **Network Facilitator**: Universities by nature connect with a wide range of public and private organizations and institutions and are in a position to act as advocates for the creation of networks able to stimulate entrepreneurship.
5. **Entrepreneurial Node**: Universities may serve as the 'go-to place' for all things entrepreneurial. As a node, entrepreneurial and innovative ventures will be attracted to it from either inside or outside the university. The notion of entrepreneurial nodes is evident when universities host a specific entrepreneurship or enterprise center or institute. The entrepreneurial node may also not be immediately evident or identifiable as a specific place or activity, and may take place as discipline specific activities of industry engagement or commercialization found in various locations distributed across the university (O'Connor & Reed, 2018).

Keeping the Schumpeterian (1934) definition of entrepreneurs as individuals who exploit market opportunities through technical or organizational innovation (with the rise of the knowledge economy the term 'market opportunity' can also be interchanged with 'research opportunity') we can deduce that the entrepreneurial process requires many inputs in order to the catalyzed. Furthermore, entrepreneurial ecosystems (discussed further in Chap. 3) require the active participation of many system actors, and rely on mechanisms that influence the emergence and identification of entrepreneurial opportunities, the individuals to identify them, their willingness to take on risk and create new ventures, and their ability to develop a project (Isenberg, 2010).

Further, the concept of entrepreneurial opportunity is not completely novel, as authors have long suggested that opportunities are the heart of entrepreneurship (Stevenson & Gumpert, 1985). Without opportunity, there is no entrepreneurship (Short, Ketchen Jr, Shook, & Ireland, 2010).

Van de Ven (1993), specifically, was one of the first authors who did not exclusively focus on individual traits of entrepreneurs, but instead focused on the process of constructing an infrastructure capable of facilitating and restricting entrepreneurship. Specifically, Van de Ven (1993) presents a "social system framework" and highlights the importance of universities, financing opportunities, human capital, and appropriate institutional arrangement to foster entrepreneurial activity.

Entrepreneurship contributes to economic prosperity by serving as an avenue for knowledge spillovers, and by assisting in the creation of marketable products and services that would otherwise not be commercialized. Entrepreneurship is an accepted dynamic of any economy (Minniti & Lévesque, 2008), and universities have long been considered as one of the essential elements of entrepreneurial development in ecosystems that strive toward a knowledge economy.

Once successful, entrepreneurs have the potential to drive significant impacts in their society and environment, but if entrepreneurs are not set up for success, their ideas will simply not get them anywhere/far.

Similarly, Moore (1993) posits that entrepreneurship does not exist in a vacuum, and that entrepreneurs are highly dependent on their environment. This finding is also shared by a number of authors who argue that entrepreneurship is a local phenomenon, shaped by the immediate environment and its available resources (Feldman, 2003; Malecki, 1993; Motoyama, Konczal, Bell-Masterson, & Morelix, 2014). This idea has led to the emergence and understanding of entrepreneurship as a system of connected networks that share resources and knowledge, and assume risks together. Furthermore, Aulet and Murray (2013) and Isenberg (2011) identify *innovation* and *growth-ambition* as the two main individual characteristics of entrepreneurship. They go on to state that innovation-driven entrepreneurship requires specific policies, support systems, and adequate environments.

The prevalent question that has been raised by authors is how entrepreneurship can be best systemically ignited, and what are the best methods for entrepreneurial activity to develop, be supported, and sustained.

Finally, even though a plethora of proposed definitions for entrepreneurship exist, and diverse conceptualizations of entrepreneurs have been proposed, we do not narrow our focus to one specific manifestation of entrepreneur or entrepreneurship. Through systems thinking, we know that food systems are composed of all actors from every sector of the food supply chain, and other industries that are interdependent with food systems, therefore, in the remaining chapters, we consider every member, or stakeholder, of the food ecosystem a potential entrepreneur.

2.4 Entrepreneurial Opportunity

Entrepreneurial opportunities have been regarded as positive and favorable circumstances that lead to entrepreneurial action, and have been lauded for their central role in igniting entrepreneurship (Aldrich & Cliff, 2003; Eckhardt & Shane, 2003; Shane, Nicolaou, Cherkas, & Spector, 2010). Schumpeter (1934) viewed opportunities as central to the innovative combination of resources, and suggested that novel combinations and exploitations of opportunities could manifest as products and services, new production methods, novel processes to organize markets, and new or raw materials' management. The appreciation of opportunities has been persistent in the literature as evidenced by Kirzner (1979) who emphasized that opportunities are at the core of market imperfections, and when identified and exploited, have the potential to generate economic returns.

Based on these two main ideas behind entrepreneurial opportunity, we can see a dichotomy of thought, i.e. the creation and discovery view. Schumpeter (1934) and his successors support the 'creation view' and posit that opportunities are not objective and must be created by the entrepreneur and his/her actions when exploring new products or services. Creation opportunities are dependent on the entrepreneur's perceptions and skills (Aldrich & Kenworthy, 1999). In this sense, Schumpeter's definition also suggests that the creation of opportunities requires both intellect and capital. The discovery view on the other hand, proposed by Kirzner (1979), assumes that the goal of the entrepreneur is to identify and exploit opportunities and existing market imperfections which give way to these opportunities exogenously, leaving the entrepreneur the responsibility to recognize and act upon these changes, which can be of a technological, social, or political nature (Shane, 2003).

The dichotomous views regarding entrepreneurial opportunities can further be explained through theory; e.g., discovery theory and creation theory. They are considered two main alternative theories of entrepreneurial opportunity; discovery posits that opportunities exist in the market independently of the entrepreneur (e.g., need for diet programs in a high obesity region), while in creation theory the assumption is that opportunities themselves do not exist, but must be created by the entrepreneur (e.g., extracting by products from food waste for later use) (Baker & Nelson, 2005; Gaglio & Katz, 2001).

Entrepreneurship engagement in the global food system is believed to be an effective solution to address the growing global challenges (Kline et al., 2017; Tripathi & Agarwal, 2014). But like most entrepreneurs in many industries, food entrepreneurs also experience their share of difficulties when faced with identifying market opportunities, creating a managerial structure behind the opportunity, and securing funding sources to scale ideas into startups or business ventures (Cranwell, Kolodinsky, Donnelly, Downing, & Padilla-Zakour, 2005; Opolot et al., 2018).

In the case of food entrepreneurs, for example, additional facilities such as certified kitchens for product preparation, permits for product or service production, and marketing channels to distribute their food products or disseminate their innovations might also be necessary (Chen & Polat, 2017).

The basic premise behind opportunities or venture creation is the introduction of new goods or services (Sarma, 2018). This relates to some of the earlier postulations of entrepreneurship, such as Stevenson (1983) who defined entrepreneurship as the pursuit of opportunity, without regarding the resources that are currently, and actually, controlled.

Furthermore, we adopt the view of Santos (2018) that entrepreneurial opportunities cannot be understood as a single factor, but as a set of conditions which allow for the viable introduction of innovations, new organizational or business models, or customer engagement strategies for improved market results (Santos, 2018).

This chapter does not intend to contribute to existing debates regarding entrepreneurial opportunities, or whether these are discovered or created; however we contend with researchers who support the idea that opportunities are both discovered and created.

In this chapter, we aim to highlight how universities, as part of innovative communities, can stimulate entrepreneurs to harness and exploit opportunities in the food system. We build our argument based on the notion that opportunity identification is not a simple "Aha!" or "Eureka!" moment, but a more circular process comprised of knowledge acquisition and creation, knowledge sharing, and individual reflection on new findings (Lumpkin & Lichtenstein, 2005). Furthermore, evidence also shows that opportunity discovery can occur during the pre-conception phase of new ventures, or in already established firms (Hayton, Chandler, & DeTienne, 2011).

A prevalent idea in the literature is that entrepreneurial opportunities arise from disequilibrium, or market needs, which can then be harnessed and exploited by individuals, and are usually interpreted as technological, political, regulatory, and social opportunities (Casson, 2005; Cohen & Winn, 2007; Holcombe, 2003; Saemundsson & Holmén, 2011). It is the recognition of these opportunities that brings forth the positive and favorable circumstances that lead to entrepreneurial actions.

Entrepreneurial opportunity has been conceptually divided into three themes; *discovery*, *creation*, and *recognition*. Sarasvathy, Dew, Velamuri, and Venkataraman (2003) further advanced these themes by distinguishing the three themes based on the preconditions of their existence (Sarasvathy et al., 2003).

In short, opportunity creation occurs when neither product nor demand exist and must be invented by the entrepreneur (Buenstorf, 2007), on the other hand, when a product or market demand exist and another condition must be identified is known as opportunity discovery, and if the product and market demand are obvious, then exploring new ways to organize these demands is considered opportunity recognition. The diverse processes for identifying opportunities, coupled with the recent stimulus to adopt systems thinking thus encourages the integration and consideration of different vantage points of entrepreneurial opportunity simultaneously rather than engaging in debates to promote individual and discipline specific views (Chiasson & Saunders, 2005; Gaglio & Katz, 2001).

Systems thinking accepts the notion that the opportunity recognition process is significantly influenced by a variety of factors, including individual cognition, social networks, personality traits, prior knowledge, knowledge sharing, environmental

2.4 Entrepreneurial Opportunity

factors, and the opportunity itself (Acs, Audretsch, & Lehmann, 2013; Acs, Braunerhjelm, Audretsch, & Carlsson, 2009; Ardichvili, Cardozo, & Ray, 2003; García-Cabrera & García-Soto, 2009; George, Parida, Lahti, & Wincent, 2016; Grégoire & Shepherd, 2012; Tang, Kreiser, Marino, Dickson, & Weaver, 2009; Tumasjan & Braun, 2012); opportunity identification is shaped by objective and subjective factors (Grégoire, Barr, & Shepherd, 2010).

Alvarez and Barney (2007) further made essential contributions proposing the idea that the formation of entrepreneurial opportunities can be explained both through discovery and creation processes rather than just one or the other.

Furthermore, based on the results from a systematic literature review of 189 articles that discussed the topic of entrepreneurial opportunity recognition, George et al. (2016) individuate a series of six influencing factors that are related to opportunity discovery and creation, which then lead individuals to evaluate and exploit the identified opportunities—(i) prior knowledge, (ii) social capital, (iii) cognition/personality traits, (iv) environmental conditions, (v) alertness, and (vi) systematic search (George et al., 2016).

The authors suggest that research emphasis should be allotted to these six influential factors that affect entrepreneurship and not on the two previously dominating opportunity identification processes (e.g., creation vs. discovery). They further evidence that these six factors are interrelated, and that excluding any of them would misrepresent an understanding of how individuals create or discover opportunities. A summary of the six factors follows:

- **Prior Knowledge:** Some individuals are able to discover opportunities due to prior information they possess and their capacity to value it (Audretsch, 2005), while an individual's lack of knowledge and skill may limit their ability to discover or create opportunities (Kourilsky & Esfandiari, 1997; Kourilsky & Walstad, 1998). Prior knowledge can further be categorized into three dimensions, (i) knowledge of markets, (ii) knowledge of ways to serve the market, and (iii) knowledge of customer problems (Shane, 2000). Furthermore, Chandra, Styles, and Wilkinson (2009) posit that prior knowledge must be combined with other information from various sources that assist entrepreneurs in recognizing, finding, and creating opportunities (Chandra et al., 2009; Van Gelderen et al., 2008). Literature also suggests that prior knowledge is a fundamental cognitive resource of an individual, a building block of the opportunity identification process, a fountain of insights that help synthesize information regarding opportunity identification, and a moderator in identifying opportunities (Grégoire et al., 2010; Haynie, Shepherd, & McMullen, 2009; Rerup, 2005; Shane & Venkataraman, 2000; Vaghely & Julien, 2010). It must also be noted that prior knowledge can also limit new ideas and creativity, as the human brain is accustomed to processing information in a certain way, certain bits of new incoming information may go unnoticed or new processes might be hard to accept over traditional methods.
- **Social Capital:** Social capital serves as a facilitator to access information and tangible resources in the entrepreneurial opportunity recognition process (Ardichvili et al., 2003; Shane & Venkataraman, 2000). Increased social capital

ensures better access to scarce resources, which in turn assist entrepreneurs to exploit opportunities (Fuentes, Arroyo, Bojica, & Pérez, 2010). Social capital plays a mediating role between human capital and opportunity recognition, as well as resource mobilization (Bhagavatula, Elfring, Van Tilburg, & Van De Bunt, 2010). Social capital is considered a critical influential factor for opportunity recognition.

- **Cognition and Personality Traits:** These are comprised of concepts discussed primarily in psychology and include personal traits such as creativity, self-efficacy, risk averseness, extraversion, need for independence, and locus of control (Ardichvili et al., 2003; Baron & Ensley, 2006; Nicolaou & Shane, 2009; Tataj, 2015; Tominc & Rebernik, 2007). Self-efficacy, for example, motivates entrepreneurs to set high objectives and achieve them (Wood & Pearson, 2009). Individuals willing to take risks are also more adept at perceiving the larger frame of opportunities that surrounds them (Baron & Ensley, 2006; Foo, 2011). Individuals who are less afraid and are not intimidated by success tend to view a new venture as an opportunity (Li, 2011). And finally, intelligence and creativity are essential for identifying a niche opportunity (George et al., 2016). It has also been found that entrepreneurs' creative capacity is higher than that of the average population (Heinonen, Hytti, & Stenholm, 2011). Finally, as posited Tataj (2015) the origin of invention is culture with its individual and collective influences to create—that is creativity. Tataj (2015) further states that invention is an idea, and that an invention is transformed into innovation in a creative process that bridges the gap between the world of ideas and market or societal reality (Tataj, 2015).

- **Environmental Factors:** Environmental factors can be viewed as an "umbrella term" for a society's economic growth, social and political contexts, geographic location, and cultural values that affect entrepreneurs in the process of finding or creating opportunity. For example, changes in available technologies, social norms, political climate, and demographic conditions create pockets of new information and necessities, which help in the processes of entrepreneurial discovery and creation (Shane & Venkataraman, 2000). Furthermore Casson and Wadeson (2007) evidence that changes in economic environments make opportunity recognition feasible, and economic stability is also important for generating a positive atmosphere for entrepreneurial activity (Global Entrepreneurship Monitor, 2019). Social and political factors refer to the availability of tangible and intangible resources, government regulations, policies, and other societal issues (e.g., the waning sustainability of food production) that may influence the opportunity recognition process (Tominc & Rebernik, 2007). Finally, it can be argued that entrepreneurial opportunity is dependent on information regarding a specific region's available resources that can be reorganized to create value for its inhabitants.

- **Entrepreneurial Alertness:** Alertness is defined as the capacity to possess insights into identifying entrepreneurial opportunities. Researchers agree that if a person's level of alertness is high, opportunities could be identified even without actively searching for them, ergo by simply observing existing phenomena (George et al., 2016). Gaglio and Katz (2001) suggest that alert individuals possess complex and adaptive mental frameworks about change, the social environment they find themselves in, and the industries that surround them, however they also suggest that the process of validating the alertness construct empirically is too complex to be quantified. In essence, alert individuals are more prone to viewing situations from new perspectives or unconventional ways more so than people with lower levels of alertness (George et al., 2016).

- **Systematic Searchers/Resources:** Systematic searches help individuals discover opportunities (Westhead, Ucbasaran, & Wright, 2009; Zahra, Gedajlovic, Neubaum, & Shulman, 2009). Research on systemic searches posits that entrepreneurial opportunity discovery can only happen when entrepreneurs have access to private information (e.g., research databases, network platforms), and are able to use this information to help themselves obtain specific additional insights to complement his/her prior knowledge (Fiet, 1996). Furthermore, Murphy (2011) specifies that systematically searching for entrepreneurial opportunities does not represent the opposite of alertness, and developed a framework that suggests that opportunities may also be discovered in situations that are high or low on both dimensions (i.e., searching and alertness). Furthermore, actively searching constitutes a key determinant of entrepreneurial success, and influences the opportunity recognition processes (Santos, 2018; Wustrow, 2018).

In addition, George et al. (2016) evidence that only a handful of authors are involved, or have been involved, in establishing the prominent dialogue supporting entrepreneurial opportunity identification (George et al., 2016). This scenario leaves room for questions such as, how, and why some individuals recognize and create opportunities while others do not. Hechavarría and Welter (2015) argue that in order to advance our understanding of entrepreneurial opportunities, scholars must analyze both sides of the debate (i.e., discovery vs. creation) to determine how to best support aspiring entrepreneurs through both perspectives.

It is quite evident that a systematic and holistic method should be considered best practice for promoting and facilitating entrepreneurial discovery and creation through universities. Integrating entrepreneurship aspects that involve technical and scientific know-how, business creation, social and environmental awareness, experiential education, and values and ethics into academic curriculums would provide universities with the increased capacity to promote entrepreneurial opportunities.

2.5 Opportunity Discovery and Creation in Food Systems

The food system is also a significant contributor to worldwide economies, and in 2016 it accounted for 8.6% of all employment in Europe (European Commission, 2019). At the same time, the food system is faced with complicated challenges such as food security, food waste, and resource over-exploitation, thus providing an ideal arena for aspiring entrepreneurs to develop innovative solutions to solve or help ameliorate these challenges. Individual entrepreneurial skills are decisive for identifying opportunities and navigating turbulent environments (Aparicio, Urbano, & Audretsch, 2016), however these skills must be complemented by personal adaptability and flexibility, strong leadership, and an environment that promotes entrepreneurial mindsets (Gibb & Hannon, 2006).

Regarding food systems, entrepreneurial and organizational competencies among farmers are considered critical in improving their productivity and market access for sustainable agriculture development through enhanced household food and income security (Opolot et al., 2018). The role of training to build farmer's capacity for successful agricultural transitions cannot be over-estimated or exaggerated (FAO, 2014), and universities are viewed as the go-to institutions in an innovation system framework with the responsibility to instill competencies for sustainable transitions among farmers. Regarding the agricultural sector, universities have been viewed as key actors in the performance of agricultural innovation system frameworks (Etzkowitz & Zhou, 2017), and have been evidenced as significant contributors to farmer's competence building (Pindado, Sánchez, Verstegen, & Lans, 2018).

This was evidenced in a study conducted by Opolot et al. (2018) that assessed the influence of a training program, conducted by Makere University in Kampala Uganda, on smallholder farmer's competencies, productivity, and organizational capacity. The farmers underwent a 4-month training on topics regarding marketing, record keeping, value addition, business planning, financial management, and budgeting in order to build entrepreneurial capacity. From this study, scholars discovered that the farmers, as a result of the training, developed value-added products such as soy, coffee, soymilk, roasted and packed groundnuts, and groundnut paste thus evidencing the efficacy of such a practical training, and outlining the power of such trainings in activating bottom up transitions (Opolot et al., 2018). Opportunity recognition, however, does not only involve the provision of sufficient and adequate resources to be used or exploited, it is also dependent on subjective efforts to comprehend the immediate, local, or regional environment and imagine the possibilities for resource utilization (e.g., introducing new technologies or processes) (Patzelt & Shepherd, 2011).

Recently, the United Nations adopted the 'UN Decade on Ecosystem Restoration', declared on March 1st, 2019 by the UN General Assembly, which aims to scale up the restoration of degraded and destroyed natural ecosystems as a proven measure to combat climate change and improve food security, water supply, and biodiversity. This initiative will be led by the UN Environment and the Food and Agriculture Organization (FAO), and offers unparalleled opportunities for job creation and food security, and paves the way for entrepreneurial endeavors and innovations to tackle climate change (United Nations Environment, 2019).

However, this, along with other efforts to support entrepreneurship will be futile if attention is not granted to the entrepreneurial opportunity identification process. The food system consists of a diverse spectrum of members, from farmers, to investors, academics, and business owners. This heterogeneity in system members suggests varying levels of preparation to tackle entrepreneurial endeavors, and while providing physical resources is a key aspect, another important area of focus is providing individuals with the necessary skills to embrace the present food system environment. In the next sections we outline how universities can engage with other ecosystem members to best ignite entrepreneurial initiatives amongst food system members.

2.5.1 Opportunity Creation: Tangible Resources

Academic institutions are perhaps the most prevalent actors in efforts to create entrepreneurial networks and intentions, this is due to the fact that beyond a focus on entrepreneurs themselves, a large section of entrepreneurial and innovation research focuses on universities and their role in creating stimulating environments, such as innovation and entrepreneurial ecosystems (Nelles, Bramwell, & Wolfe, 2005). Universities, especially, have been evidenced to maintain an active role within entrepreneurial ecosystems even when they are not a central actor (Motoyama & Knowlton, 2017).

However, providing vast networks, sufficient amounts of funding, and immersing potential entrepreneurs into environments filled with many avenues for opportunity creation will not be sufficient to ignite entrepreneurial initiatives.

2.5.2 Opportunity Recognition: Intangible Resources

Currently, economic globalization and entrepreneurship contribute to daily growth and development, and the shift from efficiency-driven to innovation-driven developments in universities have also fostered models that promote investment in emerging growth and multilateral alliances that enhance global competition (Brito, 2018). With the shift toward innovation-driven, and knowledge economies, universities have adopted a larger role than simple knowledge production, indeed they engage in a range of activities that prepare future generations to meet the requirements to drive innovations in such a new landscape.

Regarding intangible resources such as knowledge and social capital, Hmieleski, Carr, and Baron (2015) found that psychological capital such as optimism, self-efficacy, and resilience positively influence opportunity creation in dynamic industry conditions, such as the food system (Hmieleski et al., 2015). Food system members however do not always posses the entrepreneurial competencies to enhance their productivity and competitiveness such as strategic planning, relationship building, marketing, and value chain development, all of which facilitate opportunity recognition (Bergevoet, Giesen, Saatkamp, Van Woerkum, & Huirne, 2005; Holster, Klerkx, & Elzen, 2008; Morgan, Marsden, Miele, & Morley, 2010). Furthermore, stress tolerance and the willingness to bear uncertainty have been identified as antecedents of opportunity identification (Frese & Gielnik, 2014).

Product development, documentation, organizational management, and diversification are also important enablers for farmers and food producers to create new value through creativity; applying social capital and taking risks in adopting and using new technologies (Chegini & Khoshtinat, 2011; Ezeibe, Okorji, Chah, & Abudei, 2014; Rezai, Mohamed, & Shamsudin, 2011). Improving competencies in agri-food by promoting entrepreneurial mindsets is viewed as a precondition for ensuring sustainable agriculture and rural development (Opolot et al., 2018). Furthermore, Hennon (2012) posits that entrepreneurial competencies stimulate creativity and innovativeness that re-orient food system members into thinking about and applying new management practices that embolden their confidence to engage in entrepreneurial endeavors. Increasing food ecosystem members' self-efficacy in entrepreneurial activities also enables them to work in cooperative ways, thereby also benefitting from economies of scale (Basso, Fayolle, & Bouchard, 2009).

Regardless of the type of approach adopted by universities, the intended outcome should generate changes in the knowledge and behaviors that enable food system members to not only increase productivity, but also engage in practices that lead to sustainable solutions for challenges threatening our food system.

Aspiring and potential entrepreneurs need both the adequate environment and resources to be able to create opportunities, but also the personal knowledge and characteristics to identify and be able to know what to do with existing opportunities. By ensuring that the presence of explicit resources is accompanied by the substantial tacit knowledge required for the development and use of new technologies, the university then becomes an important resource for entrepreneurial activity (Zucker, Darby, & Brewer, 1994).

2.6 Entrepreneurial Universities

Universities are knowledge-intensive institutions that play an important role in today's knowledge-based entrepreneurial economies (Acs et al., 2009; Audretsch, 2014; De Bernardi, Bertello, & Forliano, 2019). Many scholars have examined the contributions of universities to the economy, including knowledge spillover theory of entrepreneurship (Audretsch, 2014), regional innovation ecosystems (Asheim & Coenen, 2005; Cooke, Uranga, & Etxebarria, 1997), entrepreneurial ecosystems (Brown & Mason, 2017), academic entrepreneurship (Bertello, Azucar, & Tirabeni, 2019; Hayter, Nelson, Zayed, & O'Connor, 2018; Siegel & Wright, 2015), and entrepreneurial universities concept (Etzkowitz et al., 2000; Guerrero, Urbano, & Fayolle, 2016).

The concept of the entrepreneurial university emerged in the 1940's and 1950's and fostered connections and collaborations with industry partners, government agencies, and society in order to stimulate applications for research, trading patents, and diffusing technological and scientific capacity.

The two go-to examples for entrepreneurial universities are the Massachusetts Institute of Technology (MIT), (i.e., the most impactful entrepreneurial university) and Stanford University in California (i.e. the most famous entrepreneurial university) (Tataj, 2015). An entrepreneurial university can be defined as a university that finds new solutions to address the pressures and challenges that stem from an uncertain and unpredictable environment (Hannon, 2013).

University entrepreneurship ecosystems can be defined as: educational programs, infrastructures, regulations, culture, and relationships with economic agents (Guerrero & Urbano, 2012) acting in the knowledge-based entrepreneurial economies as facilitators of innovation and entrepreneurial opportunities. Many initiatives have been put in place to ensure that scholars and talented individuals pursue a career or explore potential opportunities within entrepreneurship ecosystems, such as the concept of the 'entrepreneurial university'. As defined by National Center for Entrepreneurship in Education (NCEE) the entrepreneurial university can be best characterized as promoting institutional leadership and strong entrepreneurial culture, and can create the policies and practices that are conductive to the development of enterprising and entrepreneurial mindsets and behaviors throughout the organization (e.g., in management, administration, teaching, and research activities for academic staff and students alike) (Hannon, 2013). The entrepreneurial university mission is built on the traditional academic task of producing research and providing education, with entrepreneurship being added as a third mission during the course of the last two decades (Clark, 1998; Goldstein, 2010; Kirby, 2006; Wissema, 2009). The emergence of entrepreneurial universities has accelerated along with the university's adoption of new responsibilities for knowledge transfer and technological innovation (Bramwell & Wolfe, 2008; Martinelli, Meyer, & Von Tunzelmann, 2008). This is due to both the internal development of universities, and external influences such as the drive for sustainable knowledge-based solutions in high-risk regions (Etzkowitz, 2003; Etzkowitz et al., 2000; Goldstein, 2010).

The entrepreneurial university is thought of as an avenue to answer the increasing global academic competitions, and the need to support economic growth through knowledge transfer (Wissema, 2009). However, its important to note that universities are not entirely in control of their entrepreneurial transformation, and instead cope with issues regarding strategies that empower them to create and disseminate new knowledge and eventually develop such a role (Giuliani & Rabellotti, 2012).

Due to the increased focus on sustainable economic development, entrepreneurial universities actively seek ways to interact with public and private partners and communities in order to create a cohesive impact on sustainability challenges; where joint efforts are needed to combine socio-economic concerns with growing concerns regarding food nutrition and security, healthy societies, poverty, and the mounting environmental issues leading to climate change (Cohen, 2006).

In a study of the transformation of European Universities, Clark (1998) uses the term 'entrepreneurial university' to denote a characteristic of social systems, that must be adopted by the entire university, its internal departments, research centers, faculties, and schools (Clark, 1998).

Literature also highlights that universities can achieve the status of entrepreneurial university in two main ways. The first includes the concept of 'academic entrepreneurship' and focuses on the commercialization of knowledge and research findings (Hayter et al., 2018; Klofsten & Jones-Evans, 2000), through academic entrepreneurship universities are seen as knowledge hubs (Youtie & Shapira, 2008) with the associated challenges and opportunities of technology transfer (Owen-Smith & Powell, 2003). The second way includes entrepreneurial education (Gibb & Hannon, 2006) becoming part of the university's teaching mission, which includes the building of entrepreneurial competencies in students and faculty (Altmann & Ebersberger, 2013). By providing knowledge and human capital, universities also promote an entrepreneurial culture and become catalysts for entrepreneurial opportunity searching, startups, and spin-offs (Cohen, 2006; Guerrero et al., 2014).

Miller et al. (2018) further evidence that throughout the literature there is an increased interest on how to improve the effectiveness of knowledge transfer from universities to industries, and highlight that many lists that attempt to identify the type of activities that constitute university-industry knowledge transfer have been developed (Bommer & Jalajas, 2004; Miller et al., 2018).

Interestingly, the development of the entrepreneurial university is conditioned by formal and informal, and external and internal factors that relate to its available resources and capabilities (Guerrero & Urbano, 2012). External factors may include partnerships with stakeholders, industry collaborations, local policy structures, and access to new technologies to name a few (Goldstein, 2010; Guerrero & Urbano, 2012). Internal factors may include entrepreneurship centers, accelerators, and incubators (discussed in the following sections), and the individual actors, their knowledge of entrepreneurial processes, willingness to engage, and the resulting effect member behaviors impose on entrepreneurial culture, whether positive or negative.

Building on the internal factors' consideration, Goldfarb and Henrekson (2003) compare two different approaches to support entrepreneurship in universities, a top-down approach that is most prevalent in Europe with a more bottom-up approach applied in the USA. Not surprisingly, they found the bottom-up approach more successful in stimulating academics to commercialize their research results.

The attitudes of university members toward entrepreneurship are considered the most critical factors that affect the development of entrepreneurial universities (Guerrero & Urbano, 2012). One of the central preconditions for entrepreneurial universities is their academics believing in their entrepreneurial potential therefore driving a supportive atmosphere within the institution.

In addition to simply supporting and enabling the legitimacy of entrepreneurial activities among academics, in order to truly become entrepreneurial, universities must develop their dynamic capabilities, especially in sensing opportunities, seizing them by relying on strong university leadership, and be able to transform policies, strategies, and practices whenever they become unsuitable for the local environment (Leih & Teece, 2016).

As the economy has evolved from a 'managed economy' driven by physical capital, towards an 'entrepreneurial and knowledge economy' driven by knowledge (Audretsch & Thurik, 2004; Thurik et al., 2013), the role universities has also evolved (Audretsch, 2014). Universities have evolved from a Humboldtian model whose core idea is a combination of research and teaching (Rothblatt & Wittrock, 1993), towards a model that aims to naturally include industry partners in new initiatives. Known as the Third Mission, this initiative seeks to drive economic and social development for the institution and its surrounding communities, while concurrently developing the core pillars of research and teaching (Audretsch, 2014; Etzkowitz, 2004). Elements to foster entrepreneurial activities in universities and move them toward the third mission include Technology Transfer Offices, entrepreneurship courses and degrees, diverse governing models for incubators and accelerators, mentoring, business coaching, and even university venture capitalists to finance academic business ventures (Tataj, 2015).

One of the most essential considerations when creating entrepreneurial universities to drive the identification and promotion of entrepreneurial opportunities is that regional differences will always be determining factors that guide the development of an entrepreneurial identity, therefore a uniform approach to promoting the identification of entrepreneurial opportunities cannot be recommended.

In a study conducted by Gibson and Foss (2017) analyzed the significance of five university entrepreneurial architecture dimensions on the entrepreneurial 'turn' of ten universities. The five dimensions they individuate are the following:

1. **Structure**: Includes technology transfer offices, incubators, technology parks, and business portals.
2. **Systems**: Focuses on networks of communication and the configuration of linkages between structures and administration.
3. **Leadership**: Focuses on the qualification and orientation of key influencers including administrators, board of directors, department heads, and 'star scientists'.
4. **Strategies**: Refers to institutional goals elaborated in institutional planning documents, incentive structures, and policy.
5. **Culture**: Refers to institutional, departmental, and individual attitudes and norms.

From their study, Gibson and Foss (2017) emphasize the importance and impact of the regional and national context in which the university is embedded concerning the launch, development, and sustainability of programs and activities supporting entrepreneurial turns. Another major finding supports the idea that institutional change toward the development of ecosystems thinking must adopt both top-down and bottom-up approaches. Furthermore, they report that even for cases that emphasized university autonomy, a national law or environmental stimulant was important for a transition toward entrepreneurial university.

The entrepreneurial university engenders a culture of entrepreneurship as a whole institution, and creates an infrastructure that promotes knowledge sharing and open innovation, supports new ventures from established and aspiring entrepreneurs, and offers avenues for entrepreneurial education and skills development. In order to turn a university into an entrepreneurial university, top-down and bottom-up converging forces are needed.

Developing entrepreneurially is a complex endeavor that crosses levels of influence and control while being strongly impacted by broader institutional and organizational environments (Gibson & Foss, 2017).

In the following sections we provide a brief overview and best practices for creating and engaging with the main elements of entrepreneurial universities, i.e., entrepreneurial education, entrepreneurship centers (including technology transfer offices, incubators, and accelerators), the Triple-Helix approach for open collaboration, and finally, the Knowledge Triangle, which has been the driving force behind the creation of Knowledge and Innovation Communities funded by the European Institute of Innovation and Technology (EIT) (Tataj, 2015).

2.7 Entrepreneurship Education

Entrepreneurship education has been previously associated with increased entrepreneurial skills and intention, and economic growth, as well as with new knowledge and the discovery and development of competitive opportunities (Wong, Ho, & Autio, 2005). This model of education dates back decades with one of the first entrepreneurship courses developed at Harvard's Business School in 1947 (Katz, 2003). Since then, the prevalence of entrepreneurship education programs has experienced significant global increases (Katz, 2003; Autio, Nambisan, Thomas, & Wright, 2018). As summarized by Fiore, Sansone, and Paolucci (2019) the number of entrepreneurship education programs has experienced marked increases, this is also evidenced by Katz (2003) and Torrance et al. (2013) who found 2200 entrepreneurship related courses in over 1600 schools in the early 2000's, and more than 5000 in 2008 (Fiore et al., 2019; Katz, 2003; Torrance et al., 2013). Entrepreneurship education is vital for the formation of entrepreneurial activity as it provides the ability to recognize and grasp the right opportunities and to develop them into more elaborated business concepts (Marvel, 2013), meanwhile it is positively related with venture performance as it provides the requested capabilities for the daily operations of firms such as problem-solving and decision-making qualities (Chandler, & Hanks, 1994). Hence, a reinforcement of entrepreneurship education and training is strategic for the creation of business ventures, especially in high-tech sectors.

In Europe, the European Council has stressed that entrepreneurship education should be a priority strategy for sustainable, inclusive, and economic growth (Curth, Chatzichristou, Devaux, & Allinson, 2015). Due to specific policy initiatives, emerging research that highlights the positive associations between entrepreneurial education and practical entrepreneurial skills, and the idea that entrepreneurship education can foster entrepreneurial ecosystems, the increasing number of entrepreneurship education programs should come as no surprise (Cavallo, Ghezzi, & Balocco, 2018)

Despite the high prevalence of entrepreneurship education programs (Nabi, Liñán, Fayolle, Krueger, & Walmsley, 2017), most of them are designed for students from specific academic fields and specific levels of academic and professional preparation. This finding seems contradictive since Human Capital Theory suggests that multi-disciplinarity is important for innovation and entrepreneurship (Colombo & Grilli, 2005), thus combining individuals from diverse backgrounds and investigating the

2.7 Entrepreneurship Education

effect of multi-disciplinarity in entrepreneurship education programs can be of essential value.

In efforts to synthesize the way in which entrepreneurship education is executed, Béchard and Grégoire (2005) classified entrepreneurship education into three distinct models: (i) the supply model, (ii) the demand model, and (iii) the competence model. The supply model emerges as a theoretical-oriented teaching model, while the demand and competence models manifest as more practical-oriented teaching models; since a professor or faculty member acts as a tutor and facilitator in the demand model, and as a coach or developer in the competence model, the student takes on active roles and knowledge intake becomes practical and not theoretical.

The proposed practical dimension by Béchard and Grégoire (2005) proves quite useful in guiding entrepreneurship education. For example, Kassean, Vanevenhoven, Liguori, and Winkel (2015) found that students who engage in entrepreneurship experiential learning activities report higher levels of entrepreneurial intention. Their findings build on previous research by Rasmussen and Sørheim (2006) who discuss that a 'learning-by-doing' approach that involves the student is essential when teaching entrepreneurship since it promotes team work and open conduits for cooperation with more experienced entrepreneurs and mentors (Kassean et al., 2015). As reported by Pittaway and Cope (2007), in order to best promote entrepreneurial skills and assist aspiring entrepreneurs to harness opportunities in diverse and authentic environments, entrepreneurship education should aim to educate 'for' entrepreneurship by way of experiential and action learning, which includes idea generation exercises, elaboration on real case studies, startup creation, mentorship projects, exposure to experienced entrepreneurs, pitch simulations, and business case development training (Kassean et al., 2015).

These findings are further supported by the Human Capital Theory, which suggests that multi-disciplinarity is important in entrepreneurship (Colombo & Grilli, 2005). And practice-based entrepreneurship education programs have been evidenced to play a role in promoting entrepreneurship in the local entrepreneurship ecosystem (Rasmussen & Sørheim, 2006).

Shedding further light on the aforementioned ideas, Fiore et al. (2019) conducted an exploratory single case study on an entrepreneurial learning program in a multidisciplinary environment known as the Contamination Lab of Turin (CLabTo). CLabTo is a joint-entrepreneurship education program developed by the Polytechnic of Turin and the University of Turin that aims to increase entrepreneurial skills and intentions for students through challenge-based entrepreneurial learning programs. Furthermore, in order to develop the challenge-based program, entrepreneurship education and design thinking were combined, thus including design methods, cognitive processes and techniques, and sensibility toward problem-solving (Fiore et al., 2019). Furthermore, challenge-based programs allow diverse actors of the local entrepreneurship ecosystem to be integrated into a single environment.

In CLabTo, organizers employ the 'demand model' introduced by Béchard and Grégoire (2005) in order to guide student-professor interactions and enhance the active role of students. From their results, Fiore and colleagues support the idea that creating teams composed of individuals with diverse competencies and from different academic backgrounds, while adopting the principles of design-thinking are quite useful in entrepreneurial education, and that challenge-based entrepreneurship courses lead to cooperation with external actors in the local entrepreneurial ecosystem (Fiore et al., 2019). Furthermore, when seeking to develop entrepreneurial skill and ability, the authors suggest employing a practical-oriented entrepreneurship-teaching model, such as the one employed by CLabTo, which is inclusive of corporations, student-led entrepreneurial organizations, and other resources such as incubators.

Currently, there is a widespread use of experiential learning in entrepreneurial education, and experiential learning has been recognized as a model effort to integrate real world experiences with conceptual learning (Onyido & Duru, 2019).

A popular model for entrepreneurship education for food system members is the Northeast Center for Food Entrepreneurship (NECFE) in the United States. It is a collaborative effort between Cornell University and the University of Vermont, and uses a multi-institutional and regional collaboration approach to provide technical assistance and education for businesses in the food industry and promote sustainable economic development of rural communities (Cranwell et al., 2005). Furthermore, upon evaluation of the NECFE, five essential components of a model food entrepreneurship assistance and education center were identified:

1. Multi-institutional and regional collaboration.
2. Expertise (i.e., through faculty and network contacts).
3. Facilities and resources.
4. Services.
5. Evaluation of the Center.

The authors posit that these components build on each other and enable entrepreneurship education programs to provide possible entrepreneurs with access to relevant technology in the food system, technical information, and skills that are directly applicable to real world situations (e.g., opportunity identification, scale up, management) (Cranwell et al., 2005).

Finally, individuals interested in engaging in, creating, or evaluating entrepreneurial learning programs must consider that they are context-specific, and are strongly affected by the cultural and economic dimensions that characterize the entrepreneurial ecosystem in which they are imbedded; local context plays an important role in what is possible and appropriate in entrepreneurial education (Ndou, Secundo, Schiuma, & Passiante, 2018; Urban & Kujinga, 2017).

In addition to entrepreneurship education, universities are also encouraged to provide mechanisms to enable knowledge spillovers of core and applied research from the public to the private sectors, and vice versa (Lockett, Siegel, Wright, & Ensley, 2005; Lockett, Wright, & Franklin, 2003). In their attempts to remain innovative and incorporate partners from outside academia in their innovation efforts, many universities have invested into programs designed to engage students in entrepreneurial activities. For example, Technology Transfer Offices (TTOs) have emerged as one of the core methods to facilitate knowledge spillovers, by enabling patenting activity and licensing intellectual property in some instances (Siegel, Veugelers, & Wright, 2007). University science parks and incubators are other examples of mechanisms created at universities to enable these spillovers (Phan, Siegel, & Wright, 2005).

2.8 Entrepreneurship Centers

There is a clear consensus that universities should play an active role in supporting sustainable socio-economic development and prepare human capital for entrepreneurial opportunity recognition, and that the most effective way to achieve is through the adoption of an entrepreneurial university philosophy. This means creating programs, whether educational or practical, to promote knowledge sharing, and provide avenues for networking with industry partners and stakeholders from outside of the academic community. This realization has encouraged many universities to revisit their business models and adopt strategies that acknowledge the importance of entrepreneurship in socio-economic development, and to remain actively involved in the process of promoting entrepreneurship.

In order to ensure active participation in entrepreneurial developments some universities rely on the creation of specific Entrepreneurship Centers to serve as a sort of headquarters for entrepreneurial activities, while other institutions are able to weave entrepreneurial activities as part of their institutional fabric; it is important to highlight that it is the latter of these methods that gives rise to the concept of the *entrepreneurial university*. Since the introduction of entrepreneurship and entrepreneurial themes in universities, researchers have seen the emergence of a plethora of initiatives such as entrepreneurial training programs, venture creation disciplines, introduction of research streams focusing on a variety of entrepreneurial topics, creation of 'on campus' incubators, and the provision of support services for students seeking to scale their startups or business ideas. Unfortunately, reports that aim to summarize best practices for the promotion of entrepreneurship in universities oftentimes place varying levels of attention to issues ranging from entrepreneurship, innovation, research and development, and support systems. Universities are therefore not only placed in a rapidly evolving environment, but are also tasked with simultaneously finding the methods that allow them to best incorporate entrepreneurship in their institution.

In the event that universities are not well trained to incorporate entrepreneurial initiatives in their business models, they require a carefully designed entrepreneurial strategy, one that connects the overall university strategy with more innovation and entrepreneurial operational activities (Ardito, Ferraris, Petruzzelli, Bresciani, & Del Giudice, 2019). It is further recommended that such strategies consider regional and institutional differences, and because of this, a uniform strategy that provides effective results across a large pool of universities is not available (Tataj, 2015). A major way universities have tried to address this complexity, as previously anticipated, is by creating or assigning a dedicated center that can spearhead these activities within the institution; the entrepreneurial center.

Research has mainly focused on the current tangible functions of these entrepreneurial centers and disregarded their future directions, which leads to the question of whether entrepreneurial centers are engaged in activities that are in line with future expectations (Maas & Jones, 2017). For example, there is growing evidence that even though a wide range of entrepreneurial support activities are emerging within universities, some of them struggle to create the future desired state of economic growth.

Of course, as stated by Maas and Jones (2017), *"it would be an ideal environment where the Higher Education Institution's fabric is such that a dedicated center is not needed to stimulate enterprise and entrepreneurship activity"* pg. 12. However, this is not the case for a large part of universities and many of them require a dedicated center to stimulate entrepreneurial activities. Furthermore, it is commonly accepted that a considerable amount of entrepreneurial activities within universities can be attributed to entrepreneurship centers, nonetheless, these tend to experience various challenges such as lack of resources, and the responsibility of managing diverse sets of expectations from their academic stakeholders. If one center must handle the expectations from many stakeholders, from many different disciplines within the university, they may lose focus, which not only influences their direct activities but may also have negative effects on the sustainable development of regions.

Despite the possible challenges for entrepreneurial centers, research does exist that supports the importance of these centers in stimulating enterprise and entrepreneurship in universities (Finkle, Kuratko, & Goldsby, 2006; Nelles & Vorley, 2011). Furthermore, even though it is widely accepted that not every university student will be entrepreneurial, it is believed that students should be exposed to entrepreneurial learning in order to 'plant the seed' for them to develop individual interest or intention to act entrepreneurially, or engage in entrepreneurial activities. Maas and Jones (2017) also highlight that these activities should not be the sole responsibility of entrepreneurship centers within universities; further emphasizing the importance of trans-disciplinary collaborations, not only for university resource gain, but also for knowledge spillovers to potential entrepreneurs not found within universities. Finally, it should be noted that entrepreneurial centers are not homogenous in their activities, and while some may manifest as technology transfer offices, incubators, or accelerators, some may be research oriented and knowledge based nodes (Mazzarol, 2014).

In a study that analyzed ten Entrepreneurship Centers across seven Europeans countries, Ndou et al. (2018) identified some common pillars off Entrepreneurship Education (EE) as developed within these centers in terms of five key dimensions— (i) target audience, (ii) learning objectives, (iii) entrepreneurship contents, (iv) learning pedagogies, and (v) stakeholders engagement. Their analysis provided the basis to introduce a process-based framework for entrepreneurial mindset creation and recommend future EE learning programs to be organized around the following four main phases (Ndou et al., 2018):

- **Inspiration**: Focuses on generating a broad entrepreneurial awareness; which serves for opportunity identification.
- **Engagement**: Creating specific entrepreneurship capabilities in the target groups.
- **Exploitation**: Creating hands-on entrepreneurial capabilities that are aimed at taking advantage of emerging opportunities.
- **Sustainment**: Providing the targets with techniques, instruments, resources, and network to endure the growth and produce value through new endeavors.

Regardless of their documented success in stimulating entrepreneurship within universities, several challenges with the current model of 'stand alone' entrepreneurship centers have also been identified. Some of these include finding the right staff, the scarcity and variability of resources, high and diverse expectations from stakeholders, diverse sets of internal and external actors, and developing legitimacy within the university (Finkle et al., 2006; Finkle, Menzies, Kuratko, & Goldsby, 2013).

Finding the right staff has been reported as a challenge for entrepreneurship centers. This is due to the nature of the center itself, and the individuals it attracts. Entrepreneurially oriented staff might grow tired of the standby periods for promotion, and thus seek out their own employment elsewhere, or create opportunities for career advancement themselves (Clarysse, Tartari, & Salter, 2011). Furthermore, finding a balance between research and commercial staff to provide a full-immersion entrepreneurial experience, and achieving mutual respect between the integrated disciplines has been reported as a challenge in a number of case studies (Maas & Jones, 2017).

Due to the lack of uniformity in their operating environments, it comes as no surprise that the goals of individual centers vary in regard to their approach to new firm creation, research and development, instilling entrepreneurial mindsets in faculty and staff, and in their contribution to the capitalization of knowledge (Del-Palacio, Sole, & Batista-Foguet, 2008). In his work conducted in 2015, Maas also highlights that some centers provide all-inclusive services from opportunity identification, to idea creation, and commercialization, while others offer specialized services such as knowledge transfer, and leave the route-to-market aspects to other departments or services (Maas, 2015).

One important consideration is that regional differences will always be the determining factors that guide how entrepreneurship centers should be designed; therefore, a uniform approach to organizing these centers cannot be created. Furthermore, the physical location of the entrepreneurial center within the university and its staff play an important role in the promotion of an entrepreneurial mindset and culture (Maas & Jones, 2017). Depending on their environment, some centers might place higher importance on their own survival, than on creating the dynamic networks necessary for sustainable value creation. This raises the question of whether entrepreneurship centers promote entrepreneurship effectively, and whether or not they make a significant contribution toward achieving the Sustainable Development Goals discussed in Chap. 1.

There is a variety of activities performed by different entrepreneurship centers including new firm creation, market research, skills development, motivating entrepreneurial behavior, and entrepreneurial knowledge creation, just to name a few. Maas (2015) also reports that this variation of center-to-center activities is often the result of a lack of clarity regarding corporate strategy. Since the introduction of entrepreneurial themes into university environments, the resulting entrepreneurship centers have and should continue to play an important role in promoting entrepreneurship within institutions. However, as recommended by a number of authors, particular attention should be paid to ensure that the role of entrepreneurship centers is aligned with the overall strategy of its host institution.

2.8.1 Technology Transfer Offices/Centers

Technology transfer offices (TTOs), in some sense, should be considered intermediaries who must mediate between different highly educated or segmented communities, such as academic science, research bodies, and private enterprises. Universities are traditionally the most important knowledge source for nurturing technological innovation. Technological innovation is a dynamic process that, over the last decade, has become much more based upon a complex and multidisciplinary knowledge base. Accordingly, universities have been required to put more effort into coordinating different disciplines and creating industry linkages in order to shorten the time required for prototyping and identifying market needs. Indeed while many universities often have TTOs, the effectiveness of these offices in stimulating entrepreneurship within universities is debated (Chapple, Lockett, Siegel, & Wright, 2005; Siegel et al., 2007). Studies identify that TTOs are often focused on logistic processes and metrics of startups, and less on providing expert support or helping to develop academics' skills to engage in other more informal activities with industry (Abreu & Grinevich, 2013; Fini, Lacetera, & Shane, 2010; Fitzgerald & Cunningham, 2016; Miller et al., 2018).

One example of a successful TTO is found in the Waginengen University Research (WUR), a leading research institution in technology transfer in agricultural science. Researchers highlight that WUR facilitates technology transfer through four mechanisms:

1. Department independence to pursue different forms of technology transfer.
2. Implementation of general legal frameworks of technology transfer to lessen the burden for departments, scientists, and aspiring entrepreneurs.
3. Embrace a culture where the prime driver for technology transfer is a 'responsibility to give back to society" rather than income.
4. Embedding itself in a location where ties with industry are the norm, and not the exception.

Throughout the literature it is evident that technology transfer to industry is increasingly pursued at universities as a major entrepreneurial activity. However, the success of those efforts is not always guaranteed; therefore we suggest that researchers and stakeholders apply the above components when creating or exploring TTOs, always based on their specific environmental context (Hoenen, Kolympiris, Wubben, & Omta, 2018).

2.8.2 Incubators

In efforts to foster an environment that drives innovation and entrepreneurship, various universities have established mechanisms such as university business incubators (UBIs) to promote the commercialization of innovative ideas (Theodoraki et al., 2018). Incubators are key elements of sustainable entrepreneurial ecosystems (Cohen, 2006; Klofsten & Lundmark, 2016; Spigel, 2017), they act as specific entrepreneurship centers whose purpose is to function as a neutral coordinator to promote the interests of academic entrepreneurs, remove barriers to their success, and connect them to entrepreneurship support mechanisms both inside and outside the university (Hayter, 2016). The incubators within these ecosystems vary with respect to structure, support services, and operational processes, but they generally share a common purpose: to promote entrepreneurship, innovation, the creation of new firms, and economic development (Theodoraki et al., 2018). In some cases, incubators are the catalysts for the creation of sustainable university based entrepreneurial ecosystems and, more incubators may stimulate a variety of actors (e.g., schools, universities, chambers of commerce, business clubs, and so forth) to encourage the creation of programs that build awareness of entrepreneurial activity, and that further support and develop established entrepreneurs (Hackett & Dilts, 2004; Theodoraki et al., 2018). Generally, an incubator's purpose is to provide a supportive environment that enhances the probability of incubatees' survival and success. One of the main mechanisms of an incubator for helping entrepreneurs overcome resource gaps is by facilitating networking with external resources such as advisers, investors, potential partners, early-adopter customers, and potential employees (Lasrado, Sivo, Ford, O'Neal, & Garibay, 2016).

In the case of university-based incubators (UBIs), their success is thought to depend on two main factors. The first factor is related to the decline of public funding, since most incubators are publicly funded, reductions in public funds can influence incubators' survival (Tengeh & Choto, 2015). The second factor concerns the arrival of new entrants and the impact of substitutes, or UBI stakeholders. These new stakeholders usually consist of private parties (e.g., consultants, accountants, bankers, lawyers, and so forth) all of whom may increase their personal support for incubates, without threatening other public incubators that offer similar or complementary services (e.g., negative tradeoff). With respect to their structural dimension, university based entrepreneurial ecosystems are directly influenced by the UBIs since these enhance the university's networks by establishing and fostering connections among members from different departments and research fields. Internally, these networks include students (e.g., undergraduate, masters, and doctoral), university researchers, incubatees, laboratories, and research centers, and externally they include other entrepreneurship-support institutions, other incubators, experts and consultants, funders, and industry partners from certain sectors (Theodoraki et al., 2018).

With respect to the structural dimension of social capital, incubators must create dense and strong relationships with other university, industry, and community members to compensate for their usually limited availability of material and non-material resources (Hayter, 2016). With respect to the cognitive dimension of social capital, they must develop shared values, norms, and culture to ensure the sustainability of the ecosystem. With respect to the relational dimension of social capital, they must develop trust among themselves, and other members of the university ecosystem, and decrease the number of individualistic opportunistic behaviors (Tötterman & Sten, 2005).

2.8.3 Accelerators

The changing needs of society demand closer collaboration between universities and industries to address some of the significant challenges threatening Earth's natural resources (Wilson, 2012). All of this has resulted in many forward-looking universities re-evaluating their core activities and research capabilities resulting in a wide range of modes of university knowledge transfer and business engagement which is responsive to the needs of industry (Fitzgerald & Cunningham, 2016; Miller et al., 2018).

Evidence also points out that while entrepreneurship centers report having a central strategy that guides their activities, they are not always clear on *how* their strategy guides their activities. This may be due, for example, to the fact that some centers are strategically located in a certain department (e.g., business schools) while others are placed on 'neutral' campus grounds (e.g., career center) (Maas & Jones, 2017). One issue with the former model is that it is commonly assumed that when a center is placed within a specific faculty or department, then the center, naturally or by choice, will eventually adopt and prioritize the goals of its host faculty.

Entrepreneurship Centers also experience difficulties when it comes to financial resources. A lack of clarity about their corporate strategy can easily translate to insecurity regarding financial resources.

In line with the findings that entrepreneurship centers can achieve more if they are independent of a specific faculty or department, it can also be proposed that these centers should act as guardians to the entrepreneurial ecosystem within universities. A formalized university entrepreneurial ecosystem that is guided by a transparent institutional strategy can perhaps address the issues regarding acceptance and legitimacy of business creation and entrepreneurship within universities, and help these areas achieve the same recognition as research and academic publications among scholars. It is recommended that a set of carefully formulated policies, procedures, and practices be put forward in order to guide the implementation of an entrepreneurial ecosystem within universities (Maas & Jones, 2017).

2.9 Triple-Helix Approaches

The triple helix system refers to collaborations among universities, businesses, and governments (Table 2.1).

The Triple Helix Model (THM) (Gunasekara, 2006) was originally described by Etzkowitz and Leydesdorff (1997) who argued for a 'new social contract between universities and the larger society'. Etzkowitz (2003) further posits that the interaction between universities, industry, and government is the key to improving the conditions for innovation in a knowledge-based society. The THM evidences the power of creating common goals between industry, government, and the university sectors. The THM is in essence a long and evolutionary process that defines relationships among industry players, universities, public research organizations (PROs), and governmental institutions to boost local economic growth (Etzkowitz & Leydesdorff, 2000). For a brief review of the THM and its dimensions please see Table 2.1.

A first role of universities within the THM is their influence, which can be associated to issues of human capital development through higher levels of general educational attainment (Bramwell & Wolfe, 2008). Further, a second view is from the perspective of universities as a public research provider, which posits that knowledge spillovers are indicated as the main source of economic contribution and that universities are expected to act as engines of economic growth (Smith & Bagchi-Sen, 2012). This suggests that research knowledge produced by universities promotes entrepreneurship and that universities act as essential intersections in a regional network of innovation activity.

From the industry point of view, there are two main aspects when seeking to foster collaboration with universities; companies are attracted to universities if they provide both a large amount of fundamental and cutting edge research, and a selection of innovations or potential innovations along with top quality human capital (e.g., graduates and students).

Some universities experience difficulties when trying to initiate collaborations with industry partners, and oftentimes attempt to reduce the problem by setting up processes or services to promote entrepreneurship (e.g., technology transfer offices, accelerators, and incubators).

Table 2.1 Triple-Helix approaches

	Supply	Demand
University	*R&D* (E.g., Google was started by PhD students at Stanford)	*Customer Base* (E.g., Facebook at Harvard)
Business	*Funding* (E.g., many successful businesses fund startups and unicorns)	*Customer* (E.g., businesses can later become customers of the startups they financed)
Government	*Funding* (E.g., NSA and CIA funded Google)	U.S. intelligence agency funded the internet as an in house service for itself

Source: Adapted from Chinta and Sussan (2018, p. 75)

Specifically, universities have been noted to be key instruments in increasing entrepreneurial capacity among farmers, and effective tools to foster an entrepreneurial culture among them (Opolot et al., 2018). By bridging linkages between farmers and other public and private institutions, universities help expose food system members to knowledge and ideas beyond their own horizons (Abeyrathne & Jayawardena, 2014; Berggren & Silver, 2009). Finally, it has been noted that effective partnerships between universities, government agencies, private businesses, and residents are a vital element of overall community development (Etzkowitz & Zhou, 2017; Heitor, 2015).

The contribution of universities in new knowledge creation and especially the importance of their research in fostering entrepreneurial activity and economic growth are central to many theories regarding innovation and entrepreneurship. In this case 'Triple Helix Model' Model' (Etzkowitz & Dzisah, 2008; Etzkowitz & Leydesdorff, 2000). In the university context, an entrepreneurial ecosystem echoes the Triple Helix concept, in which academia, government, and industry form trilateral networks and hybrid organizations, the actions of which are often encouraged, but not controlled, by government (Carayannis, Grigoroudis, Campbell, Meissner, & Stamati, 2018; Etzkowitz & Leydesdorff, 2000).

2.9.1 The Knowledge Triangle

The Knowledge Triangle is a novel approach to designing a growth model based on a specific type of innovation network (Tataj, 2015). Unlike most linear models of knowledge transfer to the viable commercialization of scientific research, the Knowledge Triangle adopts a more systemic approach to the processes of knowledge transfer and innovation creation by linking the three areas of (academic) research and knowledge creation, education and training, and business innovation. The Knowledge Triangle is often considered as the logical evolution of other related concepts such as the 'third mission', 'entrepreneurial universities', and the 'THM' (Unger & Polt, 2017).

Even though these previous concepts, especially the THM, have some overlap with the Knowledge Triangle, the way in which these constructs are applied in practice differs. One major advancement of the Knowledge Triangle is that whereas other concepts focus on the actors within innovation systems as the starting point, the Knowledge Triangle employs an activity oriented approach to linking the dimensions of education, research, and innovation. Therefore, the Knowledge Triangle is a model that focuses on the interactions among the three dimensions, with a specific focus on the following types of interactions:

- **Research and Education**: These interactions are reflected by the geographical and sectorial mobility of students, training programs, and the fundamental idea of considering applied research as the foundation for research-based teaching, and measures to improve skill-matching between companies and graduates.

2.9 Triple-Helix Approaches

- **Research and Innovation**: This area focuses on the support and intensification of knowledge transfer. Specifically, it focuses on (i) public-private partnership models (i.e., clusters, and entrepreneurial universities), (ii) the commercialization of publicly funded research, (iii) contract research and development services from universities for the industrial sector, and (iv) university spin-offs and academic startups, (v) knowledge and technology transfer offices (TTOs), (vi) incubators, and (vii) open science or open innovation platforms (e.g., Forward Fooding).
- **Education and Innovation**: This dimension evaluates the collaboration between actors by considering the support framework for the development of an entrepreneurial culture in the ecosystem of interest, and ensures the presence of industry-focused and practical training programs, and the formation of appropriate human capital competencies through education.

The Knowledge Triangle has recently gained marked importance as a framework to conceptualize the relationships between universities, business sectors, and societies at large. This reflects the European Commission's policy strategies, and addresses the targets formulated in the European Union's 2020 Strategy for Smart Sustainable Growth (European Council, 2010). According to this strategy, effective links between research, education, and innovation are considered key prerequisites for tackling social challenges.

The Knowledge Triangle as an innovation network is discussed as a formalized collaboration of research institutions, universities, and industry partners all located in geographical proximity of an existing innovation ecosystem and linked to similar networks operating in comparable environments (Tataj, 2015). In this context, partners enter into dynamic and reciprocal relationships that are interdependent, and underlined by a series of continuous flows of information exchange that include the core drivers of innovation, i.e., talent, knowledge, and capital (Tataj, 2015). Furthermore, the Knowledge Triangle rejects the 'traditional belief' that knowledge is generated in research labs and universities, and later turned into businesses and brought to market by industry; it argues that innovations can originate in any of these settings.

In essence, the Knowledge Triangle as an innovation network can manifest in a number of different ways. An exemplary model for which the Knowledge Triangle was used as a conceptual framework is the Knowledge and Innovation Communities (KICs) of the European Institute of Innovation and Technology (i.e., EIT). KICs considered manifestations of the Knowledge Triangle and are specifically considered European innovation networks, and can be described as an "excellence-driven, autonomous partnership of higher education institutions, research organizations, companies, and other stakeholders [EIT Regulation (EC) No 294/2008] (Tataj, 2015).

To date, the EIT has established 8 KICs, each with their own focus area, including climate, innovative energy, digital technologies, health, manufacturing, raw materials, urban mobility, and of special interest to this text, food.

For further information regarding EIT's Food KIC or the 8 KICs (i.e., https://eitfood.eu/) please see Chap. 10 or the accompanying link, respectively.

2.10 Conclusion

We conclude that when structured according to the needs and resources of their local or regional environment, entrepreneurial and innovation endeavors in universities serve the following functions to assist food system entrepreneurs in identifying and exploiting entrepreneurial opportunities:

- **Environmental Opportunity:** This means networks, interactions, events, and connections that allow university members to interact with food system members and vice-versa.
- **Resource Opportunity:** Providing funding, and human capital (e.g., mentors, venture capitalists, and field experts).
- **Growth Opportunity:** teaching practical skills to individuals which take on transversal forms for easier and diversified navigation of entrepreneurial opportunities.

Furthermore, the importance of knowledge transfer from universities as a source of innovative ideas positions universities as key actors in regional and national innovation efforts (Abreu & Grinevich, 2013; Guerrero et al., 2016).

Some higher education institutions simply seem to be better at being entrepreneurial and developing an entrepreneurial culture. However, one important fact to remember, and as stated by Tataj (2015), not every member of the university's student body will become entrepreneurs. She then goes on to divide university students into three segments, (i) students who matter what is done will never become entrepreneurs, (ii) students who no matter what is done will become entrepreneurs regardless, and (iii) students who do not consider an entrepreneurial venture as their career choice (Tataj, 2015). For example, in the case of the most famous entrepreneurial university, Stanford, the university did not teach entrepreneurship, but attracted entrepreneurial people. At Stanford, students are taught to develop the necessary skills that will increase their chances of success in the business world, but they are not taught to be entrepreneurs. Instead, entrepreneurial skill can be described by their fluidity in a free market economy, by acquiring entrepreneurial skills in marketing, sales, finance, and human and environmental resource management. Teaching students how to write a business plan, what language to use when attempting to raise money from venture capitalists or in trying to secure a loan, and how to present a new venture for the purpose of selling it are the factors that drive the entrepreneurial culture at Stanford. Therefore, preparing entrepreneurs at higher education institutions should not be exclusively about teaching students how to be entrepreneurial, but to also teach them everyday techniques to aid them in success.

Furthermore, Shu, Ren, and Zheng (2018) support the notion of a positive relationship between network capabilities and opportunity discovery even after controlling for entrepreneur's prior knowledge, cognitive bias, and political skills. They go on to describe network capability as a four dimensional construct including (i) network orientation (i.e., the extent to which a person is willing to depend on social networks in their daily socializations), (ii) network building (e.g., relational

2.10 Conclusion

efforts to expand network), (iii) network maintenance (e.g., ensuring stable and long-term exchange relationships with others), and (iv) network coordination (e.g., managing multiple relationships) (Shu et al., 2018). Thus, highlighting once again the importance of a strong network, and the university's role in stimulating such.

Similarly, Feld (2012) emphasizes the critical role of university as a promoter of entrepreneurial activity due to its facilities, and abundance of potential entrepreneurs. Therefore, the entrepreneurial culture of the university has a great influence on the entrepreneurial ecosystem. Universities play a dual role in fostering entrepreneurial ecosystems (Spigel, 2017). First, they provide human capital (Motoyama, 2014) and disseminate an entrepreneurial mindset among students, encouraging them to create startups or seek experiences in innovative environments (Shah & Pahnke, 2014). Second, through academic research, they develop new technologies, hereby creating entrepreneurial opportunities (Smith, Chapman, Wood, Barnes, & Romeo, 2014). Academic entrepreneurs can then commercialize these innovations (Shane, 2004) or they can spill over to existing ventures (Kirchhoff, Newbert, Hasan, & Armington, 2007). One can conclude that in addition to being the engine for entrepreneurial activity, universities act as feeders into the entrepreneurial ecosystem (Feld, 2012).

Up until recently, the decision to become an entrepreneur and the outcomes of entrepreneurial ventures were viewed solely as dependent on the individual entrepreneur, group of individuals, or individual company characteristics. However, it was recently noted that entrepreneurship is much more than a phenomenon that manifests itself at the individual level. Through observations of clusters of entrepreneurship such as the Silicon Valley, industry experts arrived at the realization that 'place matters', and more specifically, the resources available in these places. Entrepreneurship has also been found to thrive across a broad spectrum of cultures and national contexts, and a commonality amongst these different areas is the local resources to promote entrepreneurship such as supportive local firms, engaged universities, policies, and other local institutions.

Finally, we believe that the famous African proverb "It takes a village to raise a child", transcends boundaries into the business world, and postulate that "it takes an ecosystem to raise an entrepreneur".

Entrepreneurial activity should be interpreted as a complex system, exhibiting technological, cultural, and social aspects and components that touch upon philosophical and social issues (Tataj, 2015). It is clear that universities are important members of entrepreneurial ecosystems and particularly, with respect to innovation (O'Connor & Reed, 2018).

A recurring problem with the collaboration efforts between academia and industry is the transition from prototype stage to mass manufacturing; to overcome barriers between small scale and industrial production ecosystem relationships are needed. Furthermore, policy makers consider universities important contributors to economic growth and thus allocate resources, time, and financial support at their disposal (Hyder et al., 2011; Riviezzo, Santos, Liñán, Napolitano, & Fusco, 2019; Urbano & Guerrero, 2013), further highlighting the need to establish meaningful and effective collaborations.

Hayter et al. (2018) show that the links between graduate students and individuals outside the university, and access to external resources are necessary in ensuring the success of new ventures. Luckily, we are witnessing the birth of ecosystems for collaborative research; open innovation, multiple project collaboration agreements, multiple partner consortia, and other new forms of governance have received increased attention from academia and the corporate world (Chinta & Sussan, 2018).

There is widespread recognition of the need for input reduced production to reflect the issues of climate change and population growth (i.e., exogenous shocks), an increasing awareness of environmental pollution and animal welfare (i.e., change in demand), and of new technological abilities in biotechnical and process engineering (i.e., change in supply)—the combination of which fosters entrepreneurial opportunities in food systems (Kuckertz et al., 2019).

Universities are the key elements in driving these transitions, education, and collaboration initiatives. Understanding their many roles in providing opportunities for possible entrepreneurs, whether through practical education or resource provision is critical for stakeholders wishing to stimulate entrepreneurial environments in their institutions through academic and business collaborations, and for aspiring entrepreneurs seeking a good fit of support for their nascent ventures.

References

Abeyrathne, H. R. M. P., & Jayawardena, L. N. A. C. (2014). Impact of group interactions on farmers' entrepreneurial behaviour. *E a M: Ekonomie a Management, 17*(4), 46–57.

Abreu, M., & Grinevich, V. (2013). The nature of academic entrepreneurship in the UK: Widening the focus on entrepreneurial activities. *Research Policy, 42*(2), 408–422.

Acs, Z. J., Audretsch, D. B., & Lehmann, E. E. (2013). The knowledge spillover theory of entrepreneurship. *Small Business Economics, 41*(4), 757–774.

Acs, Z. J., Braunerhjelm, P., Audretsch, D. B., & Carlsson, B. (2009). The knowledge spillover theory of entrepreneurship. *Small Business Economics, 32*(1), 15–30.

Ahmad, N., & Seymour, R. G. (2008). *Defining entrepreneurial activity: Definitions supporting frameworks for data collection.* Paris: OECD.

Aldrich, H. E., & Cliff, J. E. (2003). The pervasive effects of family on entrepreneurship: Toward a family embeddedness perspective. *Journal of Business Venturing, 18*(5), 573–596.

Aldrich, H. E., & Kenworthy, A. (1999). The accidental entrepreneur: Campbellian antinomies and organizational foundings. In J. A. C. Baum & B. McKelvey (Eds.), *Variations in organization science: In honor of Donald T. Campbell* (pp. 19–33). Thousand Oaks, CA: SAGE Publications.

Altmann, A., & Ebersberger, B. (2013). *Universities in change: Managing higher education institutions in the age of globalization.* New York: Springer.

Alvarez, S. A., & Barney, J. B. (2007). Discovery and creation: Alternative theories of entrepreneurial action. *Strategic Entrepreneurship Journal, 1*(1–2), 11–26.

Alvarez, S. A., & Busenitz, L. W. (2001). The entrepreneurship of resource-based theory. *Journal of Management, 27*(6), 755–775.

Aparicio, S., Urbano, D., & Audretsch, D. (2016). Institutional factors, opportunity entrepreneurship and economic growth: Panel data evidence. *Technological Forecasting and Social Change, 102*, 45–61.

Ardichvili, A., Cardozo, R., & Ray, S. (2003). A theory of entrepreneurial opportunity identification and development. *Journal of Business Venturing, 18*(1), 105–123.

References

Ardito, L., Ferraris, A., Petruzzelli, A. M., Bresciani, S., & Del Giudice, M. (2019). The role of universities in the knowledge management of smart city projects. *Technological Forecasting and Social Change, 142*, 312–321.

Asheim, B. T., & Coenen, L. (2005). Knowledge bases and regional innovation systems: Comparing Nordic cluster. *Research Policy, 34*(8), 1173–1190.

Audretsch, D. B. (2005). The knowledge spillover theory of entrepreneurship and economic growth. In G. T. Vinig & R. C. W. Van Der Voort (Eds.), *The emergence of entrepreneurial economics* (pp. 37–54). Bingley: Emerald Group Publishing Limited.

Audretsch, D. B. (2014). From the entrepreneurial university to the university for the entrepreneurial society. *The Journal of Technology Transfer, 39*(3), 313–321.

Audretsch, D. B., & Thurik, A. R. (2004). A model of the entrepreneurial economy. *International Journal of Entrepreneurship Education, 2*(2), 143–166.

Aulet, W., & Murray, F. (2013). *A tale of two entrepreneurs: Understanding differences in the types of entrepreneurship in the economy.* Kansas City, MO: Ewing Marion Kauffman Foundation.

Autio, E., Nambisan, S., Thomas, L. D., & Wright, M. (2018). Digital affordances, spatial affordances, and the genesis of entrepreneurial ecosystems. *Strategic Entrepreneurship Journal, 12*(1), 72–95.

Baker, T., & Nelson, R. E. (2005). Creating something from nothing: Resource construction through entrepreneurial bricolage. *Administrative Science Quarterly, 50*(3), 329–366.

Baron, R. A., & Ensley, M. D. (2006). Opportunity recognition as the detection of meaningful patterns: Evidence from comparisons of novice and experienced entrepreneurs. *Management Science, 52*(9), 1331–1344.

Basso, O., Fayolle, A., & Bouchard, V. (2009). Entrepreneurial orientation: The making of a concept. *The International Journal of Entrepreneurship and Innovation, 10*(4), 313–321.

Béchard, J. P., & Grégoire, D. (2005). Entrepreneurship education research revisited: The case of higher education. *Academy of Management Learning & Education, 4*(1), 22–43.

Belitski, M., & Heron, K. (2017). Expanding entrepreneurship education ecosystems. *Journal of Management Development, 36*(2), 163–177.

Bergevoet, R. H., Giesen, G. W. J., Saatkamp, H. W., Van Woerkum, C. M. J., & Huirne, R. (2005). Improving entrepreneurship in farming: The impact of a training programme in Dutch dairy farming.

Berggren, B., & Silver, L. (2009). The effect of bridging networks on entrepreneurial activity: The rational-legal framework and embeddedness in local social capital networks. *Journal of Enterprising Communities: People and Places in the Global Economy, 3*(2), 125–137.

Bertello, A., Azucar, D., & Tirabeni, L. (2019). The impact of digitization on motivations and institutional logics of PhD students' startup initiatives: An exploratory study. In *GIKA-global innovation and knowledge* (pp. 0–1). Valencia: Observatory of Knowledge Research.

Bhagavatula, S., Elfring, T., Van Tilburg, A., & Van De Bunt, G. G. (2010). How social and human capital influence opportunity recognition and resource mobilization in India's handloom industry. *Journal of Business Venturing, 25*(3), 245–260.

Bommer, M., & Jalajas, D. S. (2004). Innovation sources of large and small technology-based firms. *IEEE Transactions on Engineering Management, 51*(1), 13–18.

Bramwell, A., & Wolfe, D. A. (2008). Universities and regional economic development: The entrepreneurial University of Waterloo. *Research Policy, 37*(8), 1175–1187.

Brito, S. M. D. R. B. (2018). Introductory chapter: Entrepreneurship as a trend and as a challenge. In S. M. D. R. B. Brito (Ed.), *Entrepreneurship-trends and challenges* (pp. 3–7). London: IntechOpen.

Brown, R., & Mason, C. (2017). Looking inside the spiky bits: A critical review and conceptualization of entrepreneurial ecosystems. *Small Business Economics, 49*(1), 11–30.

Buenstorf, G. (2007). Creation and pursuit of entrepreneurial opportunities: An evolutionary economics perspective. *Small Business Economics, 28*(4), 323–337.

Carayannis, E. G., Grigoroudis, E., Campbell, D. F., Meissner, D., & Stamati, D. (2018). The ecosystem as helix: An exploratory theory-building study of regional co-opetitive entrepreneurial ecosystems as quadruple/quintuple Helix innovation models. *R&D Management, 48*(1), 148–162.

Carayannis, E. G., & Rakhmatullin, R. (2014). The quadruple/quintuple innovation helixes and smart specialisation strategies for sustainable and inclusive growth in Europe and beyond. *Journal of the Knowledge Economy, 5*(2), 212–239.

Casson, M. (2005). The individual–opportunity nexus: A review of Scott Shane: A general theory of entrepreneurship. *Small Business Economics, 24*(5), 423–430.

Casson, M., & Wadeson, N. (2007). The discovery of opportunities: Extending the economic theory of the entrepreneur. *Small Business Economics, 28*(4), 285–300.

Cavallo, A., Ghezzi, A., & Balocco, R. (2018). Entrepreneurial ecosystem research: Present debates and future directions. *International Entrepreneurship and Management Journal*, 1–31. https://doi.org/10.1007/s11365-018-0526-3

Chandler, G. N., & Hanks, S. H. (1994). Founder competence, the environment, and venture performance. *Entrepreneurship Theory and Practice, 18*(3), 77–89.

Chandra, Y., Styles, C., & Wilkinson, I. (2009). The recognition of first time international entrepreneurial opportunities. *International Marketing Review, 26*(1), 30–61.

Chapple, W., Lockett, A., Siegel, D., & Wright, M. (2005). Assessing the relative performance of U.K. university technology transfer offices: Parametric and non-parametric evidence. *Research Policy, 34*(3), 369–384.

Chegini, M., & Khoshtinat, B. (2011). Study of relationship between entrepreneurial skills and organizational entrepreneurship. *Australian Journal of Basic and Applied Sciences, 5*(4), 165–172.

Chen, Y. S., & Polat, I. H. (2017). Cultivating global entrepreneurs in the food supply chain. In *Agri-food supply chain management: Breakthroughs in research and practice* (pp. 287–307). Hershey, PA: IGI Global.

Chiasson, M., & Saunders, C. (2005). Reconciling diverse approaches to opportunity research using the structuration theory. *Journal of Business Venturing, 20*(6), 747–767.

Chinta, R., & Sussan, F. (2018). A triple-helix ecosystem for entrepreneurship: A case review. In A. O'Connor, E. Stam, F. Sussan, & D. Audretsch (Eds.), *Entrepreneurial ecosystems* (pp. 67–80). New York: Springer.

Clark, B. R. (1998). *Creating entrepreneurial universities: Organizational pathways of transformation. Issues in higher education*. Pergamon: Oxford.

Clarysse, B., Tartari, V., & Salter, A. (2011). The impact of entrepreneurial capacity, experience and organizational support on academic entrepreneurship. *Research Policy, 40*(8), 1084–1093.

Cogliser, C. C., & Stambaugh, J. E. (2008). A multi-level process view of new-venture emergence: Impressive first step toward a model. In *Multi-level issues in creativity and innovation* (pp. 471–477). Bingley: Emerald Group Publishing Limited.

Cohen, B. (2006). Sustainable valley entrepreneurial ecosystems. *Business Strategy and the Environment, 15*(1), 1–14.

Cohen, B., & Winn, M. I. (2007). Market imperfections, opportunity and sustainable entrepreneurship. *Journal of Business Venturing, 22*(1), 29–49.

Colombo, M. G., & Grilli, L. (2005). Founders' human capital and the growth of new technology-based firms: A competence-based view. *Research Policy, 34*(6), 795–816.

Cooke, P., Uranga, M. G., & Etxebarria, G. (1997). Regional innovation systems: Institutional and organisational dimensions. *Research Policy, 26*(4–5), 475–491.

Cranwell, M. R., Kolodinsky, J. M., Donnelly, C. W., Downing, D. L., & Padilla-Zakour, O. I. (2005). A model food entrepreneur assistance and education program: The northeast center for food entrepreneurship. *Journal of Food Science Education, 4*(4), 56–65.

Curth, A., Chatzichristou, S., Devaux, A., & Allinson, R. (2015). *Entrepreneurship education: A road to success: A compilation of evidence on the impact of entrepreneurship education strategies and measures*. Bruxelles: European Commission.

References

Del-Palacio, I., Sole, F., & Batista-Foguet, J. M. (2008). University entrepreneurship centres as service businesses. *The Service Industries Journal, 28*(7), 939–951.

De Bernardi, P., Bertello, A., & Forliano, C. (2019). Unpacking Higher Educational Institutions (HEIs) performances through the institutional logics lens. In *IFKAD 14th international forum on knowledge assets dynamics: Knowledge ecosystems and growth* (pp. 1537–1555). Matera: Institute of Knowledge Asset Management (IKAM), Arts for Business Institute, University of Basilicata.

Di Nauta, P., Merola, B., Caputo, F., & Evangelista, F. (2018). Reflections on the role of university to face the challenges of knowledge society for the local economic development. *Journal of the Knowledge Economy, 9*(1), 180–198.

Eckhardt, J. T., & Shane, S. A. (2003). Opportunities and entrepreneurship. *Journal of Management, 29*(3), 333–349.

EIT Food. (2019). *About EIT food*. Retrieved from https://eitfood.eu/about-eit-food

Etzkowitz, H. (2003). Innovation in innovation: The triple helix of university-industry-government relations. *Social Science Information, 42*(3), 293–337.

Etzkowitz, H. (2004). The triple helix and the rise of the entrepreneurial university. In K. Grandin, N. Wormbs, & S. Widmalm (Eds.), *The science-industry nexus: History, policy, implications*. Sagamore Beach, MA: Science History Publications.

Etzkowitz, H., & Dzisah, J. (2008). Rethinking development: Circulation in the triple helix. *Technology Analysis & Strategic Management, 20*(6), 653–666.

Etzkowitz, H., & Leydesdorff, L. (1997). Introduction to special issue on science policy dimensions of the triple Helix of university-industry-government relations. *Science and Public Policy, 24*(1), 2–5.

Etzkowitz, H., & Leydesdorff, L. (2000). The dynamics of innovation: From national systems and "Mode 2" to a triple Helix of university–industry–government relations. *Research Policy, 29*(2), 109–123.

Etzkowitz, H., Schuler, E., & Gulbrandsen, M. (2000). The evolution of the entrepreneurial university. In M. Jacob & T. Hellström (Eds.), *The future of knowledge production in the academy* (pp. 40–60). Buckingham: SRHE and Open University Press.

Etzkowitz, H., & Zhou, C. (2017). *The triple helix: University–industry–government innovation and entrepreneurship*. Abingdon-on-Thames: Routledge.

European Commission. (2018a). A European strategy for plastics in a circular economy. In *Single-use plastics: New measures to reduce marine litter*. Retrieved from https://ec.europa.eu/environment/waste/pdf/single-use_plastics_factsheet.pdf

European Commission. (2018b). *Research and innovation for food and nutrition security: Transforming our food system 2nd food 2030 high level event: Conference outcome report, 14–15 June 2018 in Plovdic (Bulgaria)*. Retrieved from https://publications.europa.eu/en/publication-detail/-/publication/d0e51873-4478-11e9-a8ed-01aa75ed71a1/language-en/format-PDF/source-search

European Commission. (2019). *Food and drink industry*. Retrieved from https://ec.europa.eu/growth/sectors/food_en

European Council. (2010). *Cover note from general secretariat of the council to the delegations* (EUCO 13/10, 17.06.2010). Brussels: European Council.

Ezeibe, A. B. C., Okorji, E. C., Chah, J. M., & Abudei, R. N. (2014). Impact of entrepreneurship training on rural poultry farmers adoption of improved management practices in Enugu state, Nigeria. *African Journal of Agricultural Research, 9*(20), 1604–1609.

FAO. (1989). *The state of food and agriculture* (Vol. 37). Rome: Food & Agriculture Organization of the UN (FAO).

FAO, I. (2016). WFP 2015, the state of food insecurity in the world 2015. In *Meeting the 2015 international hunger targets: Taking stock of uneven progress*. Rome: Food and Agriculture Organization Publications.

FAO, WFP. (2014). *IFAD (2012) the state of food insecurity in the world 2012: Economic growth is necessary but not sufficient to accelerate reduction of hunger and malnutrition*. Rome: FAO.

Feld, B. (2012). *Startup communities: Building an entrepreneurial ecosystem in your city*. Hoboken, NJ: John Wiley & Sons.

Feldman, M. P. (2003). Entrepreneurship and American research universities: Evolution in technology transfer. In D. M. Hart (Ed.), *The emergence of entrepreneurship policy: Governance, start-ups, and growth in the US knowledge economy* (pp. 92–112). Cambridge: Cambridge University Press.

Fiet, J. O. (1996). The informational basis of entrepreneurial discovery. *Small Business Economics, 8*(6), 419–430.

Fini, R., Lacetera, N., & Shane, S. (2010). Inside or outside the IP system? Business creation in academia. *Research Policy, 39*(8), 1060–1069.

Finkle, T. A., Kuratko, D. F., & Goldsby, M. G. (2006). An examination of entrepreneurship centers in the United States: A national survey. *Journal of Small Business Management, 44*(2), 184–206.

Finkle, T. A., Menzies, T. V., Kuratko, D. F., & Goldsby, M. G. (2013). An examination of the financial challenges of entrepreneurship centers throughout the world. *Journal of Small Business & Entrepreneurship, 26*(1), 67–85.

Fiore, E., Sansone, G., & Paolucci, E. (2019). Entrepreneurship education in a multidisciplinary environment: Evidence from an entrepreneurship programme held in Turin. *Administrative Sciences, 9*(1), 1–28.

Fitzgerald, C., & Cunningham, J. A. (2016). Inside the university technology transfer office: Mission statement analysis. *The Journal of Technology Transfer, 41*(5), 1235–1246.

Foo, M. D. (2011). Emotions and entrepreneurial opportunity evaluation. *Entrepreneurship Theory and Practice, 35*(2), 375–393.

Frese, M., & Gielnik, M. M. (2014). The psychology of entrepreneurship. *Annual Review of Organizational Psychology and Organizational Behavior, 1*, 413–438.

Fuentes, M. D. M. F., Arroyo, M. R., Bojica, A. M., & Pérez, V. F. (2010). Prior knowledge and social networks in the exploitation of entrepreneurial opportunities. *International Entrepreneurship and Management Journal, 6*(4), 481–501.

Gaglio, C. M., & Katz, J. A. (2001). The psychological basis of opportunity identification: Entrepreneurial alertness. *Small Business Economics, 16*(2), 95–111.

García-Cabrera, A. M., & García-Soto, M. G. (2009). A dynamic model of technology-based opportunity recognition. *The Journal of Entrepreneurship, 18*(2), 167–190.

George, N. M., Parida, V., Lahti, T., & Wincent, J. (2016). A systematic literature review of entrepreneurial opportunity recognition: Insights on influencing factors. *International Entrepreneurship and Management Journal, 12*(2), 309–350.

Gibb, A., & Hannon, P. (2006). Towards the entrepreneurial university. *International Journal of Entrepreneurship Education, 4*(1), 73–110.

Gibb, A., Haskins, G., & Robertson, I. (2013). Leading the entrepreneurial university: Meeting the entrepreneurial development needs of higher education institutions. In A. Altmann & B. Ebersberger (Eds.), *Universities in change* (pp. 9–45). New York: Springer.

Gibson, D. V., & Foss, L. (2017). Developing the entrepreneurial university: Architecture and institutional theory. *World Technopolis Review, 6*(1), 3.1–3.15.

Giuliani, E., & Rabellotti, R. (2012). Universities in emerging economies: Bridging local industry with international science—Evidence from Chile and South Africa. *Cambridge Journal of Economics, 36*(3), 679–702.

Global Entrepreneurship Monitor. (2019). Global Entrepreneurship Monitor. Retrieved from https://www.gemconsortium.org/

Godfray, H. C. J., Beddington, J. R., Crute, I. R., Haddad, L., Lawrence, D., Muir, J. F., ... Toulmin, C. (2010). Food security: The challenge of feeding 9 billion people. *Science, 327*(5967), 812–818.

Goldfarb, B., & Henrekson, M. (2003). Bottom-up versus top-down policies towards the commercialization of university intellectual property. *Research Policy, 32*(4), 639–658.

References

Goldstein, H. A. (2010). The 'entrepreneurial turn' and regional economic development mission of universities. *The Annals of Regional Science, 44*, 83.

Grégoire, D. A., Barr, P. S., & Shepherd, D. A. (2010). Cognitive processes of opportunity recognition: The role of structural alignment. *Organization Science, 21*(2), 413–431.

Grégoire, D. A., & Shepherd, D. A. (2012). Technology-market combinations and the identification of entrepreneurial opportunities: An investigation of the opportunity-individual nexus. *Academy of Management Journal, 55*(4), 753–785.

Grimaldi, R., Kenney, M., Siegel, D. S., & Wright, M. (2011). 30 years after Bayh–Dole: Reassessing academic entrepreneurship. *Research Policy, 40*(8), 1045–1057.

Guerrero, A. B., Granados, P. D., & González, M. D. (2014). Economy of knowledge, entrepreneurial culture and employability in the field of education. An approximation to the Spanish case. *Procedia-Social and Behavioral Sciences, 139*, 168–174.

Guerrero, M., & Urbano, D. (2012). The development of an entrepreneurial university. *The Journal of Technology Transfer, 37*(1), 43–74.

Guerrero, M., Urbano, D., & Fayolle, A. (2016). Entrepreneurial activity and regional competitiveness: Evidence from European entrepreneurial universities. *The Journal of Technology Transfer, 41*(1), 105–131.

Gunasekara, C. (2006). Reframing the role of universities in the evelopment of regional innovation systems. *The Journal of Technology Transfer, 31*(1), 101–113.

Gür, U., Oylumlu, İ. S., & Kunday, Ö. (2017). Critical assessment of entrepreneurial and innovative universities index of Turkey: Future directions. *Technological Forecasting and Social Change, 123*, 161–168.

Hackett, S. M., & Dilts, D. M. (2004). A systematic review of business incubation research. *The Journal of Technology Transfer, 29*(1), 55–82.

Hannon, P. D. (2013). Why is the entrepreneurial university important? *Journal of Innovation Management, 1*(2), 10–17.

Haynie, J. M., Shepherd, D. A., & McMullen, J. S. (2009). An opportunity for me? The role of resources in opportunity evaluation decisions. *Journal of Management Studies, 46*(3), 337–361.

Hayter, C. S. (2016). A trajectory of early-stage spinoff success: The role of knowledge intermediaries within an entrepreneurial university ecosystem. *Small Business Economics, 47*(3), 633–656.

Hayter, C. S., Nelson, A. J., Zayed, S., & O'Connor, A. C. (2018). Conceptualizing academic entrepreneurship ecosystems: A review, analysis and extension of the literature. *The Journal of Technology Transfer, 43*(4), 1039–1082.

Hayton, J., Chandler, G. N., & DeTienne, D. R. (2011). Entrepreneurial opportunity identification and new firm development processes: A comparison of family and non-family new ventures. *International Journal of Entrepreneurship and Innovation Management, 13*(1), 12–31.

Hechavarría, D. M., & Welter, C. (2015). Opportunity types, social entrepreneurship and innovation: Evidence from the panel study of entrepreneurial dynamics. *The International Journal of Entrepreneurship and Innovation, 16*(4), 237–251.

Heinonen, J., Hytti, U., & Stenholm, P. (2011). The role of creativity in opportunity search and business idea creation. *Education + Training, 53*(8/9), 659–672.

Heitor, M. (2015). How university global partnerships may facilitate a new era of international affairs and foster political and economic relations. *Technological Forecasting and Social Change, 95*, 276–293.

Hennon, C. B. (2012). Entrepreneurship, farming, and identity: A phenomenological inquiry. In T. Burger-Helmchen (Ed.), *Entrepreneurship-gender, geographies and social context* (pp. 249–294). London: InTechOpen.

Hmieleski, K. M., Carr, J. C., & Baron, R. A. (2015). Integrating discovery and creation perspectives of entrepreneurial action: The relative roles of founding CEO human capital, social capital, and psychological capital in contexts of risk versus uncertainty. *Strategic Entrepreneurship Journal, 9*(4), 289–312.

Hoenen, S., Kolympiris, C., Wubben, E., & Omta, O. (2018). Technology transfer in agriculture: The case of Wageningen University. In N. Kalaitzandonakes, E. Carayannis, E. Grigoroudis, & S. Rozakis (Eds.), *From agriscience to agribusiness* (pp. 257–276). Cham: Springer.

Holcombe, R. G. (2003). The origins of entrepreneurial opportunities. *The Review of Austrian Economics, 16*(1), 25–43.

Holster, H. C., Klerkx, L. W. A., & Elzen, B. (2008). Stimulating entrepreneurship – The impact of a new way of organizing dairy farmers. In *8th European IFSA Symposium. Empowerment of the rural actors: A renewal of farming system perspectives, 6–10 July, 2008, Clermont Farrand, France* (pp. 13–22).

Hyder, A. A., Corluka, A., Winch, P. J., El-Shinnawy, A., Ghassany, H., Malekafzali, H., . . . Ghaffar, A. (2011). National policy-makers speak out: Are researchers giving them what they need? *Health Policy and Planning, 26*(1), 73–82.

Isenberg, D. J. (2010). How to start an entrepreneurial revolution. *Harvard Business Review, 88*(6), 40–50.

Isenberg, D. (2011). The entrepreneurship ecosystem strategy as a new paradigm for economic policy: Principles for cultivating entrepreneurship. *Presentation at the Institute of International and European Affairs.*

Kassean, H., Vanevenhoven, J., Liguori, E., & Winkel, D. E. (2015). Entrepreneurship education: A need for reflection, real-world experience and action. *International Journal of Entrepreneurial Behavior & Research, 21*(5), 690–708.

Katz, J. A. (2003). The chronology and intellectual trajectory of American entrepreneurship education: 1876–1999. *Journal of Business Venturing, 18*(2), 283–300.

Kirby, D. A. (2006). Creating entrepreneurial universities in the UK: Applying entrepreneurship theory to practice. *The Journal of Technology Transfer, 31*(5), 599–603.

Kirchhoff, B. A., Newbert, S. L., Hasan, I., & Armington, C. (2007). The influence of university R & D expenditures on new business formations and employment growth. *Entrepreneurship Theory and Practice, 31*(4), 543–559.

Kirzner, I. M. (1979). *Perception, opportunity, and profit: Studies in the theory of entrepreneurship* (pp. 142–143). Chicago, IL: University of Chicago press.

Kline, K. L., Msangi, S., Dale, V. H., Woods, J., Souza, G. M., Osseweijer, P., . . . Mugera, H. K. (2017). Reconciling food security and bioenergy: Priorities for action. *GCB Bioenergy, 9*(3), 557–576.

Klofsten, M., & Jones-Evans, D. (2000). Comparing academic entrepreneurship in Europe – The case of Sweden and Ireland. *Small Business Economics, 14*(4), 299–309.

Klofsten, M., & Lundmark, E. (2016). Supporting new spin-off ventures–experiences from a university start-up program. In S. H. De Cleyn & G. Festel (Eds.), *Academic spin-offs and technology transfer in Europe: Best practices and breakthrough models* (pp. 93–107). Cheltenham: Elgaronline.

Kourilsky, M. L., & Esfandiari, M. (1997). Entrepreneurship education and lower socioeconomic black youth: An empirical investigation. *The Urban Review, 29*(3), 205–215.

Kourilsky, M. L., & Walstad, W. B. (1998). Entrepreneurship and female youth: Knowledge, attitudes, gender differences, and educational practices. *Journal of Business Venturing, 13*(1), 77–88.

Kuckertz, A., Hinderer, S., & Röhm, P. (2019). Entrepreneurship and entrepreneurial opportunities in the food value chain. *NPJ Science of Food, 3*(1), 6.

Lasrado, V., Sivo, S., Ford, C., O'Neal, T., & Garibay, I. (2016). Do graduated university incubator firms benefit from their relationship with university incubators? *The Journal of Technology Transfer, 41*(2), 205–219.

Leih, S., & Teece, D. (2016). Campus leadership and the entrepreneurial university: A dynamic capabilities perspective. *Academy of Management Perspectives, 30*(2), 182–210.

Li, Y. (2011). Emotions and new venture judgment in China. *Asia Pacific Journal of Management, 28*(2), 277–298.

References

Lindgren, E., Harris, F., Dangour, A. D., Gasparatos, A., Hiramatsu, M., Javadi, F., ... Haines, A. (2018). Sustainable food systems – A health perspective. *Sustainability Science, 13*(6), 1505–1517.

Lindqvist, G., Ketels, C., & Sölvell, Ö. (2013). *The cluster initiative greenbook 2.0*. Stockholm: Ivory Tower Publishers.

Lockett, A., Siegel, D., Wright, M., & Ensley, M. D. (2005). The creation of spin-off firms at public research institutions: Managerial and policy implications. *Research Policy, 34*(7), 981–993.

Lockett, A., Wright, M., & Franklin, S. (2003). Technology transfer and universities' spin-out strategies. *Small Business Economics, 20*(2), 185–200.

Lumpkin, G. T., & Lichtenstein, B. B. (2005). The role of organizational learning in the opportunity–recognition process. *Entrepreneurship Theory and Practice, 29*(4), 451–472.

Maas, G. (2015). *Systemic entrepreneurship: Contemporary issues and case studies*. Basingstoke: Palgrave Macmillan.

Maas, G., & Jones, P. (Eds.). (2017). *Entrepreneurship centres: Global perspectives on their contributions to higher education institutions*. Basingstoke: Palgrave Macmillan.

Malecki, E. J. (1993). Entrepreneurship in regional and local development. *International Regional Science Review, 16*(1–2), 119–153.

Martinelli, A., Meyer, M., & Von Tunzelmann, N. (2008). Becoming an entrepreneurial university? A case study of knowledge exchange relationships and faculty attitudes in a medium-sized, research-oriented university. *The Journal of Technology Transfer, 33*(3), 259–283.

Marvel, M. R. (2013). Human capital and search–based discovery: A study of high–tech entrepreneurship. *Entrepreneurship Theory and Practice, 37*(2), 403–419.

Mazzarol, T. (2014). *How do Australia's universities engage with entrepreneurship and small business?* Centre for Entrepreneurial Management and Innovation, DP 1401.

Miller, K., Alexander, A., Cunningham, J. A., & Albats, E. (2018). Entrepreneurial academics and academic entrepreneurs: A systematic literature review. *International Journal of Technology Management, 77*(1/2/3), 9–37.

Minniti, M., & Lévesque, M. (2008). Recent developments in the economics of entrepreneurship. *Journal of Business Venturing, 23*(6), 603–612.

Moore, J. F. (1993). Predators and prey: A new ecology of competition. *Harvard Business Review, 71*(3), 75–86.

Morgan, S. L., Marsden, T., Miele, M., & Morley, A. (2010). Agricultural multifunctionality and farmers' entrepreneurial skills: A study of Tuscan and Welsh farmers. *Journal of Rural Studies, 26*(2), 116–129.

Motoyama, Y. (2014). The state-level geographic analysis of high-growth companies. *Journal of Small Business & Entrepreneurship, 27*(2), 213–227.

Motoyama, Y., & Knowlton, K. (2017). Examining the connections within the startup ecosystem: A case study of st. louis. *Entrepreneurship Research Journal, 7*(1), 2194–6175.

Motoyama, Y., Konczal, J., Bell-Masterson, J., & Morelix, A. (2014). *Think locally, act locally: Building a robust entrepreneurial ecosystem*. Kansas City, MO: Ewing Marion Kauffman Foundation.

Murphy, P. J. (2011). A 2 × 2 conceptual foundation for entrepreneurial discovery theory. *Entrepreneurship Theory and Practice, 35*(2), 359–374.

Nabi, G., Liñán, F., Fayolle, A., Krueger, N., & Walmsley, A. (2017). The impact of entrepreneurship education in higher education: A systematic review and research agenda. *Academy of Management Learning & Education, 16*(2), 277–299.

Ndou, V., Secundo, G., Schiuma, G., & Passiante, G. (2018). Insights for shaping entrepreneurship education: Evidence from the European entrepreneurship centers. *Sustainability, 10*(11), 1–19.

Nelles, J., Bramwell, A., & Wolfe, D. A. (2005). History, culture and path dependency: Origins of the Waterloo ICT cluster. In D. A. Wolfe & M. Lucas (Eds.), *Global networks and local linkages: The paradox of cluster development in an open economy* (pp. 227–252). Montreal: McGill-Queen's University Press.

Nelles, J., & Vorley, T. (2011). Entrepreneurial architecture: A blueprint for entrepreneurial universities. *Canadian Journal of Administrative Sciences/Revue Canadienne des sciences de l'administration, 28*(3), 341–353.

Nicolaou, N., & Shane, S. (2009). Can genetic factors influence the likelihood of engaging in entrepreneurial activity? *Journal of Business Venturing, 24*(1), 1–22.

O'Connor, A., & Reed, G. (2018). Theorizing the university governance role in an entrepreneurial ecosystem. In A. O'Connor, E. Stam, F. Sussan, & D. B. Audretsch (Eds.), *Entrepreneurial ecosystems* (pp. 81–100). Cham: Springer.

Onyido, J. A., & Duru, D. I. (2019). Entrepreneurial education for sustainable development in Nigeria. *British Journal of Education, 7*(2), 58–72.

Opolot, H. N., Isubikalu, P., Obaa, B. B., & Ebanyat, P. (2018). Influence of university entrepreneurship training on farmers' competences for improved productivity and market access in Uganda. *Cogent Food & Agriculture, 4*(1), 1469211.

Owen-Smith, J., & Powell, W. W. (2003). The expanding role of university patenting in the life sciences: Assessing the importance of experience and connectivity. *Research Policy, 32*(9), 1695–1711.

Patzelt, H., & Shepherd, D. A. (2011). Recognizing opportunities for sustainable development. *Entrepreneurship Theory and Practice, 35*(4), 631–652.

Phan, P. H., Siegel, D. S., & Wright, M. (2005). Science parks and incubators: Observations, synthesis and future research. *Journal of Business Venturing, 20*(2), 165–182.

Pindado, E., Sánchez, M., Verstegen, J. A. A. M., & Lans, T. (2018). Searching for the entrepreneurs among new entrants in European agriculture: The role of human and social capital. *Land Use Policy, 77*, 19–30.

Pittaway, L., & Cope, J. (2007). Simulating entrepreneurial learning: Integrating experiential and collaborative approaches to learning. *Management Learning, 38*(2), 211–233.

Prost, L., Berthet, E. T., Cerf, M., Jeuffroy, M. H., Labatut, J., & Meynard, J. M. (2017). Innovative design for agriculture in the move towards sustainability: Scientific challenges. *Research in Engineering Design, 28*(1), 119–129.

Ramana, V. V., Prasad, B., & Guda, N. (2018). A study on emerging trends in business incubation & innovation. *Small Enterprises Development, Management & Extension (Sedme) Journal, 33*(1).

Rasmussen, E. A., & Sørheim, R. (2006). Action-based entrepreneurship education. *Technovation, 26*(2), 185–194.

Ratten, V., Marques, C. S., & Braga, V. (2018). Knowledge, learning and innovation: Research into cross-sector collaboration. In V. Ratten, V. Braga, & C. S. Marques (Eds.), *Knowledge, learning and innovation* (pp. 1–4). Cham: Springer.

Rerup, C. (2005). Learning from past experience: Footnotes on mindfulness and habitual entrepreneurship. *Scandinavian Journal of Management, 21*(4), 451–472.

Rezai, G., Mohamed, Z., & Shamsudin, M. N. (2011). Informal education and developing entrepreneurial skills among farmers in Malaysia. *World Academy of Science, Engineering and Technology, 79*, 254–261.

Riviezzo, A., Santos, S. C., Liñán, F., Napolitano, M. R., & Fusco, F. (2019). European universities seeking entrepreneurial paths: The moderating effect of contextual variables on the entrepreneurial orientation-performance relationship. *Technological Forecasting and Social Change, 141*, 232–248.

Rothblatt, S., & Wittrock, B. (1993). *The European and American university since 1800*. Cambridge: Cambridge University Press.

Saemundsson, R. J., & Holmén, M. (2011). Yes, now we can: Technological change and the exploitation of entrepreneurial opportunities. *The Journal of High Technology Management Research, 22*(2), 102–113.

Santos, C. J. O. (2018). *Can we model the entrepreneurial opportunity using both discovery and creation theory?*

References

Sarasvathy, S. D., Dew, N., Velamuri, S. R., & Venkataraman, S. (2003). Three views of entrepreneurial opportunity. In Z. J. Acs & D. B. Audretsch (Eds.), *Handbook of entrepreneurship research* (pp. 141–160). Boston, MA: Springer.

Sarma, S. (2018). *Opportunity recognition: A contingency framework of individual attributes, time pressure, and uncertainty* (Doctoral dissertation). Kansas City: University of Missouri. Retrieved from https://mospace.umsystem.edu/xmlui/bitstream/handle/10355/67996/Dissertation_2018_Sarma.pdf?sequence=1&isAllowed=y

Schumpeter, J. A. (1934). *The theory of economic development*. Cambridge: Harvard University Press.

Shah, S. K., & Pahnke, E. C. (2014). Parting the ivory curtain: Understanding how universities support a diverse set of startups. *The Journal of Technology Transfer, 39*(5), 780–792.

Shane, S. (2000). Prior knowledge and the discovery of entrepreneurial opportunities. *Organization Science, 11*(4), 367–472.

Shane, S. A. (2003). *A general theory of entrepreneurship: The individual-opportunity nexus*. Cheltenham: Edward Elgar Publishing.

Shane, S. A. (2004). *Academic entrepreneurship: University spinoffs and wealth creation*. Cheltenham: Edward Elgar Publishing.

Shane, S., Nicolaou, N., Cherkas, L., & Spector, T. D. (2010). Do openness to experience and recognizing opportunities have the same genetic source? *Human Resource Management, 49*(2), 291–303.

Shane, S., & Venkataraman, S. (2000). The promise of entrepreneurship as a field of research. *The Academy of Management Review, 25*(1), 217–226.

Short, J. C., Ketchen, D. J., Jr., Shook, C. L., & Ireland, R. D. (2010). The concept of "opportunity" in entrepreneurship research: Past accomplishments and future challenges. *Journal of Management, 36*(1), 40–65.

Shu, R., Ren, S., & Zheng, Y. (2018). Building networks into discovery: The link between entrepreneur network capability and entrepreneurial opportunity discovery. *Journal of Business Research, 85*, 197–208.

Siegel, D. S., Veugelers, R., & Wright, M. (2007). Technology transfer offices and commercialization of university intellectual property: Performance and policy implications. *Oxford Review of Economic Policy, 23*(4), 640–660.

Siegel, D. S., & Wright, M. (2015). Academic entrepreneurship: Time for a rethink? *British Journal of Management, 26*(4), 582–595.

Smith, H. L., & Bagchi-Sen, S. (2012). The research university, entrepreneurship and regional development: Research propositions and current evidence. *Entrepreneurship & Regional Development, 24*(5–6), 383–404.

Smith, H. L., Chapman, D., Wood, P., Barnes, T., & Romeo, S. (2014). Entrepreneurial academics and regional innovation systems: The case of spin-offs from London's universities. *Environment and Planning C: Government and Policy, 32*(2), 341–359.

Spigel, B. (2017). The relational organization of entrepreneurial ecosystems. *Entrepreneurship Theory and Practice, 41*(1), 49–72.

Steffen, W., Richardson, K., Rockström, J., Cornell, S. E., Fetzer, I., Bennett, E. M., ... Folke, C. (2015). Planetary boundaries: Guiding human development on a changing planet. *Science, 347*(6223), 1259855.

Stevenson, H. H. (1983). *A perspective on entrepreneurship* (Vol. 13). Cambridge: Harvard Business School.

Stevenson, H., & Gumpert, D. (1985). The heart of entrepreneurship. *Harvard Business Review*. Retrieved from https://hbr.org/1985/03/the-heart-of-entrepreneurship

Tang, Z., Kreiser, P. M., Marino, L., Dickson, P., & Weaver, K. M. (2009). A hierarchical perspective of the dimensions of entrepreneurial orientation. *International Entrepreneurship and Management Journal, 5*(2), 181–201.

Tataj, D. (2015). *Innovation and entrepreneurship. A growth model for Europe beyond the crisis*. New York: Tataj Innovation Library.

Tengeh, R. K., & Choto, P. (2015). The relevance and challenges of business incubators that support survivalist entrepreneurs. *Investment Management and Financial Innovations, 12*(2), 150–161.

Theodoraki, C., Messeghem, K., & Rice, M. P. (2018). A social capital approach to the development of sustainable entrepreneurial ecosystems: An explorative study. *Small Business Economics, 51*(1), 153–170.

Thurik, A. R., Stam, E., & Audretsch, D. B. (2013). The rise of the entrepreneurial economy and the future of dynamic capitalism. *Technovation, 33*(8–9), 302–310.

Tominc, P., & Rebernik, M. (2007). Growth aspirations and cultural support for entrepreneurship: A comparison of post-socialist countries. *Small Business Economics, 28*(2/3), 239–255.

Torrance, W. E., Rauch, J., Aulet, W., Blum, L., Burke, B., D'Ambrosio, T., & Jacquette, J. (2013). *Entrepreneurship education comes of age on campus: The challenges and rewards of bringing entrepreneurship to higher education.* St. Louis, MO: Ewing Marion Kauffman Foundation.

Tötterman, H., & Sten, J. (2005). Start-ups: Business incubation and social capital. *International Small Business Journal: Researching Entrepreneurship, 23*(5), 487–511.

Tripathi, R., & Agarwal, S. (2014). An empirical study of marketing for guava and its sub-products by farmers in Allahabad: An approach towards agripreneurship through food processing units. *International Journal of Business and Globalisation, 13*(1), 69–75.

Tumasjan, A., & Braun, R. (2012). In the eye of the beholder: How regulatory focus and self-efficacy interact in influencing opportunity recognition. *Journal of Business Venturing, 27*(6), 622–636.

Unger, M., & Polt, W. (2017). The knowledge triangle between research, education and innovation–a conceptual discussion. *National Research University Higher School of Economics, 11*(2), 10–26.

United Nations Environment. (2019). *New UN decade on ecosystem restoration offers unparalleled opportunity for job creation, food security and addressing climate change.* Retrieved from https://www.unenvironment.org/news-and-stories/press-release/new-un-decade-ecosystem-res toration-offers-unparalleled-opportunity

Urban, B., & Kujinga, L. (2017). The institutional environment and social entrepreneurship intentions. *International Journal of Entrepreneurial Behavior & Research, 23*(4), 638–655.

Urbano, D., & Guerrero, M. (2013). Entrepreneurial universities: Socioeconomic impacts of academic entrepreneurship in a European region. *Economic Development Quarterly, 27*(1), 40–55.

Vaghely, I. P., & Julien, P. A. (2010). Are opportunities recognized or constructed? An information perspective on entrepreneurial opportunity identification. *Journal of Business Venturing, 25*(1), 73–86.

Van de Ven, H. (1993). The development of an infrastructure for entrepreneurship. *Journal of Business Venturing, 8*(3), 211–230.

Van Gelderen, M., Brand, M., van Praag, M., Bodewes, W., Poutsma, E., & Van Gils, A. (2008). Explaining entrepreneurial intentions by means of the theory of planned behaviour. *Career Development International, 13*(6), 538–559.

Wee, C. H., Lim, W. S., & Lee, R. (1994). Entrepreneurship: A review with implications for further research. *Journal of Small Business & Entrepreneurship, 11*(4), 25–49.

Westhead, P., Ucbasaran, D., & Wright, M. (2009). Information search and opportunity identification: The importance of prior business ownership experience. *International Small Business Journal: Researching Entrepreneurship, 27*(6), 659–680.

Wilson, T. (2012). *A review of business–university collaboration.* London: Department for Business, Innovation and Skills.

Wissema, J. G. (2009). *Towards the third generation university: Managing the university in transition.* Cheltenham: Edward Elgar Publishing.

Wong, P. K., Ho, Y. P., & Autio, E. (2005). Entrepreneurship, innovation and economic growth: Evidence from GEM data. *Small Business Economics, 24*(3), 335–350.

References

Wood, M. S., & Pearson, J. M. (2009). Taken on faith? The impact of uncertainty, knowledge relatedness, and richness of information on entrepreneurial opportunity exploitation. *Journal of Leadership & Organizational Studies, 16*(2), 117–130.

Wustrow, P. (2018). *Entrepreneurial information search behavior for opportunity recognition: Measurement, antecedents, outcomes* (Doctoral dissertation). St. Gallen: University of St. Gallen. Retrieved from https://www1.unisg.ch/www/edis.nsf/SysLkpByIdentifier/4741/$FILE/dis4741.pdf

Youtie, J., & Shapira, P. (2008). Building an innovation hub: A case study of the transformation of university roles in regional technological and economic development. *Research Policy, 37*(8), 1188–1204.

Zahra, S. A., Gedajlovic, E., Neubaum, D. O., & Shulman, J. M. (2009). A typology of social entrepreneurs: Motives, search processes and ethical challenges. *Journal of Business Venturing, 24*(5), 519–532.

Zhang, Q., MacKenzie, N. G., Jones-Evans, D., & Huggins, R. (2016). Leveraging knowledge as a competitive asset? The intensity, performance and structure of universities' entrepreneurial knowledge exchange activities at a regional level. *Small Business Economics, 47*(3), 657–675.

Zucker, L. G., Darby, M. R., & Brewer, M. B. (1994). Intellectual capital and the birth of US biotechnology enterprises. *American Economic Association, 88*(1), 290–306.

Chapter 3
Innovation and Entrepreneurial Ecosystems: Structure, Boundaries, and Dynamics

Abstract Recognizing the broader dimensions of entrepreneurial and innovation activities, holistic and inclusive networked approaches pave the way to co-creation activities that are essential for achieving sustainability in food systems. Recent studies have started to deepen what are the critical enablers for creating thriving entrepreneurial and innovation ecosystems. Networks that include firms, institutions, and several other relevant stakeholders in knowledge spillovers enable to produce more social and economic value through co-creation processes. However, due to the unique complexity within ecosystems, there is no standardized framework or strategy to develop entrepreneurial or innovation ecosystems effectively. In this chapter, a synthesis of the structure, dynamics, and boundaries of innovation and entrepreneurial ecosystems is presented. In particular, the main differences between these two concepts and the traditional ecosystem concept are provided and an overview of the more well-established definitions and frameworks present in the business and management literature offered. So, the following questions and many others will be addressed: what are the critical factors that lead some ecosystems to success? What the key actors? What dynamics characterize them? Answering these questions may represent an effective solution to address sustainability in the multi-functionality of food systems collectively. Therefore, how the heterogeneous elements and complexity of entrepreneurial and innovation ecosystems can be applied in food system sustainability initiatives will be finally discussed and critical action points for policy and practice recommended.

Keywords Innovation ecosystems · Entrepreneurial ecosystems · Value co-creation · Food systems · Sustainability

---

Co-authored by Canio Forliano—Department of Management, University of Turin, School of Management and Economics, Turin, Italy
Department of Political Science and International relations, University of Palermo, Palermo, Italy, e-mail: canio.forliano@unito.it
Co-authored by Alberto Bertello—Department of Management, University of Turin, School of Management and Economics, Turin, Italy, e-mail: alberto.bertello@unito.it

© Springer Nature Switzerland AG 2020
P. De Bernardi, D. Azucar, *Innovation in Food Ecosystems*, Contributions to Management Science, https://doi.org/10.1007/978-3-030-33502-1_3

3.1 Introducing the Ecosystems Concept

Over the last few years, the concepts of systems and ecosystems have gained a surge of interest as novel forms to describe the competitive environment (Jacobides, Cennamo, & Gawer, 2018). Notably, Autio and Thomas (2014) analysed and compared the differences between these two terms, concluding that ecosystems are in their early stages and more studied in the innovation subdomain of the business and management literature, whereas the concept of systems is well established and developed among interdisciplinary scholars. In a more recent study, Hajikhani (2017) came to the same conclusions, highlighting that while systems are used 21 times more than ecosystems, they contribute only twice the former to innovation studies. Their analysis further revealed that the ecosystem concept covers more various topics and occurs without consistency and interconnectivity of authors than the system concept, thus implying higher diversity in the literature and evidencing the need for a more precise understanding of the term. In fact, as new ecosystems pursue new trajectories and processes to transform or replace traditional methods, they are often opposed by reluctant stakeholders and institutions (Adner & Kapoor, 2016).

The term "ecosystem" has emerged as an attractive metaphor to describe the range of interactions and interdependencies that currently occur between multiple institutions and stakeholders. Moore (1993) was the first to introduce the term in the fields of business and economics, using it for describing the set of organizations and consumers that interact around a central organization and contribute to its success. Iansiti and Levien (2004) further built on this conceptualization and described ecosystems as open networks of stakeholders whose activity impacts the central organization activity and is reciprocally impacted by the same. In this sense, ecosystems represent inclusive communities of both private and public institutions, organizations, and individuals (Teece, 2007) and one of their essential characteristics is that they empower coordination between subjects that would conversely be more independent (Jacobides et al., 2018). The degree to which a system is made up of relatively independent parts, namely parts that can be combined, separated, and re-combined, is called modularity. Therefore, modularity characterizes more or less every ecosystem and the interplays between its interdependent members. However, if modularity creates the conditions for an ecosystem to emerge, its survival requires a particular grade of coordination among its members. Notably, this coordination must be present regardless of the presence of a central controlling actor. Subsequently, also a specific kind of complementarity will be necessary, referring to members that reciprocally require each other for their functioning or maximizing their performances.

The idea that organizations rarely operate in perfectly competitive markets, but often act in network structures where they play complementary roles to co-create value, represents a core foundation behind the notion of innovation and entrepreneurship. This new insight has gained importance amongst innovation and entrepreneurship scholars, leading to the introduction of innovation and entrepreneurial ecosystems when adopted in their respective fields (Thomas, Sharapov, & Autio, 2018). So, the remainder of this chapter will introduce the most cited frameworks for both innovation and entrepreneurial ecosystems and provide the guidelines for how to best tailor them to be integrated into the food system.

3.2 Innovation Ecosystems

Innovation ecosystems have been defined as a "network of interconnected organizations, organized around a focal firm or a platform, and incorporating both production and use side participants, and focusing on the development of new value through innovation" (Autio & Thomas, 2014, 2016).

So, in order to stimulate value co-creation, the relationships in an ecosystem must efficiently move resources and information (i.e., knowledge spillovers) around the network. For what regards resources, it is possible to say that innovation ecosystems are systemically characterised by value co-creation objectives that need to expressly consider the complementary or conflicting role that resource providers can play towards other members (Jacobides, Knudsen, & Augier, 2006). Subsequently, the dynamics of value co-creation mean that opportunities provided by ecosystems are not always equally distributed amongst their members (Adner & Kapoor, 2010; Ceccagnoli, Forman, Huang, & Wu, 2012). Conversely, for what concerns information, since it can be moved regardless of physical boundaries, value co-creation is independent of the physical locations of the ecosystem institution or members (Thomas et al., 2018). As a consequence, even if innovation ecosystems usually are regionally located, they can be disseminated throughout the world. So, thanks to the networks created by their members, shared problems and emerging societal challenges (e.g., SDGs, food scarcity, food waste) can be addressed. In essence, an innovation ecosystem operates regionally, but its significance and impact, due nature of trade-offs within ecosystems, can have a global magnitude (Schiuma & Carlucci, 2018). The possibility of global dissemination is made possible by digital affordances and spatial affordances. Digital affordances (e.g., communication technologies) allow a faster, more connected ecosystem members, thus facilitating knowledge sharing. Spatial affordances, instead, serve more as illustrations of the trans-disciplinarity of these type of ecosystems, since they are not limited to a given industry sector or technological domain (Autio, Nambisan, Thomas, & Wright, 2018).

3.2.1 Differences Between Innovation Ecosystems and Other Cluster Approaches

Innovation ecosystems engage in a set of complex networked relationships where they combine their assets into coherent solutions, in the process of co-creating value that would not be possible for single or isolated members. In innovation ecosystems, the co-creation of value depends on investments in upcoming ventures, significant knowledge exchanges, and spillovers, as well as governance mechanisms that keep members becoming integrated into a single organization. Due to the interdependent nature of ecosystem relationships, each innovation ecosystem member is symbiotic to and co-evolves with other single members and institutions. Subsequently, each member's expected performance is tied to the expected outcomes of the ecosystem as a whole, regardless of that individual member or institution's power, or capital, in the ecosystem (Thomas et al., 2018). This characteristic represents a shift from traditional value creation, which has usually been founded on the provision of assets and vertically integrated linear chains. Therefore, in traditional networked systems, value is formed by the characteristics of network relationships and their adaptability to customer needs and goals; assets can only create value when they are embedded into consumers' own value formation (Still, Lähteenmäki, & Seppänen, 2019). A synthesis of the main characteristics of innovation ecosystems and their differences as compared to other networking concepts is provided in Table 3.1. As can be observed, even if they have traditionally been better addressed in the business and management literature, the other networking concepts result in being less comprehensive than the innovation ecosystem concept.

Therefore, innovation ecosystems primarily consist of innovative firms, which represent their key innovator actors, as well as end-users of the knowledge created through member interactions. However, other members can be: (i) public institutions and governments; (ii) research institutions and universities, which are considered to be the main contributors to knowledge production; (iii) the financial institutions, that facilitate innovations through ensuring funding; (iv) and all the other actors able to stimulate cooperation, mobility, knowledge spillovers, and social interactions (Romano, Passiante, Del Vecchio, & Secundo, 2014).

3.2.2 An Innovation Ecosystems Mapping Effort: The Ecosystem Pie Model

For better understanding and modelling innovation ecosystems for both practical and scholarly use, Talmar and colleagues (2018) developed a qualitative strategy mapping tool: the Ecosystem Pie Model (EPM) (Fig. 3.1). To do so, they integrated a structuralist tradition (Adner, 2017; Hannah & Eisenhardt, 2018; Talmar, Walrave, Podoynitsyna, Holmström, & Romme, 2018) with the approaches developed in recent academic works on ecosystems and instrumentalizing the innovation

3.2 Innovation Ecosystems

Table 3.1 From clusters to innovation ecosystems

	Key actors	Key concepts	Input into the entrepreneurial ecosystem approach	Key outcome
Cluster	Innovative firms	Factor conditions; demand conditions; related and supporting industries; firm structure, strategy and rivalry	Talent, finance, knowledge, physical infrastructure (factor conditions); market demand; support services (e.g., related and supporting industries)	National and regional competitiveness (i.e., productivity of certain industries)
Triple Helix model	Government firms and universities	Interactions between university, industry, and government, innovation, knowledge-based society	Knowledge transfer and interdependence of three sectorial actors	Innovation system
Innovation system	Innovative firms and National Government	Networks, inter-organizational learning, system	Knowledge, finance, formal institutions, demand	Innovation
Innovation ecosystem	Innovative firms	Co-innovation, adoption chain, shared value proposition	Interdependence of actors involved in innovation; global networks	Value creation and capture by the firms in the ecosystem; firm survival

Source: O'Connor, Stam, Sussan, and Audretsch (2018)

ecosystem concept. The EPM distinguishes its elements and relationships at the ecosystem level (EL) and the actor level (AL), which both interact between and within ecosystem members.

The EPM uses elements of actor-based sectors and embedded circles representing the specific characteristics of each actor. The circular shape of the EPM has two main benefits. The first is that it enables a simultaneous detailed representation of ecosystem and actor level properties. Secondly, it clearly displays the relationships that transcend the immediate boundaries in the value chain. So, the EPM serves as a tool to consider and integrate significant ecosystem properties such as interdependency, complementarities, and alignment risks. The tool serves to empower stakeholders to make informed decisions about their innovation strategies and helps them make sense of the ecosystem as complex entities. For a complete list of guidelines for the successful usage of the Pie model, please see Talmar et al. (2018).

Talmar et al. (2018) further suggest that the EPM can also deliver value to ecosystem members and to external experts that seek to map and analyze ecosystems for the evaluation of investment opportunity or developing research funding policies. Furthermore, using the EPM to explore opportunities for common innovation initiatives in efforts to guide potentially infamous conversations on topics such as dependence, risk, or environmental challenges leads to the engagement of several

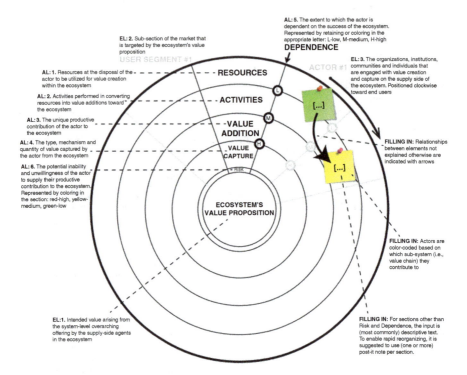

Fig. 3.1 The ecosystem pie model. Source: Talmar et al. (2018)

organizations in co-creation and collaborations. The characteristics of the EPM assist in drafting a clear strategy for ecosystem performance. This is an essential consideration regarding the use of EPM, since a significant topic of interest is ecosystem strategy, i.e., how do firms change their behavior or attempt to influence the behavior of others based on the analysis of their ecosystem setting (Adner, 2017; Dattée, Alexy, & Autio, 2018; Hannah & Eisenhardt, 2018).

The EPM framework for ecosystem modeling is also thought to empower researchers to study the topic of ecosystems in four novel ways:

(i) The main challenges in developing ecosystems strategy arise from the context of the ecosystem, as represented by the interdependence of its structural elements. The EPM explicitly considers the structural elements of ecosystems, which paves the way for contextualizing scholarly inquiries into strategic decision making in and around a particular ecosystem (Adner, 2017).

(ii) Scholars can employ the visual illustration of the EPM to create ecosystem strategies as design interventions.

(iii) Researchers may use the EPM framework to represent different ecosystems (e.g., innovation and entrepreneurial), which enables the comparability of research input and output.

3.3 Entrepreneurial Ecosystems

(iv) By presenting research outcomes in the form of a synthesized visual model accompanied by detailed and strategic implications, scholars can effectively create value for organizations that can then be exchanged for greater future entrepreneurial opportunities.

3.3 Entrepreneurial Ecosystems

In modern complex economies, it is even more challenging for companies to address the entire value chain of specific products or services, since they are progressively turning themselves into very specialized organizations (Appleyard & Chesbrough, 2017; Kapoor & Furr, 2015). Instead, they must depend on and seek collaborations with other members of their ecosystem to engage in system-wide value proposition and value creation initiatives; initiatives that materialize when diverse ecosystem members combine their single contributions (Hannah & Eisenhardt, 2018). Thus, the ecosystem concept has been associated with companies interdependent from each other frequently. According to Teece (2007), ecosystems can be depicted as the landscape in which all companies operate and that give shape to their dynamic capabilities. As a consequence, for building sustainable competitive advantages, they need to constantly keep an eye on them and be ready to react to them (Jacobides et al., 2018).

Given this scenario, entrepreneurial ecosystems can consist of various components, including tenured and experienced entrepreneurs, legal support systems, a culture that condones failure, entrepreneurship centers, and access to finances through business angels or venture capitalists (Isenberg, 2010). Therefore, they can be seen as networks that refer to the human capital, financial and professional resources, and other support systems that drive social and economic development in specific geographic locations (Graham, 2014; Isenberg, 2010). So, several actors come together and create an environment where also governing policies can encourage, protect, and stimulate entrepreneurship (Isenberg, 2010). For this reason, researches on entrepreneurial ecosystems have been driven by the realization of the importance of the institutional environment and the local context for the possible effects on entrepreneurship (Autio, Kenney, Mustar, Siegel, & Wright, 2014; Levie, 2014; Pitelis, 2012).

However, differently from the established concept of district or cluster, an entrepreneurial ecosystem emphasize its emergence around the possibility to exploit some recognized entrepreneurial opportunities, strictly relying on business model innovation, the continuous provision of human, financial, and technological resources, and the presence of horizontal knowledge spillovers (Autio et al., 2018). According to Tallman, Jenkins, Henry, and Pinch (2004), entrepreneurial ecosystems can exactly be viewed as networks in which subjects concentrate their efforts on developing and fostering knowledge. More specifically, entrepreneurial ecosystems promote horizontal knowledge sharing practices among their members, finalized, for example, in understanding how to innovate companies' business

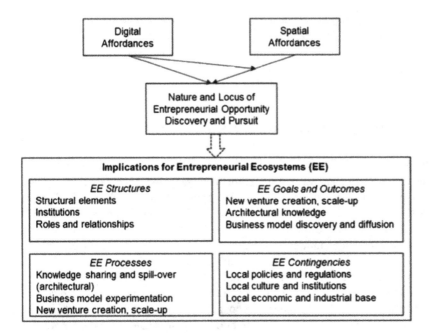

Fig. 3.2 Structural framework for entrepreneurial ecosystems. Source: Autio et al. (2018)

models properly, what entrepreneurial opportunities seize, and what businesses expand (Autio et al., 2018). As said for what regards innovation ecosystems, the combination of digital and spatial affordances further facilitates business model innovation for entrepreneurial opportunity, discovery, and pursuit, which are also characteristics of entrepreneurial ecosystems. Based on work conducted by Autio et al. (2018) regarding digital and spatial, they propose a structural framework for entrepreneurial ecosystems (Fig. 3.2).

Subsequently, a vast kind of industries, actors, and technologies can be involved. That said, entrepreneurial ecosystems can be seen as essential drivers that usually: (i) support and stimulate new venture creations, (ii) enable access to markets, (iii) and offer human capital and financial assistance for entrepreneurs seeking to scale up new businesses.

For what regards new ventures (e.g., start-ups), they emerge and grow not only because of the individual characteristics of their founding entrepreneur(s) but also because are located in networks of public and private members that nurture and help them evolve through the developmental phases. The availability of resources and entrepreneurial environment thus influences the formation and eventual trajectory of new ventures, and if thriving, potentially the economy as a whole. Importantly, the way that these resources are manifested and exploited, and how the entrepreneurial culture develops within the ecosystem is unique to specific locations—there is no universal model that can be employed to create and ensure the success of entrepreneurial ecosystems (Isenberg, 2010).

Conversely, regarding access to markets, due to the heterogeneity of new ventures and start-ups, and their anticipated effect magnitude and initial revenues, having access to sustainable revenues at critical stages is an essential aspect of every economy's social and economic development (Foster et al., 2013). Entrepreneurial ecosystems with a larger and more complex depth of skilled members create a more accommodating environment for the scaling of early-stage entrepreneurial endeavors.

Furthermore, the complex interactions amongst ecosystem members drive social and economic benefits by connecting aspiring entrepreneurs and new ventures with potential funding sources (Radojevich-Kelley & Hoffman, 2012). Moreover, it helps to accelerate the process for reaching key milestones, including raising required venture capital, and eventual independence from the ecosystem by acquisition and achievement of customer traction (Hallen, Bingham, & Cohen, 2014; Winston Smith, Hannigan, & Gasiorowski, 2013). Moreover, some authors have also suggested that entrepreneurs can reap higher benefits when embedded in multiple entrepreneurial ecosystems by exploiting differences and complementarities between ecosystems (Kulchina, 2016) and by overcoming resource scarcity in one ecosystem by accessing the needed resources in another (Thomas et al., 2018).

3.3.1 The Emergence of Entrepreneurial Ecosystems

Due to those characteristics and functions of entrepreneurial ecosystems, it is no wonder they are considered as vital elements to the success of entrepreneurial activities (Acs, Autio, & Szerb, 2014). However, up to date, researches have mainly posed their attention to individuating the key characteristics of thriving ecosystems. For example, it is well known that the most famous ecosystem, Silicon Valley, contains essential features that include a large stock of investors, professionals, knowledge spillovers opportunities, and research centers (Bahrami & Evans, 1995). It has been found that a significant role is also played by lead users, a term introduced by von Hippel (1986) to identify skilled and sophisticated consumers that actively propose innovation to companies. However, studies have also detached the critical attributes for the success of other famous ecosystems, i.e., those located in Edinburgh (Spigel, 2016) or Tel Aviv (Klingler-Vidra, Kenney, & Breznitz, 2016). So, they highlighted that to understand the phenomenon itself and its emergence better, we should understand the interdependencies among their members and attributes, rather than only taking an inventory of the latter (Auerswald, 2015; Mack & Mayer, 2016).

In efforts to accurately theorize factors that affect the emergence of entrepreneurial ecosystems, Roundy, Bradshaw, and Brockman (2018) highlighted the necessity to deepen investigate entrepreneurial ecosystems at a micro-level, for what regards individual entrepreneurs, and meso-level, concerning the enterprises themselves. From their results, the authors identified three intertwined forces that let an entrepreneurial ecosystem rise: (i) the intentionality and adaptive tensions of entrepreneurs, (ii) the coherence of entrepreneurial activities, (iii) and the injections of resources into the ecosystem. So, in the first stages, it is all linked to some entrepreneurs' willingness to start doing business differently (intentionality) (Krueger Jr, Reilly, & Carsrud, 2000; Muñoz & Encinar, 2014: 323).

However, intentionality is not enough to let an entrepreneurial ecosystem arise. Indeed, it is necessary that also a certain amount of resources is placed within that specific area (e.g., human capital, funding, facilities). In this way, particularly aspiring entrepreneurs will strive to access those resources for taking advantage of the recognized favorable circumstances and start to trigger creative answers and plans (adaptive tensions) (Lichtenstein, Carter, Dooley, & Gartner, 2007; McKelvey, 2004). Subsequently, this pressure to act will lead entrepreneurs to put their plans into action. If the plan results successful, other entrepreneurs will start structuring their business model for emulating it (Osterwalder, 2004). Conversely, if uncoordinated efforts would result in not achieving the expected results, the process that Minniti and Bygrave (2001) called entrepreneurial learning begins. Entrepreneurs start sharing information and experiences, reciprocally influencing their behaviors and results, so that undesired outcomes become the trigger of unexpected innovation (Petkova, 2009). As a consequence, in any case, activities will start being more coordinated among those subjects (coherence of entrepreneurial activities), stimulating the emergence of an entrepreneurial ecosystem.

Finally, the resulting recursive relations of the members and their reaction to the internal and external forces that intervene at all levels, from individual to system ones, will further structure the ecosystem (Spigel, 2016). For what regards external or exogenous forces, particular attention has been posed to a continue provision of resources (injections of resources into the ecosystem), which are able to influence members' behaviors and further stimulate coherence among them. For example, companies located in a region where a particular technology is well developed could be spurred to adopt the same technology if fuelled with the necessary resources to implement it.

3.3.2 Limitations and Further Developments of Current Studies

Given the above, it must be said that entrepreneurial ecosystems are not without their own set of limitations. During a review of entrepreneurial ecosystem literature Alvedalen and Boschma (2017) identified five main weaknesses: (i) a clear analytical framework that explains the cause and effects of entrepreneurial ecosystems remains absent; (ii) the ways in which the proposed elements are connected and interact with each other, and an outline of which interactions are most important are not always clear; (iii) there is no clear explanation regarding what factors really influence an entrepreneurial ecosystems structures and performances; (iv) there are no studies that compare entrepreneurial ecosystems on a large scale, overcoming the boundaries of a single case study, regionally located; (iv) entrepreneurial ecosystem literature lacks of longitudinal studies that can address how ecosystems evolve over time.

Moreover, Alvedalen and Boschma (2017) suggest the following streams on which concentrating further researches on entrepreneurial ecosystems:

(i) At a macro-level studying institutional changes, since existing institutions need to adapt themselves or new institutions need to be created for seizing the opportunities provided by entrepreneurial ecosystems.
(ii) At a meso-level, studying what organizational elements may hinder institutional changes and entrepreneurial ecosystems to emerge in certain regions.
(iii) At a micro-level, analyzing what subjects can trigger institutional changes and under what conditions, what factors empower certain subjects to create new companies or adapt to new institutions more successfully than others, and what are the drivers that lead some regions to be a more fertile ground for ecosystems to rise.

3.4 Structure of Innovation and Entrepreneurial Ecosystems

3.4.1 Similarities

One overarching similarity between entrepreneurial and innovation ecosystems is the fact they go beyond their internal perspectives and take advantage of the different support sources from various institutions (e.g., those located on industrial and governmental levels). Consequently, they both pave the way for inflows and outflows of external knowledge (Chesbrough, 2003; Scaringella & Radziwon, 2018).

Entrepreneurial and innovation ecosystems can both be described as complex adaptive systems that share the following six properties: (i) self-organization, (ii) open but distinct boundaries, (iii) complex components, (iv) non-linearity, (v) adaptability, and (vi) sensitivity to initial conditions (Roundy et al., 2018).

Innovation and entrepreneurial ecosystem and their complexity have encouraged many authors to develop conceptualizations of their existing and interacting elements. A popular conceptualization of innovation ecosystems, for example, includes the following core elements: (i) actors, (ii) infrastructure, (iii) regulations, (iv) knowledge, and (v) ideas (Durst & Poutanen, 2013; Hwang & Horowitt, 2012; Jackson, 2011).

(i) **Actors**: they include government, universities, industry, supportive institutions, field experts, entrepreneurs, financial support systems, viable markets, societies, and their (social and economic) relationships that play various roles throughout the innovation ecosystems life.

(ii) **Infrastructure**: physical and technical conditions, as well as all the general resources that are necessary to support the innovation ecosystem and the developments occurring within it.

(iii) **Regulations**: including laws and rules that frame the innovation ecosystem functioning and innovation environment.

(iv) **Knowledge**: regards existing supporting theoretical foundations, both tacit/explicit and formal/informal, and specialized knowledge that are used, generated (eventually organized and managed), made available, and learned along the innovation value chain.

(v) **Ideas**: these include intentional thoughts that trigger innovation actions and around which the whole innovation ecosystems work.

Actors can perform several roles throughout the ecosystems' life; this is in part due to the many overlapping capabilities of members. Ecosystem actors may be different in nature, internal processes, stages of evolution, and value systems. It is through the heterogeneity of its members that ecosystems can be viewed as diverse systems of systems. Even though these members are independent entities that oftentimes come from diverse institutions, they still perform actions related to sustaining the entire ecosystem. Moreover, they frequently do not limit themselves to remain within the boundaries of their innovation initiatives, e.g., some members help other members to create and evolve both directly and indirectly through system 'trade-offs' (Rabelo, Bernus, & Romero, 2015).

Innovation and entrepreneurial ecosystems have been defined differently across the literature and this can be attributed to their transversal properties, which make their concepts easily applicable in many different fields (e.g., the food system). However, attempts to consolidate the shared characteristics of innovation and entrepreneurial ecosystems have yielded results that identify seven common dimensions of the two ecosystems (Scaringella & Radziwon, 2018).

1. A given territory with a unique atmosphere, an anchoring industry, and varying sizes.
2. A set of shared values, such as trust, sense of community belonging, and mutual understanding through traditions and culture.
3. A heterogeneous pool of stakeholders, such as corporations of varying sizes, research institutions, universities, and government officials all positioned at different stages of the food value chain.
4. A strong economic foundation based on localized economies, agglomeration economies, transaction cost theory, localized spillovers, and economies of scale.
5. Social foundations based on co-existence, co-evolvement, collaboration, and competition that emphasize the increasing importance of social and human capital.
6. A core of knowledge of different natures (e.g., tacit vs. explicit), which circulates well through knowledge sharing and spillovers, and is well absorbed through practical education, and offers synergies.
7. Well-defined outcomes, which represent the catalysts of innovation and entrepreneurial initiatives and competitiveness and lead to economic growth, long-term development, performance, and success.

In both innovation and entrepreneurial ecosystems, members develop significant relationships anchored by interdependence. Interdependence offers synergetic interactions between system members. When institutional ecosystem members establish cooperation and have common interest for shared business objectives, the interdependencies between them start to become more visible, and proper management and risk mitigation strategies allow them to reduce uncertainty. Still, it is only through the knowledge sharing and spillover aspects that the creation of innovative products and services can be fostered. Ecosystem stakeholders are typically highly interconnected. Partnerships often result from this interdependence and interconnectedness, which lead to co-evolution and co-creation of value that no *one* member would be able to create in isolation.

3.4.2 Differences

Surely, entrepreneurial and innovation ecosystems are not stand-alone concepts, and other versions of ecosystems exist, however with slight variations in structure and overall aims. In fact, from a systematic literature review of 104 articles and books, Scaringella and Radziwon (2018) identified four main types of ecosystems with slight, but nonetheless existing, differences: (i) business, (ii) entrepreneurial, (iii) innovation, and (iv) knowledge ecosystems (Scaringella & Radziwon, 2018).

(i) **Business Ecosystems**: perhaps the oldest of the concepts, focuses on inter-organization networks that are in close proximity to each other and on large firms that assume the role of orchestrators. This ecosystem places heavy emphasis on the business-related value creation processes that emerge due to close collaborations between its many institutions. The emergence of entrepreneurial, innovation, and knowledge ecosystems represents a series of possible substitutes to business ecosystems and future multi-directional developments.

(ii) **Entrepreneurial Ecosystem**: these ecosystems focus on a particular region or country and highlight the importance of both governmental level actors and entrepreneurs. Entrepreneurial ecosystems acknowledge the contributions and impact of individual members as well as institutions on the economy. In order to ensure that this contribution to the economy is successful, the support of policy makers is crucial.

(iii) **Innovation Ecosystem**: these ecosystems are increasingly being associated with the digital world. Innovative products and services are developed by companies from diverse industries that are located in close (geographic or cognitive) proximity to each other. The uncertainty associated with supply and demand is higher in innovation ecosystems than in other cases.

(iv) **Knowledge ecosystem**: these bodies serve as bridges between the business ecosystem and markets. It includes essential elements of collaboration and knowledge exchange and acknowledges the value-creating intersection of the business and academic sectors.

From their synthesis, Scaringella and Radziwon (2018) developed a list of invariants, or ever-present elements in each ecosystem, to strengthen the foundations of this growing field. The list of variants is outlined in Table 3.2.

In essence, detailed knowledge about the specificities of innovation and entrepreneurial ecosystems should not be viewed as optional. It is crucial to understand that success in one context does not guarantee success in another due to the uniqueness of each ecosystem and environment in which it is located. For example, replicating Silicon Valley and its successes in other environments has not worked despite numerous attempts. However, detailed knowledge of specific elements and their expected roles in guiding ecosystem relationships in the local or regional environmental context is essential to creating adaptive networks that may later evolve to ecosystems.

Gaining a deeper understanding of the contextual relationships within ecosystems and best strategies to achieve beneficial results while avoiding those that do not is more effective than attempting to replicate the "best functioning ecosystem". Thus, future research should investigate local entrepreneurial and business perspectives on the role of institutions and policy makers in the process of ecosystem creation and development (Scaringella & Radziwon, 2018).

3.4.3 Boundaries

As noted, the idea of ecosystems is complex, never static, and influenced by the interactions of its members, which therefore raises questions regarding their boundary conditions—what are the factors that determine the vertical and horizontal sector scope and boundaries of an ecosystem? How do boundaries differ across different geographic regions and sectors? What configurations of actors within place-based ecosystems are most conducive to discovering and exploring opportunities?

Authors argue that boundary questions should also consider the relationship between ecosystems themselves. For example, to what extent does knowledge spillover across entrepreneurial and innovation ecosystems? How does the role of digitalization vary depending on whether the outcomes of ecosystems are commercial or social?

Ecosystems typically embrace many kinds of stakeholders, infrastructure, and even other ecosystems, since there is no physical or organizational border, ecosystems can embrace universities, private R&D institutions, funding agencies, and industry partners.

Subsequently, entering and exiting the ecosystem can be dynamic and single members may exit without even being noticed. Ecosystem boundaries are intrinsically 'elastic' and this means having general or less formal governance and performance management models. It is posited that ecosystems manage themselves in an organic manner rather than being managed by some central authority. Due to cultural factors and implicit social rules, it is unlikely for formal governance to forcefully coerce members and system behaviors (Rabelo et al., 2015).

Table 3.2 Invariants of the ecosystem approach

Invariants		Business ecosystem	Entrepreneurial ecosystem	Innovation ecosystem	Knowledge ecosystem
Territory	Anchoring	Platform as an anchor point to the ecosystem			Presence of an anchor tenant
	Territorial size	Close proximity; inherently local	The country or region	Spatial proximity (in case of innovative business ecosystems) or/and virtual spaces	Close proximity
	Industry		Disruption of existing industries and creation of new ones	Wide range of industries	Technological clusters
Values	Trust	Trust		Trust	Trust
	Belonging to a community	Virtual/Cocreation community		Mutual dependence on exchange relationships	Collective sense of belonging to a special group
	Mutual understanding		Understanding ones own entrepreneurial cognitions	Understanding as a key controllability factor	
	Uncertainty reduction		Visible success reduce the perception of risk	Mitigation of interdependencies risks	
	Culture, history & routines		Culture impacts the ecosystem development		Promotion of culture of innovation
Stakeholders	Firms	Internal organization networks	Entrepreneurial firms embedded in networks, interconnected companies	Firms embedded in networks	Large firms with established R&D departments, SMEs, and start-ups
	Networking among firms	Learning, connectivity, and mutually influencing interactions	Interaction between entrepreneur and ecosystem	Interdependence	Collective learning Networking between residents
	Other stakeholders	Complementors; a large volume of innovating entities	Individuals and entrepreneurial teams; social, institutional, industrial, organizational, temporal and spatial networks	Complementors, government organizations, funders, resource providers, standard	The universities, public research organization

(continued)

Table 3.2 (continued)

Invariants		Business ecosystem	Entrepreneurial ecosystem	Innovation ecosystem	Knowledge ecosystem
				setters, and complementary innovators	
	Value chain	Customers, suppliers, distributors, outsourcing firms, makers of related products or services, technology providers	Open-minded customers, specialized suppliers, service providers, training institutions, and support organizations	Customers, suppliers, intermediaries	Diversity of organizational forms
	Governance	Orchestrator	'Anchor events' as governance platform	Leading firm/ecosystem orchestrator/network orchestrator	University or public research organization (PRO)
Economics	Location economics				Collective resources
	Localized spillovers				Local spillovers
	Economies of scale	Economies of scale			Economies of scale and scope
Social	Economic and non-economic		Economic progress stimulation, social-economic interactions	Shared economic and social value	
	Collaboration versus competition	Collaboration and competition resulting in cooperation relationships; symbiosis	Private enterprises coexisting in symbiotic relationships	Simultaneous cooperation and competition	Knowledge-based R&D collaboration
	Workforce	Job creation function	Mobility of innovative entrepreneurs; job creation		Mobility of personnel

Knowledge	Type of knowledge	Protected patents			Tacit and protected
	Knowledge dynamics	Knowledge mobility	New knowledge production through interaction	Coordinated knowledge flows: Purposive knowledge inflows and outflows	Make use of knowledge available in the region: Proximity to knowledge generators
	Synergies	Synergies of innovation resources		Synergistic relationships of people, knowledge, and resources	
Outcomes	Economic	Value creation; performance enhancement	GDP growth		
	Innovation	Innovation	Radical innovation	Innovation	Innovation
	Competitiveness	Competitive advantage through collaboration in value network			
	Entrepreneurship		Venture creation		Cross-realm transposition
	Development	Adaptation and evolution	Co-creation and evolution, which are fostered by policymakers and drives innovation	Co-creation	

Source: Scaringella and Radziwon (2018)

3.4.4 Personal and Systemic

Explorations of the emergence of ecosystems have noted challenges regarding the ecosystem concept and its lingering interchangeability with the terms networks, communities, and knowledge sharing platforms. However, most importantly, they have also demonstrated that established ecosystem members have multiple innovation relationships in different ecosystems and between them (Still et al., 2019).

In order to ameliorate the vagueness between these concepts, Still et al. (2019) provide engagement guidelines for both academics and practitioners. For academics, they propose highlighting the elements of modularity, complementarity, and coordination with a shared goal, and making them explicit in the descriptions of ecosystems since they are considered the elements that separate ecosystems from networks and communities (Still et al., 2019). For practitioners, they recommend emphasizing the importance of understanding the need for those elements; however, always complementing the ecosystem level approach with the needs of individual actors. Therefore the development activities can be better designed, thus making the ecosystem management more effective (Still et al., 2019).

Furthermore, the interdependency that defines ecosystem relationships can also confine institutions and the introduction to new products and services. For example, the launch or testing of new products can be delayed by the ecosystem itself if the necessary complementary elements of the ecosystem are not readily available (Dattée et al., 2018; Overholm, 2015).

3.4.5 Dynamics

As open social systems, innovation and entrepreneurial ecosystems enable dynamic inflows and outflows of resources (e.g., funding, knowledge, members themselves, technologies) and provide a shared institutional logic for the emergence of different types of innovations (Vargo & Lusch, 2016; Vargo, Wieland, & Akaka, 2015).

The dynamics of ecosystems are analyzed by using ecological concepts such as diversity, selection, related diversification, resilience, and adaptation (Auerswald & Dani, 2017; Boschma, 2015). Ecosystems cannot be thought of as instruments for decision-making and actions, but as specialized organizational spaces, tailored to co-creation of values through collaboration. So, they constitute sophisticated pools of members, assets, and linkages, generated by the collaborative activities of networks. This idea of ecosystem corresponds to findings in the literature on complexity, viewing collaborative networks as complex adaptive systems that are inseparable from their changing environment by definition.

Schiuma and Carlucci (2018) propose a research agenda for understanding how to establish and develop strategic partnerships within innovation ecosystems, and identify four fundamental dimensions that characterize the role and function mechanisms of successful collaborative relationships:

3.4 Structure of Innovation and Entrepreneurial Ecosystems

(i) the entrepreneurial learning network dynamics and the transformation patterns that affect the development of entrepreneurial capital of ecosystems;

(ii) the role and features of the organizational units to support companies' entrepreneurial and innovative development;

(iii) the organizational models and factors that influence a company's capacity to establish successful partnerships and to develop entrepreneurial and innovation capabilities;

(iv) the approaches, models, and tools that can support the design, implementation, and assessment of partnerships and initiatives aimed to develop entrepreneurial and innovative capabilities.

Furthermore, Hakala and colleagues (2019) apply a novel literature review method, model-narrative, in order to systematically trace and reveal dominant narratives from the existing literature on ecosystems in business studies. To date, most literature on ecosystems resembles a knowledge base composed of competing overarching stories with complex members engaging in even more complex relationships. Based on their analysis, Hakala, O'Shea, Farny, and Luoto (2019) found differences around key themes used to portray relationships in an ecosystem. They then applied specific vocabularies to create intertwined characters and narrative voices to communicate different roles in the ecosystem. Their results provided further explanations between how the dynamic relationships between business, innovation, and entrepreneurial ecosystems emerge (Hakala et al., 2019). The method employed by Hakala et al. (2019) allowed for a more profound analysis of simple data-driven themes and allowed for the analysis of the tone of entire research streams, which revealed missing elements that could inform our ability to create thriving ecosystems. A summary of the model-narratives, structured along the nine identified conceptual elements of their narrative review, is presented below in Table 3.3.

3.4.6 Change, Growth, and Performance

In addition to the aforementioned human elements, certain systemic elements also have an impact on the way innovation ecosystems operate (Rabelo et al., 2015).

1. **Interface**: represents the channel to support the interactions between ecosystem members and external actors, considering their usually significant heterogeneity.
2. **Culture**: refers to the mindset of people and organizations combined with supporting and facilitating innovation initiatives and solving related problems.
3. **Architectural Principles**: refers to the way the innovation ecosystem elements are combined and orchestrated; the culture element is also reflected here. The innovation ecosystem dynamics make actors assume multiple but not fixed or pre-defined roles in the different stages involved in the innovation ecosystem's lifecycle.

Table 3.3 Conceptual overview of innovation and entrepreneurial ecosystems

	Model-narrative of business ecosystem	Model-narrative of innovation ecosystem	Model-narrative of entrepreneurial ecosystem
Thematic reading			
Key themes	Global competition, co-opetition; co-evolution, synergies, market selection	Collaboration, value co-creation, customer-facing solutions, platforms, keystones, hubs	Concentration, wealth and job creation, locality, clusters, governance, system components and attributes
Scientific puzzle	How can large companies adapt strategy to fit an ecosystem concept? The reason is changing circumstances of industrial transformation	How can keystone companies maintain health in the ecosystem? There is a shared fate and interdependence; this can reduce time-to-market for innovations	How to create wealth and employment for a defined geographic area? What elements can be influenced by regional public policy?
Enstoried reading			
Plot	• Companies must realize they are in a system—they must adapt their strategy and contrive to lead the system • They can induce ecosystem collaboration • Key purpose is to create connections • Leader role is valued—leadership through co-opetition. Impose value and supply network • A main company governs the ecosystem • Co-evolution • Market (supply/demand) is part of the story • Winners and losers—Predator seat prey • Strategy improvement tools	• Big companies now realize they are in a system—They are the key stones that can regulate ecosystem health • They can manage ecosystem collaboration • Key purpose is to create innovations • Leader through platform technology, keystone but not a leader—Co create value and supply network • Maintain ecosystem health • Platform technology governs • Co-evolution • All can be winners • Operational assessment tools	• Regional actors (governments) must realize that public policy and other elements need to be considered to create entrepreneurial ecosystems • They can create conditions for ecosystem emergence and health • Regional actors lead • System may lack governance • Interaction of the elements (not people) • Produces only winners • Regional ecosystem setup lists
Narrative setting	Industrial transformation, global competition where there is a need to collaborate US corporates 1980s and 1990s	US corporates 1990s and 2000s Innovative customer offering with collaborative arrangements between companies	Regions needing transformation
Emplotted characters	Leading company, other companies, markets, demand side	Leading companies, leading technologies, 'complementors'	Various actors or elements in the regional systems, 'silicon valleys' and 'technology parks'

(continued)

3.4 Structure of Innovation and Entrepreneurial Ecosystems

Table 3.3 (continued)

	Model-narrative of business ecosystem	Model-narrative of innovation ecosystem	Model-narrative of entrepreneurial ecosystem
Narrative voices	Leading companies eco-system as a 'deity'	Leading technologies Platform as a deity	Regional governance actors Region as a deity
Moral lesson	Society finds ways to help members of dying eco-systems move to more vital ones and stops supporting dying ones—Continuous renewal We are connected outside of the organization to serve the market	Interdependence, integra-tion, renewal We are connected outside of the organization to serve and improve a common technology	Proof and belief that such systems exist We are not connected—The system needs to be created
Rhetorical reading			
Rhetorical device	Metaphors: Predators and prey, grasslands, savan-nah, co-evolution	Metaphors: Dominators, keystones, sea otters	Metaphors: Few explicit metaphors except the general idea of ecology and ecosystem
Rhetorical strategy	Authorization by leading companies	Authorization by leading technology (companies)	Authorization from benchmark regions
	Slogan: Survival of fittest in ecosystem	Slogan: Manage to win with ecosystem	Slogan: Govern to create the ecosystem

Source: Hakala et al. (2019)

Ecosystems can also be viewed through a model developed by Rabelo et al. (2015) that illustrates the lifecycle phases and processes involved in building an innovation ecosystem. This model highlights that although separate, the activities within these processes may be circularly depending on one another. A description of the phases individuated in the model follows.

- **Strategy Formulation Phase.** It consists of three main processes. First, strategy definition, which (re)-identifies the innovation ecosystem's mission, vision, values, and strategic goals and performs feasibility analysis. Second strategy planning, which defines action plans, milestones, critical success factors, and key indicators for the innovation ecosystem to be built or that is already running. Moreover, it outlines actions to ensure the preparedness of actors, mandates, and overall plans and dedicates innovation ecosystem building or transformation programs and projects. Third, strategy analysis, that refers to the variety of strategic analyses informing the evaluation and feedback of the outcomes of the two other processes.
- **Project Phase.** This process designs and prepares the underlying conditions required for transforming an innovation ecosystem and involves two main pro-cesses: ecosystem design and ecosystem preparedness. Ecosystem design defines the ecosystems 'architecture', its components, types of actors, roles and

relationships, infrastructure requirements, governance model, operating and business models, bylaws, ethics, and stimulates the attraction of other actors. Ecosystem preparedness defines a plan of actions related to preparing the ecosystem members, infrastructure, and laws and regulations to handle the ecosystem's requirements, along the future stages of evolution.

- **Deployment Phase.** This regards formally establishing the designed innovation ecosystem, transforming specifications into infrastructures, and populating them with real actors. This phase consists of four main processes—actor's attraction & marketing, actor's recruiting, physical building, and ecosystem foundation. *Actors' attraction & marketing* designs and executes actions to disseminate knowledge of the ecosystem to attract qualified actors. *Actors' recruiting* aims to attract new members according to preparedness directives and rules. *Physical building* is the availability of suitable facilities to support the diverse types of actions required throughout an innovation's lifecycle, following the requirements and guidelines indicated in the design sub-process. *Ecosystem foundation* refers to the official organizational foundation of the ecosystem, when pertinent. Depending on the deployment model and taxation laws as well as legal incentive mechanisms, this can involve a legal or more formal establishment of the innovation ecosystem, or, in other extreme cases, this may simply take the form of an official 'announcement'.
- **Execution Phase.** It can be defined as the set of processes involved in operating the entire ecosystem and consists of two main processes: ecosystem operation and ecosystem management. Ecosystem operation includes the activities involved in creating and ensuring the success of the many innovation activities occurring within the ecosystem. Ecosystem management can function on two levels. The first is the strategic management of the ecosystem itself (e.g., identifying opportunities, threats, and issues, and initiating other relevant lifecycle processes as above). The second is the tactical and operational management of the ecosystem, which involves human resources, financial, organization, technological, and governance issues. It is likely to be a delegated set of activities rather than being consolidated into a central role performed by one particular institution or member.
- **Conclusion Phase.** This phase holds the responsibility for handling issues that significantly affect the continuation of the ecosystem's life and also consists of two main processes; ecosystem decommission and ecosystem disbanding. Ecosystem decommission refers to managing the entering and exiting of actors within the ecosystem along with its developmental phases. Ecosystem disbanding refers to a gradual exiting of members from the ecosystem due to strategic changes or general disagreements.
- **Sustenance Phase.** This final phase is responsible for anticipating the future evolution and viability of the ecosystem. This phase impacts and receives feedbacks from all the other sub-processes. Ecosystem sustainability corresponds to tactical and strategic management levels that all phases have when performing their actions.

It is holistic approaches such as the one above that complete the view of the entire ecosystem creation process and its life cycle. Models such as these may prove helpful for stakeholders who desire to better plan and manage their time, allocate resources, and manage the degree of complexity of actions in different stages of the ecosystem creation. This can be helpful for anticipating points of higher risk of failure and preventing the entire ecosystem from achieving an undesirable state (Rabelo et al., 2015).

Adner (2012) introduces a list of recommendations to assist stakeholders in creating and developing an ecosystem. They propose that (i) designing the ecosystems 'value blueprint' (i.e., locations and links between ecosystem members), (ii) foreseeing risks to value creations, (iii) determining the value of leadership and followership roles in the ecosystem, (iv) timing of innovation introductions, and (v) the dynamic reconfiguration of the ecosystem over time are the elements that drive ecosystem success.

Most studies have focused on isolating entrepreneurial ecosystem components, but few theories that embrace the complexity of entrepreneurial ecosystems exist to date. To address this gap in ecosystem research, Roundy and colleagues posit that entrepreneurial ecosystems can be more fully understood if they are examined through a lens of complexity and conceptualized as complex adaptive systems. Roundy et al. (2018) go on to propose three related forces that act as important influencers to the emergence of entrepreneurial ecosystems—(i) intentionality of entrepreneurs, (ii) coherence of entrepreneurial activities, and (iii) injections of resources.

Recognizing the social and cultural dimensions' involvement of entrepreneurial activities has been accompanied by a shift of focus from studies of entrepreneurs and ventures to the creation of (entrepreneurial) ecosystems, which includes the sets of stakeholders, institutions, social networks, and cultural values that produce and sustain entrepreneurial activity (Acs, Stam, Audretsch, & O'Connor, 2017; Auerswald, 2015; Brown & Mason, 2017; Roundy et al., 2018; Stam, 2015).

3.4.7 Drivers

Building innovation ecosystems is a more complex task than building other environments that are usually less open and more controlled (e.g., incubators, technology and science parks, innovation habitats, and entrepreneurship centers) (Romero, Rabelo, & Molina, 2012). When viewed as a whole, this organic task comprises different and independent but interrelated activities that must be carefully undertaken while considering different tangible and intangible factors. These activities (e.g., implicit or deliberate, emergent or planned, static or evolving, loosely or tightly managed) span the innovation ecosystems life through all stages of its evolution (Rabelo et al., 2015).

It is a shared vision, a clear mission statement, and an overarching unified sense of direction are the elements that promote bonding among ecosystem members, enable collaborations, and guide the ecosystem's focus (Järvi, Almpanopoulou, & Ritala, 2018).

In order to give more detail to the characteristics of the main actors, their interactions, and cognitive mindsets within the ecosystems, Brown and Mason (2017) proposed a taxonomy that features four main coordinative aspects of entrepreneurial ecosystems: (i) entrepreneurial actors, (ii) entrepreneurial resource providers, (iii) entrepreneurial connectors, and (iv) entrepreneurial culture.

In essence, they highlight that when examining entrepreneurial ecosystems, it is important to examine structure and agency simultaneously in order to appreciate the full complexity of the dynamics of entrepreneurial activity in any given context (Brown & Mason, 2017). Given the heterogeneity of ecosystems, a 'one-size fits all' policy or approach for developing different types of ecosystems remains absent from the literature.

Regarding innovation ecosystems, specifically, based on a systematic review, Dedehayir, Mäkinen, and Ortt (2018) propose several roles that are critical to innovation ecosystem creation and classify them into four groups that are defined by the specific activities they carry out during ecosystem birth—(i) leadership roles, (ii) direct value creation roles, (iii) value creation support roles, (iv) entrepreneurial ecosystem roles.

1. **Leadership roles**: It initiates, maintains, and develops ecosystem functionality. Forges partnerships by creating networks provide the basis for market to function by ensuring alignment between innovation and markets, helps create and capture value by stimulating value appropriation, and as a dominator that conducts mergers and acquisitions in related fields.
2. **Direct value creation roles.** They serve as a supplier of materials, technologies, and services. Also as assemblers that provide products and services, then as complementors who utilize the design of other ecosystem offerings, and users who usually define a problem or need, and develop innovations under the ecosystem leaders guidance.
3. **Value creation support roles.** These involve experts and champions. Experts support primary value creators by generating knowledge from basic and applied research, provide consultation and expertise, and encourage technology transfer and commercialization. Champions support ecosystem construction by building connections and alliances between members, interacting between partners and sub-groups, and by providing access to local and non-local markets.
4. **Entrepreneurial ecosystem roles.** These roles have been sub-grouped into entrepreneurs, sponsors, and regulators. Entrepreneurs start new ventures around a vision by co-locating in a region with others and coordinating collaboration between research and commercial partners. The sponsor supports the new venture creation by giving resources to entrepreneurs and linking entrepreneurs to other system actors. The regulator supports entrepreneurial activity and opens avenues for ecosystem emergence by providing economic and political reform, and loosening regularity restrictions.

These roles clearly assist in highlighting the implications for a range of stakeholders (e.g., university, industry, and government partners) who are ultimately concerned with the formation of innovation ecosystems to enhance economic welfare (Dedehayir et al., 2018).

3.4.8 Challenges

The emergence of ecosystems is constrained by a host of institutional and system-level barriers in the existing organizational field that inhibit the legitimacy, resourcing, and growth of new initiatives. Furthermore, scholars have mostly focused on entry barriers for single actors rather than on the dynamic counterforces that prevent the emergence of whole ecosystems.

An empirical study by Almpanopoulou, Ritala, and Blomqvist (2019) analyzed the institutional barriers for innovation ecosystem emergence and individuated four ecosystem emergence barriers and related-field sustaining mechanisms.

1. **Incumbent actor inertia.** These are actors or stakeholders who are hesitant to drive change; they adhere to traditional business logic and modus operandi, thus sustaining the existing norms and industry cultures instead of stimulating innovation and novel transitions. The concentration of influence with these traditional closed and static networks also functions as an enabler for their bargaining power and legitimacy.
2. **Regulation and policy-making ambiguities.** The length of time required by policy makers and the policymaking environment reinforces ambiguities related to policy vision and the actual action plan. The unhurried pace of policymaking, also referred to shortsighted political view (e.g., election, or re-elections, of political leaders after a brief amount of time).
3. **Cognitive constraints for opportunity recognition.** This deals with perceived uncertainty over market opportunities, which makes it difficult to identify viable entrepreneurial opportunities. The dispersion of necessary capabilities and resources further creates constraints for collectively recognizing and exploiting opportunities.
4. **Institutional complexity.** This involves system-level challenges with the required system-level transitions being accepted by all segmented stakeholders. For example, European and national climate or circular economy policies are oftentimes broken down into smaller objectives, which further increases ecosystem complexity. In the food industry, this could manifest as large corporations investing in new fertilizers for crop growth, but coming at a higher cost to farmers, therefore creating a rift between aims and best practices to achieve them. The complexity of the food system can slow down the decision-making process, and therefore slow down development as well.

Based on these barriers further highlight how the mutual reinforcement of regulation, policymaking ambiguities, the inertia of incumbent actors, and cognitive constraints for opportunity recognition inhibit innovation ecosystem emergence (Almpanopoulou, Ritala, and Blomqvist 2019). Furthermore, the perceptions of ecosystem members, the legitimacy of existing modus operandi (Markard, Wirth, & Truffer, 2016; Suddaby, Bitektine, & Haack, 2017), and the stabilizing influence of shared norms and culture provide barriers to the successful identification of opportunities for business creation. Furthermore, cognitive constraints for opportunity identification can also reinforce existing operating procedures and strengthen an industry's inability to engage in sustainability transitions (Almpanopoulou et al., 2019).

3.5 Food Systems

For what specifically regards food systems, they can be effectively analyzed through the five systems thinking principles proposed by Gharajedaghi (2011): (i) openness, (ii) purposefulness, (iii) multi-dimensionality, (iv) emergent property, and (v) counterintuitive behavior. Indeed, food systems can be described as dynamic open systems (Pigford, Hickey, & Klerkx, 2018) that are influenced by several external factors (e.g., social, economical, technological, political, environmental) (openness), in which multiple actors (multi-dimensionality) operate for achieving specific purposes (purposefulness). Notably, these purposes are all somehow related to producing value along the food supply chain up to the final consumer (De Bernardi, Bertello, Venuti, & Zardini, 2019; Lioutasa, Charatsarib, De Rosac, & La Roccad, 2018). However, a high degree of uncertainty in every intentionally generated action can lead to an undesired or opposite outcome (counterintuitive behaviour). Thus, performances often depend more on the quality of the interactions among actors rather than on the quality of the actors themselves (emergent property).

Furthermore, the infamously low-technological presence and a high degree of complexity hamper both innovation processes and knowledge production in food systems (Lioutasa et al., 2018). Moreover, the high degree of interdependence among food system actors and a lack of control over their market environments contribute to this complexity. Luckily, innovation and entrepreneurship are rapidly emerging like the combination of evolving competencies and knowledge, leading to new methods of resource integration among interrelated stakeholders of the dynamic food system (De Bernardi, Bertello, & Venuti, 2019; Lioutasa et al., 2018). Recent manifestations of entrepreneurship and innovation in the food system involve forms of alternative methods for food production such as aquaponics, vertical farming, urban agriculture, precision farming, and social and smart farming (Dell'Olio, Hassink, & Vaandrager, 2017; Ingram, 2018; Junge, König, Villarroel, Komives, & Jijakli, 2017; Muller et al., 2017; Orsini, Kahane, Nono-Womdim, & Gianquinto, 2013; Wolfert, Ge, Verdouw, & Bogaardt, 2017). However, individual startups and standalone ventures that emerge from entrepreneurial and innovation activities are seldom sufficient to tackle the sustainability and environmental issues threatening the food system. Networked approaches to innovation and entrepreneurship are, therefore, necessary in order to facilitate trans-disciplinary co-creations across food systems (Hermans, Roep, & Klerkx, 2016; Pigford et al., 2018). Infact, well designed and supportive innovation and entrepreneurship environments, as well as the adoption of holistic and inclusive approaches to achieve sustainability pave the way for a spectrum of possible solutions, including agroecology, place-based food systems, and other social innovations (De Bernardi, Bertello, & Venuti, 2020; De Bernardi, Forliano, Rotti, & Franco, 2019; Pigford et al., 2018).

3.6 Conclusion

As innovative as the concept of systems thinking to create entrepreneurial and innovation ecosystems, future attempts to create sustainable solutions, especially in food systems, should consider them as interlinked, and co-existing; one cannot exist without the other. Stakeholders aiming to merge these two concepts should consider lessons from previous explicit attempts to link entrepreneurial and innovation ecosystems.

Like innovation and entrepreneurial ecosystems, food systems should also be thought of as dynamic, open systems that operate in order to produce value. The combination of innovation and entrepreneurship, emerge as the simultaneous evolution of competencies and knowledge, and lead to new methods of resource integration and exploitation while always considering the context in which these transitions are planned to occur, thus sustaining the capacity of such systems (Lioutasa et al., 2018).

Given the unique characteristics and specificities within the interrelations of ecosystems, there is no standardized framework or strategy to effectively develop entrepreneurial or innovation ecosystems (Audretsch, 2015; Brown & Mason, 2017).

Therefore, in order to address to complex and ubiquitous threatening food system sustainability, it is imperative to design appropriate and culturally relevant systems that can stimulate transitions and recommend key action points for policy and practice (Pigford et al., 2018).

Innovation and entrepreneurial ecosystems may offer a useful umbrella concept that is appropriate for the wider multi-functionality of food systems, with the potential to better support the development of trans-disciplinary ecosystems designed to realize the collective and integrated innovations in support for sustainability. Systems thinking complements and advances the established foundation of food system innovation toward more sustainable production and consumption methods and practices.

The application of innovation and entrepreneurial ecosystem principles and frameworks to food systems would expand food systems in three ways:

1. Be more explicit on the power dynamics in innovation platforms or communities.
2. Include both human and non-human change agents across the innovation ecosystem.
3. Be more cognizant of boundary crossing and potential trade-offs.

Food system innovation approaches might be opened to better include innovation and entrepreneurial ecosystems as well. The existence of innovation and entrepreneurial ecosystems thus has the potential to broaden food systems by emphasizing their role and power in shaping directionality in innovation platforms or communities that are connected to other networks. By highlighting the plurality of members and the integral role of ecological catalysts of innovation, entrepreneurial and innovation ecosystems offer umbrella terms that may guide sustainable transitions in the food sector (e.g., by engaging with a variety of ecosystem members in other agricultural landscapes or systems.

Agricultural, or food, innovation ecosystems approach may help design and support the development of trans-boundary, inter-sectorial, innovation niches that can realize more collective and integrated innovation to support sustainability transitions and help enact mission-oriented food system policies.

The ecosystem concept enhances our understanding of complex interactions that make up innovation and entrepreneurial ecosystems, as well as food systems. Ecosystems thinking has the potential to provide novel ways of approaching structure, interaction, and exchanges among institutions that are dependent on one another, and moves our focus toward analyzing the many relationships that operate at the system level of organizations, technologies, products and customers (Hakala et al., 2019).

References

Acs, Z. J., Autio, E., & Szerb, L. (2014). National systems of entrepreneurship: Measurement issues and policy implications. *Research Policy, 43*(3), 476–494.

Acs, Z. J., Stam, E., Audretsch, D. B., & O'Connor, A. (2017). The lineages of the entrepreneurial ecosystem approach. *Small Business Economics, 49*(1), 1–10.

Adner, R. (2012). *The wide lens: A new strategy for innovation.* London: Penguin.

Adner, R. (2017). Ecosystem as structure: An actionable construct for strategy. *Journal of Management, 43*(1), 39–58.

Adner, R., & Kapoor, R. (2010). Value creation in innovation ecosystems: How the structure of technological interdependence affects firm performance in new technology generations. *Strategic Management Journal, 31*(3), 306–333.

Adner, R., & Kapoor, R. (2016). Innovation ecosystems and the pace of substitution: Re-examining technology S-curves. *Strategic Management Journal, 37*(4), 625–648.

Almpanopoulou, A., Ritala, P., & Blomqvist, K. (2019). Innovation ecosystem emergence barriers: Institutional perspective. In *Proceedings of the 52nd Hawaii International Conference on System Sciences.*

Alvedalen, J., & Boschma, R. (2017). A critical review of entrepreneurial ecosystems research: Towards a future research agenda. *European Planning Studies, 25*(6), 887–903.

References

Appleyard, M. M., & Chesbrough, H. W. (2017). The dynamics of open strategy: From adoption to reversion. *Long Range Planning, 50*(3), 310–321.

Audretsch, D. B. (2015). *Everything in its place: Entrepreneurship and the strategic management of cities, regions, and states.* Oxford: Oxford University Press.

Auerswald, P. E. (2015). Enabling entrepreneurial ecosystems: Insights from ecology to inform effective entrepreneurship policy. *Kauffman Foundation Research Series on city, metro, and regional entrepreneurship.*

Auerswald, P. E., & Dani, L. (2017). The adaptive life cycle of entrepreneurial ecosystems: The biotechnology cluster. *Small Business Economics, 49*(1), 97–117.

Autio, E., & Thomas, L. (2014). Innovation ecosystems: Implications for innovation management. In M. Dodgson, D. M. Gann, & N. Phillips (Eds.), *The Oxford handbook of innovation management* (Vol. 1, pp. 204–288). Oxford: Oxford University Press.

Autio, E., & Thomas, L. D. (2016). Tilting the playing field: Towards an endogenous strategic action theory of ecosystem creation. In *Academy of management proceedings* (Vol. 2016, No. 1). Briarcliff Manor, NY: Academy of Management.

Autio, E., Kenney, M., Mustar, P., Siegel, D., & Wright, M. (2014). Entrepreneurial innovation: The importance of context. *Research Policy, 43*(7), 1097–1108.

Autio, E., Nambisan, S., Thomas, L. D., & Wright, M. (2018). Digital affordances, spatial affordances, and the genesis of entrepreneurial ecosystems. *Strategic Entrepreneurship Journal, 12*(1), 72–95.

Bahrami, H., & Evans, S. (1995). Flexible re-cycling and high-technology entrepreneurship. *California Management Review, 37*(3), 62–89.

Boschma, R. (2015). Towards an evolutionary perspective on regional resilience. *Regional Studies, 49*(5), 733–751.

Brown, R., & Mason, C. (2017). Looking inside the spiky bits: A critical review and conceptualisation of entrepreneurial ecosystems. *Small Business Economics, 49*(1), 11–30.

Ceccagnoli, M., Forman, C., Huang, P., & Wu, D. J. (2012). Co-creation of value in a platform ecosystem: The case of enterprise software. *MIS Quarterly, 36*(1), 263–290.

Chesbrough, H. W. (2003). *Open innovation: The new imperative for creating and profiting from technology.* Boston: Harvard Business Press.

Dattée, B., Alexy, O., & Autio, E. (2018). Maneuvering in poor visibility: How firms play the ecosystem game when uncertainty is high. *Academy of Management Journal, 61*(2), 466–498.

De Bernardi, P., Bertello, A., & Venuti, F. (2019). Online and on-site interactions within alternative food networks: Sustainability impact of knowledge-sharing practices. *Sustainability, 11*(5), 1457.

De Bernardi, P., Bertello, A., & Venuti, F. (2020). Community-oriented motivations and knowledge sharing as drivers of success within food assemblies. In *Exploring digital ecosystems* (pp. 443–457). Cham: Springer.

De Bernardi, P., Bertello, A., Venuti, F., & Zardini, A. (2019). Knowledge transfer driving community-based business models towards sustainable food-related behaviours: A commons perspective. *Knowledge Management Research & Practice,* 1–8. https://doi.org/10.1080/14778238.2019.1664271

De Bernardi, P., Forliano, C., Rotti, R., & Franco, M. (2019). Innovazione e sostenibilità nei nuovi modelli di business del settore vitivinicolo. Analisi del caso Fontanafredda. In F. Moreschi (Ed.), *Il paesaggio vitivinicolo come patrimonio europeo: Aspetti gius-economici, geografici, ambientali, contrattuali, enoturistici, di marketing* (pp. 27–41). Torino: Giappichelli.

Dedehayir, O., Mäkinen, S. J., & Ortt, J. R. (2018). Roles during innovation ecosystem genesis: A literature review. *Technological Forecasting and Social Change, 136,* 18–29.

Dell'Olio, M., Hassink, J., & Vaandrager, L. (2017). The development of social farming in Italy: A qualitative inquiry across four regions. *Journal of Rural Studies, 56,* 65–75.

Durst, S., & Poutanen, P. (2013). Success factors of innovation ecosystems-initial insights from a literature review. In R. Smeds & O. Irrmann (Eds.), *Co-create 2013: The boundary-crossing conference on co-design in innovation* (pp. 27–38). Espoo: Aalto University.

Foster, G., Shimizu, C., Ciesinski, S., Davila, A., Hassan, S., Jia, N., & Morris, R. (2013). *Entrepreneurial ecosystems around the globe and company growth dynamics* (Vol. 11). Geneva: World Economic Forum.

Gharajedaghi, J. (2011). *Systems thinking: Managing chaos and complexity: A platform for designing business architecture.* Amsterdam: Elsevier.

Graham, R. (2014). *Creating university-based entrepreneurial ecosystems: Evidence from emerging world leaders.* Cambridge, MA: Massachusetts Institute of Technology.

Hajikhani, A. (2017). Emergence and dissemination of ecosystem concept in innovation studies: A systematic literature review study. In *Proceedings of the 50th Hawaii International Conference on System Sciences.*

Hakala, H., O'Shea, G., Farny, S., & Luoto, S. (2019). Re-storying the business, innovation and entrepreneurial ecosystem concepts. The model-narrative review method. *International Journal of Management Reviews, 00,* 1–23.

Hallen, B. L., Bingham, C. B., & Cohen, S. (2014). Do accelerators accelerate? A study of venture accelerators as a path to success?. In Academy of management proceedings (Vol. 2014, No. 1, p. 12955). Briarcliff Manor, NY: Academy of Management.

Hannah, D. P., & Eisenhardt, K. M. (2018). How firms navigate cooperation and competition in nascent ecosystems. *Strategic Management Journal, 39*(12), 3163–3192.

Hermans, F., Roep, D., & Klerkx, L. (2016). Scale dynamics of grassroots innovations through parallel pathways of transformative change. *Ecological Economics, 130,* 285–295.

Hwang, V. W., & Horowitt, G. (2012). The rainforest: The secret to building the next Silicon Valley.

Iansiti, M., & Levien, R. (2004). *The keystone advantage: What the new dynamics of business ecosystems mean for strategy, innovation, and sustainability.* Boston: Harvard Business Press.

Ingram, J. (2018). Agricultural transition: Niche and regime knowledge systems' boundary dynamics. *Environmental Innovation and Societal Transitions, 26,* 117–135.

Isenberg, D. J. (2010). How to start an entrepreneurial revolution. *Harvard Business Review, 88*(6), 40–50.

Jackson, D. J. (2011). *What is an innovation ecosystem* (p. 1). Arlington, VA: National Science Foundation.

Jacobides, M. G., Cennamo, C., & Gawer, A. (2018). Towards a theory of ecosystems. *Strategic Management Journal, 39*(8), 2255–2276.

Jacobides, M. G., Knudsen, T., & Augier, M. (2006). Benefiting from innovation: Value creation, value appropriation and the role of industry architectures. *Research Policy, 35*(8), 1200–1221.

Järvi, K., Almpanopoulou, A., & Ritala, P. (2018). Organization of knowledge ecosystems: Prefigurative and partial forms. *Research Policy, 47*(8), 1523–1537.

Junge, R., König, B., Villarroel, M., Komives, T., & Jijakli, M. (2017). Strategic points in aquaponics. *Water, 9,* 182.

Kapoor, R., & Furr, N. R. (2015). Complementarities and competition: Unpacking the drivers of entrants' technology choices in the solar photovoltaic industry. *Strategic Management Journal, 36*(3), 416–436.

Klingler-Vidra, R., Kenney, M., & Breznitz, D. (2016). Policies for financing entrepreneurship through venture capital: Learning from the successes of Israel and Taiwan. *International Journal of Innovation and Regional Development, 7*(3), 203–221.

Krueger, N. F., Jr., Reilly, M. D., & Carsrud, A. L. (2000). Competing models of entrepreneurial intentions. *Journal of Business Venturing, 15*(5–6), 411–432.

Kulchina, E. (2016). A path to value creation for foreign entrepreneurs. *Strategic Management Journal, 37*(7), 1240–1262.

Levie, J. (2014). The university is the classroom: Teaching and learning technology commercialization at a technological university. *The Journal of Technology Transfer, 39*(5), 793–808.

Lichtenstein, B. B., Carter, N. M., Dooley, K. J., & Gartner, W. B. (2007). Complexity dynamics of nascent entrepreneurship. *Journal of Business Venturing, 22*(2), 236–261.

References

Lioutasa, E. D., Charatsarib, C., De Rosac, M., & La Roccad, G. (2018). Knowledge and innovation in the agrifood supply chain: Old metaphors and new research directions. In *13th European International Farming Systems Association (IFSA) Symposium, Farming systems: facing uncertainties and enhancing opportunities, 1–5 July 2018, Chania, Crete, Greece* (pp. 1–13). Europe: International Farming Systems Association (IFSA).

Mack, E., & Mayer, H. (2016). The evolutionary dynamics of entrepreneurial ecosystems. *Urban Studies, 53*(10), 2118–2133.

Markard, J., Wirth, S., & Truffer, B. (2016). Institutional dynamics and technology legitimacy–a framework and a case study on biogas technology. *Research Policy, 45*(1), 330–344.

McKelvey, B. (2004). Toward a complexity science of entrepreneurship. *Journal of Business Venturing, 19*(3), 313–341.

Minniti, M., & Bygrave, W. (2001). A dynamic model of entrepreneurial learning. *Entrepreneurship Theory and Practice, 25*(3), 5–16.

Moore, J. F. (1993). Predators and prey: A new ecology of competition. *Harvard Business Review, 71*(3), 75–86.

Muller, A., Ferré, M., Engel, S., Gattinger, A., Holzkämper, A., Huber, R., . . . Six, J. (2017). Can soil-less crop production be a sustainable option for soil conservation and future agriculture? *Land Use Policy, 69*, 102–105.

Muñoz, F. F., & Encinar, M. I. (2014). Agents intentionality, capabilities and the performance of systems of innovation. *Innovations, 16*(1), 71–81.

O'Connor, A., Stam, E., Sussan, F., & Audretsch, D. B. (2018). Entrepreneurial ecosystems: The foundations of place-based renewal. In A. O'Connor, E. Stam, F. Sussan, & D. Audretsch (Eds.), *Entrepreneurial ecosystems. International studies in entrepreneurship* (Vol. 38). Cham: Springer.

Orsini, F., Kahane, R., Nono-Womdim, R., & Gianquinto, G. (2013). Urban agriculture in the developing world: A review. *Agronomy for Sustainable Development, 33*(4), 695–720.

Osterwalder, A. (2004). *The business model ontology a proposition in a design science approach* (Doctoral dissertation, Université de Lausanne, Faculté des hautes études commerciales).

Overholm, H. (2015). Collectively created opportunities in emerging ecosystems: The case of solar service ventures. *Technovation, 39*, 14–25.

Petkova, A. P. (2009). A theory of entrepreneurial learning from performance errors. *International Entrepreneurship and Management Journal, 5*(4), 345.

Pigford, A. A. E., Hickey, G. M., & Klerkx, L. (2018). Beyond agricultural innovation systems? Exploring an agricultural innovation ecosystems approach for niche design and development in sustainability transitions. *Agricultural Systems, 164*, 116–121.

Pitelis, C. (2012). Clusters, entrepreneurial ecosystem co-creation, and appropriability: A conceptual framework. *Industrial and Corporate Change, 21*(6), 1359–1388.

Rabelo, R. J., Bernus, P., & Romero, D. (2015). Innovation ecosystems: A collaborative networks perspective. In *Working conference on virtual enterprises* (pp. 323–336). Cham: Springer.

Radojevich-Kelley, N., & Hoffman, D. L. (2012). Analysis of accelerator companies: An exploratory case study of their programs, processes, and early results. *Small Business Institute Journal, 8*(2), 54–70.

Romano, A., Passiante, G., Del Vecchio, P., & Secundo, G. (2014). The innovation ecosystem as booster for the innovative entrepreneurship in the smart specialisation strategy. *International Journal of Knowledge-Based Development, 5*(3), 271–288.

Romero, D., Rabelo, R. J., & Molina, A. (2012). On the management of virtual enterprise's inheritance between virtual manufacturing & service enterprises: Supporting "dynamic" product-service business ecosystems. In *2012 18th international ICE conference on engineering, technology and innovation* (pp. 1–11). Munich: IEEE.

Roundy, P. T., Bradshaw, M., & Brockman, B. K. (2018). The emergence of entrepreneurial ecosystems: A complex adaptive systems approach. *Journal of Business Research, 86*, 1–10.

Scaringella, L., & Radziwon, A. (2018). Innovation, entrepreneurial, knowledge, and business ecosystems: Old wine in new bottles? *Technological Forecasting and Social Change, 136*, 59–87.

Schiuma, G., & Carlucci, D. (2018). Managing strategic partnerships with universities in innovation ecosystems: A research agenda. *Journal of Open Innovation: Technology, Market, and Complexity, 4*(3), 25.

Spigel, B. (2016). Developing and governing entrepreneurial ecosystems: The structure of entrepreneurial support programs in Edinburgh, Scotland. *International Journal of Innovation and Regional Development, 7*(2), 141–160.

Stam, E. (2015). Entrepreneurial ecosystems and regional policy: A sympathetic critique. *European Planning Studies, 23*(9), 1759–1769.

Still, K., Lähteenmäki, I., & Seppänen, M. (2019). Innovation relationships in the emergence of Fintech ecosystems. In *Proceedings of the 52nd Hawaii International Conference on System Sciences.*

Suddaby, R., Bitektine, A., & Haack, P. (2017). Legitimacy. *Academy of Management Annals, 11*(1), 451–478.

Tallman, S., Jenkins, M., Henry, N., & Pinch, S. (2004). Knowledge, clusters, and competitive advantage. *Academy of Management Review, 29*(2), 258–271.

Talmar, M., Walrave, B., Podoynitsyna, K. S., Holmström, J., & Romme, A. G. L. (2018). Mapping, analyzing and designing innovation ecosystems: The ecosystem pie model. *Long Range Planning.*

Teece, D. J. (2007). Explicating dynamic capabilities: The nature and microfoundations of (sustainable) enterprise performance. *Strategic Management Journal, 28*(13), 1319–1350.

Thomas, L. D., Sharapov, D., & Autio, E. (2018). Linking entrepreneurial and innovation ecosystems: The case of AppCampus. In *Entrepreneurial ecosystems and the diffusion of startups.* Cheltenham, UK: Edward Elgar Publishing.

Vargo, S. L., & Lusch, R. F. (2016). Institutions and axioms: An extension and update of service-dominant logic. *Journal of the Academy of Marketing Science, 44*(1), 5–23.

Vargo, S. L., Wieland, H., & Akaka, M. A. (2015). Innovation through institutionalization: A service ecosystems perspective. *Industrial Marketing Management, 44*, 63–72.

Von Hippel, E. (1986). Lead users: A source of novel product concepts. *Management Science, 32*(7), 791–805.

Winston Smith, S., Hannigan, T. J., & Gasiorowski, L. (2013). Accelerators and crowd-funding: Complementarity, competition, or convergence in the earliest stages of financing new ventures?. In *University of Colorado-Kauffman Foundation Crowd-Funding Conference, Boulder, CO.*

Wolfert, S., Ge, L., Verdouw, C., & Bogaardt, M. J. (2017). Big data in smart farming–a review. *Agricultural Systems, 153*, 69–80.

Chapter 4
Innovation for Future Proofing the Food Ecosystem: Emerging Approaches

Abstract The European food ecosystem is not well-prepared for the looming future global challenges. However through research and innovation, and the ensuing open innovation activities, food ecosystems may become the perfect arena for combining the knowledge specificities of its many actors, especially SMEs and startups in efforts to create effective and sustainable transformations in the food ecosystem. This chapter aims to present an up-to-date reflection on the dynamics and drivers of innovation in food ecosystems and their related challenges in ensuring human health and environmental sustainability. We discuss the concept of innovation specifically in food ecosystems and present a synthesis of the current limitations and opportunities to improve food ecosystem sustainability. We then discuss the implications that foster regional innovation cultures within food ecosystems and present the main areas in need for innovation in food ecosystems, as identified by diverse food ecosystem members. Furthermore, we introduce examples of noteworthy food startups that seek to drive sustainability either by changing consumer behavior, or providing more efficient farming techniques. Finally, we briefly discuss the future directions with food ecosystem research and innovation, and suggest the employment of both top-down and bottom-up approaches to identify areas in need of transformation in food ecosystems.

Keywords Food innovation · Research and innovation · Open research and innovation · Food startup · Multi-layered innovation

4.1 Introduction

The food ecosystem is one of the largest manufacturing sectors in the European Union, it alone employs 2.24 million people, consists of about 289,000 companies, and is characterized by €102 billion in exports and €71.9 billion in imports (Food Drink Europe, 2017).

Due to its importance in maintaining a standard quality of daily living, and the economic benefits (e.g., employment opportunities and investment) it provides to

© Springer Nature Switzerland AG 2020
P. De Bernardi, D. Azucar, *Innovation in Food Ecosystems*, Contributions to Management Science, https://doi.org/10.1007/978-3-030-33502-1_4

European governments, efforts to maintain our food ecosystem and prepare it for future challenges is a topic that cannot be ignored.

The European food ecosystem however is not well-prepared for the looming future global challenges; its methods of producing, processing, transporting, consuming, and discarding food is not sustainable, especially if it is expected to provide the projected growing populations with food nutrition and security (De Bernardi, Bertello, & Venuti, 2019; De Bernardi, Bertello, & Venuti, 2020; Gill et al., 2018). By 2050 food demand will increase by 60% and 'future proofing' (i.e. ensuring resilience and sustainability) our food ecosystem proves to be a massive challenge.

Engaging in efforts toward sustainability will require collective action (De Bernardi, Bertello, Venuti, & Zardini, 2019), and improved research and innovation is considered an excellent place to start. This idea has been quickly adopted by European policy makers, and is evidenced by the creation of 'Food 2030', which is the European Commission's research and innovation policy blueprint for transforming food ecosystems and places nutrition, circularity, climate resilience, and innovation at the core of these possible transformations (European Commission, 2018). Food 2030 aims to support scientific and technological breakthroughs to (i) reduce the rate of non-communicable diseases associated with overwhelming food consumption; (ii) foster smart and resilient food ecosystems that yield 50% less carbon emissions, and (iii) build public trust and involvement between consumers and large food industries. Future proofing our food ecosystem also constitutes ensuring economic growth and job creation, engaging in new partnerships, empowering communities through practical education, and achieving healthy and sustainable food access for all populations. In essence, efforts should be directed to create a food ecosystem where people can monitor their food intake and access foods according to their specific health and cultural needs, where farmers can run their farms and cultivate necessary amounts of food without the use of harmful chemical pesticides, where restaurants and food retailers can operate as usual while reducing or eliminating their food waste output, and where no individual suffers from malnutrition and its related effects (European Commission, 2018).

The current food ecosystem scenario (see Chap. 1) thus calls for an increased focus on sustainability, and the creation of a food ecosystem that meets the needs of current world populations while at the same time preparing for the needs of future generations. Some authors argue that developing this sustainable food ecosystem demands a multi-level approach that considers (i) the international, national, regional and local legislature, (ii) the food production industry, (iii) public health and preventive medicine, and (iv) communities, companies, schools and every days citizens (Anderson et al., 2019).

Food nutrition and security, the cultivation of quality products, and access to diets that provide optimal nutrition are all some of the key challenges for the future of our food ecosystem. While our current methods of food production do meet the need of providing access to healthy and nutritious food for much of the world's population, it still does not grant every individual equal access to food in terms of both quantity and quality. Even though the dynamics and structures of the global food ecosystem are complex, gaining a better understanding of how the variety of challenges affecting our food ecosystem interact is fundamental for future sustainability efforts and the resulting innovations and entrepreneurial initiatives that will drive its transformation. Research and innovation, due to their ability to reorganize and reallocate resources in novel ways so that they can be used more efficiently, are considered as the ideal vehicles to transform our food ecosystem.

4.2 Innovation in Food Ecosystems

Innovation is often the result of the entrepreneur's activities. Innovation can be defined as the process of creating a new product, service, market, process, or organization. Innovation can exist in degrees running from "new to the world" (most innovative) to "new only to the individual" (least innovative). Accordingly, based on proposed conceptualizations by previous authors we posit that entrepreneurship and innovation in the food ecosystem can be thought of as the place in supply chains where individuals create, discover, and exploit market opportunities through the creation and dissemination of new ventures related to food processes (Aldrich & Cliff, 2003; Gries & Naudé, 2010).

Current discussions regarding innovation in food ecosystems usually contest the overwhelming 'top-down' models of innovation, which are thought to be a significant limit for food ecosystem progress (Touzard, Temple, Goulet, Chiffoleau, & Faure, 2018). Evidence suggests that instead of focusing on the 'leaders', we must actively seek to involve the heterogeneous actors that make up the entirety of the food ecosystem in the development and creation of innovations, in order to create a food ecosystem that is more representative of the globalized populations, and based on collective decision making (Von Hippel, 2005). Furthermore, certain research streams posit that 'agricultural entrepreneurs' have weaker entrepreneurial capabilities than in other sectors (Pindado & Sánchez, 2017), but nonetheless share a number of characteristics with entrepreneurs in different fields, e.g., a personalized motivation to commercialize products or services, thus evidencing the need to integrate their efforts for more impactful results.

Innovation is often driven not by individual factors but systemic ones such as policy changes (e.g., the ban of certain materials or processes), private industry forces (e.g., increased investment in researching alternative protein products), public health objectives (e.g., bringing to light current trends in community health such as obesity), and individual or community level approaches that can later serve as conduits for further collaboration between private and public sectors. Furthermore, the Food and Agriculture Organization (FAO) define 'food ecosystem innovation' as *"the process whereby individuals or organizations bring new or existing products, processes or ways of organization into use for the first time in a specific context in order to increase effectiveness, competitiveness, resilience to shocks or environmental sustainability and thereby contribute to food security and nutrition, economic development or sustainable natural resource management"* (FAO, 2018 pg. 3). Innovations are not restricted to those who employ disruptive technologies, but also include social, organizational, institutional, or marketing processes to rearrange resources and provide increased value for food ecosystems. Importantly, one type of innovation that is central to food ecosystem transformation is the notion of social innovation, which is usually delivered within the context of the non-profit sector by social entrepreneurs, brings economic and social impact, and specifically, develops sustainability models and new business models that cater to underprivileged communities (Tataj, 2015).

Innovation is a system where institutions interact with their surrounding environment. However, the diverse nature of members that participate in these processes as a whole may also be a limiting factor to effective information spillovers and knowledge sharing between them. This can be attributed to fears of disclosing protected information (e.g., intellectual property), lack of a clear understanding of discipline specific goals (perhaps through the use of complicated nomenclature), and conflicting interests in goals and objectives. Therefore creating and implementing a culture of trust and open communication in food ecosystems may be more conducive to open innovation and more effective than top-down strategies (Tataj, 2015).

Food ecosystem transformations should also be founded on a combination of global and local knowledge, and the distribution of challenges and good practices. The FAO (2018) recommends that in order to set up local systems for knowledge creation and dissemination, clear and sustainable pathways for knowledge sharing between core food ecosystem members and local and regional 'knowledge providers' (e.g., extension services, research institutes, laboratories, and knowledge networks) must be created and promoted.

4.3   Open Innovation in Food Ecosystems

A food ecosystem can be described as an adaptive system that exhibits complex dynamics (Ingram, 2011; Zhang et al., 2018), has a multi-actor, multi-function, and multi-factor nature that shapes the way it evolves through its emerging complex relationships.

Therefore, in order to transform a system as complex as the food ecosystem, we must attempt to improve our understanding of the technological, political, economic, and social dynamics that give it shape, and also successfully identify the leverage points where entrepreneurship and innovations will be most effective (Gill et al., 2018). Furthermore, various sources posit that the successful identification of these leverage points will require a systems approach, one that illustrates the moving and evolving roles of multiple actors, at various levels, along with different policy fields (European Commisson, 2018). The notion of a holistic view of food systems signifies taking into account both the horizontal (i.e., fields of action such as the environment, health, infrastructure, and education) and vertical (i.e., the range of stages of the food value chain) dimensions (Moragues et al., 2013). It is through the employment of a systems approach that researchers and food ecosystem stakeholders can appreciate the interrelated impacts (e.g., benefits and side effects) of research and innovation initiatives, whether technological in nature or not, on other parts of the food system and be able to introduce newer innovations that better reinforce benefits across multiple segments of the food system.

These innovations and entrepreneurial endeavors should further capitalize on the fundamental need to redesign production in food ecosystems, and seek to create products and services that can potentially yield co-benefits across the food system; e.g., for the environment and for health, simultaneously (Parsons & Hawkes, 2018). Innovation and entrepreneurship are two distinct but intertwined components of economic growth in the knowledge economy (Tataj, 2015). Specifically, innovation is a social process of knowledge production and dissemination, during which human creativity leads to translation of knowledge into shared and enriched capacities (Tataj, 2015).

Food institutions and firms traditionally innovate by looking internally for new ideas, technologies, products, and services that may grant them a sustainable advantage. But by looking only inward, and ignoring the range of potential in the immediate outside environment, firms miss out on ideas, knowledge, and technology that resides outside of their institutional barriers. However, some firms are aware of these boundaries and have shifted from a closed innovation strategy to an open innovation strategy, a term originally introduced by Chesbrough (2003). The basic idea behind open innovation is that institutions should combine internal and external ideas and technologies when innovating. Specifically, as defined by Chesbrough, "Open Innovation is the use of purposive inflows and outflows of knowledge to accelerate internal innovation, and expand the markets for external use of innovation, respectively" (Chesbrough, Vanhaverbeke, & West, 2006). It can be described as a broad concept that is usually distinguished by inbound and outbound open innovation activities.

Ramirez-Portilla, Cagno, and Zanatta-Alarcon (2016) investigated how the adoption of open innovation influences activities driven by food ecosystem stakeholders in order to complement a larger image of open innovation, and found that large institutions in food ecosystems are not the only actors that propose and drive lasting initiatives through open innovation. SMEs, non-profit foundations, collective community actions, startups, and individual consumers are also cited to catalyze significant transformations (Ramirez-Portilla et al., 2016). Furthermore, scholars posit that collaborations under the umbrella of open innovation seem to be based on a foundation of trust (Ramirez-Portilla et al., 2016). Based on their results, the authors coin the term *'open food'* as a label for food innovation that adopts an open innovation approach. The authors define open food as a collective of initiatives and practices empowered by small organizations, users, communities, and citizens sharing a common objective of creating, adapting, capturing, adopting, and disseminating food related value, knowledge, and innovations that may be leveraged by for-profit actors (Ramirez-Portilla et al., 2016). Even though it is considered as a low-tech and a 'traditions bounded' industry, food production and food ecosystems, especially, have the power to innovate with its variety of internal and external stakeholders (Sarkar & Costa, 2008). In fact, this inclusion of diverse stakeholders has greatly increased in the last years due to the heterogeneous needs of consumers, which have driven food firms to open up their innovation processes (Bigliardi & Galati, 2013) from traditional innovation partnerships in the food industry

(Lazzarotti & Manzini, 2013) to more advanced innovation ecosystems (Bresciani, 2017; Saguy & Sirotinskaya, 2014; Santoro, Vrontis, & Pastore, 2017).

In essence, through research, innovation, and entrepreneurship and the ensuing open innovation activities, food ecosystems become the perfect arena for combining the knowledge specificities of its many actors, especially SMEs and startups in efforts to create effective and sustainable transformations in the food ecosystem. In order to achieve the best possible mix of innovation and inclusion Saguy and Sirotinskaya (2014) offer certain recommendations, including practicing collaboration and involvement of SMEs, new intellectual property models for complex collaborations, and the creation of new innovation ecosystems within food that can easily adapt to external demands.

To shed light on these initiatives, Gillebo and Hugo (2006) explored key the characteristics and dynamics of ongoing regional innovation cultures within the food sector, and found that a common denominator of the cases they analyzed is a strong community of innovative practitioners that shape their activities around intentional interactions, dialogue, and inquiry that revolves around long-term commitments. They discuss four strategies to develop regional innovation cultures within food ecosystems:

1. Build strategies for the activity of pioneering local and regional cultures of practice.
2. Analyze their entrepreneurial uniqueness and social ecology.
3. Facilitate a broader co-involvement of institutional, market, and cultural entrepreneurship.
4. Develop competency and cultures of inquiry linked to interdependent entrepreneurship.

Furthermore, in a survey conducted by the research team at Food 2030 on 100 respondents from the areas of education and research, business, government, non-governmental organizations, and civil society answered questions related to the future of research and innovation breakthroughs, identifying the main areas of interest for innovative action (Fernandez & Lazaro-Mojica, 2018).

4.4 Emerging Food Approaches

The current food system strongly needs transformative changes to address the twenty-first century grand food challenges, among others: (i) population growth and climate change; (ii) the degradation of public health due to unhealthy diets; (iii) the pollution of our environment due to intensive food production and (iv) the over-population of rural areas among other due to poor economic viability.

Innovative approaches are emerging to stimulate and to contribute to future-proofing the food system, overcoming the grand challenges. These included new breeding techniques for animals and plants either by generating new varieties of plants, by crosslinking species, or by introducing new growth methodologies. Smart farming techniques, which include developments in the increase of productivity and efficiency, using precise farming for planting seeds, watering, fertilizing, and harvesting to get the best possible use of land are some of the most promising transitions. Other promising products include the use of new agriculture techniques such as hydroponics as a system of plant growth and development in controlled environments, higher intelligence on crop rotation to enrich soil nutrients, and the use of agro-ecology principles for improving local farming, and a reduction of synthetic pesticides and fertilizers. These innovations have been identified as the main drivers of changes in dietary habits including plant-based alternatives for meat products, and a decrease in the overall consumption of nutritional "unhealthy" ingredients such as sugar and salts. More recent approaches to tranform food approaches include adopting a circular economy, which includes reuse of fresh water supplies, as is the case with vertical gardens, repurposing of food waste in order to create fertilizers or feed for animals, and even the use of edible insects based on the consumption of non-used byproducts from the food industry. These examples however are not exhaustive and present only a summary of findings from Food 2030's survey results (Fernandez & Lazaro-Mojica, 2018). For a more detailed summary of possible research and innovation breakthroughs as identified by Food 2030 see Table 4.1.

Finally, research has shown that citizens and end-users are perhaps some of the most influential players in ensuring the success of emerging innovations. They are the food ecosystem members who either adopt innovations or reject them by adapting to current trends. In relation to this, Ramirez-Portilla et al. (2016) provide different notions that can be considered a baseline for trends, and a breakdown of areas of need in current food innovation projects in food ecosystems. Their categorization is as follows:

- Fresh, local, and convenient:

  - New ingredients
  - Emerging regulations
  - Foods on the go
  - Proximity to customers

- Automated solutions:

  - Food bots
  - Advanced processing
  - Waste and resource minimization

- Safety and Quality:

  - Food authenticity and traceability
  - Quality management across the supply chain
  - Sanitation

- Supply Chains:

  - Short product life cycles
  - Intelligent packaging
  - Sustainable sourcing

Table 4.1 Inventory of possible R&I breakthroughs

Domain	R&I breakthrough	Specific R&I breakthrough topics	Impact	Food 2030
The new approach of primary food production and distribution	Breeding new techniques and applications	– New varieties of animals and plants – New genetic methodologies and new applications	Plants: Increase of drought resistance, "less water" resistance, more resilient varieties, pest resistant or less fertilizers' dependency	Climate, nutrition
	Smart farming	– Precision farming: Use of local data (e.g., apps, terrain data, irrigation data, foliar growth) – Use of global data (e.g., web platforms, forecasts) – Applied mechatronics – Artificial intelligence applied	Higher quality, ensured food safety, better traceability, improved productivity, higher efficiency, less fraud, lower costs and more benefits to a new era of higher sustainability of the agricultural ecosystem	Climate, circularity
	Non-conventional production systems	– Hydroponics – Vertical agriculture – Intelligent – Cropping – Agro-ecology – Permaculture – Organic awareness – Urban farming – Biodiversity	Higher quality of crops, better use of resources and land, less "intensive" agriculture, use of waste streams, higher sustainability of the agricultural ecosystem	Climate, nutrition, circularity
	Reduction of impact of production enhances	– New approaches to fertilizers – New approaches to pesticides – New approaches to animal antibiotics	Better footprint of production, better use of natural resources, less environmental impact	Innovation, climate
	New value systems	– Business model for the primary sector – Short value chain – New models on developing countries (microcredits, crowd funding) – Social innovation relating to food production and distribution, food coops, social markets etc.	New policies and management of the agricultural system towards a new food revolution on the supply chain and use of resources for a more sustainable trade from the first producer to the final consumer. Thus taking into account the margins gained on the process by middle-men and a more balanced equity on the costs of production	Climate, circularity, innovation

	New aquaculture	– Advanced fish farms – New feeds – New on sea production with lower impact on nature	There is potential for a better exploitation of our seafood resources, from the feeding system to food safety and authenticity	Climate, circularity
An engaged and healthy consumer	Empowered consumer	– Innovation in social sciences – Living labs – Optimized use of big databases – Informed consumer – Active and engaged consumer – Co-creation – Due diligence – Value based food system – Domotics (technologies at home for preparation, storing, menu selection, etc.)	Consumers from the point of view of society can be part of the research and innovation inputs into the food system. There is a space for innovative ways to empower consumers in a supply driven food chain	Innovation, nutrition
	Change of dietary habits	– Awareness of healthy habits – Reduction of targeted ingredients (salt, sugar, trans saturated fats) – Reduction of targeted additives (clean label)	A healthier population with all the consequences this enables: Less communicable diseases, healthier growth and ageing of individuals, a sustainable lifestyle...	Nutrition
	New tools to improve nutrition and health	– Personalized nutrition – Multi-Omics – Nutraceuticals – Functional foods – Human genome knowledge and application	Further knowledge on human health and the tools available to measure and to influence an adequate nutrition and healthy habits	Nutrition
	New methods in education	– New models for education (e.g. learner cantered/personalized education, new approach to MOOCs—Massive online open courses, do it yourself education, problem solving learning—Participatory research) – Awareness of food-system – Innovation and entrepreneurial behavior (e.g. innovation through Hackathons, MakerSpaces, FabLabs, science shops) – Guidance to start ups and SMEs, new models of collaboration and impact – Open research and open innovation concepts	Society and new generations need to think differently to achieve new solutions to the actual and future incoming challenges	Innovation

(continued)

Table 4.1 (continued)

Domain	R&I breakthrough	Specific R&I breakthrough topics	Impact	Food 2030
The tools of a future proof food system	Logistics—New systems	– Physical internet – Service "at the door at any time"	A new way of transferring materials from one place to another globally would change the way we understand trade and acquisition of goods in a rapid market	Innovation, circularity
	Smart traceability in the food supply chain	– Transparency and trust through the value chain	Blockchain could allow a quick tracing of food products to their source for enhanced food authenticity, therefore increasing transparency and trust in the food value chain	Circularity
	A novel approach to biotechnology	– New biotechnological tools – New applications	The further exploitation of microbiota/microbiome knowledge can impact the way that foods are produced and the nutrients that they provide. The development of biotechnological tools on the knowledge of genome and its sequencing, opens the possibility of new applications and implementations. Some examples were the conversion of biomass and residues into a new range of new sub-products and ingredients, the use of actual biorefineries to separate protein and energy into protein usable for humans, or the use of microalgae to produce nutraceutic components without impacting food agriculture	Innovation, nutrition, circularity
	Information and communication technologies (ICT) applied to food system	– Full exploitation of big data – Internet of things – New sensors applied to multiple applications – Digitalization of industry – Robotics – Augmented reality – Artificial intelligence	Transversal to many sectors in the food system, from the efficiency of industrial processes to new business models on the interaction with consumers	Innovation

	Food industry 4.0—Novel and efficient food processing	– Mild processing – Low input technologies – New robotic applications – Nanotechnology – Integrated input-output responses – 3D printing – Preservation (IR, UV, radiowaves, pulsed electric fields, high pressure treatment, osmosis, cold plasma) – Filling (aseptic filling, clean room tech, super cooling)	More efficient processes in productivity and energy consumption, more environmentally sustainable processes, less production of waste, products of higher nutritional quality	Innovation, circularity, nutrition
	Sustainable packaging	– New materials – Biodegradable materials – New recycling methods – Reduction of package – New models in the food system	Higher sustainability of the food system, less environmental impact, better use of resources and waste streams	Circularity, climate
	Diversity on the diet	– New sources not fully exploited – New protein sources – Full exploitation of algae – Full exploitation of insects – Cultured meat	Exploring new ingredients allows a higher diversity on use of resources, technological applications and health impact on consumers. Always from a sustainable perspective and environmental impact perspective	Climate, circularity, nutrition
	The global food analysis	– Higher efficiency, better detection, global standardization, world food regulatory standards	Food analysis is basic for the correct use and interpretation of data. The importance of the information output requires evolvement for higher capacity and impact	Innovation
A sustainable and dynamic value based food system	Circularity in food systems	– Reduction of waste (zero waste) – New uses of waste – New recycling business models – New structure in food system	Transversal to all value chain, the use of waste streams has a greater impact on efficiency and sustainability of the food system	Circularity
	Efficient use of resources	– Efficient use of water – Efficient use of land – Efficient use of nutrients – Efficient use of energy	Optimization of our processes from agricultural input up to consumer behavior is relevant for the overall sustainability of the food system	Circularity

(continued)

Table 4.1 (continued)

Domain	R&I breakthrough	Specific R&I breakthrough topics	Impact	Food 2030
	Food for society	– Community driven social innovations (City labs, community based participatory research, citizen science, urban cropping, urban beekeeping, rent a tree) – Innovative public procurement (meals in nurseries, schools, residences, senior people's homes) – Social entrepreneurship – Awareness of waste in social context (homes, schools, restaurants, take waste food at home) – Trade norms (dismissed fruits by shape or form) – Do it yourself – Collaborative production – The European cultural food heritage (maintaining the local characteristics considering new options of geographic diversity)	How the society interacts with the food system and how there is an overall awareness on the impact of the power of small individual actions and public policies is relevant for a social innovation breakthrough	Innovation, circularity
	Policy and management within the food system	– Applying responsible research and innovation – Improving the R&I network – Public-private transfer – Impact of research and innovation – Higher implementation of knowledge – Regional aspects of food system – Food marketing and labeling (new approaches)	Optimization of our processes for knowledge transfer, for implementation of knowledge, for a full public-private collaboration, for better measurements of impact	Innovation

Source: Fit4Food2030 Towards Food 2030—Future proofing the European Food systems through Research&Innovation—Deliverable 4.1 (Fernandez & Lazaro-Mojica, 2018) (Adapted)

Based on these conceptualizations that describe the major topic areas of interest for interventions and their sub-categories that describe innovations in food ecosystems, respectively, we present the following discussion of real examples of the most trending and current food production innovations.

4.5 Vertical Farms

Gilbert Ellis Bailey was the first to define "vertical farming" in 1915 through his book titled "Vertical Farming". His main argument was that hydroponic farming[1] in a controlled and vertical environment would provide certain economic and environmental benefits (Bailey, 1915). Furthermore, urban planners and food ecosystem stakeholders propose that cities will be required to provide food 'in house' in order to be able to adapt to the increasing urban population and its ensuing demands, and avoid threatening food security and nutrition (Al-Kodmany, 2018a). Urban agriculture has been put forth as a solution to these challenges as it consolidates food production and consumption in a single location; in the case of urban areas where fertile land is scarce and expensive, vertical farms seem like the hero we need.

With the expected increased in global population and its effect on urban cities, a key emerging challenge is the question of how food will be transported into cities in sufficient quantities to effectively nurture and maintain the health of dense populations; it is here where the vertical farming models can provide an innovative solution (Al-Kodmany, 2015; Al-Kodmany, 2018b; Corvalan, Hales, McMichael, Butler, & McMichael, 2005).

Moreover, a few diverse yet specific cultivation techniques and technologies that complement vertical farms' success in ensuring food security in cities exist. The first type regards the construction of tall vertical structures with several levels of seed beds lined with artificial lights. Many cities across the world have embraced this model, and in some instances re-structure industrial buildings to make them appropriate for food production activities (Despommier, 2013). Another type of vertical farming uses rooftops of both residential and commercial buildings, and other city structures, e.g., restaurants (Birkby, 2016; Thomaier et al., 2015).

Furthermore, vertical farms manifest in a couple of different ways, from simple two-level or wall-mounted systems to occupying large warehouse spaces reaching several stories high. However, one common denominator of all vertical farms is the use of one of three soil-free systems for providing nutrients to plants, i.e. aeroponics, aquaponics, and hydroponics. These high-technology processes reflect an important

---

[1]Hydroponic farming is a method of growing plants without soil by instead using mineral nutrient solutions in a water solvent.

shift in farming and food production processes, that offer timely and effective methods for urban farming, while minimizing maintenance, and maximizing yield (Al-Kodmany, 2018a).

4.5.1 Aeroponics

This indoor growing technique was developed by the National Aeronautical and Space Administration (NASA) out of an interest to find efficient methods to grow plants in outer space. Aeroponics can be defined as growing plants in an air or mist environment with no soil and very little water (Al-Kodmany, 2018a; Birkby, 2016). This technique is still rare in the vertical farming world, but has recently been generating interest. An aeroponic system is the most efficient of the three techniques for vertical farming, since it uses around 90% less water than even the most efficient hydroponic system (Birkby, 2016). Plants grown in aeroponic systems also have been evidenced to contain more vitamins and minerals, which make them healthier and with an added nutritional value.

An aeroponic system is an enclosed air and water, nutrient rich, ecosystem that fosters rapid plant growth with little water and direct sun, and does not require soil (Al-Kodmany, 2018a). This technique uses mist or nutrient solutions instead of water, so it does not require containers or trays to hold water.

4.5.2 Aquaponics

Aquaponic techniques can be seen as an upgrade on the hydroponic system (discussed next), and is a bio-system that combines recycled aquaculture (e.g., fish farming) with hydroponic plant production to create mutually beneficial interactions between the plants and the fish (Birkby, 2016). It achieves this mutuality due to the nutrient-rich waste from fish tanks that is used to simultaneously fertilize and irrigate (i.e., fertigate) hydroponic seedbeds. The hydroponic seedbeds also serve as bio-filters that remove unwanted chemicals and gases from the water. Fish are usually grown indoors, and produce nutrient-rich waste that is re-used as a feed source for the plants in the system. The plants therefore act as filters for the wastewater, which is then recycled back into the fishponds. Some researchers even suggest that aquaponic techniques might in themselves serve as a model for sustainable food production by achieving a true model of the 3 R's, i.e. **reduce**, **reuse**, and **recycle** (Al-Kodmany, 2018b; Graber & Junge, 2009) and cite the following added benefits.

- Automatically cleans water for fish ecosystems.
- Provides plants with organic fertilizers that foster their healthy growth.

- Provides efficiency and circularity since the waste products of one biological ecosystem serve as nutrients to the other.
- Recycles water since it is automatically re-used through biological filtration and recirculation. A function that is crucial in drought-prone regions.
- Reduces and removes the need for chemical and artificial fertilizers.
- Results in a polyculture that increases biodiversity.
- May be an attractive business that generates two products, vegetables and fish, from one ecosystem.

Finally, aquaponics is sometimes preferred over hydroponics (Al-Kodmany, 2018b). Nonetheless, it remains at experimental and pilot stages with limited commercial success. This might be due to the fact that the technologies required to build an aquaponic ecosystem are quite complex since they require the mutual interdependence of two different agricultural ecosystems.

4.5.3 Hydroponics

The dominant technique employed in vertical farms, hydroponic systems grow plants in nutrient solutions that are free of soil. The plant's roots are sub-merged in the solution, which is then monitored and circulated so make sure that the nutrient solution ph is maintained (Birkby, 2016). This technique can be further defined as *'the cultivation of plants in nutrient-enriched water, with or without the mechanical support of an inert medium such as sand or gravel'* (Al-Kodmany, 2018a, p. 7). And while the use of water as a method to grow crops is not exactly novel, its commercial introduction is a recent phenomenon.

One of the main innovative elements of this technique is its potential to eliminate, or reduce, soil related cultivation problems such as pesticides, fungus, and bacteria that are found in the soil (García-Caro Briceño, 2018). Further, because this system is closed, the nutrient solution is fully recycled, meaning significant water conservation. Due to this, this method could be especially appropriate for water-scarce regions. Furthermore, this method is free of animal manure, fertilizers, and pesticides (Birkby, 2016; García-Caro Briceño, 2018). For a description of the top 3 techniques for high-tech indoor farming please see Table 4.2.

These techniques, made possible by certain technologies, have raised vertical farms to be considered a revolutionary approach to producing high quality and fresh produce all year round, with minimal reliance on physical labor, adequate weather conditions, fertile land, and high amounts of water use (Baudoin et al., 2013). Vertical farming is a forward thinking approach that aims to ensure food sustainability in cities by directly tackling the issue of food security in urban areas. As a significant tool in the quest for sustainability, vertical farms are able to grow food efficiently and sustainably.

One example of a current startup seeking to implement hydroponic technology is 'Phytophonics', which was founded to bring advanced crop production technology

Table 4.2 High tech indoor farming

Farming method	Key characteristics	Major benefits	Common/applicable technologies
Hydroponics	Soil-less, uses water as the growing medium	Rapid plant growth; reduces and even eliminates soil-related cultivation problems; decreases the use of fertilizers and pesticides	Computerized and monitoring systems; cell phones, laptops, and tablets; food growing apps; remote control systems and software; automated racking, stacking systems, moving belts, and tall towers; programmable LED lighting systems; renewable energy applications (e.g., solar panels); closed-loop systems, anaerobic digesters; programmable nutrient systems; climate control, HVAC systems; water recirculating and recycling systems; rainwater collectors; insect-killing systems; robots.
Aeroponics	A variant of hydroponics; it involves spraying the roots of plants with mist or nutrient solutions	Includes those for hydroponics, and the additional benefit of using less water	
Aquaponics	It integrates aquaculture (fish farming) with hydroponics	Creates synergies between plants and fish; it uses the nutrient-rich waste from fish tanks to 'fergitate' hydroponic seedbeds; the seedbeds filter the water for the fish	

Source: Al-Kodmany (2018a)

to the food ecosystem by introducing new technology that is highly productive, efficient, and resilient to climate change. The startup was founded in 2016 and has turned their original vision for the future of agriculture into a reality. They have currently developed, tested, and trialed a deep-water culture growing system for tomatoes. In 2008, the company raised enough funding worth of investment to test their hydroponic system as an 'all in one' greenhouse. The company grows plants from transplant into crop, and works with growing tomatoes, pepper, medical cannabis, cucumbers, and strawberries among others. Furthermore, their state of the art technology offers a high return on investment, rapid deployability, and automated nutrient system (Phytoponics, 2018).

4.6   Short Food Supply Chains

Recently, short food supply chains (SFSCs), the creation of local and regional food ecosystems, and efforts to reconnect consumers with food producers have gained international attention from both researchers and policy makers (Kneafsey et al., 2008; Marsden, Banks, & Bristow, 2000). The European Union's rural development regulation (1305/2013), for instance, outlines a number of measures to promote SFSCs with the main aim of enhancing farmer's incomes and thereby helping to support rural economies (European Commission, 2013; Schmutz, Kneafsey, Kay, Doernberg, & Zasada, 2018). SFSCs as legally defined by Reg. (1302/2013) are expected to be able to reach the goals and objectives of 'sustainable agriculture' through the reduction of transportation costs and the resulting reduction in CO2 emissions, and promotion of biodiversity, e.g., products are recognized as 'local' by consumers. (Canfora, 2016). Considering their role in reaching certain levels of environmental protection, it is not surprising that interest in SFSCs is growing in the European Union and other national member-state legislations.

However, current reservations about the economic relevance of SFSCs are ever present. This relates to the consideration of costs associated with small-scale productions when compared to the traditional quantitative mass production and large food producers, especially when taking into account the relative advantages of economies of scale, as well as the costs associated with producing products in specific geographic regions that are inadequate for growing certain products.

For instance, large food retailers have been slow to adopt direct-to-consumer distribution, something that is slowly beginning to change (CB Insights, 2018). Large food retailers such as Coca-Cola and General Mills do not operate their own point of sale, and have traditionally relied on large retailers to sell their products. With the emergence of e-commerce, many of these large industries turn to online retailers such as Amazon to get their products to customers.

However these retailers and distributors often invest in smaller and private labels, thus becoming competitors, and not collaborators with food giants. This is made more evident since many of the companies retailers invest in are usually SMEs and startups, which offer direct-to-customer purchasing options almost by default. Moving to direct-to-consumer business models, large food companies would grant themselves more control over their image with customers, and the representation of their products. They might also further their personal relationship with customers thus achieving higher 'buy in' for future innovations and products (CB Insights, 2018).

Furthermore, some authors argue that a narrow view of supply chains focused on economic advantage must be assessed against the evaluation of both social and environmental benefits that might come from reducing the physical distance from farm to fork, maintaining farm activities in local areas, and connecting to consumers (Canfora, 2016). For example, by simply evidencing the potentially significant reduction in CO2 emissions, we can see that SFSCs have a positive effect on public goods, with clear environmental benefits when compared to the traditional, economically comfortable, long supply chains.

Furthermore, in a study conducted by Schmutz et al. (2018), the researchers employed a participatory Sustainability Impact Assessment (SIA) in which local food ecosystem stakeholders were asked to rank the perceived impacts of five diverse urban SFSCs over the traditional food supply system, e.g., mass production, supermarkets as large retailers, and standardized food products. From their analysis, they identified that stakeholders perceive SFSCs as generally out-performing more mainstream, traditional, global food supply chains (Schmutz et al., 2018).

This might be due to the many benefits that that SFSCs provide to the many challenges affecting our food ecosystem. Through SFSCs, consumers will have access to food and produce that is fresh and of a higher quality and nutritional value. With SFSCs food ecosystem stakeholders and consumers can support jobs in their local region, their local environmental resilience, and food ecosystem member cohesion for increased impact when pursuing common goals. For producers, SFSCs enable a more equal remuneration through increased and personalized price control (Staes & Heubuch, 2019). One example of a successful SFSC network, is the Gasap-network in Brussels, where about 4000 community members have established direct and long-term relationships with around 30 small-scale farmers, thus yielding a stable and equal economical basis for sustainable food production (Christophe, 2013).

Due to many environmental and social benefits generated by SFSCs, it is no wonder that a growing number of startups and new ventures seek to reduce the distance in supply chains between farmers, retailers, and consumers. These efforts include traceability technologies, robotics, environmental sensing and tracking technologies, and logistics.

One major example of a successful startup that promotes SFSCs is "NinjaCart", originally a hyper-local grocery delivery platform in 2015; it is now India's largest B2B[2] fresh produce supply chain company. With their technologies and user centric solutions they have disrupted the way produce is delivered to people's plates, thereby improving the lives of producers, businesses, and consumers in a meaningful way (NinjaCart, 2019). NinjaCart's short-term target is to build a food distribution network of a million retailers, restaurants, and food service providers in the next 3 years, while their long-term target is to ensure that safe and healthy food is affordable and accessible for millions of people in India.

Their 'Eureka!" moment occurred when they identified a large consumer demand for an online fruits-and-vegetables-only marketplace, however the supply side from farmers and retailers was too fragmented to accommodate the demand, this proved problematic for both customers and farmers. For small retailers, problems regarding complex procurement processes and proper management of quality, hygiene, price, logistics and customer understanding were a main challenge. For farmers, unfair prices, high food wastes due to a mismatch in supply and demand and lower incomes were the biggest barrier. Therefore, NinaJaCart created their agri-tech platform in efforts to build reliable, cost-effective, and high-speed infrastructure, thus enabling retailers and merchants to source fresh produce directly from farmers.

Their premise is to solve the inefficiencies in the food supply chain through their state-of-the-art supply chain innovation, while adding value to stakeholders and changing the way fresh food reaches consumer plates in regards to quality, affordability, and accessibility.

Through their business model, NinjaCart is perfectly positioned to assist farmers get better prices and handle the consistent consumer demand, and to help retailers source fresh vegetables at competitive prices directly from farmers. They are able to do this successfully at a lower cost, faster speeds, and larger scales using an

---

[2]**Business-to-business (B2B** or, in some countries, **BtoB**) is a situation where one business makes a commercial transaction with another.

integrated supply chain that is powered by technology, data science, and a logistics network.

Since its inception, NinjaCart has disrupted the way fruits and vegetables move from farms to consumers. In essence, they source fruits and vegetables from farmers from over 20 different Indian states, and deliver these to over 17,000 local small retailers and restaurants across 7 major cities, everyday in less than 12 h. Their focus is to make the Ninjacart innovation more accessible and leverage their strengths to innovate for new product categories and customer segments while solving complex supply chain problems. Importantly their technology enabled supply chain, with an always-connected logistics network helps them lower costs, and increase speeds of food delivery thus reduce waste. For example, its model of delivering food in less than 12 h comes at half the cost of those from traditional market, with less than 1% food waste. Traditional supply chains take more than 12 h to deliver products to retailers, on average, and food waste with this method is more than 30% (LinkedIn, 2019).

4.7 Precision Agriculture

Like many other facets of daily life, agriculture and food ecosystems have also gone through a technological evolution. Technology has become an indispensible part of doing business for every farmer, and food producer. This is evident in recent technique adopted by farmers to improve their production outputs. Precision agriculture (PA), or precision farming, for example, comprises a set of technologies that combines sensors, information systems, enhanced machinery, and informed management to optimize production by accounting for variability and uncertainties within food ecosystems (Gebbers & Adamchuk, 2010). Precision agriculture (PA), satellite farming, or site-specific crop management (SSCM) is a crop management concept that is based on observing, measuring, and responding to inter and intra-field variability in crops, this technique has been increasing in recent years and reports suggest that precision agriculture is projected to grow into a $43.4 billion industry by 2025 (Business Wire, 2017).

Initially used as a tool to adapt fertilizer distribution to varying soil conditions across farming fields, PA has gone through some evolutions in its employment, such as automatic guidance of agricultural vehicles, autonomous machinery and cultivation processes, product traceability, on-farm research, and new software and technologies for the overall management of food production systems (Gebbers & Adamchuk, 2010). Perhaps one of the simplest ways to explain PA is by thinking of it as any activity that makes farming processes more accurate, controlled, and precise when it comes to growing crops or raising livestock. Key technologies used for this approach include GPS guidance, control systems, sensors, robotics, drones, autonomous farming vehicles, GPS-based soil sampling, automated hardware, telematics, and other software.

PA first emerged in the 1990's with the introduction of GPS guidance for farm tractors. The adoption of this GPS guidance is now so globally widespread that it is probably the most common used type of PA today.

John Deere was the first to adopt this technology employing GPS location data from satellites. A GPS-connected controller in a farm tractor automatically steers itself based on the coordinates of a field. This automated steering of farm vehicles thus reduces steering errors by human drivers, and therefore avoids overlap on the field. This in turn results in less wasted seeds, fertilizers, fuel, and time. Reducing the amount of natural resources that go waste, and resulting in less wasted fertile seeds, fuel, fertilizer, and time (Schmaltz, 2017).

A current startup that provides PA services to farmers is known as "xFarm". xFarm is comprised of farmers who provide first hand advise about the challenges and complexities of managing a company. xFarm can be considered a collaboration between farmers and computer and electronic engineering to empower farmers to be able to employ the best available technologies and achieve adaptability in the global food ecosystem. xFarm was born from the collaborative experiences of farmers who struggled to solve their farm managing challenges, and technicians who managed to create technological solutions for farmer's challenges.

xFarm is a software that helps farmers improve data management through a digital log of field activities and creating all the necessary documents to track their activities and ensure their products are yielding the best possible output. The team at xFarm aims to make modern technologies easy to use, and help farmers manage their personal data and their field data; xFarm's software records all activities and prepares the crops on farmer's fields. Farmers can then manage this data from their computer, tablet, or smartphone.

Once farmers collect their data on their mobile device, they can then analyze it to improve the efficiency of their farming procedures. Farmers are also empowered to identify areas to be corrected or improved. xFarm helps farmers estimate and prepare their stock, and helps them manage their required reports by authorities and certification bodies. Furthermore, the real-time data provided by xFarm includes current field work, which is displayed on farmer's mobile devices while they are physically on the field, this provides them with a live feed of their activities, which can indicate to farmers what needs to be done based on the soil and based on their physical location. With xFarm farmers can also manage other features such as entrances and exits in stocks, and get alerts for when farming equipment is in need of maintenance. In essence, xFarm assists farmers in managing their land and crop output, operates a software that is compatible with computer desktops and mobile devices, works with arable crops, vegetables, and fruits, functions in fields and land registries creating maps, lists of tasks, stocks, crops, and equipment and safety. Furthermore the data provided by xFarm can indicate a farmer's compatibility for certain certifications (xFarm, 2019).

4.8 Bio-Fertilizers

Much of the increases in food production have been a direct result of the increased use of chemical fertilizers and pesticides, however this increase in greater production of food has some side effects as well. Some fertilizing chemicals are expensive, and reduce microbial activity in agricultural soils and accumulate in the food chain, thereby posing potential harmful effects for humans. Along with many of the transitions in food systems, shifting way from chemical fertilizers and exploring more sustainable solutions is a key issue in achieving overall food ecosystem sustainability.

One possible solution for this transition is bio-fertilizers, which consists of plant bi-products, organic matter, and microorganisms, and are natural, organic, biodegradable, eco-friendly and cost effective (Bhardwaj, Ansari, Sahoo, & Tuteja, 2014). Furthermore, bio-fertilizers are composed of microbes that are essential because they produce nutrients that are necessary for plant growth (e.g., nitrogen, phosphorus, and potassium), and other chemicals that are crucial for plant growth (e.g., auxins & cytokinins). Biofertilizers also help to improve the physical properties, fertility, and productivity of soil, thus decreasing or removing the need for chemical fertilizers while simultaneously producing expected crop yields. Hence, bio-fertilizers are a powerful vehicle for sustainable food ecosystems (Win, Barone, Secundo, & Fu, 2018).

Furthermore, the European Consortium of the Organic-Based Fertilizer Industry (ECOFI) is the representative body of European producers of organic fertilizers. ECOFI members operate in many European countries and also export to, and engage in interactions with, other non-EU regions such as the Mediterranean and the Middle East. Collectively, ECOFI memberships make up about 60% of the European market in organic-based fertilizers, which is worth about 250 million Euros (ECOFI, 2019). Furthermore, ECOFI categorizes bio-fertilizers and defines them as follows:

- **Organic fertilizer**: A fertilizer whose main function is to provide nutrients under organic forms from organic materials of plant and/or animal origin.
- **Organo-mineral fertilizer**: a complex fertilizer obtained by industrial co-formulation of one or more inorganic fertilizers with one or more organic fertilizers and/or organic soil improvers into solid forms (with the exception of dry mixes) or liquids.
- **Organic soil improver**: a soil improver containing carbonaceous materials of plant and/or animal origin, whose main function is to maintain or increase the soil organic matter content.

A novel startup that has truly harnessed the power of bio-fertilizers is 'Mama Organa' from North Macedonia. This startup focuses on creating organic fertilizers from food waste, essentially cleaning the planet and feeding people (F6S, 2019). It is a company that was formed to collect food waste by adding value to it, produce organic fertilizers in order to help farmers in growing healthy and clean food, and also provide job opportunities for socially excluded single mothers (European Commission, 2019). Furthermore, Mama Organa was awarded the 'Best Job Growth Startup' prize at the 'StartUp Europe Awards', thus highlighting the importance of engaging in sustainable initiatives while simultaneously providing job opportunities and economic growth.

Another related yet different venture is 'InnovaFeed'. InnovaFeed is a pioneer in the production of high-quality protein, oil, and fertilizers from insect farms that are then used for animal feed and aquaculture. It is a biotech company that produces a new source of protein from insects, and has raised a whopping €55 million since its launch in 2016, and hopes to reach a production capacity of more then 10,000 tons per years before their international launch in 2022. Their model is based on technology that allows them to place the insect at the heart of the food ecosystem and restore its natural place in their smaller ecosystem; they give it its function of recycling nutrients to then feed fish, birds or small mammals.

Given the imminent and fast-growing world population, InnovaFeed's activities respond swiftly and competitively to an increase in protein demands, with simultaneously contributing to developing more sustainable food ecosystems, in this case especially through the improvement of quality aquaculture (InnovaFeed, 2019).

4.9 Meat Alternatives

Traditionally, meat has been considered an important component of a healthy diet, as socially accepted and desirable, and as an indicator of societal development (Biesalski, 2005). Animal-sourced foods are rich in nutrients and provide us with an array of high quality proteins, essential fatty acids, and vitamins and minerals that are present in lower quantities in plant based foods. However, the massive production and consumption of meat at global levels has ignited relevant concerns about the natural resources required, resulting pollution, and GHG emissions (Steinfeld et al., 2006) and biodiversity loss (Machovina, Feeley, & Ripple, 2015). Furthermore, the current amounts of meat production by agriculture and consumption by individuals not only exceed the dietary protein requirements, but also are actually unsustainable (van der Weele, Feindt, van der Goot, van Mierlo, & van Boekel, 2019). This unsustainability of meat production is a result of a mix of current production methods such as the inefficient use of resources per protein consumed (Tilman, Balzer, Hill, & Befort, 2011) and the large amounts of GHG emissions from animal production, which have also ignited efforts to reduce meat consumption (Gill, Feliciano, Macdiarmid, & Smith, 2015).

Furthermore, raising livestock has an enormous environmental footprint as it contributes to land and water degradation, biodiversity loss, acid rain, and deforestation. However, this environmental impact is most evident in climate change, with livestock contributing to 18% of GHG emissions worldwide (FAO, 2019); more GHG emissions than ships, planes, cars, and all other forms of transportation taken together (Pimentel & Pimentel, 2003). Therefore, driving reductions in the consumption of meat products and animal products in general is essential if we are to meet the sustainable food systems and the SDGs. Meat production is quite inefficient, and this is especially true for red meat. For example, the production of a kilogram of beef requires 25 kg of grain, and roughly about 15,000 L of water (Pimentel & Pimentel, 2003). The inefficiency that characterizes meat production is also evident when it comes to land use, since around 30% of the Earth's land is current occupied for livestock farming (Pimentel & Pimentel, 2003).

These severe environmental challenges with meat production and consumption however do not have to seem bleak, since they provide an array of opportunities for innovation and entrepreneurial endeavors.

For example, "This.co" produces plant-based meat alternatives that are mostly made from soybean proteins, water, and pea protein. This.co offers its customers wide option of products, ranging from meals that are 'ready to cook' to meals that are 'ready to eat'; and all made with sustainable plant based meat alternatives. Furthermore, This.co ensures their products are full of iron and B12, high in protein, have a longer shelf-life than real meat to help reduce waste, and uses 90% less plastic to package (This.co, 2019).

Furthermore, 'The Meatless Farm Co' was founded in 2016 to help people reduce their meat consumption. Since then the company has developed plant-based mince and burger patties that best replicate the taste and texture of meat. This startup created these products with the goal of helping people reduce their meat consumption and ease the process of adopting more plant based products. The mince and burgers are high in protein, a great source of fiber, and vegan friendly. 'The Meatless Farm Co' is a British company that has been met with success in outside market such as the United Arab Emirates (UAE), Canada, China, and Europe. Finally, it is easy to use; consumers must only follow the cooking instructions included in the packaging and can also be included into regular meals (TMF, 2019).

4.10   Waste Reduction

Food ecosystem stakeholders are increasingly becoming aware of the issues related to food waste, and are also recognizing their potential and responsibility in preventing it. For example, research shows that most Europeans identify an individual responsibility when it comes to methods of reducing food waste, with 63% stating that improved food related processes in terms of shopping and budgeting food items would help reduce waste (Romani, Grappi, Bagozzi, & Barone, 2018). It is no secret that food waste is a major global challenge, and therefore innovative efforts are needed to tackle it.

'Too Good to Go' is an innovative app that allows users to do their share in reducing food waste, while at the same time getting access to healthy and nutritious food and supporting local businesses. Too Good to Go is an innovative app that lets everyone do their bit to reduce waste, while also getting delicious food and supporting local businesses. The businesses get to reduce their waste and also have potential new customers try out their food. Both contribute to a better environment. Too Good To Go is an app that functions as a marketplace that connects businesses with surplus food to regular consumers who want to 'rescue' this food. Customers order this surplus food at a discounted price and then collect it from the participating stores in a pre-set collection window. Customers have to simply choose which store (from existing app members) they would like to rescue from, place and pay for their order, and then go to allotted collection window and show their in-app receipt to the staff in the store or restaurant of interest (TooGoodtoGo, 2019).

'Wasteless' on the other hand is the world's first machine learning approach with real-time tracking for grocery stores that seeks to offer customers dynamic pricing based on when a product is set to expire. This results in reduced food waste and increased revenue by enabling adjusted pricing. To reduce waste and optimize revenue, the Wasteless' pricing engine employs a branch of machine learning that enables the engine to adapt quickly to how consumers respond to adjusted pricing, thus being able to identify the optimal discount policy. With the current advances in technological know-how and products, supermarkets cannot be left behind. Wasteless takes the most advanced machine learning, forecasting, and analytical techniques, and applies them to brick and mortar or online stores. With Wasteless, business owners and entrepreneurs will be able to manage their business inventory the smart way, always having control over their supply, inventory, and pricing (Wasteless, 2019).

4.11 Health and Wellbeing

Unfortunately, the current global challenges posed by our food ecosystem are not limited to environmental consequences as these transcend boundaries into the actual well-being of individuals. While food ecosystems have been designed to ensure food access and availability for all, there are still some issues with doing this equally; this is evidenced by the co-existing alarming rates of obesity and wide availability of processed foods, and severe undernourishment and limited access to basic dietary needs such as fresh produce and fresh drinking water (Shamsuzzoha, Rasheduzzaman, & Ghosh, 2018). With the projected population growth by 2050, increased demands for food, changes in dietary habits due to availability of resources, or increased consumer information will create new challenges to provide universal access to nutritious and high quality food, while avoiding negative trade-offs in environmental, economic, or social arenas (Lindgren et al., 2018).

The 2017 Global Nutrition Report detailed the health and well being crisis associated with food ecosystems, and highlights that it is especially prominent in

4.11 Health and Wellbeing

the Asia Pacific region. Furthermore, 155 million children under the age of 5 are current stunted and malnutrition costs amount to about \$3.5 trillion every year. Interestingly enough, around 3.4 million people die every year due to overweight and obesity (Aid Forum, 2018).

Furthermore, increased food options and a saturation of food availability might make it difficult for individuals to choose the healthier option, and many opt out for the 'easy choice', which in the end might be detrimental to their health. For this reason, startups focusing on maintaining and improving human health and wellbeing are mostly focusing on providing personalized nutrition guidance.

One example of such a startup can be found in an Irish biotech company which was founded in 2014, 'Nuritas'. Nuritas combines artificial intelligence and genomics to discover peptides, i.e. molecules in food and food by products, that can be repurposed by scientific teams and used in supplements and new drugs. To date, the startup has recused a €30 million in investments. Nuritas states that it can find peptides 10 times faster and 500 times more accurately than existing methods, and does so at a lower cost. It has developed and patented health-improving innovations that can address a wide range of health challenges ranging from inflammation, to diabetes, and even Methicillin-Resistant Staphylococcus Aureus (MRSA). Furthermore, Nuritas states their goal as a global ambition to improve the lives of billions of people (Irish Times, 2018; Nuritas, 2019).

Furthermore, 'myDNAhealth' is a startup that combines science, human behavior, and technology to facilitate a shift from a 'one-size-fits-all' approach to diets to a personalized nutritional approach aimed at preventing health problems and improving life expectancy (myDNAhealth, 2019). To do this, customers complete a DNA-type test, which helps them take advantage of their inherited strengths while overcoming their limitations. Upon completion of tests by customers, the company then provides customers with 16 reports with risk scores and explanations, personalized wellness guide and tips, methods to increase nutritional intake based on their genetic make-up, and provides lifestyle suggestions to improve overall wellness and performance. The multivariate algorithms provided by myDNAhealth provides personalized recommendations, including nutrient values, from a database of 2.5 million recipes designed to reduce risk of disease (myDNAhealth, 2019).

Finally, 'FoodSay' is a free of charge dietician app. A real-time food consumption-learning platform that provides recommendation for the most nutritionally appropriate and goal specific food depending on the time of day, season, and activity levels. FoodSay works in three easy steps, (i) users initially input their allergies, diet plan goals and receive diet recommendations almost immediately, (ii) then populate their food diary by ordering food via FoodSay, and (iii) FoodSay then suggests best meal options based on locations and diet profile. FoodSay aims to gradually help each user easily follow a diet plan without any pressure and with all their diet goals in consideration. The first version of prototype is also available at: https://share.protopie.io/W4c68BhfsUi (FoodSay, 2019).

4.12 Conclusion

The recent emergence of the knowledge economy, which includes intangibility, high level of interactions, and increasing importance of organizational innovation in global value chains, has triggered important shifts from traditional food production models. Food ecosystems are slowly moving from quantitative and economy focused production, to smarter agricultural processes that are designed to ensure the maintenance of the food ecosystem itself. However, these transitions have also highlighted significant system limitations on innovation themselves.

In traditional linear models of innovation, science was always thought to be the originating point of innovation. However, the recently emerging chain like, and circular, model of innovation emphasizes that science is an element of the innovation process and not necessarily the context in which innovation originates. For example, increased attention is being given to farmers as entrepreneurs, since they are the individuals who directly come in contact with crops, animal, and sometimes consumers, it would be them to hold key insights to innovative solutions for food ecosystems transformation.

The essence of systems thinking and open innovation considers the interaction among elements. This perspective thus illustrates the innovation process of knowledge production, turning knowledge into practice, and dissemination as occurring within a non-hierarchical, dynamic, and open environment where many kinds of knowledge spillovers occur, which are then harnessed by entrepreneurial talent to create valuable innovations for societies (Tataj, 2015).

The importance of research and innovation for sustainable developments in food ecosystems is evident, and the proposed research and innovation frameworks themselves can serve as guides to identify specific problem areas that are in particular need for sustainable transformation. Specifically, the intervention points that emerged from Food 2030's survey, serve as important indicators for researchers and entrepreneurs seeking to create impactful innovations toward sustainability. One reason for this is that those topics emerged from a systemic representation of food stakeholders, and not from personal preferences of institutions or individual members. These transformations in production should be based on a mix of bottom-up and top-down approaches, with innovations being led by farmers and citizen demand, but at the same time accompanied by more influential actors from the food supply chain such as industry, food processing sites, and retailers (Meynard et al., 2017).

Even strict research streams that often identify issues in one area oftentimes fail to see appreciate their relationships and interdependencies with other related or unrelated topics.

As originally proposed by Gill et al. (2018), the next logical step to effectively engage research and innovation activities in food ecosystems, is for researchers themselves to realize that research and innovation itself is in need of a systems approach (Gill et al., 2018). This, however, remains a challenge since private sector investment in such integrated and holistic research and innovation approaches remains modest and fragmented, this fact outlines the need for strategies that trigger a double transformation, both in food ecosystems and in R&I approaches (Gill et al., 2018).

References

Aid Forum. (2018). *41 countries face triple threat of malnutrition, anaemia and obesity, FAO reports*. Retrieved from http://www.aidforum.org/topics/food-security/41-countries-face-triple-threat-of-malnutrition-anaemia-and-obesity-fao-rep/

Aldrich, H. E., & Cliff, J. E. (2003). The pervasive effects of family on entrepreneurship: Toward a family embeddedness perspective. *Journal of Business Venturing, 18*(5), 573–596.

Al-Kodmany, K. (2015). *Eco-towers: Sustainable cities in the sky*. Southampton: WIT Press.

Al-Kodmany, K. (2018a). The vertical farm: A review of developments and implications for the vertical city. *Buildings, 8*(2), 24.

Al-Kodmany, K. (2018b). *The vertical city: A sustainable development model*. Southampton: WIT Press.

Anderson, C. A., Thorndike, A. N., Lichtenstein, A. H., Van Horn, L., Kris-Etherton, P. M., Foraker, R., & Spees, C. (2019). Innovation to create a healthy and sustainable food system: A science advisory from the American Heart Association. *Circulation,* CIR-0000000000000686.

Bailey, G. E. (1915). *Vertical farming [by] Gilbert Ellis Bailey*. Wilmington, DE: E. I. Dupont de Nemours Powder Co.

Baudoin, W., Nono-Womdim, R., Lutaladio, N., Hodder, A., Castilla, N., Leonardi, C., ... Duffy, R. (2013). *Good agricultural practices for greenhouse vegetable crops: Principles for mediterranean climate areas*. Rome: FAO plant production and protection paper (FAO).

Bhardwaj, D., Ansari, M. W., Sahoo, R. K., & Tuteja, N. (2014). Biofertilizers function as key player in sustainable agriculture by improving soil fertility, plant tolerance and crop productivity. *Microbial Cell Factories, 13*(1), 66.

Biesalski, H. K. (2005). Meat as a component of a healthy diet–Are there any risks or benefits if meat is avoided in the diet? *Meat Science, 70*(3), 509–524.

Bigliardi, B., & Galati, F. (2013). Models of adoption of open innovation within the food industry. *Trends in Food Science & Technology, 30*(1), 16–26.

Birkby, J. (2016). *Vertical farming. ATTRA sustainable agriculture*. NCAT IP516, 12.

Bresciani, S. (2017). Open, networked and dynamic innovation in the food and beverage industry. *British Food Journal, 119*(11), 2290–2293.

Business Wire. (2017). *Global precision culture agriculture market analysis*. Retrieved from https://www.businesswire.com/news/home/20170313006084/en/Global-43.4-Billion-Precision-Agriculture-Market-Analysis

Canfora, I. (2016). Is the short food supply chain an efficient solution for sustainability in food market? *Agriculture and Agricultural Science Procedia, 8*, 402–407.

CB Insights. (2018). *Food and beverage trends, 2019*. Retrieved from https://www.cbinsights.com/research/report/food-beverage-trends-2019/

Chesbrough, H. W. (2003). *Open innovation: The new imperative for creating and profiting from technology*. Boston, MA: Harvard Business Press.

Chesbrough, H., Vanhaverbeke, W., & West, J. (Eds.). (2006). *Open innovation: Researching a new paradigm*. Oxford: Oxford University Press on Demand.

Christophe. (2013). *Sustainable food in urban communities*. Retrieved from http://www.sustainable-everyday-project.net/urbact-sustainable-food/2013/05/21/gasap-network/

Corvalan, C., Hales, S., McMichael, A. J., Butler, C., & McMichael, A. (2005). *Ecosystems and human well-being: Health synthesis*. Geneva: World Health Organization.

De Bernardi, P., Bertello, A., & Venuti, F. (2019). Online and on-site interactions within alternative food networks: Sustainability impact of knowledge-sharing practices. *Sustainability, 11*(5), 1457.

De Bernardi, P., Bertello, A., & Venuti, F. (2020). Community-oriented motivations and knowledge sharing as drivers of success within food assemblies. In *Exploring digital ecosystems* (pp. 443–457). Cham: Springer.

De Bernardi, P., Bertello, A., Venuti, F., & Zardini, A. (2019). Knowledge transfer driving community-based business models towards sustainable food-related behaviours: A commons perspective. *Knowledge Management Research & Practice, 1–8.* https://doi.org/10.1080/14778238.2019.1664271

Despommier, D. (2013). Farming up the city: The rise of urban vertical farms. *Trends in Biotechnology, 31*(7), 388–389.

ECOFI. (2019). *Representing European producers of organic fertilizers, organo-mineral fertilizers and organic soil improvers.* Retrieved from http://www.ecofi.info/

European Commission. (2013). *Agriculture and rural development.* Retrieved from https://ec.europa.eu/agriculture/rural-development-2014-2020/legislation_en

European Commission. (2018). *Food 2030.* Retrieved from https://ec.europa.eu/research/bioeconomy/index.cfm?pg=policy&lib=food2030

European Commission. (2019). *Startup awards recognize the best startups in a special edition focused on social impact.* Retrieved from https://ec.europa.eu/digital-single-market/en/news/startup-europe-awards-recognize-best-5-startups-special-edition-focused-social-impact

F6S. (2019). *Mama Organa.* Retrieved from https://www.f6s.com/mamaorgana1

FAO. (2018). *International symposium on agricultural innovation for family farmers.* Retrieved from http://www.fao.org/3/CA2588EN/ca2588en.pdf

FAO. (2019). *Key facts and findings.* Retrieved from http://www.fao.org/news/story/en/item/197623/icode/

Fernandez R., & Lazaro-Mojica, J. (2018). *fit4food deliverable 4.1.* Retrieved from https://fit4food2030.eu/wp-content/uploads/2019/01/FIT4FOOD2030_D4.1_Report-on-inventory-of-RI-breakthroughs.pdf

Food Drink Europe. (2017). *Data and trends. EU food and drink industry.* Retrived from https://www.fooddrinkeurope.eu/uploads/publications_documents/DataandTrends_Report_2017.pdf

FoodSay. (2019). *Get the best food for you, always.* Retrieved from https://foodsay.co/

García-Caro Briceño, D. (2018). *Vertical farming sustainability and urban implications.* Uppsala: Uppsala University.

Gebbers, R., & Adamchuk, V. I. (2010). Precision agriculture and food security. *Science, 327*(5967), 828–831.

Gill, M., Den Boer, A. C. L., Kok, K. P., Cahill, J., Callenius, C., Caron, P., … Lappiere, A. (2018). *A systems approach to research and innovation for food system transformation.* Retrived from https://arrow.dit.ie/cgi/viewcontent.cgi?article=1001&context=resdirotn

Gill, M., Feliciano, D., Macdiarmid, J., & Smith, P. (2015). The environmental impact of nutrition transition in three case study countries. *Food Security, 7*(3), 493–504.

Gillebo, T., & Hugo, A. (2006). Sustainable entrepreneurship: Regional innovation cultures in the ecological food sector. *International Journal of Agricultural Sustainability, 4*(3), 244–256.

Graber, A., & Junge, R. (2009). Aquaponic systems: Nutrient recycling from fish wastewater by vegetable production. *Desalination, 246*(1–3), 147–156.

Gries, T., & Naudé, W. (2010). Entrepreneurship and structural economic transformation. *Small Business Economics, 34*(1), 13–29.

Ingram, J. S. I. (2011). *From food production to food security: Developing interdisciplinary, regional-level research.* Wageningen: Wageningen University.

InnovaFeed. (2019). *Natural and sustainable solutions to feed the world.* Retrieved from https://innovafeed.com/en/

Kneafsey, M., Cox, R., Holloway, L., Dowler, E., Venn, L., & Tuomainen, H. (2008). *Reconnecting consumers, producers and food: Exploring alternatives.* Oxford: Berg.

Lazzarotti, V., & Manzini, R. (2013). Partnering with public research centres and private technical and scientific service providers for innovation: The case of Italian rice company, Riso Scotti. In *Open innovation in the food and beverage industry* (pp. 97–108). Cambridge: Woodhead Publishing.

References

Lindgren, E., Harris, F., Dangour, A. D., Gasparatos, A., Hiramatsu, M., Javadi, F., ... Haines, A. (2018). Sustainable food systems—A health perspective. *Sustainability Science, 13*(6), 1505–1517.

LinkedIn. (2019). *NinjaCart. Indias largest B2B fresh produce supply chain*. Retrieved from https://www.linkedin.com/company/ninja-cart/about/

Machovina, B., Feeley, K. J., & Ripple, W. J. (2015). Biodiversity conservation: The key is reducing meat consumption. *Science of the Total Environment, 536*, 419–431.

Marsden, T., Banks, J., & Bristow, G. (2000). Food supply chain approaches: Exploring their role in rural development. *Sociologia Ruralis, 40*(4), 424–438.

Meynard, J. M., Jeuffroy, M. H., Le Bail, M., Lefèvre, A., Magrini, M. B., & Michon, C. (2017). Designing coupled innovations for the sustainability transition of agrifood systems. *Agricultural Systems, 157*, 330–339.

Moragues, A., Morgan, K., Moschitz, H., Neimane, I., Nilsson, H., Pinto, M., ... Halliday, J. (2013). *Urban food strategies. The rough guide to sustainable food systems*.

myDNAhealth. (2019). *Intelligent health and nutrition*. Retrieved from https://mydnahealth.co.uk/

NinjaCart. (2019). *Quality food for everyone*. Retrieved from http://ninjacart.in/

Nuritas. (2019). *Life changing discoveries for a changing world*. Retrieved from https://www.nuritas.com/applications/

Parsons, K., & Hawkes, C. (2018). *Connecting food systems for co-benefits: How can food systems combine diet-related health with environmental and economic policy goals?* Copenhagen: WHO.

Phytoponics. (2018). *Home. Our story*. Retrieved from https://phytoponics.com/

Pimentel, D., & Pimentel, M. (2003). Sustainability of meat-based and plant-based diets and the environment. *The American Journal of Clinical Nutrition, 78*(3), 660S–663S.

Pindado, E., & Sánchez, M. (2017). Researching the entrepreneurial behaviour of new and existing ventures in European agriculture. *Small Business Economics, 49*(2), 421–444.

Ramirez-Portilla, A., Cagno, E., & Zanatta-Alarcon, A. (2016). *Open food–Revisiting open innovation in the food industry*.

Romani, S., Grappi, S., Bagozzi, R. P., & Barone, A. M. (2018). Domestic food practices: A study of food management behaviors and the role of food preparation planning in reducing waste. *Appetite, 121*, 215–227.

Saguy, I. S., & Sirotinskaya, V. (2014). Challenges in exploiting open innovation's full potential in the food industry with a focus on small and medium enterprises (SMEs). *Trends in Food Science & Technology, 38*(2), 136–148.

Santoro, G., Vrontis, D., & Pastore, A. (2017). External knowledge sourcing and new product development: Evidence from the Italian food and beverage industry. *British Food Journal, 119*(11), 2373–2387.

Sarkar, S., & Costa, A. I. (2008). Dynamics of open innovation in the food industry. *Trends in Food Science & Technology, 19*(11), 574–580.

Schmaltz, R. (2017). *What is precision agriculture?* Retrieved from https://agfundernews.com/what-is-precision-agriculture.html

Schmutz, U., Kneafsey, M., Kay, C. S., Doernberg, A., & Zasada, I. (2018). Sustainability impact assessments of different urban short food supply chains: Examples from London, UK. *Renewable Agriculture and Food Systems, 33*(6), 518–529.

Shamsuzzoha, M., Rasheduzzaman, M., & Ghosh, R. C. (2018). Building resilience for drinking water shortages through reverse osmosis technology in coastal areas of Bangladesh. *Procedia Engineering, 212*, 559–566.

Staes, B., Heubuch, M. (2019). *Europe must get serious about short food supply chains*. Retrieved from https://www.euractiv.com/section/agriculture-food/opinion/europe-must-get-serious-about-short-food-supply-chains/1250375/

Steinfeld, H., Gerber, P., Wassenaar, T. D., Castel, V., Rosales, M., Rosales, M., & de Haan, C. (2006). *Livestock's long shadow: Environmental issues and options*. Rome: Food & Agriculture Org.

Tataj, D. (2015). *Innovation and entrepreneurship: A growth model for Europe beyond the crisis*.

The Irish Times. (2018). *Nuritas secures €30m investment from EU's financial arm*. Retrieved from https://www.irishtimes.com/business/technology/nuritas-secures-30m-investment-from-eu-s-financial-arm-1.3715140

This.co. (2019). *Why eat this?* Retrieved from http://this.co/why/

Thomaier, S., Specht, K., Henckel, D., Dierich, A., Siebert, R., Freisinger, U. B., & Sawicka, M. (2015). Farming in and on urban buildings: Present practice and specific novelties of Zero-Acreage Farming (ZFarming). *Renewable Agriculture and Food Systems, 30*(1), 43–54.

Tilman, D., Balzer, C., Hill, J., & Befort, B. L. (2011). Global food demand and the sustainable intensification of agriculture. *Proceedings of the National Academy of Sciences, 108*(50), 20260–20264.

TMF. (2019). *The home of fresh plant based food*. Retrieved from https://meatlessfarm.com/

Too Good to Go. (2019). *Save delicious food and fight food waste*. Retrieved from https://toogoodtogo.co.uk/en-gb

Touzard, J. M., Temple, L., Goulet, F., Chiffoleau, Y., & Faure, G. (2018). *Innovation and development in agricultural and food systems*. Quae.

van der Weele, C., Feindt, P., van der Goot, A. J., van Mierlo, B., & van Boekel, M. (2019). Meat alternatives: An integrative comparison. *Trends in Food Science & Technology, 88*, 505–512.

Von Hippel, E. (2005). *Democratizing innovation: Users take center stage*. Boston, MA: MIT Press.

Wasteless. (2019). *Increase sales and reduce food waste with dynamic pricing*. Retrieved from https://www.wasteless.co/

Win, T. T., Barone, G. D., Secundo, F., & Fu, P. (2018). Algal biofertilizers and plant growth stimulants for sustainable agriculture. *Industrial Biotechnology, 14*(4), 203–211.

xFarm. (2019). *Software company xfarm*. Retrieved from https://www.xfarm.ag/xfarm/

Zhang, W., Gowdy, J., Bassi, A. M., Santamaria, M., deClerck, F., Adegboyega, A., ... Darknhofer, I. (2018). Systems thinking: An approach for understanding 'eco-agri-food systems'. In *TEEB for agriculture and food: Scientific and economic foundations report: Work in progress*. Geneva: The Economics of Ecosystems and Biodiversity.

Chapter 5
Entrepreneurial Food Ecosystem: Strategic Driver to Boost Resilience and Sustainability

Abstract Food is connected to a variety of fields such as agriculture, environment, energy, health, education, infrastructure, and urban planning to name a few. Given the threats of population growth, climate change, and the waning health of our natural resource base, broadening our R&I methods to be more systems-based, and building public-private partnerships around shared interests and objectives are two key approaches that can be employed to address challenges to food ecosystem resiliency and sustainability. A better understanding of the linkages between food ecosystem sustainability (and consequently food ecosystem sustainability transitions) and food security is necessary to achieve 'future proof' food ecosystems. However, R&I efforts have failed to adequately respond to the urgent and system wide challenges that threaten food sustainability. A reason for this includes the fact that much like linear ideas of food systems, R&I streams too suffer from compartmentalization. Furthermore, the engagement of all stakeholders, shifting mindsets and approaches from mainstream linear models toward holistic approaches, and involving public and independent R&I could be an appropriate response to challenges regarding food ecosystems' complexity, and address the dominant and established pathways that are difficult to transform. In this chapter we introduce the concept of Responsible Research and Innovation (RRI) as the adequate vehicle for holistically assessing food ecosystems and innovations toward sustainability while truly considering potential trade-offs from proposed innovations.

Keywords Entrepreneurship center · Knowledge spillover · Entrepreneurship · Higher education institution · Innovation

5.1 Introduction

In order to tackle the ever-present and multifaceted societal challenges, and contribute to the achievement of the Sustainable Development Goals (SDGs) it is essential, once food ecosystems are created, to make them "future proof", i.e. resilient, sustainable, responsible, diverse, competitive, and inclusive (European Commission, 2018). The main outcome of the food system has traditionally been to achieve food and

© Springer Nature Switzerland AG 2020
P. De Bernardi, D. Azucar, *Innovation in Food Ecosystems*, Contributions to Management Science, https://doi.org/10.1007/978-3-030-33502-1_5

135

nutritional security, and only relatively recently has our global food system been challenged to achieve this task while simultaneously considering and protecting the Earth's natural resources. However, even though food availability and access are the main goals of food systems, about half of the global population remains affected by food insecurity and the triple burden of malnutrition, all while food systems continue to be one of the main contributors to the degradation of natural resources—two factors that are clear symptoms of the inadequacy of current processes.

'Sustainability' has recently become a 'buzzword' amongst researchers and scholars, as it has been catapulted into everyday discussions by worldwide media, politicians, and general public opinions (Bertoni et al., 2018). This increased global attention to sustainable initiatives and increased awareness of the potential future damages associated with 'business as usual' have led to a convergence of efforts by communities in attempts to identify effective strategies that are capable of promoting sustainable development (e.g., short food supply chains, insects as proteins, and sustainable or edible plastic packaging) (Akhtar & Isman, 2018; Bertoni et al., 2018; Dankhade, Kazi, & Gophane, 2018; De Bernardi & Tirabeni, 2018).

Recent findings from a recent systematic review aimed to yield greater insight into the state of research on the sustainability of agro-food transitions suggest that in order to become 'future proof', food systems must (i) venture beyond their traditional segments to foster trans-disciplinary and multi-institutional collaborations, and (ii) integrate their varied sustainability transitions regarding food security, nutritional interests, and environmental protection into consolidated regional, community, or organizational goals (El Bilali, 2019). Unfortunately, when it comes to food and sustainability, food security and nutrition and their relationships with sustainability transitions remains a scant topic in research literature (El Bilali, 2019).

The European Commission's Food 2030 Expert Group describes the food system as follows: *'The food system incorporates all elements and activities that relate to food production, processing, distribution, preparation, and consumption, as well as its disposal. This includes the environment, people, processes, infrastructure, institutions, and the effects of their activities on our society, economy, landscape, and climate'* (Gill et al., 2018, p. 2). In essence, 'food system' refers to the actors within the food supply chain, and their interactions with each other and overall system activities, as well as between environmental, economic, and technical dimensions (Rundgren, 2016). These conceptualizations of food systems provide a novel point of view, one that appreciates their complexity beyond traditional and segmented linear production-focused or consumption-focused models. Furthermore, in adopting this holistic view, it is clear to see the overlap in the literature regarding the use of the term 'system' or 'ecosystem' to describe the processes related to bringing food from 'farm to fork'. For consistency purposes, we consider 'food systems' the physical structures of food supply chains (e.g., stakeholders, institutions, farms, retailers, producers, etc.), and posit that these systems evolve into an 'ecosystem' when the interdependent relationships between members, and systems themselves, are recognized as drivers of overall system procedures, culture, and transformation. Throughout the rest of the chapter we employ the term 'food ecosystem' when discussing food supply chain processes.

Holistic views of food ecosystems provide several benefits, especially since traditional models have been evidenced as unsustainable and inadequate in driving the transformational capacity of a system, mainly due to the fact that current segmented approaches result in a range of heterogeneous sustainability initiatives (e.g., depending on the sector) that are usually conducted by members in isolation, and are therefore characterized by a narrow scope of solutions and limited research and innovation (R&I) agendas (FEC, 2018).

Bertoni et al. (2018) also demonstrate that the path towards sustainable development is related to environmental protection. They further suggest that a combination of agricultural policies aimed at protecting and preserving the environment and innovation along the agri-food chain, in concurrence with consumer engagement towards ameliorating environmental issues can play an important role in achieving sustainability objectives (Bertoni et al., 2018). Finally, even though research efforts to understand and achieve sustainability have skyrocketed in the recent years (Fischer et al., 2015), field experts acknowledge that research alone is not enough as successful transitions also require the translation of research into practice in order to effectively stimulate innovations for sustainability and change consumer behavior patterns to truly deliver social impact (Tataj, 2015). This of course, requires a more thorough understanding of the interactions and dynamics between the individual and institutional stakeholders found in food ecosystems, and the provision of evidence based guidance for stimulating positive change with desired outcomes (FAO, 2018).

5.2 Beyond Linearity in Food Supply Chains: Systems Thinking

When it comes to sustainability, our food system is plagued with multi-faceted challenges (De Bernardi, Bertello, & Venuti, 2019; De Bernardi, Bertello, Venuti, & Zardini, 2019). For example, the industrial approach to food production and its resulting food surplus in many communities have caused a reduction of the perceived value of food as a highly critical and important product; this is evidenced by the ominous fact that about one-third of global food goes to waste (FAO, 2019). Even more alarming, global population growth, and changes in dietary patterns require an increase in overall food production of more than 60% to feed the ten billion projected world inhabitants by 2050 (Alexandratos & Bruinsma, 2012). Furthermore, highly fragmented food supply chains, and unbalanced trading practices put limits on the potential for efficiency gains and advances in food systems that could build consumer trust and promote disruptive innovations (EIT Food Strategic Agenda, 2019). These multi-faceted barriers to food sustainability, coupled with the global challenges outlined by the SDGs and their individual connections to the overall food ecosystem (Rockström & Sukhdev, 2016) illustrate why systems' thinking, in multiple domains, is an important and necessary approach for sustainable food production and consumption.

We know that when we seek to tackle global challenges, they must be considered along with their accompanying causes, consequences, and benefits, and we must keep in mind that every single one of these challenges cannot be solved in isolation. This remains a troublesome scenario since the current segregated components and processes of the food ecosystem directly impede its members from engaging with each other, and thus limits its potential for achieving sustainability.

On a global scale, innovation and entrepreneurship have emerged as two prominent vehicles to drive transformations in food ecosystems (De Bernardi, Bertello, & Venuti, 2020; Vrontis, Bresciani, & Giacosa, 2016). However, in the case of the European Union, food ecosystems are characterized by low entrepreneurial engagement; this is reflected by a low share of representation, i.e. 2.6%, of food and agricultural startups among all European startups from various industries (EIT Food Strategic Agenda, 2019). This reluctant nature of food ecosystem stakeholders when it comes to adopting innovations (e.g., new technologies and procedures) should be interpreted as a challenge to scholars and field experts to attempt to shift stakeholder mind-sets in order to develop a common culture that fosters entrepreneurial and innovative spirits for trans-disciplinary collaborations.

The well documented interdependencies between food production and consumption procedures, environmental degradation, climate change, and unequal concentration of research in specific food areas provide the perfect recipe for additional and intricate challenges such as increased inequalities along socio-economic status (SES), caused mainly by increased stressors for farmers, disconnect between rural and urban areas, and conflicts related to natural resources (Gill et al., 2018). The many interdependencies, e.g., feedback loops, synergies, and trade-offs, not only between ecosystem members but also between the food ecosystem and other societal systems (e.g., technology and health ecosystems), can oftentimes lead to undesired side effects when specific interventions or innovations are introduced to particular sectors (Gill et al., 2018).

Therefore, not only do the traditional food production systems of 'make, use, and dispose' pose severe challenges to environmental sustainability and food security and nutrition, but their very nature, which remains significantly divided, poses significant challenges to current R&I efforts. The idea of food ecosystems as holistic organisms has yet to experience widespread adoption, and a segmented view of the food scenario from a research perspective, will produce segmented results.

The well-known need to transform the current nature of food systems has shifted to an urgent and active call to arms from food system members (Caron et al., 2018). Specifically, for the creation of holistic approaches that allow for the identification of inter-sectorial and individual power imbalances, that are inclusive of all stakeholders, and seek to involve even the most vulnerable members to shape innovations and interventions for the improvement of food systems (Gill et al., 2018).

A positive step in the right direction is the existing element of novelty that is inherent in conversations about food ecosystems; discussing ecosystems in itself, is quite novel since it is has recently been adopted as a metaphor for agricultural systems and their complex network of satellite systems that make the food system function as an organic whole (e.g., farmers, retail, processing, health systems,

5.2 Beyond Linearity in Food Supply Chains: Systems Thinking

environmental systems, and waste management). One principle that can be easily identified in food ecosystems is that they are essentially a collection, or network, of heterogeneous subsystems that are themselves heavily institutionalized (e.g., even though food and health ecosystems are interdependent, they often have little to do with each other in practice). When we discuss the notion of food ecosystems, the idea is to consider all of the moving parts and consolidate them, for example, not looking at excessive food access as a factor for obesity and lower health outcomes, without also taking into account where the food is produced and how it is delivered to consumers (e.g., short or extended supply chains). Ecosystems thinking also means producing food to be economically viable and environmentally sustainable, while also considering the people who will be purchasing, consuming, and disposing the food. Many attempts have been made to illustrate this complex process, and naturally, most depictions end up adopting a simplified and linear approach in their processes. One such example of a simplified linear representation of the food ecosystem is shown in Fig. 5.1.

Even in more complex depictions, however, the evident 'researcher' tendency is to try and make sense of complexity by breaking the whole system into smaller parts (Broerse, 2018).

As suggested by the research team at Food 2030, a more detailed way to look at food systems is through a lens of multi-functionality. Food ecosystems consist of heterogeneous factors, multiple levels, and a selection of diverse members that must be considered as moving parts of a larger whole, and as a system of complex dynamics. These dynamics, when not coordinated, result in trade-offs and synergies that are difficult to understand. It is a useful notion for authors and experts to

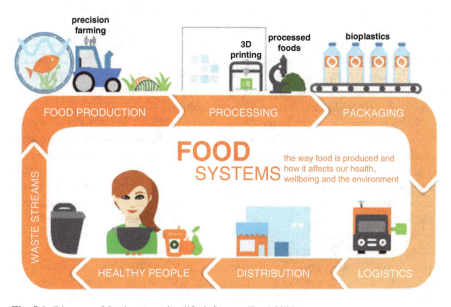

Fig. 5.1 Diagram of food system simplified. Source: Food 2030

appreciate that the complex dynamics of food systems, specifically, are far from being understood. As stated by a leading member of the Food 2030 research team, 'we can increase our understanding of the complexity, but we cannot truly understand it, it is too complex' (Broerse, 2018).

5.3 Resilience and Sustainability in Food Ecosystem

Resilience can be defined as the emergent characteristic of a system that encompasses the ability to absorb internal and external shocks and to adapt and transform in response to, and in anticipation of, these shocks (Béné, Newsham, Davies, Ulrichs, & Godfrey-Wood, 2014). Resilience, even though related to sustainability, is distinguished by its specific association with adaptation and transformation (Doherty, Ensor, Heron, & Prado, 2019; Folke et al., 2010). Based on these conceptualizations of resilience, we can conclude that its functionality depends on three distinct abilities, i.e. (i) absorptive capacity (enabling system persistence), (ii) adaptive capacity (enabling incremental system adjustments), and (iii) transformative capacity (enabling profound systems change by intentionally crossing thresholds).

When discussing resilience, scholars typically distinguish between 'engineering' and 'ecological' perspectives (Holling, 1996; Marchese et al., 2018; Walker & Cooper, 2018). In this chapter, we adopt the ecological perspective, which is rooted in the study of living systems, and is usually understood as complex, nonlinear, and adaptive. This concept of resilience has quickly infiltrated many areas of the social sciences, becoming a key concept in fields such as finance, banking, psychology, development, corporate strategy, education, public health, and now ecosystem management (Walker & Cooper, 2018). Through this view, the notion that a system has a single and static state is discarded and replaced with the idea that multiple interactions with complex natures are constantly transforming the ecosystem. For example, a natural lake may function as both a productive resource for fishing and cultivating certain plants, or may develop into a turbulent environment due to overfishing or uncontrolled nutrient runoff from farming.

When it comes to food ecosystems, resilience regards the amount of system shocks (internal and external) that can be absorbed before it is forced to change structures and functions. One example of current shocks to the food ecosystem includes the waning availability of natural resources, these excessive pressures have caused disturbances that are not linear, and involve many segments simultaneously trespassing the many thresholds, thus leading to a need for system wide transformation into a new and viable state. The social-ecological perspective of resilience is inherent of significant analytical potential, since a resilient social-ecological system has greater capacity to avoid unwelcome surprises and trade-offs resulting from external disturbances, and therefore has a greater capacity and increased certainty to continue to provide its intended goods and services that support quality of life; e.g., food ecosystems providing healthy and nutritious foods for all global communities (Doherty et al., 2019; Walker et al., 2006).

5.3 Resilience and Sustainability in Food Ecosystem

Resilience and sustainability appear as interchangeable concepts in the literature, but some authors discuss that it is more accurate to describe resilience as a required but insufficient condition for sustainability (Domptail & Easdale, 2013; Leach, Scoones, & Stirling, 2010). Resilience has thus been described as an essential means to promote sustainability, given that it implies a specific system's capacity to continue functioning in its intended way, over time, despite external or internal shocks (Tendall et al., 2015). Thus contributing to the evidence that resilience can serve as a vector to achieve sustainability. As argued by authors, efforts to achieve resilience toward sustainability should be adaptive and flexible, and open to knowledge sources from outside of the immediate ecosystem members in order to avoid 'lock-ins' (Leach et al., 2010). In this sense, a system's ability to adapt is central to resilience since this is a quality that truly reflects the learning aspects, and knowledge sharing behaviors of a system (Fait, Scorrano, Mastroleo, Cillo, & Scuotto, 2019; Robinson & Berkes, 2011).

In our case, the ecological perspective of resilience removes the idea that a food ecosystem has a single, normal state, and is replaced with the notion of continuous equilibrium as an ever-present component between ecosystem members and 'regime shifts' (Doherty et al., 2019).

This equilibrium further highlights the importance of adopting systems approach to engaging in resilience initiatives, especially in the food ecosystem. Integrating the countless food ecosystem functions, its accompanying environmental factors, interactions, and stress-related responses requires a systems approach to effectively address the context dependency of resilience in agricultural landscapes (Brock et al., 2018).

5.3.1 Barriers to Resilience

Barriers to resilience can be considered the existing consequences of mismatches between implicit an explicit food ecosystem stakeholder aims, and the structural, institutional, and informal obstacles (e.g., culture and behaviors) that impede their success.

Community engagement is not an easy task, and researchers have proposed Responsible Research and Innovation (RRI) in order to drive the sustainability agenda forward. RRI is an uncertain and somewhat unpredictable process that is value-based, and therefore allows for controversial debates about differences in individual values regarding food ecosystems. RRI suggests that some innovations will be more successful than others, namely the 'responsible ones'. The task of identifying which innovations will be successful is difficult in any type of ecosystem, especially when there is some uncertainty as to what exactly a 'responsible innovation' is, and who will be the stakeholders that get to determine this. This promotes questions on various levels of food ecosystems. Even though new avenues for food ecosystem transformation are being explored, we still witness gaps between RRI and how research funding in food ecosystems conceives innovation (Khan et al., 2016). There are a number of significant barriers both at governmental and organizational levels to fully disseminate RRI. These mostly relate to conflicting priorities and incentives agendas, but also simply to the lack of adequate resources to engage in RRI in food research and innovation (Martinuzzi, Blok, Brem, Stahl, & Schönherr, 2018).

In food ecosystems, attention is often directed to the potential for uncertainty, change, and cross-scale interactions (e.g., between geographic, institutional, or temporal scales). Under these circumstances, interventions can yield unanticipated results and impacts that occur in areas beyond their immediate intended application. This failure of 'command and control' approaches to provide predictable responses in the management of real, complex food ecosystems has in part driven research and policy agendas toward holistically assessing ecosystem resilience through systems thinking and RRI. Relational dimensions must also consider truly assessing the extent to which ecosystem members consider the needs and goals of others, including aspects such as trust, norms, and members' obligations and expectations (Fang, Tsai, & Lin, 2010; Tötterman & Sten, 2005).

Another well-documented barrier to achieving resilience in food ecosystems regards the uncertainty of starting a new venture or innovative business. As previously stated, entrepreneurs are the drivers of innovation who, in the food ecosystem context, face the challenge of coordinating a complex network of stakeholders while attending to individual and collective business uncertainties (York & Venkataraman, 2010). From an analysis of five longitudinal, inductive, in-depth case studies of startups and their innovation ecosystems, it was demonstrated that the current methods employed by entrepreneurs in these cases to cope with uncertainties go beyond the mainstream approaches to manage uncertainties, which are mostly individualistic in nature (De Vasconcelos Gomes, Salerno, Phaal, & Probert, 2018). Furthermore, this study revealed three aspects that characterize how entrepreneurs cope with uncertainties at the innovation ecosystem level. First, entrepreneurs initially focus on their own, individual, uncertainties, and entrepreneurs decide to consider uncertainties that affect the entire ecosystem partners when facing specific contingencies (e.g., achieving right market sales, difficulties with product performance, low investor willingness to invest in new technologies and products). Second, by engaging in uncertainty management in isolation (e.g., not paying mind to ecosystem partners), entrepreneurs themselves may contribute to the dissemination of uncertainties throughout the ecosystem to other individual members. Finally, similar behavior patterns were observed among the entrepreneurs that *do* engage in managing collective uncertainties, which are summarized in the following process: (i) Identifying collective uncertainties that affect many ecosystem members, (ii) building bridges between ecosystem uncertainties, and (iii) engaging in strategic action to mitigate these uncertainties through collective learning and instilling common goals (De Vasconcelos Gomes et al., 2018).

De Vasconcelos Gomes et al. (2018) further describe this process as the 'bridging uncertainties processes', and posit that this building of bridges occurs when entrepreneurs connect the many perceived uncertainties, into a collective uncertainty, even though individual ecosystem members may perceive this uncertainty differently. Finally, they conclude by suggesting that forming this collective view of uncertainty involves a high degree of exploration processes from entrepreneurs. Much like knowledge, individual uncertainties may spillover throughout innovation ecosystems and evolve into collective uncertainties that affect more than one ecosystem actor or sector; therefore by keeping procedures at business as usual, and failing to adopt a holistic mind-set, entrepreneurs themselves may be contributors to the propagation of uncertainties in innovation ecosystems.

Successful ecosystem members know best how to use the structure and the culture to their own advantage. The ones that lose out are the ones who don't know how to use the culture and structure. In a 'Darwinistic' sense, this also ensures resilience, and stability in the system, because the actors that stand out the most are likely to want to keep this culture and structure as it is because they stand to benefit from it.

5.4 Holistic Innovation and Entrepreneurship

Food ecosystem stakeholders have increasingly begun to stimulate transitions through R&I, but for some reason, the available initiatives have yet to yield the desired results. So what, or why, is this happening? To answer this question, we turn to the model of 'Diffusion of Innovations' that analyzes factors that influence the diffusion of an innovation (Greenhalgh, Robert, Macfarlane, Bate, & Kyriakidou, 2004). Some researchers suggest that this has to do with our traditional and linear approach to R&I, which is still the dominating method in most Western societies. These traditional approaches state that we can solve problems by breaking them into small parts (Lovett & Forbus, 2017). Even in highly rigorous research environments professional scholars engage in this linear type of problem solving, moving systematically from beginning to end, they begin with a grand challenge, then break it up into small parts, analyze the segments, and bring the fragmented solutions to the implementation phase, e.g. intervention, innovation, or policy, etc.

This approach, as identified by the Diffusion of Innovations theory, is viewed as the main contributor to reluctance in new innovation adoption from food ecosystem members. The adopters of innovations must be able to identify the perceived advantage, must be convinced through being able to try the product or service, be able to observe its simplicity and possible added value, and should be able to assess the innovation's compatibility to the environmental contexts and culture. The subject of compatibility is key for product adoption and can only be fully considered through a multi and trans-disciplinary perspective. Consumers want to identify what the relative advantage is when compared to other existing products, e.g., is the innovation in line with the contextual culture, values, and behaviors. Systems thinking helps developers assess if innovations fit with the manner consumers perceive things, the way the environment is structured, and the way expected consumers engage in diurnal activities.

The idea of adapting innovations to fit current behaviors is also a tricky discussion, since in order to tackle the global challenges to sustainability, we must aim to change producer and consumer behavior. Therefore, many of the innovations that are needed to reduce the threat of global challenges, are by nature incompatible with our current modus operandi, this means that the most effective innovations and their interventions will naturally face a lot of resistance from proponents of the current method of doing things (Broerse, 2018).

This points to a clear divide between what R&I propose to what society and policy require on two different levels. The first divide happens within industries when divisions or compartmentalization of challenges occur (e.g., tackling overfishing only at fisheries and fishing locations without consider the amount of sea food waste generated at large retailers or distributors). The second occurs between society and science, the combination of which leads to an implementation gap—which in the case of startups is referred to as the 'death valley', where innovative products and services fail to achieve market attraction. This second divide is recognizable throughout R&I in many sectors and is not specific to food ecosystems.

The European Commission's Food 2030 framework is the EU's R&I policy response to the growing international policy developments including the Sustainable Development Goals. It aims to find solutions to the challenges facing our current food systems such as climate change, limited resources, high levels of waste, and the triple threat of malnutrition (i.e., undernourishment, micro-nutrient deficiencies, and over nutrition) through R&I (Gill et al., 2018). Furthermore, it is built on the four key Food and Nutrition Security (FNS) priorities, i.e., (i) nutrition, (ii) climate, (iii) circularity, and (iv) innovation, and treats these priorities as necessary for EU food systems to become 'future proof', i.e., sustainable, resilient, responsible, competitive, diverse, and inclusive.

This integrated approach that considers the synergies between these four research areas further recognizes that, much like food ecosystems themselves, the traditional 'linear' R&I which studies properties of subsystems individually (e.g., consumer behavior, crop yields, animal safety) blindly assumes that improving conditions in one specific sector will lead to ecosystem wide benefits. This approach is of course limited due to the fact they fail to attribute sufficient consideration to the trade-offs, externalities, uncertainties, and systemic feedback loops (Zhang et al., 2018).

Currently, the R&I landscape is quite fragmented as academic disciplines and their researcher are often segmented into different colleges, which are then further broken down into discipline specific specialties, e.g., schools of medicine which further segment into pediatrics or internal medicine, and law schools which then further break down into criminal law or human rights laws. Innovations discovered and created by these highly specialized research teams have been able to successfully deal with individual compartmentalized challenges facing our food ecosystem, but have oftentimes neglected an integrated perspective, the active involvement of citizens, Civil Society Organizations (CSOs), and less influential food ecosystem members such as farmers and consumers (FEC, 2018; Gill et al., 2018).

Furthermore, academic incentive structures and R&I funding programs often give increased attention to food production-oriented research (SCAR, 2018), while the support for employing multi and trans-disciplinary approaches fails to gain equal momentum (FEC, 2018).

As previously mentioned, there is no 'one size fits all' approach to ensuring sustainable food ecosystem transformation; recommendations however suggest that researchers must seek to stimulate collaborations and adapt their practices based on the local makeup of their region, while always keeping in mind the convergence of regional and global priorities (Caron et al., 2018).

Although scholars agree that a food ecosystem transformation perspective should frame and guide the sustainable transitions, such a perspective is the exception rather than the rule in the field (El Bilali, 2019). Current R&I strategies are not equipped to deal with the persistent food system complexity, which leads researchers to ask what *is* needed?

Based on a speech by Broerse (2018), what is needed is to realize that we too need to change our thinking, as researchers and scientists, from traditional ways to systems thinking.

5.5 Systems Thinking for Food System Transformation

'Systems thinking' should be employed not only for effective business creations through entrepreneurship, but also as a guiding principle towards R&I for food ecosystem transformation. When it comes to R&I, systems thinking is described as a subjective process that focuses on recognizing the interconnection between parts of a system, then synthesizing them into a unified view of the whole (Broerse, 2018).

Furthermore, when analyzing food system sustainability education (FSSE), Valley and colleagues identified systems thinking, multi-inter- and trans-disciplinary use of experimental learning approaches, and participation in collective action projects as central themes within SSE signature pedagogy (i.e., the educational practices and disciplinary assumptions about that educational process are a relatively new phenomenon) (Valley, Wittman, Jordan, Ahmed, & Galt, 2018). These findings are backed by Hartmann and Siegrist (2017), who posit that in order to achieve more sustainable behavior, consumers and citizens need to have better knowledge about the environmental consequences of their food behavior.

Therefore systems thinking also means that when we try to develop new products and services, these must be research based and able to comprehend the system in which, and how, the intervention needs to function. Understanding the system will also help us anticipate the synergies and the trade-offs so that if we are going to try to and drive changes in one part of the system, we can predict where other inevitable changes will also occur (Woods, 2011). Taken together, this signifies that R&I cannot be fully effective if researchers cannot fully anticipate emerging trade-offs within food ecosystems. The turbulent nature of food ecosystems requires research approaches to also become more fluid and be ready to adapt to environmental conditions, which is difficult because most scientific disciplines instill strict protocols, where willingly changing research elements throughout the research process directly questions the quality and integrity of the research (Casadevall & Fang, 2016).

R&I in food ecosystems must therefore transition in order appreciate sets of problems, not attempt to break them apart, and look at the entirety of members and their interactions that might contribute to current challenges. This may begin with including food ecosystem and local community stakeholders at the beginning of research processes, considering them as consultants to inform the ongoing research processes, and therefore support the translation of emerging research results into practice and viable business creations that will be adopted by consumers and be considered market successes.

A holistic approach to R&I naturally encompasses the inclusion of every member of the ecosystem, and the European Commission provides the following five suggestions towards fostering inclusiveness in food ecosystems by 2030; (i) identify the best ways to integrate and innovate across various R&I disciplines, such as economics, finance, arts and social sciences, ecology, education, health, digital sciences, and connect them with traditional knowledge, (ii) frame connections within a multiple-objective mission-type approaches that lead to innovation-driven and socially relevant solution, (iii) provide place-based solutions in local settings and actions, offering integration and innovation capacity from a technical, institutional, and social viewpoint, (iv) promote stakeholder engagement across cultures and different innovation streams, and provide open spaces for collective intelligence, information and participation, transparency and accountability, mediation or arbitration, trade-offs and progress toward convergence, and (v) integrate technical innovation along with social and organizational innovation to systemically address challenges in the food system (European Commission, 2018). Figure 5.2 provides an illustration of this holistic approach to viewing food ecosystems, is a more complex depiction than previously demonstrated, and highlights all the ecosystem actors and segments that must be considered when embarking on R&I initiatives.

Furthermore, diversity has been cited as being more sustainable than homogeneity, and with Europe being an extremely diverse place in terms of culture, terrain, and business, efforts to maintain diversity must also be carefully assessed. Some action steps to ensuring this include (i) the development of more pluralistic and diverse European R&I programs that provide equal opportunities and representation for all members, (ii) business strategies in public and private business sectors that favor culturally relevant product and raw material diversification over the long-standing traditional methods, (iii) understanding the mechanisms and role of diversity, what are the policies and norms that can make diversity models more practical in global competition, and (v) explore and apply diversity across all related policies regarding food systems and their processes (European Commission, 2018).

For quite some time, researchers and field experts have acknowledged the need to transform our food ecosystem since it no longer fulfills its main goal of providing

5.5 Systems Thinking for Food System Transformation

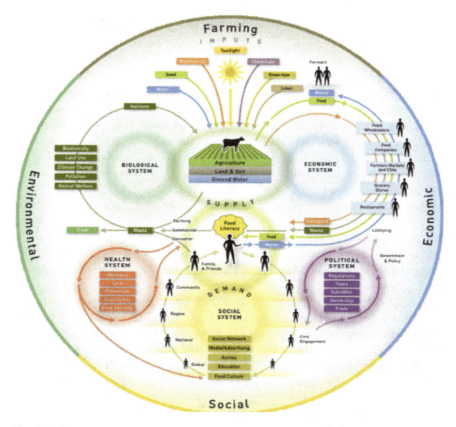

Fig. 5.2 Holistic model of food ecosystems. Source: NourishLife.Org (2019)

food security and nutrition, and it is currently threatened with persistent and emerging problems. Since R&I is usually the 'go to' method to improving the food system, we can assume in order to help food ecosystems become more systemic, then R&I must become more systemic as well. Therefore highlighting the need for a double transition.

When we look at the food ecosystem and the amount of funding that is invested from private sources to fund its research we see that it is fairly low. The main sources of funding for academic research comes in the form of open calls in many European countries (e.g., Horizon 2020). This process is problematic since national calls for research funding are considered a 'bottom-up' process where researchers and applications are mainly judged on academic excellence. One important fact to remember in this scenario is that excellence does not equal relevance, meaning that no matter how state-of-the-art or innovative a solution might be, if it is not connected to consumers and their overall needs then the solution will most likely fail (Broerse, 2018).

5.6 Responsible Research and Innovation (RRI) and Food Systems

R&I have provided people with the ability to alter ecosystems, the Earth's climate, and drive new technologies that improve everyday life. However, in parallel to the large positive impacts on human well-being and quality of life, R&I sometimes create new risks and ethical dilemmas. R&I as an instrument to solve the most pressing challenges with our food ecosystem is nothing new, this concept has been historically tasked with providing solutions to a spectrum of challenges (Cash et al., 2003; Godfray et al., 2010). However, up to date we have mostly witnessed innovations that, even though may be effective at resolving challenges in one area, oftentimes worsen problems in other areas (e.g., trade-offs). Perhaps due to a more interconnected society by way of emerging communication technologies (e.g., social network sites, email, cellphones, instant messaging, etc.), we are increasingly confronted with greater side effects that affect not only other parts of the food ecosystem itself, but also other ecosystems in general (e.g., health, transportation, employment).

Throughout the past years, many efforts have been proposed in attempts to reduce the distance between scientific research (e.g. R&I) and societies. Some of these efforts then culminated in the European-wide approach in Horizon 2020 called Responsible Research and Innovation (RRI). RRI seeks to bring issues related to research and innovation to light, to anticipate their unintended effects, and to include society in discussions about how R&I can help create a more sustainable food ecosystem.

RRI has emerged as the key framework for science and technology governance in addressing the limited attention to societal impact, and the lack of involvement of civil society in the R&I process. The concept outlines the need for mutual exchanges by which food ecosystem members become responsive to each other in the very early stages of the innovation process, and together facilitate the creation of ethically acceptable and sustainable innovation (Khan et al., 2016).

RRI is considered a dynamic, repetitious process where all stakeholders involved in the R&I practice become mutually responsive and share responsibility for the outcomes and process of R&I. RRI activities aim to unite the wide range of diverse actors and processes involved in R&I, and align them towards desirable, sustainable, and acceptable future outcomes (Ingram, 2011). The unification of different fields and areas of research is what paves the way for RRI, when research streams become inclusive, transparent, inter-sectorial, multi-stakeholder, multi-factorial, interdisciplinary, and trans-disciplinary; clearly moving R&I beyond the traditional linear models toward adopting a circular approach (Gill et al., 2018).

RRI means that every member of the food ecosystem works together during the entire R&I process to best align both processes and outcomes with the values, needs, and expectations of society (Von Schomberg, 2013). Thus, RRI helps us ask two very important questions; what type of innovations and what kind of economic or environmental conditions do we want? And who is the 'we' (Zwart, Landeweerd, &

Van Rooij, 2014)? In practice, RRI is implemented as a package that includes multi-actor and public engagement in R&I, enables easier access to scientific results, and stimulates strategic actions on thematic issues, i.e. public engagement, open access, gender ethics, and science education (European Commission, 2018b).

Furthermore, a recent study titled "A Report on Responsible Research and Innovation" summarized the five main points characterizing RRI (Sutcliffe, 2011), and described them as follows:

1. The deliberate focus of research and the products of innovation to achieve a social or environmental benefit.
2. The consistent, ongoing involvement of society, from beginning to end of the innovation process, including the public and non-governmental groups, who are themselves mindful of the public good.
3. Assessing and effectively prioritizing social, ethical and environmental impacts, risks and opportunities, both now and in the future, alongside the technical and commercial impact.
4. Where supervision mechanisms are better able to anticipate and manage problems and opportunities and to adapt and respond quickly to changing knowledge and circumstances.
5. Where openness and transparency are an integral component of the research and innovation process.

Furthermore, a concept that is essential to RRI is open science and open innovation (see Chaps. 4 and 5). Open science and open innovation seek to make scientific research, data collection and dissemination accessible to other scholars at various levels of society to better facilitate collaborations. It encompasses the full spectrum of practices to make knowledge sharing and communication easier. In the context of food and nutritional security, open science entails the development and implementation of 'open access' data infrastructures to allow different stakeholders to benefit from the 'big data revolution' in responsible ways. With the increasing access to large amounts of data regarding everyday topics involving individuals and institutions, open science is a critical component of RRI.

By adopting RRI and open innovation approaches, progress toward solutions of the grand societal challenges, e.g., SDGs and food security and nutrition, are expected to accelerate. Achieving a holistic system therefore implies the involvement of a wide variety of stakeholders and experts in the R&I processes. Being more responsible in R&I, and achieving RRI in food ecosystems means that they will become:

1. **Diverse and Inclusive**: Involve a wide range of actors that engage in R&I practice, deliberation, and decision-making to yield more useful knowledge.
2. **Anticipative and Reflective**: Envision impacts and acknowledges the underlying assumptions, values, and motives to understand how R&I will shape the future, which can happen through two main ways. The first, open and transparent—communication in significant ways through methods, results, and a community effect to enable public dialogue. The second—to be able to fully modify

traditional ways of thought or behaviors, and adapt overarching structures to evolving contexts, knowledge, and perspectives. Finally, RRI calls for specific attention to R&I activities to public engagement, gender equality, ethics, science education, and open science.

Given these two characteristics of RRI, one can see how it is quite an interesting approach to combine with 'systems thinking'. When adopting a combination of systems thinking and RRI approaches to R&I, one can more easily visualize all the stakeholders and dimensions that must be involved in the research process when truly adopting a systems approach (Gill et al., 2018).

It has been documented that the scientific knowledge and human capital necessary for developing innovative food products and services can be found internally through R&D or externally via collaboration with other firms in the food, or related systems (Sarkar & Costa, 2008). Unfortunately, cooperation and co-creation are not quite common in food ecosystems as in other sectors; this is in part due to the preference of confidentiality to protect new product formulations (Tanguy, 2016). However, this overprotection of intellectual property directly evidences how food ecosystem members may willingly ignore vital talent sources and thereby limit their innovation and entrepreneurial potential. Recent endeavors to ameliorate these challenges have resulted in researchers and field experts stimulating interactions between universities and food ecosystem members, since these interactions are considered an important element for product innovation (see Chap. 2).

However, the very nature of food ecosystem makes the initiation of these interactions a difficult concept. The food sector is composed of many SMEs, which naturally have fewer scientific and technological resources than large institutions. And while larger institutions have an increased capacity to launch product innovation due to their increased ability to invest in research and development (R&D) and capture knowledge they are known as 'late adopters' of innovative technologies and processes, and the food industry is general is classified as a low tech-sector (Lin, 2017; Triguero, Moreno-Mondéjar, & Davia, 2013). Therefore, a major remaining challenge is to improve our understanding of how, depending on their size, food institutions mobilize the scientific knowledge needed to innovate (Lascialfari, Magrini, & Triboulet, 2019). Studying the co-evolution of food consumption and agricultural production is crucial if we want to assess the impact of their contributions to food ecosystem transitions. Public, or community, support is also required to encourage these kinds of connections between the upstream and the downstream of value chains (Lascialfari et al., 2019).

The desire to achieve sustainable food systems supposes that stakeholders (e.g., researchers, farmers, manufacturers, and consumers) show a great degree of creativity, and open up to the possibilities of departing from traditional research and innovation practices (Meynard et al., 2017). Basically, the need to increase the effectiveness of R&I in food ecosystems requires much more than just empowering food system stakeholders with specialized skills, and more than the usual forms of coordination between major players, or trend setters, in the ecosystem (Meynard et al., 2017).

5.6 Responsible Research and Innovation (RRI) and Food Systems

In one of the first steps toward this agenda, Dunning, Bloom, and Creamer (2015) explored the possibilities for creating synergies between mainstream food systems with local food systems, by pairing localized procurement and distribution centers with mainstream super-market industry infrastructure to increase food system resiliency (Dunning et al., 2015). They undertook this initiative with the premise that mutually beneficial interactions to local food markets is one way to make food ecosystems more diverse, and allows them to function at multiple levels, thus enhancing ecological and community resilience (King, 2008). In their specific study, Dunning et al. (2015) were successful in demonstrating that researchers and scholars can leverage existing consumer demands for 'local food' as a strength to form partnerships between bigger industries and smaller retailers to drive effective change.

This seminal work to create public-private partnerships could be seen as a model for stimulating relationships amongst big and small food ecosystem members. Given the rapidly changing climatic conditions, increasing the diversification of production areas, products, and improving local and regional self-sufficiency can serve as effective antidotes to the growing challenges in key areas that could disrupt food supply chains, nutrition, and security as a whole. In the case of Dunning et al. (2015) they found that maintaining connections to a national distribution system may help smaller industries strengthen and supplement local food ecosystem during times of crises (Dunning et al., 2015).

These findings share complementarities with other works in the literature that evidence that efforts to mobilize science and technology for sustainability are more likely to be effective when they manage boundaries between knowledge and practice in ways that simultaneously enhance the salience, credibility, and legitimacy of the information they produce (Cash et al., 2003). Essentially, when food ecosystems apply a variety of institutional mechanisms that facilitate communication, translation, and mediation across boundaries is when they become effective actors toward sustainability.

Finally, there is a consensus among scholars that R&I regarding food need to be conducted in a holistic manner in order to capture the multiple activities, interactions, and outcomes associated with its production, exchange, consumption and governance (Ericksen, 2008; Gregory, Ingram, & Brklacich, 2005; Horton et al., 2017). This task however is much easier 'said than done' given the complexity of the food ecosystem and the various ways it interacts with other global ecosystems.

The migration from thinking about food systems as linear production machines to multi-faceted food ecosystems makes it easier to consider the entire 'value chain' from inputs, to primary production (e.g., agriculture, aquaculture, and fisheries), harvesting, processing, packaging, and waste management. This change in perception also considers more complex food ecosystem outputs than just the production of sufficient amounts of food for global populations, and adds the component of sustainability in all of its activities. To become future proof, food ecosystems need to become more resilient and be ready to function with the challenges posed by climate change, environmental sustainability of food production and consumption, nutrition related diseases, and trade and policy issues at the EU level that might interplay and affect their processes. A holistic food ecosystem approach can thus help leaders to more effectively organize discussions regarding how to make food systems more resilient and readily adaptable, and ensures that all the necessary stakeholders are engaged in these discussions.

Especially with food ecosystems, researchers must be diverse and inclusive in order to increase their capacity to reflect on activities and anticipate trade-offs. Ecosystems require diverse teams in order to tackle their complexity, and need to be open and transparent in order to effectively interact well, receive new knowledge as inputs, and deliver appropriate and tailored outputs.

5.7 Multi-level Innovation and Entrepreneurship

The overall literature on sustainability transitions emphasizes the importance and significance of radical innovations in a systemic perspective (Lachman, 2013). Innovations are deemed radical based on their degree of knowledge that must be understood by consumers and any associated learning barriers (Kline & Rosenberg, 1986). In acknowledging the fact that they are needed to reach sustainability goals, radical innovations have been analyzed through a combination of tangible and intangible factors such as technology, scientific knowledge, values, and practices (Rip & Kemp, 1998). In line with systems thinking, multiple dimensions of radical innovations have been found: i.e., (i) technological uncertainty (the degree to which the technology used in the innovative undertaking is not well developed or understood in by the scientific community), (ii) technological inexperience (a lack in the required technological experience and knowledge), (iii) business experience (the degree to which the firm lacks required business experience and knowledge, as is the case with many startups), and (iv) the technology development costs (Green, Gavin, & Aiman-Smith, 1995).

One of the most popular frameworks used by transition scholars is the Multi-Level Perspective (MLP) approach (Geels, 2014). The MLP is based on three levels (i) socio-technical landscape, (ii) socio-technical regime, and (iii) niche innovations. If we imagine the MLP as a top-down perspective, we find the socio-technical landscape that includes the socio-political context, environmental problems, demographics, and other global tendencies. The socio-technical regime is comprised of all the rules and behaviors that are responsible for the system's stability and reproduction. The niche innovations are at the bottom, and are grassroots for alternative socio-technical systems. These niches are composed of external actors, who are able to introduce new knowledge, and mobilize new skills that lead to more radical innovations, while the existing socio-technical system is locked-in to an incremental and linear innovation pathway (Rip & Kemp, 1998).

At the landscape level, we find the larger, or 'eco', trends, economic changes, and changes in the environment that put pressure on the regime to change. The niche level, on the other hand, is the level of experimentation; where actors, within the regime or outside actors experiment with new ways of working.

As proposed by Geels (2011), an important implication of MLP is that it moves beyond simple causality in transitions. With MLP, there is no single cause or driver, instead there are processes in multiple dimensions and at different levels which link up with, and reinforce each other. In a study conducted by Lascialfari et al. (2019) they combined literature from innovation emergence studies and built comprehensive guidelines to explore the multiple aspects of innovations. By combining MLP principles and insights from innovative transitions the authors drafted a group of six relevant questions that help us better understand the multiple dimension influencing innovation; (i) market/user preferences and culture, (ii) scientific knowledge, (iii) technology, (iv) industry infrastructure and networks, (v) policy-institutions, and (vi) niche innovations. Niche innovation refers specifically to niche actors in order to better understand their interactions, since MLP considers that they are the main drivers of radical innovations (Lascialfari et al., 2019). Finally the authors conclude by discussing that even though innovative products and services are launched by both incumbent and niche firms, the most radical innovations came from new small firms (e.g., startups). Furthermore, they demonstrate that product innovation is strongly influenced by consumer trends, with the most prominent example being the increased availability of vegetarian and flexitarian diets, the substitution between vegetable and animal proteins, and other tendencies toward more functional and health products to meet specific demands such as low-carb or gluten-free diets (Lascialfari et al., 2019). Most importantly however, they propose that still too few links exist between food system areas to foster sustainable transitions for the food ecosystem.

It can be considered common knowledge that every ecosystem has a regime; a dominant culture, structure, and practices that are shared by most members, but nonetheless remains unstable even though it is resilient and likes to remain unchanged. However a static nature of an ecosystem is not truly possible, due to the ever-evolving nature of ecosystems themselves, and the individual member interactions that shape this nature (Broerse, 2018).

5.8   Conclusions

When thinking about food in the context of food ecosystems, we can see that food is connected to a variety of fields such as agriculture, environment, energy, health, education, infrastructure, and planning (Gill et al., 2018). Given the threats of population growth, climate change, and the waning health of our natural resource base, broadening our R&I methods to be more systems-based and building public-private partnerships around shared interests and objectives are two key approaches that can be employed to address challenges to food ecosystem resiliency and sustainability (Dunning et al., 2015). Improving the adaptability to ever-changing environmental contexts, and the overall sustainability of food are also viewed as endeavors that can be accomplished without losing ground on the advantages provided with the current food production procedures. Selective engagement and strategic partnerships with large and smaller food businesses is one promising avenue to build stronger food ecosystems (Dunning et al., 2015). In fact, the food policy councils (FPCs) are argued to play a decisive role in strengthening urban-rural linkages, which is recognized as a key factor for promoting future-proof food ecosystems (Fattibene, Maci, & Santini, 2019).

As stated by Gill et al. (2018), systemic efforts to transform the food system need to take into account all three constituent elements of the food system (e.g., food environment, consumer behavior, and food supply chains), and must emphasize the need to re-connect a diversity of actors. Efforts have been made to develop toolkits and frameworks to help cities in their transformations toward more sustainable food systems, such as the City Region Food System Indicator Framework, by applying a 'whole food system approach' (FAO & RUAF). Sustainable food systems can be achieved through support for a systemic and integrated vision of technological, institutional, and social innovations, social inclusion, and wide stakeholder engagement, and specifically, future R&I initiatives need to be designed and implemented in this context. Reconnecting people to food systems needs evidence-based approaches that recognize the link between healthy diets and environmental sustainability (European Commission, 2018). The 2030 Agenda for Sustainable Development clearly shows that transition towards sustainable food systems is crucial to achieving sustainable development (El Bilali, 2019).

A better understanding of the linkages between food ecosystem sustainability (and consequently food ecosystem sustainability transitions) and food security is necessary to achieve 'future proof' food ecosystems. Any transition in food ecosystems, e.g. moving beyond efficiency-oriented and demand restraint narratives toward distribution of locally harvested foods, should strive to achieve sustainable food security and improved nutrition as its final outcome.

Large food organizations and institutions need to encourage a culture of collaboration, teamwork, and knowledge sharing (Tataj, 2015). Only through openness in innovation and knowledge can R&I anticipate and assess the potential implications and societal expectations with the aim of designing inclusive and sustainable R&I.

The discussed need for a systems approach, with specific attention to the relationships within food ecosystems, encompasses also the need for R&I to support this transformation. Furthermore, most R&I efforts have failed to adequately respond to the urgent and system wide challenges that threaten food sustainability. A reason for this includes the fact that much like linear ideas of food systems, R&I streams too suffer from compartmentalization, as we can clearly see in the divide between disciplines such as health, law, and engineering; each is a science that often times is segregated into specific schools, which are further broken down into sub-topics that make up the whole of the science (e.g., public health, occupational therapy, psychology, criminal law, human rights law, civil engineering, and chemical engineering to name a few).

Due to this divide between disciplines, those that do not actively seek out interdepartmental and multidisciplinary collaborations will produce R&I results that do not adequately appreciate the interconnectedness of the different parts of the food ecosystem. For example, much of the R&I produced by the European Union

5.8 Conclusions

is directed toward production processes and ensuring food security (i.e., quantitative food production). Furthermore, the Standing Committee on Agricultural Research (SCAR) conducted a qualitative and quantitative mapping of food related policies and food systems related to public R&I funds in EU member states, and found that overall R&I input for the food system is low, and there are not enough projects related to food consumption, household food waste, distribution methods, or their interaction with production processes, and food security (SCAR, 2018). From their assessment they go on to conclude that in order to achieve food systems transformation, there is an urgent need to directly engage consumers, citizens, and economic actors to a greater extent, given their central role (SCAR, 2018).

Furthermore as recommended by Gill and colleagues, the engagement of all stakeholders, shifting mindsets and approaches from mainstream linear models toward holistic approaches, and involving public and independent R&I could be an appropriate response to challenges regarding food ecosystems' complexity, and address the dominant and established pathways that are difficult to transform (Gill et al., 2018). Finally, during the Research and Innovation for Food and Nutrition Security, a high-level conference held at the Agricultural University of Plovdiv under the auspices of the Bulgarian Presidency of the Council of the European Union, it was agreed that supporting sustainable and nutritious diets, would guarantee a healthier future by decreasing the risk of chronic, non-infectious diseases, while assuring the sustainable use of resources and respecting planetary boundaries (European Commission, 2018). They go on to conclude that R&I initiatives should be better aligned since most initiatives that seek to address the challenges in food systems are largely conducted in a scattered manner and usually under a sector-oriented focus. They close with the following suggested actions: (i) Support Food 2030 R&I—through a multi-objective, cross-scale, inter- and trans-disciplinary, systemic, and integrated multi-stakeholder vision, (ii) Address the SDGs with a mission type approach, while simultaneously meeting human needs, respecting planetary boundaries, and attempting to close gaps between theoretical constructs and place-based projects, (iii) Provide evidence-based explanations for the associations between healthy diets and environmental sustainability, (iv) connect agricultural production with food manufacturing and consumer health through open innovation approaches, and (v) to provide a better understanding of the complexity of food systems, determine co-benefits, and how to reduce unwanted trade-offs.

Resilience in food systems, and in general, revolves around standing up to change (e.g., climate, technological, and societal) and mobilizing the correct stakeholders to understand the trade-offs, and applying the best governance models to overcome eventual shocks (European Commission, 2018). Resilience and food security is a complex issue that encompasses many vantage points and therefore must be embraced and applied throughout a wide range of ecosystem levels including cities and rural communities. This obviously includes aspects such as the role of cities in food systems transformation and innovation, the potential of new technologies, providing food from marine ecosystems, and the importance of international co-creation with neighboring regions (i.e., North Africa and the Balkans). However, resilience in food will also require a multi-faceted approach including individuating the best methods to integrate technical, social, and industrial innovation to address resiliency issues, redesign the specific type of R&I programs needed to re-orient our food ecosystems, and create networks, communities, or governance structures that attract new actors and that are trans-disciplinary in order to cultivate new knowledge on sustainable initiatives. Furthermore, closing the knowledge gap between science providers and consumers by means of ensuring equal communication and transparency are viewed as key for ensuring food system resilience (European Commission, 2018a).

References

Akhtar, Y., & Isman, M. B. (2018). Insects as an alternative protein source. In *Proteins in food processing* (pp. 263–288). Duxford: Woodhead Publishing.

Alexandratos, N., & Bruinsma, J. (2012). *World agriculture towards 2030/2050: The 2012 revision*. Rome: FAO.

Béné, C., Newsham, A., Davies, M., Ulrichs, M., & Godfrey-Wood, R. (2014). Resilience, poverty and development. *Journal of International Development, 26*(5), 598–623.

Bertoni, D., Cavicchioli, D., Donzelli, F., Ferrazzi, G., Frisio, D., Pretolani, R., … Ventura, V. (2018). Recent contributions of agricultural economics research in the field of sustainable development. *Agriculture, 8*(12), 200.

Brock, T., Bigler, F., Frampton, G., Hogstrand, C., Luttik, R., Martin-Laurent, F., … Rortais, A. (2018). Ecological recovery and resilience in environmental risk assessments at the European Food Safety Authority. *Integrated Environmental Assessment and Management, 14*(5), 586–591.

Broerse, J. (2018). *FIT4FOOD2030: System thinking, system innovation and system transformation* [Video presentation]. Retrieved from https://www.youtube.com/watch?v=z7RJjVldXs0

Caron, P., y de Loma-Osorio, G. F., Nabarro, D., Hainzelin, E., Guillou, M., Andersen, I., … Bwalya, M. (2018). Food systems for sustainable development: Proposals for a profound four-part transformation. *Agronomy for Sustainable Development, 38*(4), 41.

Casadevall, A., & Fang, F. C. (2016). *Rigorous science: A how-to guide*. Washington, DC: American Society for Microbiology.

Cash, D. W., Clark, W. C., Alcock, F., Dickson, N. M., Eckley, N., Guston, D. H., … Mitchell, R. B. (2003). Knowledge systems for sustainable development. *Proceedings of the National Academy of Sciences, 100*(14), 8086–8091.

Dankhade, T. S., Kazi, T. A., & Gophane, A. A. (2018). Alternative solutions over plastics. *International Journal of Electronics, Communication and Soft Computing Science & Engineering (IJECSCSE)*, 82–85.

De Bernardi, P., & Tirabeni, L. (2018). Alternative food networks: Sustainable business models for anti-consumption food cultures. *British Food Journal, 120*(8), 1776–1791.

De Bernardi, P., Bertello, A., & Venuti, F. (2019). Online and on-site interactions within alternative food networks: Sustainability impact of knowledge-sharing practices. *Sustainability, 11*(5), 1457.

De Bernardi, P., Bertello, A., & Venuti, F. (2020). Community-oriented motivations and knowledge sharing as drivers of success within food assemblies. In *Exploring digital ecosystems* (pp. 443–457). Cham: Springer.

De Bernardi, P., Bertello, A., Venuti, F., & Zardini, A. (2019). Knowledge transfer driving community-based business models towards sustainable food-related behaviours: A commons perspective. *Knowledge Management Research & Practice*, 1–8.

References

De Vasconcelos Gomes, L. A., Salerno, M. S., Phaal, R., & Probert, D. R. (2018). How entrepreneurs manage collective uncertainties in innovation ecosystems. *Technological Forecasting and Social Change, 128*, 164–185.

Doherty, B., Ensor, J., Heron, T., & Prado, P. (2019). Food systems resilience: Towards an interdisciplinary research agenda. *Emerald Open Research, 1*.

Domptail, S., & Easdale, M. H. (2013). Managing socio-ecological systems to achieve sustainability: A study of resilience and robustness. *Environmental Policy and Governance, 23*(1), 30–45.

Dunning, R., Bloom, J. D., & Creamer, N. (2015). The local food movement, public-private partnerships, and food system resiliency. *Journal of Environmental Studies and Sciences, 5*(4), 661–670.

EIT Food Strategic Agenda. (2019). *Strategic agenda 2018–2024*. Retrieved from https://www.eitfood.eu/media/documents/EIT-StrategicAgenda-Booklet-A4-Final_disclaimer.pdf

El Bilali, H. (2019). Research on agro-food sustainability transitions: Where are food security and nutrition? *Food Security, 11*(3), 559–577.

Ericksen, P. J. (2008). Conceptualizing food systems for global environmental change research. *Global Environmental Change, 18*(1), 234–245.

European Commission. (2018a). *Research and innovation for food and nutrition security. Transforming our food systems 2nd food 2030 high level event: Conference outcome report, 14–15 June 2018 in Plovdic (Bulgaria)*. Retrieved from https://publications.europa.eu/en/publication-detail/-/publication/d0e51873-4478-11e9-a8ed-01aa75ed71a1/language-en/format-PDF/source-search

European Commission. (2018b). *Responsible research and innovation*. Retrieved from https://ec.europa.eu/programmes/horizon2020/en/h2020-section/responsible-research-innovation

Fait, M., Scorrano, P., Mastroleo, G., Cillo, V., & Scuotto, V. (2019). A novel view on knowledge sharing in the agri-food sector. *Journal of Knowledge Management, 23*(5), 953–974.

Fang, S. C., Tsai, F. S., & Lin, J. L. (2010). Leveraging tenant-incubator social capital for organizational learning and performance in incubation programme. *International Small Business Journal, 28*(1), 90–113.

FAO. (2018). *Outcome of the regional symposium on sustainable food systems for healthy diets in Europe and Central Asia*. Retrieved from http://www.fao.org/3/mw166en/mw166en.pdf

FAO. (2019). *Save food: Global initiative on food loss and waste reduction*. Retrieved from http://www.fao.org/save-food/resources/keyfindings/en/

Fattibene, D., Maci, G., & Santini, G. (2019). *Feeding cities. Putting food on the urban planning agenda*. European Think Tanks Group (ETTG).

FEC. (2018). *For whom? Questioning the food and farming research agenda*. London: Good Ethics Council. Retrieved from https://www.foodethicscouncil.org/programme/democratising-food-farming-research/

Fischer, J., Gardner, T. A., Bennett, E. M., Balvanera, P., Biggs, R., Carpenter, S., . . . Luthe, T. (2015). Advancing sustainability through mainstreaming a social–ecological systems perspective. *Current Opinion in Environmental Sustainability, 14*, 144–149.

Folke, C., Carpenter, S., Walker, B., Scheffer, M., Chapin, T., & Rockström, J. (2010). Resilience thinking: Integrating resilience, adaptability and transformability. *Ecology and Society, 15*(4), 20.

Geels, F. W. (2011). The multi-level perspective on sustainability transitions: Responses to seven criticisms. *Environmental Innovation and Societal Transitions, 1*(1), 24–40.

Geels, F. W. (2014). Regime resistance against low-carbon transitions: Introducing politics and power into the multi-level perspective. *Theory, Culture and Society, 31*(5), 21–40.

Gill, M., Den Boer, A. C. L., Kok, K. P., Cahill, J., Callenius, C., Caron, P., . . . Lappiere, A. (2018). *A systems approach to research and innovation for food system transformation*. Retrived from https://arrow.dit.ie/cgi/viewcontent.cgi?article=1001&context=resdiroth

Godfray, H. C. J., Beddington, J. R., Crute, I. R., Haddad, L., Lawrence, D., Muir, J. F., . . . Toulmin, C. (2010). Food security: The challenge of feeding 9 billion people. *Science, 327*(5967), 812–818.

Green, S. G., Gavin, M. B., & Aiman-Smith, L. (1995). Assessing a multidimensional measure of radical technological innovation. *IEEE Transactions on Engineering Management, 42*(3), 203–214.

Greenhalgh, T., Robert, G., Macfarlane, F., Bate, P., & Kyriakidou, O. (2004). Diffusion of innovations in service organizations: Systematic review and recommendations. *The Milbank Quarterly, 82*(4), 581–629.

Gregory, P. J., Ingram, J. S., & Brklacich, M. (2005). Climate change and food security. *Philosophical Transactions of the Royal Society B: Biological Sciences, 360*(1463), 2139–2148.

Hartmann, C., & Siegrist, M. (2017). Insects as food: Perception and acceptance. Findings from current research. *Ernahrungs-Umschau, 64*(3), 44–50.

Holling, C. S. (1996). Engineering resilience versus ecological resilience. *Engineering Within Ecological Constraints, 31*(1996), 32.

Horton, P., Banwart, S. A., Brockington, D., Brown, G. W., Bruce, R., Cameron, D., . . . Jackson, P. (2017). An agenda for integrated system-wide interdisciplinary agri-food research. *Food Security, 9*(2), 195–210.

Ingram, J. S. I. (2011). *From food production to food security: Developing interdisciplinary, regional-level research.* Retrieved from https://library.wur.nl/WebQuery/wurpubs/fulltext/176450

Khan, S. S., Timotijevic, L., Newton, R., Coutinho, D., Llerena, J. L., Ortega, S., . . . Urban, C. (2016). The framing of innovation among European research funding actors: Assessing the potential for 'Responsible research and innovation' in the food and health domain. *Food Policy, 62*, 78–87.

King, C. A. (2008). Community resilience and contemporary agri-ecological systems: Reconnecting people and food, and people with people. *Systems Research and Behavioral Science: The Official Journal of the International Federation for Systems Research, 25*(1), 111–124.

Kline, S. J., & Rosenberg, N. (1986). *An overview of innovation. The positive sum strategy: Harnessing technology for economic growth.* Washington, DC: The National Academy of Science.

Lachman, D. A. (2013). A survey and review of approaches to study transitions. *Energy Policy, 58*, 269–276.

Lascialfari, M., Magrini, M. B., & Triboulet, P. (2019). The drivers of product innovations in pulse-based foods: Insights from case studies in France, Italy and USA. *Journal of Innovation Economics Management, 1*, 111–143.

Leach, M., Scoones, I., & Stirling, A. (2010). Governing epidemics in an age of complexity: Narratives, politics and pathways to sustainability. *Global Environmental Change, 20*(3), 369–377.

Lin, J. (2017). *Innovation in low-tech industries – An example of the food industry in China.* Retrieved from http://lup.lub.lu.se/luur/download?func=downloadFile&recordOId=8917545&fileOId=8917546

Lovett, A., & Forbus, K. (2017). Modeling visual problem solving as analogical reasoning. *Psychological Review, 124*(1), 60.

Marchese, D., Reynolds, E., Bates, M. E., Morgan, H., Clark, S. S., & Linkov, I. (2018). Resilience and sustainability: Similarities and differences in environmental management applications. *Science of the Total Environment, 613*, 1275–1283.

Martinuzzi, A., Blok, V., Brem, A., Stahl, B., & Schönherr, N. (2018). Responsible research and innovation in industry—challenges, insights and perspectives. *Sustainability, 10*(3), 702.

Meynard, J. M., Jeuffroy, M. H., Le Bail, M., Lefèvre, A., Magrini, M. B., & Michon, C. (2017). Designing coupled innovations for the sustainability transition of agrifood systems. *Agricultural Systems, 157*, 330–339.

NourishLife.Org. (2019). *Food systems map.* Retrieved from https://www.nourishlife.org/teach/food-system-tools/

Rip, A., & Kemp, R. (1998). Technological change. *Human Choice and Climate Change, 2*(2), 327–399.

References

Robinson, L. W., & Berkes, F. (2011). Multi-level participation for building adaptive capacity: Formal agency-community interactions in northern Kenya. *Global Environmental Change, 21*(4), 1185–1194.

Rockström, J., Sukhdev, P. (2016). *Keynote speech: Prof. Johan Rockström & CEO Pavan Sukhdev* [Video file]. Retrieved from https://www.stockholmresilience.org/research/research-news/2016-06-14-how-food-connects-all-the-sdgs.html

Rundgren, G. (2016). Food: From commodity to commons. *Journal of Agricultural and Environmental Ethics, 29*(1), 103–121.

Sarkar, S., & Costa, A. I. (2008). Dynamics of open innovation in the food industry. *Trends in Food Science & Technology, 19*(11), 574–580.

SCAR. (2018). *Assessment of research and innovation on food systems by European Member States Policy and Funding Analysis*. Retrieved from https://ec.europa.eu/research/bioeconomy/pdf/publications/Assessment_of_R_and_I_on_food_systems.pdf

Sutcliffe, H. (2011). *A report on responsible research and innovation*. http://ec.europa.eu/research/science-society/document_library/pdf_06/rri-report-hilary-sutcliffe_en.pdf

Tanguy, C. (2016). Cooperation in the food industry: Contributions and limitations of the open innovation model. *Journal of Innovation Economics Management, 1*, 61–86.

Tataj, D. (2015). *Innovation and entrepreneurship. A growth model for europe beyond the crisis*. New York: Tataj Innovation Library.

Tendall, D. M., Joerin, J., Kopainsky, B., Edwards, P., Shreck, A., Le, Q. B., ... Six, J. (2015). Food system resilience: Defining the concept. *Global Food Security, 6*, 17–23.

Tötterman, H., & Sten, J. (2005). Start-ups: Business incubation and social capital. *International Small Business Journal, 23*(5), 487–511.

Triguero, A., Moreno-Mondéjar, L., & Davia, M. A. (2013). Drivers of different types of eco-innovation in European SMEs. *Ecological Economics, 92*, 25–33.

Valley, W., Wittman, H., Jordan, N., Ahmed, S., & Galt, R. (2018). An emerging signature pedagogy for sustainable food systems education. *Renewable Agriculture and Food Systems, 33*(5), 467–480.

Von Schomberg, R. (2013). A vision of responsible research and innovation. In *Responsible innovation: Managing the responsible emergence of science and innovation in society* (pp. 51–74).

Vrontis, D., Bresciani, S., & Giacosa, E. (2016). Tradition and innovation in Italian wine family businesses. *British Food Journal, 118*(8), 1883–1897.

Walker, J. J., & Cooper, M. K. (2018). Resilience. In *Companion to environmental studies* (Vol. 90, No. 94, pp. 90–94). ROUTLEDGE in Association with GSE Research.

Walker, B., Gunderson, L., Kinzig, A., Folke, C., Carpenter, S., & Schultz, L. (2006). A handful of heuristics and some propositions for understanding resilience in social-ecological systems. *Ecology and Society, 11*(1), Art. 13.

Woods, D. D. (2011). Resilience and the ability to anticipate. In *Resilience engineering in practice: A guidebook* (pp. 121–125). Boca Raton, FL: CRC Press.

York, J. G., & Venkataraman, S. (2010). The entrepreneur–environment nexus: Uncertainty, innovation, and allocation. *Journal of Business Venturing, 25*(5), 449–463.

Zhang, W., Gowdy, J., Bassi, A. M., Santamaria, M., deClerck, F., Adegboyega, A., ... Darknhofer, I. (2018). Systems thinking: An approach for understanding 'Eco-agri-food systems'. In *TEEB for agriculture and food: Scientific and economic foundations report: Work in progress*. Geneva: UN Environment.

Zwart, H., Landeweerd, L., & Van Rooij, A. (2014). Adapt or perish? Assessing the recent shift in the European research funding arena from 'ELSA' to 'RRI'. *Life Sciences, Society and Policy, 10*(1), 11.

Chapter 6
Startups and Knowledge Sharing in Ecosystems: Incumbents and New Ventures

The value of an idea lies in the using of it.
Thomas A. Edison

Abstract The daily challenges that are created by our global food systems are in need of novel solutions that cannot be found within established companies or large organizations. Efforts to transition food systems toward more sustainable processes and behaviors have usually been executed via a top-down approach through legislations or by introducing new products or services, albeit without consumer engagement. These efforts have yielded unremarkable results, and thus new bottom-up, or consumer centered and collaborative efforts are warranted. A startup is a newly emerged and fast-growing business seeking to meet the marketplace by developing a business model around an innovative idea. The projects pursued by startups are very risky, so their survival rates are quite low. However, the startups that survive and succeed may have large economic impacts. In this chapter we discuss how food startups engage with larger food companies to deliver increased value to consumers and ameliorate societal issues. We further provide a sort of 'route map' for startup founders to prepare to get their innovations to market. Finally, research streams have identified that neither investigating entrepreneurs and their psychological characteristics, nor investigating the contextual elements surrounding startups and entrepreneurs provide a clear explanation for successful development of startups. Based on these findings we suggest that future research seeking to explain the startup journey should analyze both individual entrepreneurial characteristics, as well as the contextual environment where they operate.

Keywords Food startup · Knowledge sharing · Market research · Startup phases · Value creation

© Springer Nature Switzerland AG 2020
P. De Bernardi, D. Azucar, *Innovation in Food Ecosystems*, Contributions to Management Science, https://doi.org/10.1007/978-3-030-33502-1_6

6.1 Introduction

Global food ecosystems put a never-ending strain on the planet. Food production and consumption, for example, contribute to 19–29% of global greenhouse gas (GHG) emissions (Vermeulen, Campbell, & Ingram, 2012). Providing food and nutritional security requires a considerable amount of resources such as fertile land, energy, and fresh water supplies, all while the total surface of arable land is constantly shrinking. Our current food systems, due to growing populations and increased technologies to enhance human connectivity, are in desperate need of a transformation to make sure it utilizes Earth's resources not for simply producing sufficient amounts of food, but also for making products and services that provide meaningful value to communities' everyday lives, while simultaneously reducing the strain on, and protecting the planet's resources. Therefore, it is clear that food ecosystems are in need of more than just better production and consumption practices, they also require innovations that increase the appreciation of the food that has been produced. Many problems and challenges exist in achieving this overarching goal, and this is evidenced by the Food and Agriculture Organization (FAO) that reports that one-third of all globally food produced gets lost through expiration or wasted by consumers (FAO, 2019).

In addition to the environmental challenges posed by food ecosystems, the World Health Organization (WHO) cites a tripled increase in obesity since 1975. In 2016, for example, 39% of adults over the age of 18 were overweight and 13% were obese (WHO, 2018). This is alarming since obesity is linked to a range of associated health problems, from cardiovascular disease, to diabetes and cancer, to the actual physical immobility of individuals (Forhan & Gill, 2013). Interestingly, while the availability of food and caloric intake is no longer an issue for most societies, quality nutrition is.

Research suggests a link between traditional modus operandi of food ecosystems that aims to provide access to food to all populations, sometimes through highly processed foods that can cause adverse health outcomes due to the existing levels of sugar, salt, and fat (Cordain et al., 2005)

Furthermore, the negative impacts of our food ecosystem are not limited to natural resource degradation and nutritional health. With its complex interdependencies, a wide range of social issues emerge from food ecosystems, such as low pay and forced labor, low acceptability of new innovation (e.g., GMOs, meat substitutes, insects as food), gender inequality, and many more (Taub, Minch-Dixon, & Gridley, 2019). In essence, the food ecosystem does not need any new businesses, but more sustainable food businesses either through innovative redesigns of incumbent food sector businesses, or by introducing new ventures (startups) to that provide novel products and services to ameliorate problems.

One avenue that merits exploration is that of 'agri-FoodTech', which is the emergent sector "exploring how technology can be leveraged to improve efficiency and sustainability in designing, producing, choosing, delivering & enjoying food"; basically, this represents all the innovations, mostly driven by startups, that aim to improve the food ecosystem with a final goal of making it more sustainable. This model of innovation that harnesses the flexibility and adaptability of young businesses and startups is a promising sector for future global economies. For example, in 2018 alone, around 16 billion Euros were invested in Agri-FoodTech companies across 1450 deals, overall representing a 40% increase compared to 2017 (AgFunder, 2019). In European food ecosystems, some of the biggest supporters of Agri-FoodTech were the UK and France, with around 300 million and 290 million Euros raised in 2018.

Many authors posit that there is a misconception that innovation automatically translates to technology, and that some sort of digital aspects must be involved to be truly innovative. In reality, innovation can happen anywhere, with little or no technology or including very intricate digital systems (Tataj, 2015). Due to this lay-mans perspective of startups, for the rest of the text the term *startup* is used a representation of the range of startups in the food ecosystem, ranging from those high on technological aspects and digitization, to those with traditional business models that are organized in innovative ways.

Product innovation is a complex process as several innovations are often implemented together, involving new products, processes, marketing approaches, organizational methods, and internal or external network interactions (OECD, 2018).

With the organizational evolution, triggered by diversification of markets and increasing unpredictability of consumer demands, the mass model was replaced by flexible models (Cohen & Zysman, 1987). These new flexible models were manifested by different approaches, such as mass-customization, craftsmanship model, and dynamic flexibility. These new approaches to production, not based on mass quantity but on personal consumer preference led to an eventual decentralization of large companies, and the rise in importance of small companies and startups as critical agents of innovation (Tataj, 2015).

As the global ecosystem is projected to reach a worth of over 700 billion Euros by 2020 new perspectives and emerging solutions are needed, and startups have emerged as the driving forces of the upcoming future. Innovative ideas might already exist, but often it's startups that create viable business models for these ideas. For example, meat replacements, initiatives to reduce food waste, food safety, technological innovations and personal nutrition plans; all of which are innovation that provide marked benefits to food ecosystems (Foodware, 2019).

Entrepreneurship has often been described as the glue behind knowledge triangles (i.e. research, education, and innovation), and the driver of innovations. Innovations introduced by entrepreneurs usually begin with an idea, and their business creation process begins when they take the necessary steps to eventually raise a startup into a small and medium enterprise (SME).

In public policy and economy, entrepreneurship is referred to as a sector of small and medium-sized companies (Tataj, 2015). EUROSTAT further defines SMEs as "businesses with less than 250 employees, with a total turnover not exceeding 50 million Euro, or a balance sheet total not exceeding 43 million Euro, and that are independent" (EUROSTAT, 2003). Furthermore, there are actually a small number of highly successful entrepreneurs, and most businesses remain small even after surviving the 'valley of death', i.e. the time between when a startup receives initial funding to when it is adopted by consumers and begins generating revenues that are sufficient enough to cover its own costs and be self-sustaining (Tataj, 2015). This reluctance in consumer adoption is most often attributed to a disconnect between the value that is proposed by new innovations and what consumers actually want (De Jong, Gillert, & Stock, 2018).

However, consumer buy-in for economic benefit should not be the end goal of startups, but an essential component in their business creation process. For example, startup founders should seek customers that can serve as consultants and validate their ideas at the earliest stage of development possible. As Lynde (2018) states—"The greatest learning is derived from solving real problems with real customers—that's the foundation of any great innovation." Much like most initiatives that adopt systems change, there is also no one formula to provide the adequate type of support for startups, however, some authors have put forth suggestions for effective support systems based on their developmental stage—(i) early, (ii) mid-stage, and (iii) advanced (Taub et al., 2019).

(i) Early Stage:

  (a) Online tools: Guides to help startups develop their business models.
  (b) Legal and accounting support: Economical, or budget friendly, accounting support to help new startups get registered and establish accounting practices.
  (c) Hackathons: Network of events across Europe to help aspiring entrepreneurs find solutions to pressing challenges in the food ecosystem.
  (d) Mentors and Networks: A process of online and offline interactions where entrepreneurs meet individuals who are key to their development.
  (e) Entrepreneurial Training: Practical training for startups to help them develop the necessary skills to be successful.

(ii) Mid Stage:

  (a) Innovation Grants: Funding that startups need in order to get their new products or services to market.
  (b) Co-working spaces in offices, farms, and factories: Places like these help entrepreneurs develop their businesses surrounded by stimulating environments.
  (c) Demo Days: A series of events where startups and their members can present their business idea and meet stakeholders from their industry of interest (e.g., investors, industry partners).
  (d) Incubators: Developmental programs for startups with a durations of a few weeks that grants entrepreneurs the tools, resources, knowhow, and networks to test their idea with potential customers.

(iii) Advance Stage:

  (a) Accelerator Networks: Programs that help startups grow and disrupt the food system. Here, entrepreneurs meet with industry professionals who help fix any possible issues and attempt to design startups to perfection. Usually the best performing startups throughout this process earn prize money as funding.

(b) Business Services: A portfolio of business services to help European startups grow including access to large networks of investors.

(c) Specialized industry networks: In our case, in food ecosystems, the Rising Food Star program can be a great example. It is a network of agri-food startups in Europe that can participate in large-scale, and European funded innovation projects with larger governing bodies (e.g., EIT Food).

The importance of food startups and the great positive impact they can provide to food ecosystems is becoming increasingly known at the European level. One example of this realization is the creation of European Institute of Innovation & Technology (EIT) Food; a consortium of food system stakeholders who, in 2019 is projected to invest 56.4 million Euros in innovative food projects, which is an increase of 44% compared to 2018. The EIT has set goals such as making the food chain more sustainable, improving customer confidence and informing customers about making healthier choices. The belief that startups play an important role in achieving these goals is clear (Foodware, 2019).

6.2 Knowledge into Practice

Applying science and implementing both incremental improvements and breakthrough technology has played a vital role as a driving force behind innovation and startups (Tataj, 2015).

Lascialfari, Magrini, and Triboulet (2019) indicate that innovative products can be launched both by incumbent and niche firms, but that the most radical innovations come from new small firms (Lascialfari et al., 2019). SMEs and startups form a significant component of a country's economy due to their potential to help amelioratee issues such as poverty, income inequality and unemployment (Ayyagari, Demirguc-Kunt, & Maksimovic, 2011). It is not uncommon for SMEs to create relationships with others as a way to achieve greater value creation with limited strain on their resources—a process referred to as co-opetition (Mitev, de Vaujany, Laniray, Bohas, & Fabbri, 2019). This process occurs when competitors, or units of competing organizations, become partners in strategic alliances united by the specifications and purpose of a project in which they have mutually agreed to participate. This tangible and tacit knowledge constitutes their value in their respective ecosystem and protects their interests.

It is no longer an individual company, but interdisciplinary collaborations that hold the element of competitiveness in industries; oftentimes linked by a number of multi-party contractual agreements limited to achieving a particular objective over a specified period of time. Due to this, young entrepreneurs should do as much diligence and research on potential investors and partners, as they are doing on them (Lynde, 2018). Thus assisting entrepreneurs in aligning themselves and their startups with larger organizations that share the same mission, values, and beliefs and can therefore more fittingly assist the startup's evolution.

Furthermore, the relationships that entrepreneurs engage in with investors may be some of the most important relationships they will build throughout the startup creation cycle; mainly due to the financial capital they can provide. Without capital that accepts the risk of investing in innovation, there is little chance that new knowledge turns into innovative businesses (Tataj, 2015).

The food ecosystem and its associated challenges call for knowledge sharing practices to enhance businesses' performance. Knowledge sharing has been evidenced to be influenced to a great deal by outcome expectation, e.g., personal and community expectations, and three forms of dimensions of social exchange; (i) structural, (ii) relational, and (iii) cognitive (Fait, Scorrano, Mastroleo, Cillo, & Scuotto, 2019). These findings further highlight the importance of aligned company and startup values for knowledge sharing, and also evidence that knowledge sharing is facilitated when stakeholders perceive that a personal or communal benefit will arise from the interaction.

6.3 Startups and High Growth Firms (HGFs)

Not all entrepreneurs approach their ventures in the same way, and important distinctions have been made between ventures that interact with the entrepreneurial ecosystem in terms of their speed of development, namely high growth firms (HGFs) and more traditional startups.

The organization for Economic Co-operation and Development defines HGFs as 'enterprises with average annualized growth greater than 20% per annum, over a 3 year period (OECD, 2018); therefore the main characteristic of HGFs, as its name states, is rapid growth (Fuentelsaz, Maícas, & Mata, 2018). Furthermore, a distinctive feature of HGFs is their innovative capability. A major difference between HGFs and traditional startups is the importance given to innovation for their growth (Coad & Rao, 2008). Furthermore, Frederiksen (2018) identifies six characteristics of HGF's that other startups should consider adopting, in summary he suggests that HGFs:

1. Conduct systemic, structured research at least annually to understand target market and consumers.
2. Tend to be specialized:

    (a) Offering specialized services.
    (b) Focusing on specific industries and business issues.

3. Invest significantly in marketing undertaking a variety of tactics and strategies.
4. "Productize" their services.
5. Target new markets.
6. Invest in the training and development of their personnel.

The journey for startups from idea to viable business is anything but straightforward, and entrepreneurs are encouraged to adopt systems thinking in order to effectively appraise the different contextual elements found throughout each phase of their development (Taub et al., 2019).

"Creating your business is not an easy endeavor, if it was then everyone would do it". Due to this simple truth, entrepreneurs are encouraged to work on something that they are passionate about, instead of going for the 'low-hanging' fruit in search of any market opportunity. Research shows that entrepreneurs who think solely about the long-term financial gain, will eventually burn out and will not endure the many setbacks and re-designs that are innate of entrepreneurial endeavors. Due to these factors, two recommendations are proposed for young entrepreneurs wanting to 'startup' (Taub et al., 2019).

1. Creating a startup is time intensive. Much of the entrepreneur's time is spent on activities such as sales, marketing, customer service, networking, business strategy development, and other administrative tasks. So even when a startup aims to ameliorate a problem the entrepreneur is passionate about, they should be cautious and prepared to spend a lot of time on tasks that might seem secondary, but in reality are the foundation for the success of their idea. As a business owner, entrepreneurs must get comfortable with being uncomfortable and willing to embrace uncertainty.
2. Its important for entrepreneurs to be personally invested in what they do, but field experts caution against falling in love with their own idea. Holding any original idea to such a high esteem prevents entrepreneurs from accepting constructive feedback and making any necessary adjustments to their idea. Entrepreneurs are encouraged to get feedback as early as possible, and listen to consumer feedback without taking any possible negative comments personally.

At the initial phase of creating a startup, entrepreneurs are recommended to equip themselves with as much knowledge as possible (Politis, 2008). Entrepreneurs should aim to understand what waits them and have some understanding on general business concepts (Table 6.1). Importantly, besides diving into the literature, another method to generate knowledge about the field and their startup idea itself is to talk to as many as people about the startup and its goals. Many entrepreneurs might feel the need for secrecy regarding their idea, but one thing to keep in mind is that most people do not understand 'business', and there is quite some variation between having an idea an actually executing it. Finally, starting a business requires many disciplines, and as the founders of startups entrepreneurs need to be informed, or at least understand the following concepts.

Furthermore, creating a startup and giving rise to a viable business is a complex process filled with a plethora of uncertainties. With this in mind, entrepreneurs are encouraged to consider whether their startup development should be a solo task (Table 6.2), or something that requires co-founders.

Finally, when working with partners, it is important to reflect and clarify if both founders are equally committed to the success of the startup, what is the dynamic between the founders, and do they have complementary skills?

Creating a sustainable business and transforming the food system is a difficult task. An undertaking that is not only necessary to meet the needs of future

Table 6.1 Business concepts 101

Strategy: This refers to determining how your company will achieve its objectives and vision for the next few years. It's essential to plan how you will do things
Accounting: This is the process of keeping financial accounts and recording transactions in your business such as what goes in (revenue) and what goes out (expenses)
Financing: The process of obtaining or providing capital (i.e.: money) to fund business activities
Sales: The backbone of any business. Without sales, you cannot have revenue and turn a profit, meaning you cannot survive
Marketing: The process of promoting and selling products and services. This includes disciplines like advertising, PR, and pricing strategies
Operations: Refers to functions relating to how products and services are made, like managing your supply chain and logistics
Human resources: Refers to people management, taking care of your team
Return on investment (ROI): This refers to how much benefit is derived as a result of an investment. This tends to refer to a financial return, though it can refer to wider returns (environmental, social) in the case of sustainable companies. Investors will be looking to understand what kind of return they can expect if they invest in your business
Supply and demand: Every market is composed of a supply side and a demand side. The supply side consists of sellers, people or businesses selling products and services, and the demand side refers to buyers, people (consumers) or businesses buying products and services. As an entrepreneur, you should see yourself on the supply side as it's what you sell that will determine your business's success. You'll of course be on the demand side too as you buy products and services from others in your value chain
Competitive advantage: What makes your product or service stand out against the competition. It may be price related (e.g.: you stand out because you are cheaper than your competitors) or may refer to a certain attribute or condition that means what you offer is superior

Source: Taub et al. (2019)

Table 6.2 Solo and partnered—what's in it for me?

Solo entrepreneur	Partnered entrepreneur
Potential for less startup costs (fewer salaries, fewer people to support)	More likely to have a broader range of skills and experiences (which can only be a good thing)
Allows you to set your vision by yourself, and you make all the decisions	Less likely to head in the wrong direction as you can bounce ideas off each-other and act as sounding boards
Less potential for conflict (well none as long as you're by yourself), BUT...	You get to share the stress, the costs and responsibility, BUT...
It can get very lonely and carrying all the responsibility yourself is daunting	Conflicts can happen and having a co-founder is very much like being in a relationship (or a marriage) and takes a lot of work
Investors often refuse to back solo founders and prefer backing teams	

Source: Taub et al. (2019)

generations, but one that also has many economic advantages. This requires a holistic approach that considers environmental and social impacts, throughout every aspect of the business' activities. However, this holistic approach must be adopted with caution, especially for early stage startups.

Due to the limited capital, startups face barriers that are quite significant in addressing the entirety of possible trade-offs from their value proposition, and therefore will need to make some compromises regarding the trade-offs that it seeks to ameliorate. Sustainability issues are often seen as the product of a whole system that does not work properly, and startups must resist the temptation to fix them all; startups are only a small player in a much bigger game (Taub et al., 2019).

SMEs, especially startups, cannot solve every problem from their very beginning. These small companies should have clear and specific vision of the value they propose for sustainability and ameliorating societal challenges, and always adjust this vision to their business capabilities.

Doing things differently (e.g., employing individuals from different backgrounds, introducing new types of packaging, or new production processes) requires a lot of patience and grit. Entrepreneurs naturally challenge traditional embedded business processes, which means they will experience some resistance from markets when they introduce their startups. This is another reason why startups should find equilibrium between ameliorating global challenges and their current capacities. They are encouraged to identify a core mission, focus on the core mission, and build capacities to consider trade-offs throughout the startup's development.

6.4   Aligning Solutions to Consumer Needs

Once entrepreneurs have identified the market or social problem, and proposed their solution, its time to understand whether their proposed idea is fit to tackle the problems its intended to. After this step, entrepreneurs should identify if potential consumers will actually buy their product or pay for their service. Creating a perfect solution to a problem is great, but will be futile if no one is willing to pay for the product. Entrepreneurs are encouraged to identify if their ideas will work before engaging in the practical business creation processes (e.g., attaining funding, joining incubators and accelerators); success rates will seldom reach 100%, but entrepreneurs can increase the chances for their startup's success through various research streams, namely feasibility studies (Guerrero, Rialp, & Urbano, 2008; Lehmann, 1989; Sudrajat, Rahman, Sianturi, & Vendy, 2016).

Feasibility studies aim to assess whether an idea is feasible and in entrepreneurship, helps entrepreneurs write solid business plans for their startups (Arain, Campbell, Cooper, & Lancaster, 2010). It is quite common for feasibility studies to continue throughout the developmental stages of a startup as they adapt to local contexts and further develop their product or service. The information gathered during this process can be categorized into different sections looking at the market, technical, commercial, and financial and organizational feasibility (Taub et al., 2019). More in detail, there are three main strategies for feasibility research, which include (i) market research, (ii) competitive landscape, and (iii) SWOT assessment. In the following section, these terms are explored with greater detail.

6.4.1 Market Research

Whether a startup is in its initial stages, or the entrepreneurs are making changes to an existing product or service, or if an established firm is looking to develop a new product, market research will need to be conducted at a certain point. Market research, in essence, helps entrepreneurs make informed decisions about their startups by helping them understand the current market they are working in (e.g., gaining contextual insight). Having a clear understanding of the current market forces enables entrepreneurs to better align their product or service and marketing strategies to customer needs, and to better prepare pitching strategies to convince investors and other professionals to join or support their venture. Market researches could be classified by primary or secondary as well as qualitative or quantitative.

Primary market research is information that the entrepreneur gathers for themselves by interviewing stakeholders, or observing the behavior patterns of a target customer group to draw conclusions. Secondary market research relates to information gathered from existing literature sources, such as research articles, publications, books, and market reports. These two types of market research approaches thus yield one important question, is one more effective than the other?

The answer is no. Entrepreneurs should strive to collect both types of documents for their market research. Direct information and insights from leaders in the industry is quite valuable, but secondary information also helps to illustrate the context of the overall system that the entrepreneur is probably unlikely to be able to gather on their own (Chandler & Lyon, 2001).

Qualitative research focuses on how and why people think and feel about a topic, while quantitative research delivers facts and figures about how people relate to the topic; both provide great benefits to startups, especially in the food industry. Food, perhaps due to its strong cultural ties, invokes strong emotions in people (Desmet & Schifferstein, 2008). In this case, qualitative research is the perfect vehicle to understanding why some individuals make certain choices or feel a certain way around food (e.g., consumption, buying habits, spending) and how they perceive certain food innovations (e.g., disgust at 3D printed food, or reluctance to eat alternative proteins). One major limitation to qualitative research however is response bias, in which people's actual behaviors differ from their intentions, and their reported behaviors or attitudes (Paulhus, 1991). For instance, individuals may report choosing a more eco-friendly brand over another due to ethical implications, unconsciously however they may actually choose the product due to economic benefits or taste preferences. On the other hand, quantitative research is data driven, and is conducted through questionnaires, surveys, and psychometric instruments. This approach also falls victim to limitations regarding response bias but is much more data driven, therefore specific statistical methods can be applied to reduce bias or untrue responses. Despite its data driven nature, quantitative research can still be used to understand certain consumer behaviors, and in addition, the probability of adopting or rejecting a new product or service.

6.4.2 Competitive Landscape

Competitive landscape is often considered a sub-component of market research. It offers insights into what potential competitors are doing as far as business creation and innovation. This information is crucial to gaining an understanding of what threats competitors may pose to a startup, what key takeaway messages they might have to improve performance, and how new ventures can learn from their mistakes and do things differently. This type of analysis is mostly conducted qualitatively with secondary materials (i.e., by finding information that is publicly available). Furthermore, some recommendations for conducting competitive analysis are as follows, (i) aim to find the top ten performing companies; this number may be adjusted based on personal, or contextual, needs, and (ii) once the companies have been identified, begin to gather information about them. The type of information gathered will vary according to the business, product, or service in question, but in general, entrepreneurs are advised to investigate the following competitor dimensions (Taub et al., 2019):

- **Product/service**: What is their product or service(s)? How are they different, or better, regarding price, and design, and how much of the market share do they have?
- **Business Model**: How does their business model differ? Are there gaps in their business models or possible areas where they can improve?
- **Marketing**: How do they communicate with consumers, and in what way? Do they engage in open communication with consumers through digital technologies (e.g., Facebook, email, reviews etc.)? Do these feedback loops inform their business practices? What is their relationship with the media, are they often promoted?
- **Organization**: Who is on their team, managing bodies, and who are their advisors? Where are they located, and how does their location compare to other markets in launching successful startups?

A solid understanding of market competitors will help entrepreneurs develop their own company's competitive advantage, and set them on a path that is distinct from that of their competitors, which is particularly important in a crowded market since in entrepreneurship and innovation, invisibility is not a superpower.

6.4.3 SWOT Analysis

SWOT (i.e., Strengths, Opportunities, Weaknesses, and Threats) is a strategic analysis that looks at the strengths, weaknesses, opportunities, and threats to the entity being studied. This method is not limited to startups, or entrepreneurship for that matter, and can be used throughout the lifetime of any organization, or project, as a useful tool to navigate competitor strategies in order to stay competitive, or to inform entrepreneurs when its time to engage in practical business creation.

Fig. 6.1 SWOT analysis grid output—food system example. Source: Author's elaboration

Strengths

- Strong team with relevent experience
- Unique product proposition
- First mover advantage

Weaknesses

- Established market with large existing businesses
- No reputation
- Lack of funding

Opportunities

- Growing market
- Veganism trend

Threat

- Lack of existing legislation of new technology

Strengths and weaknesses are factors the entrepreneur can directly control since they are internal to the startup, while opportunities and threats are external factors of the environment the startup operates in, and out of the entrepreneur's control. SWOT results are usually depicted as a grid with four quadrants that is quite simple to interpret (Fig. 6.1)—each quadrant, or dimension, can be interpreted as follows.

- **Strengths**: Lets the entrepreneur know if they have a strong competitive advantage over others in the industry. Are you the first or one of the first to bring this type of product or service to market?
- **Weaknesses**: Helps entrepreneurs identify if there obvious gaps or limitations in their organization? For example, a startup around 'food tech' would require someone relevant in technical knowledge. Also helps assess if there is a lack of funding for the venture.
- **Opportunities**: Functions to help entrepreneurs identify market trends they can capitalize on e.g., a growth in vegetarianism can lead to developing of plant based products in addition to original value creation. This also helps entrepreneurs assess changes in legislation and determine if certain changes will support or hinder their vision.
- **Threats**: This lets the startup team assess if their idea can be replicable by other competitors, e.g., flavored sweeteners to avoid sugar has both a business model and product that can be easily copied. Also helps identify environmental threats that might impact business, e.g., if legislation is introduced that prohibits giving away food due to safety reasons, a startup that re-distributes food for waste control will find itself in trouble.

When trying to figure out whether startup will work, there is no substitute for actually trying it out and seeing how it does in real markets, with real people. This may seem like an unrealistic goal as products and services need funding to be developed and this is usually granted once startups have proven a concept.

6.5 From Ideas to Business Models and Business Plans

Once entrepreneurs determine they have a viable startup and decide to go through the practical process of development (e.g., attaining funding, joining incubators and accelerators) they have to begin to draft a strategy to make it self-sustaining, ergo how can they make profit from it; basically entrepreneurs need to figure out what their business model is (Taub et al., 2019).

In order to create their business model, startup members must figure who their customer is, what problem they are trying to solve, what their cost structure is, and what profits they would like to cultivate from the services rendered. A useful instrument for startups is the business model canvas (BMC) (Osterwalder & Pigneur, 2012). It is a user-friendly visual template that is divided into nine sections that cover all elements of a business model. Important to note is that some versions of the BMC contain 11 sections, which is due to the addition of 'eco-social costs' and 'eco-social benefits' dimensions. Therefore, in addition to economic criteria, this new version of the model also focuses on ecological and social consequences of the business activities (CASE, 2018), and aims at maximizing positive and avoiding negative impacts on society and nature. By adopting this new version of the BMC, sustainability is automatically integrated into the core business processes. The BMC in general is an excellent starting point when trying to illustrate the inputs and outputs of a potential business. It helps entrepreneurs focus, have clarity on key parts of the business, and is easily adaptable since business models naturally and continually evolve (Osterwalder & Pigneur, 2012). Once a startup's business model is laid out, the process of writing a business plan begins. In this next section we discuss the processes and strategies to creating a business strategy, for further details regarding the BMC and its properties see Chap. 7.

6.5.1 Writing a Business Plan

One of the main functions of writing a successful business plan is to use it as a tool to help generate interest from potential investors or partners (Chen, Yao, & Kotha, 2009). Business plans are not usually shared among other stakeholders, but it more so acts like a guide for entrepreneurs to use as a basis for pitches, presentations, and other communications regarding the startup and its activities (Chen et al., 2009). Business plans should also be adapted, not changed however, depending on who the entrepreneur presents it to, i.e., for investors one might emphasize the possible return of investments, while for scholars or governmental agents one might shift the emphasis to possible opportunities for university collaboration and scientific advance and, or savings in healthcare costs respectively. Even though, to some, writing a business plan may seem like a daunting task, entrepreneurs should see it as an opportunity to organize the processes of their startup, to illustrate its goals and objectives, long term vision, and the mechanisms that will employed to achieve these goals.

Not surprisingly, due to the complex and ever-changing nature of business creation, there is no *one* exact method to write a business plan but critical components that should be included have been identified (Taub et al., 2019), these components are expanded on in the following section.

In essence, a business plan is about nicely illustrating the startup's vision for the future, but it is also about showing any existing traction, experience, and successes that may support a business' effective evolution. Throughout the remainder of this section, we present a brief overview of the individual components of how to draft a solid business plan.

6.5.2 Company Overview: 'About Us'

This section is sometimes referred to as an executive summary. Usually it is the first thing stakeholders and consumers read about a startup, therefore is of the essence to make it as impactful and concise as possible, while always remembering to sell the bigger picture. For example, if a startup's aim is to provide a personalized shopping experience via an app, the positive impact in the food ecosystem should come across as part of the business plan. In this part of the business plan, it is also a good idea to display the startup's vision and values. The unique element of your startup should be key in this section, without mentioning other competitors.

6.5.3 Product or Service Offered

In the business plan, entrepreneurs should clearly illustrate what their product or service their startup is introducing to the market. They should also draft creative ways to demonstrate how this unique startup stands out, and what the unique selling points (USPs) are.

6.5.4 Target Market, Customers, and Competition

This section should highlight the market research previously conducted; basically, a greater understanding of the market translates to greater chances of success. In conveying an understanding of the market, entrepreneurs should be careful to demonstrate a mastery of the following three aspects of their venture:

- **Market**: Entrepreneurs are urged to share key insights regarding the size of the market they are going to try to enter, how the specific market is projected to grow, and any important contextual factors that are relevant for their startup. Lastly, entrepreneurs need to show an understanding of how their startup fits in the overall environment.

- **Customers**: An essential dimension of any business' success is knowing who their customer is, and understanding the drivers that lead them to pay for their specific products or services. Finally, this section of the business plan should demonstrate the need that the startup is meeting, or a pain point they are addressing for possible interested stakeholders.
- **Competition**: In order to grant a competitive element to the business plan, entrepreneurs must understand the 'ins and outs' of their relevant competitors. This is the section where entrepreneurs should highlight their competitors, and clearly indicate how their startup distinguishes itself, such as lower prices, higher quality, company values, and marketing, to name a few.

6.5.5 Sales and Marketing Strategies

In this section entrepreneurs should aim to explain how they plan to reach markets and attract customers, and should include the following information:

- **Overview of the startup brand**: This section will set the overall tone of the business plan and the startup, therefore giving readers a first 'taste' of your startup brand. This is a good place to also include detail on the startup mission, values, and how consumers should perceive the brand.
- **Sales strategy**: This section should outline the route-to-market strategy, i.e., sales process and communication channels, the startups pricing strategy, and any existing market traction.
- **Marketing strategy**: This is linked with the sales strategy, but focuses more on *how* entrepreneurs will disseminate information about their startup and what marketing strategies will achieve the best possible dissemination (e.g., public relations, social media, digital marketing, TV commercials, etc.)

6.5.6 Operations

This section varies depending on the type of business being considered but should include an overview of the startup's operational plan. Basically, here entrepreneurs should discuss any support systems that are needed in order to bring their startup to markets. This can include information such as locations needed where product development is expected to happen, the human capital needed to perform the startup functions, e.g. technical expertise, engineering, and psychology for consumer behavior, manufacturing process, and packaging if it is applicable. In this section, entrepreneurs should also discuss any legal considerations in making their startup successful.

6.5.7 The Startup Team

An essential component of a startup's success is the team behind it. In this section entrepreneurs should provide an overview of their team's core skills and backgrounds, highlighting their complementarities and multi-disciplinarity, if any. Entrepreneurs should also mention mentors and outside consultants who have been, and will continue to be involved in the startup's growth.

6.5.8 The Financial Plan

In this section it is important to outline how much the expected business activities will cost, and how much revenue it is expected to generate. This section can be further broken down into different components (Taub et al., 2019) as follows:

- **Profit & Loss (P&L)**: Is a financial statement that summarizes the revenues, costs, and expenses incurred during a specified period. A solid business plan should include a forecast of P&L for the next 5 years.
- **Balance sheet**: This is a statement of assets, liabilities, and capital of a business or institution at a specific point in time, it details the balance of the income and expenditure over the preceding period.
- **Cashflow statement**: A document that displays cash entering and leaving the business over a given period of time which is broken down into operating, financing, and investment processes. If the main goal of the current entrepreneur is to raise funds, then it is recommended that they outline the sum of investment needed, and how it will be distributed over a specified period of time.

When considering business plans, it is interesting that usually they are not followed as originally and thoroughly planned out. In order to stay competitive in ever-changing markets, startups and businesses must also be ready to change along with the external environment, and thus, so must their business plans. What potential investors and other stakeholders look for business plans is that the entrepreneur has holistically considered the business, and has a concrete understanding of the market, the core business proposition and processes, and that the startup and the entrepreneur are able to adapt as the startup grows into a business or as external factors demand it.

Financial plans can be considered one of the most important components of business plans, and when properly written, show that there is an economically viable business model behind and a startup or entrepreneurial idea. The financial plan should consist of three parts, (i) a profit and loss statement, (ii) a balance sheet and (iii) cashflow statement. Financial plans should also never cover both short-term and long-term perspectives, in this case, two different financial plans should be considered. Short-term business plans should be presented on a month period, while long-term plans can think up to 5 years ahead. Furthermore, the entrepreneur needs specific type of information before beginning to draft a business plan, namely information on direct costs of developing goods or services; fixed operating costs, such as employees, marketing, and office space rentals; capital costs which include investments in machinery, development; the startup's product or service pricing, and payment modes; company objectives regarding sales targets and margin expectations; and sales forecast.

Finally we would like to highlight that this is only an overview of the processes and components necessary to crate a financial plan. For more information on specific funding schemes and opportunities for new ventures see Chap. 9.

6.6 Digitalization as a Driver for Entrepreneurial Ecosystems and Business Creation: Fact or Fiction

Entrepreneurial ecosystems are distinguished from other forms of regional networks or communities due their relative lack of confinement to specific industries and technologies, by their processes in supporting the emergence of startups, by the way they combine and leverage spatial and digital affordances, and by their shared experiential knowledge base on business model innovation.

Moreover, the bulk of the research on entrepreneurial ecosystems has, arguably, failed to recognize the most fundamental driver of the phenomenon—that of digitalization (Malecki, 2018).

New business ventures are an extremely heterogeneous collection of, nascent, or upcoming businesses. When it comes to levels of technology intensity, food startups comprise 'low-technology' service ventures (e.g., street food vendors, food trucks, and small scale farmers), to low-to-medium tech manufacturing SMEs, to the 'high-technology' new ventures that focus on transforming R&I advances into new commercialized products and services (e.g. high growth firms) (Autio, Nambisan, Thomas, & Wright, 2018). These high-tech, or digital, startups can be found in many diverse sectors, and are usually distinguished by their ability to harness digital affordances brought about by advances in digital technologies and improvements in infrastructures for business model innovation (see Chap. 8), which translates into four distinctive characteristics of digital startups.

1. In addition to harnessing general-purpose technology, digital startups are for the most part **technology and industry agnostic**, meaning they are not limited to a specific sector and can design business models to target customers in virtually any sector (Basu & Fernald, 2007).
2. They tend to **emphasize service and business model innovation** instead of technology-push, product, or process as the key source of opportunities for startups. Business model innovation refers to the novel design to coordinate and leverage interactions for value co-creation, and can be defined as the 'implementation of non-trivial changes to at least two business model elements resulting

in a business model configuration that is new to the organization's industry and market' (Bock & George, 2017).

3. They **leverage ecosystem architecture as a source of competitive advantage**.
4. They **harness the structural malleability afforded by digital technologies** to support exponential scalability.

Therefore, the ability to harness digital affordances makes digital startups unique from more traditional business creation initiatives. This means that digital startups operate under a distinctive operational logic, one that draws on distinctive managerial recipes for innovative business model design (Autio & Cao, 2019).

Furthermore, Autio and Cao (2019) argue that a fundamental driver of entrepreneurial ecosystems is digitalization. Therefore it can be assumed that entrepreneurial ecosystems represent a novel and unique type of a regional network that facilitates the creation of digital startups. They define digital startups as 'new ventures that harness digital affordances for business model innovation.' These findings are supported by other studies that suggest that entrepreneurial ecosystems are ultimately driven and enabled by advances in digital technologies and infrastructures and the related process of digitalization (Autio et al., 2018), or the socio-technical process of integrating digitalization techniques to broader social and institutional contexts that render digital technologies infrastructural (Tilson, Lyytinen, & Sørensen, 2010).

At the same time, the researchers stated that entrepreneurial ecosystems also specialize in facilitating the startup and scale-up of new entrepreneurial ventures through the combination of digital affordances (i.e., potentialities to either perform existing functions in novel ways or perform entirely novel functions). Such digital affordances are important to highlight because they shape the locus of entrepreneurial opportunities, as well as effective practices to pursue such opportunities. Being able to successfully harness digital affordances allows new ventures to dramatically lower their startup costs, enabling them to adopt an iterative, experimentation-driven approach to their business model design; an approach that differs drastically from the traditional, linear and plan-oriented approach to new venture creation (Ewens, Nanda, & Rhodes-Kropf, 2018; Romme, 2003).

Attempts to shed light on the concept of entrepreneurial and innovation ecosystems have generally emphasized descriptions and best practice lessons, rather than their prediction power based on theoretical causation (e.g., success of startups, possible trade offs with innovation activities). Entrepreneurial ecosystems have emerged as a response to opportunities provided by digitalization to facilitate digital startups, by cultivating generic business process knowledge, and providing a munificent resource community.

In essence, the very nature of ecosystems facilitates the emergence of startups, with their distinctive structural elements, such as new venture accelerators, co-working spaces, incubators, and venture challenges (Autio et al., 2018).

6.7 Startups and Innovation Ecosystems: Do They Work?

Audretsch and Feldman (2004) describe that one of the greatest insights to innovation is that geography and location matter, and that a long tradition of observing the low effectiveness of innovation processes within the boundaries of the firm with disregard for the spatial context has paved the way for the integration of spatial context when analyzing firms. Mainstream literature also shared this belief and considers geographic location, specifically proximity, to be a driver of innovation (Letaifa & Rabeau, 2013). Theories as to why location and context matter include that the concentration of firms improves innovation and output efficiency and facilitates access to needed resources; a highly competitive environment can encourage firms to be proactive and quickly build needed competencies (Porter & Porter, 1998), and knowledge spillovers are especially effective when geographic distances are lessened (Singh, 2005). Specifically, proximity based networks of startups and entrepreneurs create a critical mass of local knowledge, human capital, and resources used by new ventures and established firms to gain competitive advantages (Carayannis, Popescu, Sipp, & Stewart, 2006).

Most newly created businesses struggle to survive beyond the first 5 years of operation, and higher than usual survival rates have been attributed to a well-organized entrepreneurial ecosystem. Even though a clear-cut definition of entrepreneurial ecosystems is still missing from the literature, some models have been proposed to illustrate their complexity. One of these models distinguished four of their distinctive elements, (i) the ecosystem community, (ii) resource dynamics, (iii) knowledge spillovers, and (iv) general framework conditions. Furthermore Autio and Cao (2019) suggest four common elements of entrepreneurial ecosystems that are featured in existing definitions and propose the following four-point structural model:

1. Regional (rather than national) focus.
2. Emphasis on new firm creation.
3. Emphasis on multi-laterality and interdependencies across ecosystem stakeholders.
4. Emphasis on system-level welfare benefits.

Entrepreneurial ecosystems are, in essence, regional communities of stakeholders organized around the new startup creation process.

Entrepreneurial ecosystems offer entrepreneurs a range of services, network outlets, and state-of-the-art support systems. However, it's not quite clear if the simple availability of such resources and support systems directly translate to an entrepreneur's proficiency in harnessing benefits from the ecosystem (Cruz, Rosekranz, & Giliberti, 2019).

According to an article on 'How to Start an Entrepreneurial Revolution', entrepreneurs are most successful when they have access to the human, financial, and professional resources they need (Isenberg, 2010). However, even more important are the government policies that help encourage and safeguard entrepreneurs, as well as the support networks of fellow entrepreneurs and experienced business leaders, or mentors, who may be able to provide personalized guidance on ameliorating some of the challenges they are facing, especially if these mentors themselves have experienced similar obstacles previously (Isenberg, 2010).

Unfortunately, some research streams have demonstrated that simply creating opportunities to raise funds, network with other entrepreneurs, and receive personalized feedback from seasoned entrepreneurs is not enough to support successful startups (Isenberg, 2014). This leads us to a narrower questions of, what kind of services do startups need, and at what phase can these services yield strong and sustainable startups and ecosystems?

Cruz et al. (2019) posit that collaborating with other startups, and the ability to engage in knowledge sharing with experienced food ecosystem institutions, practical training, and transparent access to resources are among the elements that render ecosystems productive for startups. In this case, authors agree that the idea of ecosystems is a necessary, but insufficient condition for success (Cruz et al., 2019). One important aspect for collaborations with other ecosystem startups is that it must be the startup founders themselves, the entrepreneurs, to take the initiative and connect with the networks they belong to through indirect or direct connections. However, there are still many young startup teams, who do not invest the time to seek the necessary support to reduce costs, provide seed funding, and access crucial knowledge pools (Cruz et al., 2019).

Furthermore, based on the structural model proposed by Autio and Cao (2019), we can conclude that entrepreneurial ecosystems are, in essence, regional networks of stakeholders organized around the new venture startup process.

Innovation ecosystem on the other hand may include technology parks, incubators, universities, and others, to achieve a high density of startups that is equipped with social capital to help its members evolve (Bandera & Thomas, 2018). Social capital in entrepreneurship and its endeavors has been broadly acknowledged (Stam, Arzlanian, & Elfring, 2014; Westlund & Adam, 2010). Innovation ecosystems have become popular notion that describes the networked and systemic nature of innovation, and focuses on innovation activities and the important interactions and interdependencies amongst its member (Ritala & Almpanopoulou, 2017).

One common context in which entrepreneurship and social capital encounter each other is that of the innovation ecosystem. Innovation ecosystems support startups in their development process by serving as conduits for an effective and holistic support network (Tötterman & Sten, 2005). An innovation ecosystem is defined by the complex relationships formed between actors, whose objective is to enable technology development and innovation thereby growing the economy and creating jobs (Jackson, 2011).

Like entrepreneurial ecosystems, innovation ecosystems also lack a central definition, but a few common features have been identified throughout. A first commonality is the availability of research and commercial resources. A second common feature is that entities in an ecosystem are geographically localized, and focus on a few overlapping industries (e.g. climate change, food ecosystems, water supplies).

6.7 Startups and Innovation Ecosystems: Do They Work?

Innovation ecosystems attract new ventures and aspiring entrepreneurs with resources such as lower cost facilities, business services, and opportunities for collaboration.

Due to the importance allocated to social capital, Bandera and Thomas (2018) conducted a study that analyzed access to social capital, its use, and startup success. From their analysis, they found that the availability of social capital did not correlate to startup survival, but that the startups that actively use social capital by collaborating with other system members (e.g., universities, large industries) significantly outperform startups that do not. Furthermore, they highlight that the availability of social capital in an ecosystem does not correlate with the utilization of social capital by startups in that ecosystem. Dense ecosystems composed of numerous talents can offer many benefits as far as resources, networking, and expertise, but this does not guarantee that aspiring entrepreneurs and startups will capitalize on those benefits (Bandera & Thomas, 2018).

In other words, even though entrepreneurial ecosystems may offer a range of services, and innovation ecosystems offer access to large pools social capital, it is the entrepreneurs driving the startups who hold the decisive power engage in these activities, and will do so regardless of where they are, whereas those who choose not to engage will on average produce mediocre, if any, impacts, and will remain reluctant to new processes. Finally, Bandera and Thomas (2018) find a strong positive relationship between the utilization of social capital and startup survival, more so among high-tech firms than among low-tech firms.

Furthermore, Stuart and Sorenson (2003) suggest that even though a large percentage of entrepreneurs prefer to establish startups in entrepreneurial or innovation ecosystems, the most productive new ventures are not located in regional clusters, and posit that this may be due to the highly competitive environment that exists in geographically concentrated networks. They further go on to discuss that the benefits from ecosystem clustering may disappear as new ventures create direct networks of their own, thus expanding the geographic reach of a startups firm's social network. This argument is supported by Schwartz (2013) who reveals that startup survival is statistically significantly better among companies that never participated in an incubator, or other type of designed ecosystem service.

Entrepreneurs may, or may not, have the specialized skills or the required social competence (i.e. the ability to engage in effective interactions with other ecosystem members) needed to capitalize from the present conditions of the ecosystems (Baron & Markman, 2000; Battisti & McAdam, 2012). Entrepreneurs may also be blinded by personal biases which may give them an unrealistic boost of confidence or control over their startup; they convince themselves that they can draw no additional benefit from networking with the ecosystem (Baluku, Kikooma, & Kibanja, 2016; De Carolis & Saparito, 2006; Koellinger, Minniti, & Schade, 2007). Importantly, Baluku et al. (2016) also support the notion that both startup capital and the psychological capital of the entrepreneur are significant predictors for entrepreneurial success; however, psychological capital is the better predictor.

6.8 Your Startup, Your Brand

A strong brand focuses on providing a better and more recognizable solution than competitors can offer. Through the delivery of its unique value proposition, a brand grows its consumer market and benefits from the word of mouth of loyal consumers; these statements remain true even with all the emerging digital technologies to promote products and services through different avenues. Creating a viable and recognizable brand is not about using the newest digital methods, but about using human capital such as creativity to leverage own, paid, and earned channels to reach, convert, and retain customers. In the age of technology, the traditional promotional mix (i.e., promotion, advertising, public relations, and personal contacts) continues to provide optimal results (Meng-Mei, 2019). A brand can be considered as the expectations, memories, relationships, and personal experiences with a company, that, when looked at holistically, can explain a customer's decision to choose one product or service over another. In the context of entrepreneurs and startups, brand reflects what they stand for, and lets markets and customers know the company values, even if a company is not directly interfaced with customers. The initial mission, vision, and values identified in the business planning phase play an important role in how entrepreneurs build their business. When starting a business, it's very easy to get distracted by different opportunities and challenges. Therefore having a strong mission and vision early on will act as a compass and help guide strategic business decisions. Defining value and vision early on also help startups engage with future employees and overall consumer markets (Taub et al., 2019).

- **Mission**: A mission statement expresses why a business exists; it states their purpose and lays out the impact they want to achieve. A company providing technology to reduce water usage on agricultural land could, for example, state its mission as follows: "We exist to increase water efficiency on farms to benefit farming communities in the developing world". An easy way to start putting together your mission statement is to start with "we exist to. . . .".
- **Vision**: This defines the startups idea for the future focusing more on long-term aspirations and the wider context of its mission. In this example, the company's vision statement could be: "Our vision is to create sustainable farming practices and contribute to the development of a better and more environmentally friendly food system."
- **Values**: Similarly to the mission and the vision, startups' values matter as they guide how to build the business and the type of company culture it creates. Company values should come from the founders and what is important to them. These terms are not easy to express, therefore young entrepreneurs are encouraged to look at the companies they are loyal to for examples.

6.8.1 Brand Positioning

One of the first steps in developing a viable brand and marketing strategy is figuring out who the startup's target customers are specifically, and how the startup will differentiate itself from its competitors in doing so. Consumers respond more positively to personalized messages rather than to generic ones, so it's important for startups to have a clear understanding of their brand positioning and develop strategies to exploit it. Companies are generally more likely to be successful if they create a niche rather than try to please everybody. When trying to figure out their brand positioning, entrepreneurs are encouraged to ask themselves the following questions:

- What customer segments exist within the market my startup operates in?
- Which of those customer segments is most likely to respond positively to our value proposition?
- How are competitors in this market positioning themselves, e.g. which customer segments are they trying to attain?
- How will we distinguish ourselves from the competition, especially if we're going after the same customer segments?

When we think about brand positioning, entrepreneurs should have a clear idea of the impression, or brand perception, their customers should have of their brand. Furthermore, brand statements can be structured in a number of ways as long as it answers the key points addressed in the questions above.

6.8.2 Sustainability and Brand Creation

As widely noted in the literature, sustainable food systems have gained the attention of many food ecosystem members, from farmers, to retailers, to consumers. Therefore the companies that are able to embed sustainability from the very beginning of their creation can achieve a number of relative advantages.

1. **Consumers Care**: Studies increasingly show that consumers want to choose products that are positive for the environment and society (at least when they're asked about it). A 2017 Unilever global consumer study found an over "$1 trillion market opportunity for brands that can effectively and transparently market the sustainability of their wares" (SB, 2019).
2. **Business customers care**: The EU requires large companies to report on the social and environmental impact of their activities. Therefore, most companies have sustainability targets to meet so they are increasingly looking to work with suppliers and partners who can help them fulfill these; an optimal opportunity for startups.
3. **Positive differentiation in marketplaces**: Positive impact provides a marketing advantage that can help startups stand out from competition, especially against more established businesses. The greater the positive impact from startups, the

greater the media attention will be, thus shedding light on the startups' processes and helping generate interest from local communities. Sustainability can also help startups create loyalty as they help others contribute to initiatives they care about, or consider important.

4. **Attracting a motivated and committed team**: Consumers like working with and being part of businesses that are mission driven. Recent surveys show, for example, that millennials prefer companies who strive for more than just ROI and that sustainability and environmental regard is a key motivator when they look for work (Taub et al., 2019).

5. **It's a market reality**: The growing threats to natural resources signifies that if startups and companies can exist and function in more efficient and sustainable ways, they will be less vulnerable to market forces that affect daily operations.

6.9 Conclusion

The importance of food startups and what they can do for the food industry is becoming increasingly known.

No matter the motivation for entrepreneurs, the SME sector in Europe has been generating more jobs than large enterprises, and innovation-driven SMEs are engines of growth and job creation.

First, when policy makers refer to the ecosystems concept they invariably pre-fix the term with the term 'startup' (Schreiber & Pinelli, 2013). This could be labeled the 'startup monoculture' (Brown & Mason, 2017). This can be damaging for several reasons. It ignores the fact that the needs of firms change as they evolve (Brown & Mason, 2017).

Slapping the 'startup' in front of many new initiatives is quite attractive, but field experts should keep in mind that a startup is just the initial phase of venture creation. They should offer transfer officers to help them grow, and now face the too big for the pond scenario.

Within the sustainability context, competitive companies may be happy to share information. It makes sense, as the motivation behind these companies is to create positive change in the world and so knowledge sharing benefits a greater cause (Taub et al., 2019). Although literature tends to assume that geographic proximity is a driver of innovation understanding why some startups utilize the social capital available to them while others do not is an important question. The answer will undoubtedly lie in part within the personality traits of the individual entrepreneur. For example, researchers have used the Five Factor model of personality traits (openness to experience, conscientiousness, extraversion, agreeableness, and neuroticism) to model entrepreneurs and the performance of their firms. Several of these personality traits influence not only an entrepreneur's willingness to interact with others but also the willingness of others to interact with her/him (Bandera & Thomas, 2018).

For food startups that want to innovate faster, it is crucial to keep up with current markets. Working together with other innovate food startups can ensure that, together, startups can innovate a lot quicker by assisting each other with risk management and therefore reducing single liabilities.

Furthermore, collaborations with larger companies can also provide immense benefits for the companies and the startups. In this case, startups provide innovative ideas to improve procedures of larger companies, and larger companies very often have the resources to invest in these ideas and to produce new knowledge. Therefore, larger companies work as funders for startup's innovative solutions that can later on be implemented at a large company scale; therefore truly driving a food ecosystems transformation toward sustainability.

Literature streams have reported that focusing on the psychology of entrepreneurs alone is not enough to assess their entrepreneurial success, and the provision of resources for business creation does not signify that they will be exploited or utilized by entrepreneurs to startup enhancement. Based on the literature, we propose that future studies of entrepreneurs and their propensity to engage in open communication with regional support systems should investigate both individual entrepreneurial characteristics, and environmental conditions in order to gain a more holistic picture of the startup creation, development, and overall success in market strategies.

References

Agfunder. (2019). *Why foodtech and agtech?* Retrieved from https://agfunder.com/

Arain, M., Campbell, M. J., Cooper, C. L., & Lancaster, G. A. (2010). What is a pilot or feasibility study? A review of current practice and editorial policy. *BMC Medical Research Methodology, 10*(1), 67.

Audretsch, D. B., & Feldman, M. P. (2004). Knowledge spillovers and the geography of innovation. In *Handbook of regional and urban economics* (Vol. 4, pp. 2713–2739). Amsterdam: Elsevier.

Autio, E., & Cao, Z. (2019). Fostering digital startups: Structural model of entrepreneurial ecosystems. In *Proceedings of the 52nd Hawaii International Conference on System Sciences*.

Autio, E., Nambisan, S., Thomas, L. D., & Wright, M. (2018). Digital affordances, spatial affordances, and the genesis of entrepreneurial ecosystems. *Strategic Entrepreneurship Journal, 12*(1), 72–95.

Ayyagari, M., Demirguc-Kunt, A., & Maksimovic, V. (2011). *Small vs. young firms across the world: Contribution to employment, job creation, and growth*. Washington, DC: The World Bank.

Baluku, M. M., Kikooma, J. F., & Kibanja, G. M. (2016). Psychological capital and the startup capital–entrepreneurial success relationship. *Journal of Small Business & Entrepreneurship, 28*(1), 27–54.

Bandera, C., & Thomas, E. (2018). The role of innovation ecosystems and social capital in startup survival. *IEEE Transactions on Engineering Management, 99*, 1–10.

Baron, R. A., & Markman, G. D. (2000). Beyond social capital: How social skills can enhance entrepreneurs' success. *Academy of Management Perspectives, 14*(1), 106–116.

Basu, S., & Fernald, J. (2007). Information and communications technology as a general-purpose technology: Evidence from US industry data. *German Economic Review, 8*(2), 146–173.

Battisti, M., & McAdam, M. (2012). Challenges of social capital development in the university science incubator: The case of the graduate entrepreneur. *The International Journal of Entrepreneurship and Innovation, 13*(4), 261–276.

Bock, A. J., & George, G. (2017). *The business model book: Design, build and adapt business ideas that drive business growth.* London: Pearson.

Brown, R., & Mason, C. (2017). Looking inside the spiky bits: A critical review and conceptualisation of entrepreneurial ecosystems. *Small Business Economics, 49*(1), 11–30.

Carayannis, E. G., Popescu, D., Sipp, C., & Stewart, M. (2006). Technological learning for entrepreneurial development (TL4ED) in the knowledge economy (KE): Case studies and lessons learned. *Technovation, 26*(4), 419–443.

CASE. (2018). *Sustainable business model canvas.* Retrieved from https://www.case-ka.eu/index. html%3Fp=2174.html

Chandler, G. N., & Lyon, D. W. (2001). Issues of research design and construct measurement in entrepreneurship research: The past decade. *Entrepreneurship Theory and Practice, 25*(4), 101–113.

Chen, X. P., Yao, X., & Kotha, S. (2009). Entrepreneur passion and preparedness in business plan presentations: A persuasion analysis of venture capitalists' funding decisions. *Academy of Management Journal, 52*(1), 199–214.

Coad, A., & Rao, R. (2008). Innovation and firm growth in high-tech sectors: A quantile regression approach. *Research Policy, 37*(4), 633–648.

Cohen, S. S., & Zysman, J. (1987). *Manufacturing matters: The myth of the post-industrial economy.* New York: Basic Books (AZ).

Cordain, L., Eaton, S. B., Sebastian, A., Mann, N., Lindeberg, S., Watkins, B. A., . . . Brand-Miller, J. (2005). Origins and evolution of the western diet: Health implications for the 21st century. *The American Journal of Clinical Nutrition, 81*(2), 341–354.

Cruz, M., Rosekranz, N., & Giliberti, T. (2019). *Is an entrepreneurial ecosystem beneficial for startups?* Retrieved from https://hospitalityinsights.ehl.edu/entrepreneurial-skills-ecosystem-startups

De Carolis, D. M., & Saparito, P. (2006). Social capital, cognition, and entrepreneurial opportunities: A theoretical framework. *Entrepreneurship Theory and Practice, 30*(1), 41–56.

De Jong, J. P., Gillert, N. L., & Stock, R. M. (2018). First adoption of consumer innovations: Exploring market failure and alleviating factors. *Research Policy, 47*(2), 487–497.

Desmet, P. M., & Schifferstein, H. N. (2008). Sources of positive and negative emotions in food experience. *Appetite, 50*(2–3), 290–301.

Eurostat. (2003). *Concepts and definitions.* Retrieved from https://ec.europa.eu/eurostat/ramon/ nomenclatures/index.cfm?TargetUrl=DSP_GLOSSARY_NOM_DTL_VIEW& StrNom=CODED2&StrLanguageCode=EN&IntKey=17399050&RdoSearch=& TxtSearch=&CboTheme=&IsTer=&ter_valid=0&IntCurrentPage=1

Ewens, M., Nanda, R., & Rhodes-Kropf, M. (2018). Cost of experimentation and the evolution of venture capital. *Journal of Financial Economics, 128*(3), 422–442.

Fait, M., Scorrano, P., Mastroleo, G., Cillo, V., & Scuotto, V. (2019). A novel view on knowledge sharing in the agri-food sector. *Journal of Knowledge Management.* 3 5, 953–974

FAO. (2019). *SAVE FOOD: Global initiative on food loss and waste reduction.* Retrieved from http://www.fao.org/save-food/resources/keyfindings/en/

Foodware. (2019). *How startups bring innovation to the food industry.* Retrieved from https:// www.foodware365.com/en/news/knowledge-base/2019/how-startups-bring-innovation-to-the-food-industry/

Forhan, M., & Gill, S. V. (2013). Obesity, functional mobility and quality of life. *Best Practice & Research Clinical Endocrinology & Metabolism, 27*(2), 129–137.

Frederiksen, L. (2018). *The 2018 high growth study is here.* Retrieved from https://hingemarketing. com/blog/story/the-2018-high-growth-study-is-here

Fuentelsaz, L., Maícas, J. P., & Mata, P. (2018). Institutional dynamism in entrepreneurial ecosystems. In *Entrepreneurial ecosystems* (pp. 45–65). Cham: Springer.

References

Guerrero, M., Rialp, J., & Urbano, D. (2008). The impact of desirability and feasibility on entrepreneurial intentions: A structural equation model. *International Entrepreneurship and Management Journal, 4*(1), 35–50.

Isenberg, D. J. (2010). How to start an entrepreneurial revolution. *Harvard Business Review, 88*(6), 40–50.

Isenberg, D. (2014). What an entrepreneurship ecosystem actually is. *Harvard Business Review, 5*, 1–7.

Jackson, D. J. (2011). What is an innovation ecosystem. *National Science Foundation, 1*.

Koellinger, P., Minniti, M., & Schade, C. (2007). "I think I can, I think I can": Overconfidence and entrepreneurial behavior. *Journal of Economic Psychology, 28*(4), 502–527.

Lascialfari, M., Magrini, M. B., & Triboulet, P. (2019). The drivers of product innovations in pulse-based foods: Insights from case studies in France, Italy and USA. *Journal of Innovation Economics Management, 1*, 111–143.

Lehmann, D. R. (1989). *Market research and analysis* (Vol. 3). Homewood, IL: Irwin.

Letaifa, S. B., & Rabeau, Y. (2013). Too close to collaborate? How geographic proximity could impede entrepreneurship and innovation. *Journal of Business Research, 66*(10), 2071–2078.

Lynde, R., (2018). *Accelerating entrepreneurship in the food system*. Retrieved from https://foodtank.com/news/2018/12/accelerating-entrepreneurship-in-the-food-system/

Malecki, E. J. (2018). Entrepreneurship and entrepreneurial ecosystems. *Geography Compass, 12*(3), e12359.

Meng-Mei, M. (2019). *Brand building for entrepreneurs: A more cost-effective way to raise your company's profile?* Retrieved from https://hospitalityinsights.ehl.edu/brand-building-entrepreneur?hsCtaTracking=aff45519-534e-4996-bdad-f4bcc87befea%7Ca8498e66-996e-4e59-a0e9-6dee8fa93f54

Mitev, N., de Vaujany, F. X., Laniray, P., Bohas, A., & Fabbri, J. (2019). Co-working spaces, collaborative practices and entrepreneurship. In *Collaboration in the digital age* (pp. 15–43). Cham: Springer.

OECD. (2018). *Defining innovation*. Retrieved from https://www.oecd.org/site/innovationstrategy/defininginnovation.htm

Osterwalder, A., & Pigneur, Y. (2012). Designing business models and similar strategic objects: The contribution of IS. *Journal of the Association for Information Systems, 14*(5), 3.

Paulhus, D. L. (1991). Measurement and control of response bias. In J. P. Robinson, P. R. Shaver, & L. S. Wrightsman (Eds.), *Measures of personality and social psychological attitudes* (pp. 17–59). New York: Academic.

Politis, D. (2008). Does prior start-up experience matter for entrepreneurs' learning? A comparison between novice and habitual entrepreneurs. *Journal of Small Business and Enterprise Development, 15*(3), 472–489.

Porter, M. E., & Porter, M. P. (1998). Location, clusters, and the "New" microeconomics of competition. *Business Economics, 33*(1), 7–13.

Ritala, P., & Almpanopoulou, A. (2017). In defense of 'eco' in innovation ecosystem. *Technovation, 60*, 39–42.

Romme, A. G. L. (2003). Making a difference: Organization as design. *Organization Science, 14*(5), 558–573.

SB. (2019). *The bridge to better brands*. Retrieved from https://sustainablebrands.com/

Schreiber, U., & Pinelli, M. (2013). *The power of three: Together, governments, entrepreneurs and corporations can spur growth across the G20*. The EY G20 Entrepreneurship Barometer.

Schwartz, M. (2013). A control group study of incubators' impact to promote firm survival. *The Journal of Technology Transfer, 38*(3), 302–331.

Singh, J. (2005). Collaborative networks as determinants of knowledge diffusion patterns. *Management Science, 51*(5), 756–770.

Stam, W., Arzlanian, S., & Elfring, T. (2014). Social capital of entrepreneurs and small firm performance: A meta-analysis of contextual and methodological moderators. *Journal of Business Venturing, 29*(1), 152–173.

Stuart, T., & Sorenson, O. (2003). The geography of opportunity: Spatial heterogeneity in founding rates and the performance of biotechnology firms. *Research Policy, 32*(2), 229–253.

Sudrajat, J., Rahman, M. A., Sianturi, A., & Vendy, V. (2016). Entrepreneurship learning process by using SWOT analysis. *The Winners, 17*(1), 67–75.

Tataj, D. (2015). *Innovation and entrepreneurship. A growth model for Europe beyond the crisis.* New York: Tataj Innovation Library.

Taub, I., Minch-Dixon, M., & Gridley, J. (2019). *Better businesses for a better food ecosystem.* Retrieved from https://www.eitfood.eu/media/documents/EIT_Food_Start-Up_Manual_Final.pdf

Tilson, D., Lyytinen, K., & Sørensen, C. (2010). Research commentary—Digital infrastructures: The missing IS research agenda. *Information Systems Research, 21*(4), 748–759.

Tötterman, H., & Sten, J. (2005). Start-ups: Business incubation and social capital. *International Small Business Journal, 23*(5), 487–511.

Vermeulen, S. J., Campbell, B. M., & Ingram, J. S. (2012). Climate change and food systems. *Annual Review of Environment and Resources, 37*, 195–222.

Westlund, H., & Adam, F. (2010). Social capital and economic performance: A meta-analysis of 65 studies. *European Planning Studies, 18*(6), 893–919.

WHO. (2018). *Obesity and overweight.* Retrieved from https://www.who.int/news-room/fact-sheets/detail/obesity-and-overweight

Chapter 7
Innovative and Sustainable Food Business Models

Abstract Companies are called upon to solve the great challenges of the new millennium. The food sector, from this point of view, plays a strategic role. Poverty, malnutrition, hunger, climate change, and social inequalities are just some of the trends which the agri-food sector has to cope with. The digital transformation that companies will need to embrace to survive requires new ways of creating, thinking, and working with technology-driven tools to provide value for their businesses and customers. Digitization, whether it pertains to new technologies, the analysis of big data or the development of on-line and spatial applications, can contribute to achieving systemic food production transformation in a way that aligns the sector more closely with contemporary sustainability and health challenges. Digital techniques are leading established companies to renew and innovate their business models by connecting producers to consumers, setting up innovative marketing channels, and improving logistics. Artificial intelligence for smart farming, precision and urban farming, data management for waste-less, blockchain for supply chain traceability and auditability are just some of the disruptive technologies which have been adopting by both start-ups and an increasing number of established companies, redefining their business models. This chapter aims to analyse how these new paradigms are impacting the food sector by providing examples from the real world.

Keywords Business model · Food industry · Business model innovation · Grand challenges · Sustainability

---

Co-authored by Canio Forliano—Department of Management, University of Turin, School of Management and Economics, Turin, Italy
Department of Political Science and International relations, University of Palermo, Palermo, Italy, e-mail: canio.forliano@unito.it
Co-authored by Mattia Franco—Department of Management, University of Turin, Turin, Italy, e-mail: mattia.franco@unito.it

© Springer Nature Switzerland AG 2020
P. De Bernardi, D. Azucar, *Innovation in Food Ecosystems*, Contributions to Management Science, https://doi.org/10.1007/978-3-030-33502-1_7

7.1 Introduction

Research on business models has drawn the attention of a vast number of scholars over the last decades. However, there is still no general agreement among researchers on the theoretical definition of this construct (Evans et al., 2017). The concept of business model commonly refers to the architecture for how a firm does business (Foss & Saebi, 2018), and, more specifically, how it creates, delivers, and captures value (Magretta, 2002; Teece, 2010). For this reason, this chapter will first present a summary of the main definitions of business models that are most established in the scientific literature. Next, the reflection will move to the concept of innovative and sustainable business models, with a particular focus on the disruptive changes that both the sustainability and the circular economy paradigms have brought in recent years. In doing so, the most recent changes which have been emerging in the competitive landscape will be taken into consideration (Nielsen et al., 2018). The final part of the chapter will focus on several practical examples of sustainable business model innovation in the food system. As a consequence, possible future scenarios will be analyzed, reflecting on how they can guarantee the food sector to prosper in compliance with new governmental guidelines and modern consumers' needs, that are both increasingly oriented towards giving attention to the sustainability paradigm.

7.2 Business Model

Scholars have not provided a generally accepted definition of business model so far. This absence can be well reassumed through Porter's word (2001, p. 73), when he stated that "the definition of a business model is murky at best". In particular, there are at least two different problems that may hinder providing a unique and shared definition of business model.

First, to date, practitioner insights have played an essential role in forming and developing the field through frameworks and definitions (Petrovic, Kittl, & Teksten, 2001; Timmers, 1998). Consequently, they have developed business model concepts that are very specific to each analyzed scenario and that have been used in practice as a means to capture the underlying architecture regarding how a company does business (Foss & Saebi, 2018).

Second, researches on business models have been addressed from different domains, contributing to the fuzziness of this term. For what concerns the main disciplines that have paid attention to the concept of business model so far, they are mainly related to e-business, information systems, strategy, innovation, entrepreneurship, management, and economics (Chesbrough, 2006; Chesbrough & Rosenbloom, 2002; Osterwalder & Pigneur, 2010; Porter, 2001; Teece, 2010; Zott & Amit, 2010). Nevertheless, differences can also be linked to national cultural characteristics. In fact, according to de Reuver, Bouwman, and Haaker (2013), American and European scholars have different approaches to business model research. Indeed, while Americans are more concentrated on classifying business models and their relationship with open innovation, Europeans focus on causal modeling and design approaches. In his review of the scholarly literature, Lambert (2015) as well revealed that empirically grounded taxonomies of business models are still limited and characterized by classification schemes with no explicit criteria.

The remainder of this paragraph will present an evolution of the main researches and definitions regarding the business model concept. Research on business models started during the late 1990s and the early 2000s in some famous studies (Mahadevan, 2000; Slywotzky, 1996; Timmers, 1998; Weill & Vitale, 2001), even if similar concepts had already appeared in the previous Drucker's "theory of business" (Drucker, 1994). However, one of the first definitions of business model can be traced back to Slywotzky (1996), who described a business model as a mix of decisions related to customer selection, creation of utility for customers, and profits capturing. Conversely, Timmers (1998) pointed out a broader and generic definition of business model, differentiating it from a more marketing-focused model and considering it as a "representation of a firm's underlying core logic and strategic choices for creating and capturing value in a value network". This definition also influenced those from Mahadevan (2000) and Weill and Vitale (2001). Mayo and Brown (1999) and Stewart and Zhao (2000), instead, turned their attention to the achievement of sustainable financial competitiveness. Finally, moving away from the strategic dimension of a business model, in her famous definition Magretta (2002) stressed the relationship among its various components. In doing so, she stated that a business model has to satisfy two conditions: it must have a sound logic (i.e., who customers are and what they value) and it has to focus on how firms can make money by providing customers that value. By the way, the organizational entity of business models is not clear since some of the definitions above mentioned were referring to the firm level while others to the network level.

In that regard and due to its comprehensiveness, Chesbrough and Rosenbloom's (2002) definition still represents one of the reference points of the literature on business models. More precisely, the authors intended business models as the enablers to convert technologies into economic outcomes. Indeed, they argued that "firms need to understand the cognitive role of the business model, to commercialize [the] technology in ways that will allow firms to capture value from their technology investments" (Chesbrough & Rosenbloom, 2002, p. 532). Moreover, this definition identifies several attributes of a business model that enable firms to articulate their value proposition, identify their market segments, define the best structure of the value chain, estimate the potential profit, recognize the position of the value network, and develop a competitive strategy. Another famous definition of business model, mainly centered on its components and the relationship among them, came from Osterwalder and Pigneur (2010), who described the business model as the rationale of how an organization creates, delivers, and captures value. However, to be effective, it must identify nine building blocks: (i) customer segments; (ii) value propositions; (iii) channels; (iv) customer relationships; (v) revenue streams; (vi) key resources; (vii) key activities; (viii) key partnerships; (ix) cost structure.

Four years later his study with Rosenbloom, Chesbrough (2006) stated that business models perform two main functions: value creation and value capture. The former was referred to a series of activities regarding new products or services in such a way that there is net value created throughout these various activities. Value capture, instead, was referred to as seizing value from a portion of those activities for the firm developing the model. In the two following years, another well-established definition of business model will be released. Firstly, Rasmussen (2007) defined a business model as the way through which firms assume: (i) what competitive strategy adopt, deciding what products (services) offer to the market and how much ask for selling (providing) them, as well as identifying their production costs; (ii) through what value proposition differentiate themselves from other firms; (iii) how integrate their own value chain with those of other firms that are involved in the same value network. Secondly, Richardson (2008), after an in-depth analysis of the previous literature, pointed out a framework that integrates all the already established ideas about business models in a logical structure. Notably, in this structure the key components are the value proposition (in terms of the offer and the target customer segment), the value creation and delivery systems, and the value capture system. Thirdly, according to Teece (2010), the essence of a business model regards how enterprises deliver value to customers, convince customers to pay for that value, and convert the received payments to profit.

In any case, over the years, the concept of business model has begun to increasingly consider not only the aspects related to value created by companies, but also to shared value. Therefore, in their work Zott and Amit (2010) conceptualized a company's business model as a system of interrelated activities that transcend the focal firm and its boundaries. In this case, firms are called to weave together different activities that are performed by the company itself or by its suppliers, partners, and customers to co-create shared value. The concept of value, however, remained too vague in many studies and most of the authors have not clearly explained the meaning of "value" or "customer value", making the comprehension of their definition too abstract. Table 7.1 shows the main definitions of a business model that can be found in the literature.

7.3   Business Model Innovation

The concept of business model has been further challenged by the emergence of two major factors that have radically changed the competitive landscape (Nielsen et al., 2018): the advent of the digital era and the globalization of markets, two phenomena that are strongly related to each other. For example, stating that great technologies are becoming ever more rapidly commoditized, Chesbrough (2007) reflects on the role of new technologies in enhancing companies' performances. Moreover, the global economy is leading companies to transform manufacturing processes, supply chains, marketing tools, governance mechanisms, and organizational strategies to compete internationally, which has become a necessity for companies' survival

7.3 Business Model Innovation

Table 7.1 Definitions of a business model

Source	Definition
Slywotzky (1996)	[Business model refers to] "the totality of how a company selects its customers, defines and differentiates it offerings, defines the tasks it will perform itself and those it will outsource, configures its resources, goes to market, creates utility for customers and captures profits."
Timmers (1998)	[Business model stands for] "architecture of the product, service, and information flows, including a description of the various business actors and their roles, the potential benefits for the various business actors; a description of the sources of revenues." (p. 4)
Porter (2001)	"The definition of a business model is murky at best. Most often, it seems to refer to a loose conception of how a company does business and generates revenue. Yet simply having a business model is an exceedingly low bar to set for building a company. Generating revenue is a far cry from creating economic value." (p. 73)
Chesbrough and Rosenbloom (2002)	The business model is "the heuristic logic that connects technical potential with the realization of economic value." (p. 529) "The business model provides a coherent framework that takes technological characteristics and potentials as inputs and converts them through customers and markets into economic outputs." (p. 532)
Magretta (2002)	"Business models are stories that explain how the enterprises work [...] Business models describe, as a system, how the pieces of a business fit together, but they don't factor in one critical dimension of performance: competition" [...] "A good business model has to satisfy two conditions. It must have a good logic—who the customers are, what they value, and how the company can make money by providing them that value. Second, the business model must generate profits."
Osterwalder (2004)	"A conceptual tool that contains a set of elements and their relationships and allows expressing the business logic of a specific firm. It is a description of the value a company offers to one or several segments of customers and the architecture of the firm and its network of partners for creating, marketing and delivering this value and relationship capital, to generate a profitable and sustainable revenue stream."
Chesbrough (2007)	"The business model is a useful framework to link ideas and technologies to economic outcomes" [...] "It also has value in understanding how companies of all sizes can convert technological potential (e.g. products, feasibility, and performance) into economic value (price and profits)" [...] "Every company has a business model, whether that model is articulated or not."
Richardson (2008)	A business model is "a conceptual framework that helps to link the firm's strategy, or theory of how to compete, to its activities, or execution of the strategy. The business model framework can help to think strategically about the details of the way the firm does business." (p. 135) "The three major components of the framework the value proposition, the value creation and delivery system, and value captured reflect the logic of strategic thinking about value. The essence of strategy is to create superior value for customers and capture a greater amount of that value than competitors." (p. 138)
Skarzynski and Gibson (2008)	"The business model is a conceptual framework for identifying how a company creates, delivers, and extracts value. It typically includes a whole set of integrated components, all of which can be looked on as opportunities for innovation and competitive advantage."

(continued)

194 7 Innovative and Sustainable Food Business Models

Table 7.1 (continued)

Source	Definition
Teece (2010)	"A business model articulates the logic, the data and other evidence that support a value proposition for the customer, and a viable structure of revenues and costs for the enterprise delivering that value." (p. 179)
Zott and Amit (2010)	"We conceptualize a firm's business model as a system of interdependent activities that transcends the focal firm and spans its boundaries. The activity system enables the firm, in concert with its partners, to create value and also to appropriate a share of that value [and is defined by] design elements—content, structure, and governance—that describe the architecture of an activity system; and design themes."
Wirtz, Pistoia, Ullrich, and Göttel (2016)	"A business model is a simplified and aggregated representation of the relevant activities of a company. It describes how marketable information, products and/or services are generated by means of a company's value-added component. In addition to the architecture of value creation, strategic as well as customer and market components are taken into consideration, in order to achieve the superordinate goal of generating, or rather, securing the competitive advantage. To fulfil this latter purpose, a current business model should always be critically regarded from a dynamic perspective, thus within the consciousness that there may be the need for business model evolution or business model innovation, due to internal or external changes over time." (p. 41)
Massa, Tucci, and Afuah (2017)	"A business model is a description of an organization and how that organization functions in achieving its goals (e.g., profitability, growth, social impact, . . .)." (p. 73)
Müller, Buliga, and Voigt (2018)	"The present paper defines business model as a sum of the value creation mechanisms, value offer, and value capture mechanisms."

Source: Authors' elaboration

(Onetti, Zucchella, Jones, & McDougall-Covin, 2012). Together with the expansion of their customer base by entering new markets, companies have been increasingly required also to develop appropriate information systems to gather and analyze data of their potential and actual customers (Gnizy, 2019). In this regard, several famous companies (e.g., Amazon, Netflix, Walmart), independently from offering traditional physical services or virtual ones, are taking advantage of business analytics to meet their customers' needs.

Those changes led scholars to stop considering business models as a given picture. For instance, Demil and Lecocq (2010) highlighted that business models should be analyzed in a dynamic way, capturing innovation and changes in organizations and, consequently, within their business models. In a similar vein, Chesbrough's thought (2010) that for companies innovating their business model is much more important than adopting innovative technologies. Moreover, Amit and Zott (2012) found that, whereas most of the innovations and cost savings have already been achieved, companies would receive the main benefits of innovating their business models. Nowadays, innovation must regard the whole business models rather than providing just new products and processes or performing organizational changes since product quality and production scale do not necessarily represent a competitive advantage anymore (Vrontis, Bresciani, & Giacosa, 2016). Therefore, companies should focus their efforts on where the competition does not act at all, but they keep showing a stronger shared sense of how to innovate technology rather than their business models. Some examples of industries that have somewhat disrupted the traditional ways of doing business by adopting agile technology-based businesses (Nielsen et al., 2018) are Uber (transportation), Airbnb (accommodation), Spotify (music), Amazon (retail), Skype (telecommunications), Just Eat (food).

Considering the above, the main literature that has analyzed business model innovation will now be presented, even if this concept, such as the business model

Table 7.2 Business model innovation definitions

Source	Definition
Mitchell and Bruckner Coles (2004)	"By business model innovation, we mean business model replacements that provide product or service offerings to customers and end-users that were not previously available. We also refer to the process of developing these novel replacements as business model innovation." (p. 17)
Lindgardt, Reeves, Stalk Jr., and Deimler (2012)	"Innovation becomes BMI [business model innovation] when two or more elements of a business model are reinvented to deliver value in a new way. [...] BMI can provide companies a way to break out of intense competition, under which product or process innovations are easily imitated." (p. 2)
Romero and Molina (2009)	"Business models as definers of the value creation priorities in an organisation should be continuously reviewed in response to actual and possible changes in the perceived market conditions and evolve the enterprise strategy as the business environment and customers' needs change." (p. 3)
Johnson (2010)	"[Seizing the white space] calls for the ability to innovate something more core than the core, to innovate the very theory of the business itself. I call that process business model innovation." (p. 13). "Business model innovation is an iterative journey." (p. 114)
Björkdahl and Holmén (2013)	"Business model innovation refers to a new integrated logic of how the firm creates value for its customers or users and how it captures value, and is the implementation of a business model that is new to the firm."
Geissdoerfer, Bocken, and Hultink (2016)	"Business model innovation describes either a process of transformation from one business model to another within incumbent companies or after mergers and acquisitions, or the creation of entirely new business models in start-ups." (p. 1220)
Bouwman, de Reuver, and Nikou (2017)	"Business model innovation as a change in a company's business model that is new to the firm and results in observable changes in its practices towards customers and partners."
Foss and Saebi (2017)	"We define BMI [business model innovation] as designed, novel, nontrivial changes to the key elements of a firm's business model and/or the architecture linking these elements."

Source: Authors' elaboration

one, is still not so clear. Table 7.2 collects some of the main definitions of business model innovation that can be found in the literature. Many authors described business model innovation as a process (Foss & Saebi, 2017; Schallmo & Brecht, 2010) to develop a new business model (Björkdahl & Holmén, 2013; Foss & Saebi, 2017) or an entire industry (Santos, Spector, & Van der Heyden, 2009; Schallmo & Brecht, 2010). Notably, it can be referred to "incremental changes in individual components of business models, [an] extension of the existing business model, [the] introduction of parallel business models, right through to disruption of the business model, which may potentially entail replacing the existing model with a fundamentally different one" (Khanagha, Volberda, & Oshri, 2014, p. 324). Moreover, Nielsen and Lund (2018) highlighted the importance of scalability in business model innovation. According to main findings of their research: (i) scalable business models are flexible and turn new resources into increasing returns; (ii) scalability often involves connecting strategic partners to a company's value proposition; and (iii) one key is to find smart ways to leverage the resources of partners.

The concept of business model innovation can be seen as the result of the resources and the capabilities which are available within the respective company (Teece, 2008). Firms can be sustainable over time if they successfully adapt to the environment in which they are nested. The company's dynamic capabilities represent, in this case, the proper perspective to understand how firms can cope with volatile environments. According to Schweizer (2005, p. 6), a "dynamic capability can be considered as the ability to seize new opportunities and to change the existing business model by reconfiguring the value chain constellation and protecting knowledge assets, competences and [the access to] complementary assets and technologies in order to achieve sustainable competitive advantage". Many recent studies adopted dynamic capabilities frameworks to explain business model innovation triggered by digitalization. Rachinger, Rauter, Müller, Vorraber, and Schirgi (2018), for instance, framed a conceptual setting based on the business logic triangle (Osterwalder & Pigneur, 2002). In their analysis of companies from the automotive and media industry, they found that the perceived available options for business model innovation by digitalization are determined by the firm's value proposition and the position in the value network itself, as well as the position in the value network. Another empirical evidence of business model innovation is provided by Amit and Zott (2012) with the Apple case from the real world. Apple became famous for the innovative production of hardware and software and, particularly, personal computers. Nevertheless, through the creation of the iPod and its associated software (iTunes), some years later they introduced a legal online music download service that has represented a radical innovation of the company's business model. In doing so, Apple has been the first computer company that included music distribution as a linked activity to the development of the iPod's hardware and software. In this way, Apple transformed its business model including an ongoing relationship with its customers, who consequently obtained an ongoing and shared value from using Apple devices and software. Hence, the process of innovation extended from the product to the overall business model.

7.4 Business Model Innovation for Sustainability

Sustainability issues, like social imbalances (Hart & Dowell, 2011), climate change (Reid & Toffel, 2009), and environmental matters (Seuring & Müller, 2008), are increasingly asking to redesign modern economic systems, realizing a transition toward the sustainability paradigm. Since they control the majority of both resources and capabilities, companies are considered central actors to address these issues (Porter & Kramer, 2011) and "important and necessary social change agents" (Aguilera, Rupp, Williams, & Ganapathi, 2007, p. 857). Therefore, they have been innovating their business models in a more sustainable and socially responsible way since the introduction of the United Nations Global Compact in 1999. The Global Compact represents a non-binding framework that states ten principles in the areas of human rights, labor, environment, and anti-corruption and asks companies to give evidence of both their economic and non-economic value creation processes in their reports. With the purpose of spreading the same message to more actors than just companies, in 2015 the United Nations General Assembly also released a set of 17 Sustainable Development Goals (e.g., no poverty, zero hungry, climate action, decent work, economic growth). Moreover, the recent global crises have questioned the impact of existing corporate business models on the sustainability of the global economy and society (Schaltegger, Lüdeke-Freund, & Hansen, 2016). Therefore, policy makers, practitioners, and scholars have been reconsidering the contribution of firms to sustainable development.

According to the definition given by Lüdeke-Freund (2010, p. 23), a sustainable business model is "a business model that creates competitive advantage through superior customer value and contributes to the sustainable development of the company and society". The core of a sustainable business is still thus linked to create, deliver, and capture economic value (Osterwalder & Pigneur, 2010; Teece, 2010; Zott & Amit, 2010), but including social and environmental values as well (Boons, Montalvo, Quist, & Wagner, 2013; Schaltegger, Lüdeke-Freund, & Hansen, 2012; Stubbs & Cocklin, 2008; Yang, Evans, Vladimirova, & Rana, 2017). Built upon Bocken, Short, Rana, and Evans (2014) and Lüdeke-Freund, Massa, Bocken, Brent, and Musango (2016), Ritala, Huotari, Bocken, Albareda, and Puumalainen (2018) have identified some of the main archetypes that characterize environmental and social issues in business models. The environmentally oriented archetypes which have been found are maximizing material and energy efficiency, closing resource loops, and substituting with renewables and natural processes. The socially-oriented archetypes, instead, are delivering functionality rather than owner-ship, adopting a stewardship role, and encouraging sufficiency. As argued by Zollo, Cennamo, and Neumann (2013), a business that just predicates on the hunt for an immediate profit actually ends up hurting its capacity to create both economic and non-economic value for the long term. Thus, nowadays, companies need to take into consideration both long-term value creation and systemic thinking as drivers of success (Stubbs & Higgins, 2018). As a result, if business model innovation can provide companies higher yields than just innovating their products or processes

(Chesbrough, 2007; Lindgardt et al., 2012), adopting a sustainable business model could also help companies to better-facing risks (Choi & Wang, 2009) and catch more value co-creation opportunities (De Bernardi, Forliano, Rotti, & Franco, 2019; Nidumolu, Prahalad, & Rangaswami, 2009; Porter & Kramer, 2011; Tukker & Tischner, 2006). The adoption of sustainable business models was also encouraged by Laurence D. Fink, chairman and chief executive officer at the world's biggest investor BlackRock. Indeed, in January 2018, in his annual letter sent to CEOs of the S&P 500, he stated that "Society is demanding that companies, both public and private, serve a social purpose. To prosper over time, every company must not only deliver financial performance but also show how it makes a positive contribution to society". In any case, since progressing towards sustainability requires more than just adopting new and innovative technologies (Girotra & Netessine, 2013), achieving this paradigm can represent a difficult task for some companies. Therefore, business model innovation can represent an effective solution to align internal rewarding mechanisms to leverage sustainability (Rashid, Asif, Krajnik, & Nicolescu, 2013). This led to the concept of sustainable business model innovation (Boons & Lüdeke-Freund, 2013; Schaltegger et al., 2012; Yang et al., 2017), whose implementation can follow two different approaches according to Inigo, Albareda, and Ritala (2017). The first one, preferred by well established, large companies, is called "evolutionary approach" and is based on adjusting value creation for responding to environmental changes, gradually incorporating sustainability objectives in the market. Conversely, the second approach, most suitable for novel companies or spin-offs, is called "radical approach" and is based on introducing a completely new value proposition either to match a new sustainability challenge or to tackle an issue in a radically novel manner.

For what concerns the value concept linked to sustainable business model innovation, Yang et al. (2017) have highlighted the necessity to enlarge the traditional perspectives of value proposition, value capture, value creation, and value delivery by introducing the concept of value uncaptured. This new perspective allows a more comprehensive understanding of value to promote sustainability, focusing not just on "how", "what" and "with whom" the value is shared, but also "how much" and "to what extent" the value is shared. Particularly, the paper develops four specific forms of value uncaptured: value surplus, value absence, value missed, and value destroyed.

Tables 7.3 and 7.4 show the main definitions of sustainable business models and sustainable business model innovations in the literature.

7.5 Circular Business Models

It is estimated that around nine billion people will leave on Earth by 2050 and this will require three times more resources than the one that is actually consumed (Godfray et al., 2010). However, in current linear economic systems, ruled by the "make-use-dispose" model (Stahel, 2016), approximately 80% of those resources

7.5 Circular Business Models

Table 7.3 Sustainable business model definitions

Source	Definition
Stubbs and Cocklin (2008)	A sustainable business model is "a model where sustainability concepts shape the driving force of the firm and its decision making [so that] the dominant neoclassical model of the firm is transformed, rather than supplemented, by social and environmental priorities." (p. 103)
Lüdeke-Freund (2010)	"A business model that creates competitive advantage through superior customer value and contributes to the sustainable development of the company and society."
Garetti and Taisch (2012)	Sustainable business models "have a global market perspective, taking into account the development of new industrialised countries as well as the need for more sustainable products and services." (p. 88)
Bocken, Short, Rana, and Evans (2013)	"Sustainable business models seek to go beyond delivering economic value and include a consideration of other forms of value for a broader range of stakeholders." (p. 484)
Boons and Lüdeke-Freund (2013)	A sustainable business model is different from a conventional one through four propositions, "(1) The value proposition provides measurable ecological and/or social value in concert with economic value [...] (2) The supply chain involves suppliers who take responsibility towards their own as well as the focal company's stakeholders [...] (3) The customer interface motivates customers to take responsibility for their consumption as well as for the focal company's stakeholders. [...] (4) The financial model reflects an appropriate distribution of economic costs and benefits among actors involved in the business model and accounts for the company's ecological and social impacts." (p. 13)
Wells (2013)	A business model for sustainability "would assists in the achievement of sustainability [by] following major principles [...] for sustainability", which Wells defines as (1) resource efficiency, (2) social relevance, (3) localisation and engagement, (4) longevity, (5) ethical sourcing, and (6) work enrichment. (p. 65)
Schaltegger et al. (2016)	A business model for sustainability helps describing, analysing, managing, and communicating (i) a company's sustainable value proposition to its customers, and all other stakeholders, (ii) how it creates and delivers this value, (iii) and how it captures economic value while maintaining or regenerating natural, social, and economic capital beyond its organizational boundaries
Upward and Jones (2016)	A (strongly) sustainable business model "is the definition by which an enterprise determines the appropriate inputs, resource flows, and value decisions and its role in ecosystems, [in a way that] sustainability measures [which] are those indicators that assess the outputs and effects of business model decisions [...] might be claimed as successfully sustainable." (p. 98)
Abdelkafi and Täuscher (2016)	Sustainable business models, "incorporate sustainability as an integral part of the company's value proposition and value creation logic. As such, [Business models for Sustainability] provide value to the customer and to the natural environment and/or society." (p. 75)
Geissdoerfer et al. (2016)	"We define a sustainable business model as a simplified representation of the elements, the interrelation between these elements, and the interactions with its stakeholders that an organisational unit uses to create, deliver, capture, and exchange sustainable value for, and in collaboration with, a broad range of stakeholders." (p. 1219)

(continued)

Table 7.3 (continued)

Source	Definition
Evans et al. (2017)	Sustainable business models are described with five propositions: "(1) Sustainable value incorporates economic, social and environmental benefits conceptualised as value forms. (2) Sustainable business models require a system of sustainable value flows among multiple stakeholders including the natural environment and society as primary stakeholders. (3) Sustainable business models require a value network with a new purpose, design and governance. (4) Sustainable business models require a systemic consideration of stakeholder interests and responsibilities for mutual value creation. (5) Internalizing externalities through product-service systems enables innovation towards sustainable business models." (p. 5)

Source: Authors' elaboration

become waste just after the first use and that percentage rises to 99% within 6 months (Sempels & Hoffmann, 2013). A stronger sensitivity towards these issues, a change in people's attitude toward consumption, and the existence of enabling technology conditions have led to the introduction of new models with specific additional characteristics. These models have assumed the following labels: product-service systems, green business models, and circular business models (Bocken et al., 2014; Linder & Williander, 2017; Reim, Parida, & Örtqvist, 2015). Circular business models do not only aim to create sustainable value, but they also employ a proactive multi-stakeholder management (Geissdoerfer et al., 2018; Pieroni, McAloone, & Pigosso, 2019), adopting a long-term perspective majorly oriented to (i) close, (ii) slow, (iii) intensify, (iv) dematerialise, (v) and narrow resource loops (Tunn, Bocken, van den Hende, & Schoormans, 2019). Closing a loop means that "the goods of today are the resources of tomorrow at yesterday's prices" (Stahel, 2013, p. 55) since produced waste can be reintegrated into companies' supply chains through reuse or recycle. For example, Biochair, a biofuel produced from beer production scraps, or Rise Flour, a flour made from wasted grains with more nutraceutical properties than traditional ones. Slowing, instead, regards extending products' life cycles, reducing the amount of produced waste and, consequently, reducing costs connected to inventory, transportation, and distribution activities (e.g. Cambridge Crops, which has developed a natural coating for extending food freshness). With the term intensifying a loop, it is intended that products are transformed into services, according to people's reduced interest in possessing a specific good rather than using it (Ellen MacArthur Foundation, 2014). Several examples can be found within the so-called sharing economy phenomenon (e.g., cars or bikes sharing, video and audio broadcasting, clothes rentals). Dematerialise means that digital resources are preferred to their physical alternatives, which requires both technological and cultural changes in the way products or services are produced and consumed. Finally, narrowing concerns improving products or companies' internal or external processes, so that the used resources (energy, water, raw materials, packages, stock areas, transportation needs, etc.) can be reduced, as well as the consequent produced emissions and wastes.

7.5 Circular Business Models

Table 7.4 Sustainable business model innovation definitions

Source	Definition
Boons and Lüdeke-Freund (2013)	"Sustainable business model innovation is understood as the adaption of the business model to overcome barriers within the company and its environment to market sustainable process, product, or service innovations." (p. 13)
Casadesus-Masanell and Zhu (2013)	"Business model innovation refers to the search for new logics of the firm and new ways to create and capture value for its stakeholders; it focuses primarily on finding new ways to generate revenues and define value propositions for customers, suppliers, and partners." (p. 464)
Loorbach and Wijsman (2013)	Sustainable business model innovation describes businesses' "searching for ways to deal with unpredictable [. . .] wider societal changes and sustainability issues." (p. 20)
Girotra and Netessine (2013)	"A sustainable business is not only achieved through innovation in technologies, products or services, but also through BMI, namely a different approach to value creation."
Bocken et al. (2014)	"Business model innovations for sustainability are defined as: Innovations that create significant positive and/or significantly reduced negative impacts for the environment and/or society, through changes in the way the organisation and its value-network create, deliver value and capture value (i.e. create economic value) or change their value propositions." (p. 44)
Geissdoerfer et al. (2016)	"Sustainable business innovation processes specifically aim at incorporating sustainable value and pro-active management of a broad range of stakeholders into the business model." (p. 1220)
Roome and Louche (2016)	Sustainable business model innovation describes the "processes through which [. . .] new business models are developed by businesses and their managers [. . .] how companies revise and transform their business model in order to contribute to sustainable development." (p. 12)
Schaltegger et al. (2016)	Sustainable business model innovation describes the creation of "modified and completely new business models [that] can help develop integrative and competitive solutions by either radically reducing negative and/or creating positive external effects for the natural environment and society." (p. 3)
Yang, Evans, Vladimirova, and Rana (2016)	"Sustainable business model innovation can be more easily achieved by identifying the value uncaptured in current business models, and then turning this new understanding of the current business into value opportunities that can lead to new business models with higher sustainable value." (p. 2)
Baldassarre, Calabretta, Bocken, and Jaskiewicz (2017)	"The sustainable business model innovation approach aims at achieving sustainability objectives by generating economic value. In this context, the development of a sustainable value proposition—that is, an offering addressing a sustainability problem, creating shared value for a network of stakeholders—is central. User-driven-innovations is an approach to business innovation that can help overcome some key challenges in the development of sustainable value propositions."
Geissdoerfer, Vladimirova, and Evans (2018)	"[. . .] incorporate pro-active multi-stakeholder management, the creation of monetary and non-monetary value for a broad range of stakeholders, and hold a long-term perspective."

Source: Authors' elaboration

Furthermore, regarding the circular business model, relevant is the study of Heyes, Sharmina, Mendoza, Gallego-Schmid, and Azapagic (2018), who applied the principles of the circular economy to the nine building blocks of the business model canvas theorized by Osterwalder and Pigneur (2010). Moreover, Todeschini, Cortimiglia, Callegaro-de-Menezes, and Ghezzi (2017) stressed the need to develop value propositions that can reduce environmental impacts. They conducted eight case studies on start-ups, identifying the concept of "born sustainable", which drives entrepreneurs in accomplishing the circular economy goals by designing sustainable value propositions. Geissdoerfer et al. (2018) proposed further research on sustainability-oriented and circular economy-oriented business models by highlighting that these kinds of business models are not always able to capture the full potential of sustainability. Some circular economy-oriented business model, for instance, may generate negative secondary effects. For example, Andersen (2007) focused his attention also on the costs that are linked to building circular systems, rather than just their related benefits, while Allwood (2014) pointed out the technical impossibility of closing some resources' loops. Indeed, in some instances, it could be required more energy to recycle materials than acquiring them in traditional ways. In addition to that, some other scholars (Murray, Skene, & Haynes, 2017) stated that the circular economy has brought considerable attention to some sustainability aspects, especially the environmental ones, overlooking the social sustainability dimension.

7.6 Business Modelling: Tools for Designing New Business Models

Over the last years, the technological advances and the grand challenges that the food sector is called to face are providing ideas for the creation of new and disruptive start-ups. These start-ups need the support of a framework that allows giving architecture to their business idea. One of the most successful tools which have been recently developed is the so-called Business Model Canvas (Osterwalder & Pigneur, 2010). This framework is composed of nine building blocks (Fig. 7.1) which enable companies answering to the following questions:

- *Customer segments*: for whom are we creating value? Who are our most important customers?
- *Value propositions*: what value do we deliver to the customer? Which one of our customer's problems are we helping to solve? Which customer needs are we satisfying? What bundles of products and services are we offering to each customer segment?
- *Channels*: through which channels do our customer segments want to be reached? How are we reaching them now? How are our channels integrated? Which ones work best? Which ones are most cost-efficient? How are we integrating them with customer routines?

7.6 Business Modelling: Tools for Designing New Business Models 203

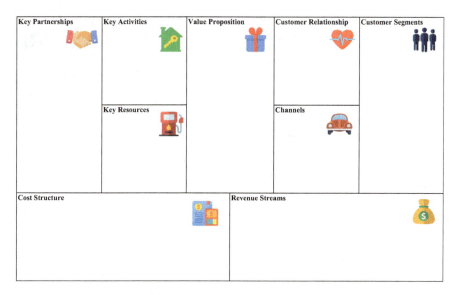

Fig. 7.1 Business model canvas. Source: Based on Osterwalder and Pigneur (2010)

- *Customer relationships*: what type of relationship does each of our customer segments expect us to establish and maintain with them? Which ones have we established? How costly are they? How are they integrated with the rest of our business model?
- *Revenue streams*: for what value are our customers willing to pay? For what do they currently pay? How are they currently paying? How would they prefer to pay? How much does each revenue stream contribute to overall revenues?
- *Key resources*: what key resources do our value propositions require? Our distribution channels? Customer relationships? Revenue streams?
- *Key activities*: what key activities do our value propositions require? Our distribution channels? Customer relationships? Revenue streams?
- *Key partnerships*: who are our key partners? Who are our key suppliers? Which key resources are we acquiring from partners? Which key activities do partners perform?
- *Cost structure*: what are the most important costs inherent in our business model? Which key resources are most expensive? Which key activities are the most expensive?

Due to the complexity of identifying some of the blocks that constitute the business model canvas for some companies, especially start-ups, this framework has been revisited by numerous scholars. For instance, Maurya (2012) theorized the lean canvas (Fig. 7.2), which is built upon the nine blocks concept of the traditional business model canvas, but with some of those building blocks that have been modified in order to suit the needs and purposes of a lean start-up. Each of these blocks is shortly described below:

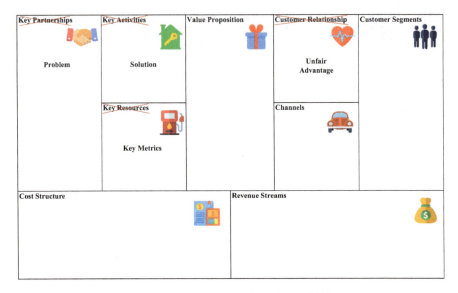

Fig. 7.2 Lean business model canvas. Source: Based on Maurya (2012)

- *Problem*: each customer segment you are thinking to work with will have a set of problems that need to be solved. Therefore, for a start-up could be easier identifying those problems and assess if the project is worthwhile, rather than recognizing its key partners in the early-life stages.
- *Customer Segments*: once a problem has been identified, a specific customer segment that experiences it should come up into the mind. So, those two dimensions can be viewed as intrinsically connected—without having a customer segment in mind problems cannot be addressed, and vice versa.
- *Solution*: the identified problem will need to be addressed and, eventually, overcome by the company. Therefore, even if key activities are still not well structured or difficult to be identified, the solution the company is going to provide to its customers should be clear since the beginning of its activities. The solution cannot be found in an office. It instead requires going out in the streets, interviewing customers, asking them questions, and interiorizing those learnings.
- *Value Proposition*: the value proposition is the core of the canvas, representing the company's promise of value that is intended to be delivered and the primary reason why a customer would buy a product or service. Thus, start-ups need to understand what differentiates them from other companies.
- *Channels*: channels represent the ways the customer segment will be reached. In the initial phase, it is crucial to think more about learning than scaling and, consequently, choosing channels that can provide information and feed-backs or allow direct contact with the customer segment.

7.6 Business Modelling: Tools for Designing New Business Models 205

- *Revenue Streams*: despite some products or services can be offered for free in order to gain traction—being careful to not affect their perceived value—it is imperative to have one principal revenue stream and eventually to build other secondary ones.
- *Cost Structure*: identifying the cost structure means understanding which elements are burdening it more than others or recognizing the company's cost centers. Some of the following questions could help to do that: how much will it cost to build the landing page? What is the burn rate of the firm? What are the total monthly running costs? How much will it cost to interview the customer segment? How much do market research papers cost? And so on.
- *Key Metrics*: every business, no matter what industry or size, will have some key metrics that are used to monitor performance. The best way to help with this is to visualize a funnel top-down that flows from the large open top, through multiple stages to the narrow end.
- *Unfair Advantage*: if relationships with customers cannot be already set-up, the company needs to at least own an unfair advantage compared to its competitors. A real unfair advantage is something that cannot be easily copied or bought by competitors (e.g., insider information, a dream team, significant networks effects, the right "expert" endorsement).

The business model canvas has also been reviewed in view of the social and environmental concerns that characterize companies nowadays. Changes in the context surrounding companies lead in fact to the reconfiguration of the instruments to design the start-up business models. As a consequence, the nine building blocks of the traditional canvas have been recently enriched by two additional blocks, respectively referring to social and environmental costs and benefits (Fig. 7.3).

In conclusion, it is presented the circular business model (Fig. 7.4), developed by Planing (2015) on the basis of the hierarchical model originally theorized by Stahel and Reday-Mulvey (1981). Indeed, even if scholars still do not agree on what elements should be part of a circular business model, it is generally accepted that the hierarchical order of those elements exists and represent one of the key factors of such a business model. Starting from the circle IV, the model takes into account material processors that can recoup every raw material from a product whose operating life has ended. Even if this means perfectly closing the resource loop associated with that specific product, this represents the most expensive activity in terms of required resources and technologies. Then, in circle III, processes that enable manufacturers to reconfigure products or upgrade some of their components with better ones are considered. These processes are referred to as narrowing a resource loop, but it is necessary that the remanufacturing process requires fewer resources than the traditional production one for respecting the sustainability paradigm. Subsequently, activities that can be performed by sellers and service providers are assessed, since circle II contemplates dematerializing products, affecting their delivery, turning them into services or extending their life-cycle. These activities are respectively connected to what has been called: dematerializing, intensifying, and slowing resources' loop. In this regard, products could additionally be reconditioned

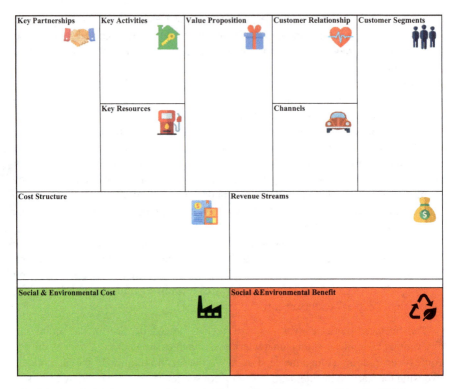

Fig. 7.3 Sustainable business model canvas. Source: Based on Joyce and Paquin (2016)

or sold back to different, more price-sensitive, customer segments. Finally, the tighter circle contemplates what customers can realize through their consumption habits to achieve circularity, for example preferring long-lasting products or consuming them in a more efficient way. So, in circle I activities that are able to slow loops are considered again. It must be highlighted that this circle also includes the activities that can be conducted requiring the lower amount of resources, respecting the above-mentioned hierarchical order of factors composing the model. Additionally, the hierarchy can also be observed in the efforts that are required to adapt a business model in order to go up from circle I to circle IV. In this vein, for example, Lewandowski (2016) added to the traditional framework developed by Osterwalder and Pigneur another block, referred to as the adoption factors. The adoption factors are those reasons that can hinder companies from turning their business model from linearity to circularity and that should be prevented (Ellen MacArthur Foundation, 2015; Scott, 2013). They can concern both internal and external factors, where the former are connected to various organizational capabilities (e.g., human, knowledge, and intellectual resources), procedures, and tools to design business models and assessment systems. Conversely, the latter refers to (i) technological possibilities; (ii) laws and political incentives; (iii) socio-cultural issues, such as consumer attitude

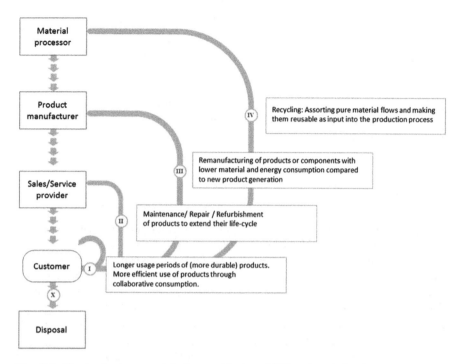

Fig. 7.4 Circular business model. Source: Planing (2015), adapted from Ellen MacArthur Foundation (2014) and Stahel and Reday-Mulvey (1981)

and public opinion); (iv) and economic forces, like the expected market demand or difficulties encountered by other companies.

7.7 Business Models in the Food Sector: Where Are We Going?

The growing concern towards sustainability-related aspects and the technological progress of the whole society are changing the competitive landscape, leading companies to explicitly address social and environmental issues and to adapt and (or) innovate their business models. Food companies are no exception (De Bernardi, Bertello, Venuti, & Zardini, 2019; De Bernardi & Tirabeni, 2018) since they also are called to face many grand challenges for years to come. The generally increasing attention to sustainability has been spurred by the adoption of the 17 Sustainable Development Goals (SDGs) by all the Members of the United Nations in 2015 as well (De Bernardi, Venuti, & Bertello, 2019). In fact, nowadays, they still represent the heart of the 2030 Agenda for Sustainable Development. For what regards food and nutrition security, in 2015 also the European Commission released his research and innovation policy. In this way, it answered to the international policy developments of those years (SDGs and the COP21 commitments), identifying the following priorities: nutrition for sustainable and healthy diets, climate-smart and environmentally sustainable food systems, the circularity of food systems, and innovation and empowerment of communities. Not facing those challenges could have relevant consequences. In the next sections, it will be presented the major paradigms and innovations that have been redefining the food sector in recent years.

7.7.1 Food-Tech

The use of technology in the food sector (food-tech) has allowed new ventures to meet the expectations of the society in a more efficient way than before. So, it has increasingly offered the opportunity to consider new solutions for achieving sustainable goals such as human health, climate change, constraints on natural resources, and animal welfare.[1] The food sector, for example, is increasingly looking for nutritional solutions tailored to specific diseases: currently, in fact, seven of eight major risk factors for premature death are linked to the way we eat, drink and exercise. Non-communicable diseases and obesity account for 63% of all annual deaths and are related to eating habits (European Commission, 2018). Companies are developing strategies to deliver nutrition advice tailored to the individuals' biological readouts (e.g., DNA, microbiome, neuroscience). Moreover, an increased number of mobile applications aim nowadays to provide specific diets for diseases such as diabetes and Alzheimer. MySugr,[2] for instance, founded in 2012 in Vienna (Austria), is currently one of the most famous apps in the world for diabetes patients, this start-up makes it easier both for the patient and the healthcare staff to manage the disease. The main features of this app are: customized screen for every user; blood sugar charts presented clearly and with an eye-catching design; daily, weekly, and monthly analysis of blood service values; exciting challenges for achieving personal goals; motivational feedbacks.

An increasing orientation towards the grand challenges of the new century has also led several companies (e.g., Beyond Meat, Impossible Foods, Moving Mountains) to base their business models on the production of plant-based meat, contributing to growing issues attributed to livestock production. For example, Beyond Meat[3] states that producing their burgers requires 99% less water, 93% land, and 50% energy than producing a beef burger, with 90% fewer greenhouse gas emissions.

But, besides these kinds of product/service innovations, the fourth industrial revolution has opened up even greater opportunities for firms, in terms of process

---

[1] https://eatforum.org/content/uploads/2019/01/EAT-Lancet_Commission_Summary_Report.pdf

[2] https://mysugr.com

[3] https://www.beyondmeat.com

7.7 Business Models in the Food Sector: Where Are We Going?

efficiency, cost reduction, productivity improvements, and in the rethinking of products and services for addressing new market needs (Bagnoli, Massaro, Bravin, & Vignotto, 2018). The Industry 4.0 phenomenon has in fact let untouched no industries (Bresciani, Ferraris, & Del Giudice, 2018; Bunn, Savage, & Holloway, 2002; De Bernardi, Bertello, & Shams, 2019; Rachinger et al., 2018) and technologies such as cloud computing, mobile computing, 3D printing and big-data analytics can represent a powerful tool in this regard (Bagnoli et al., 2018). However, the revolution will allow a radical competitive repositioning of the food system only if the opportunities offered by the enabling technologies of Industry 4.0 will be exploited to design new business models (Chesbrough, 2007).

In particular, the blockchain has attracted the attention of both scholars and practitioners. This new technology, in fact, allows overcoming the traditional certification mechanisms by tracking real-time information whose truthfulness is guaranteed by the participation of all the actors in the food chain (Perboli, Musso, & Rosano, 2018; Tirabeni, De Bernardi, Forliano, & Franco, 2019). The blockchain technology has already been applied by both large companies and start-ups operating in the food sector. For example, the French multinational retailer Carrefour has used it for the Auvergne chicken product line. Thanks to the blockchain, consumers can find out how each animal has been bred (e.g., what feed has been used, if antibiotic treatments have been adopted or not), where and by what farmer, where it was slaughtered, and so on. Barilla, on the other hand, has entered into a partnership with IBM as regards the basil product, in order to certify the quality level of the product and its sustainability-related aspects, providing consumers all data concerning cultivation, such as irrigation and treatments (i.e., pesticides), as well as reducing costs for wasted goods. Similarly, the Ambrosus start-up,[4] headquartered in Zug (Switzerland), has adopted both blockchain and Internet of Things (IoT) technologies to centralize information whereas different actors of the supply chain can keep retaining its ownership and assigning specific access rights to it. Thus, IoT sensors automatically collect environmental, positioning, and quality assurance data, which feeds a blockchain-based database that stores information in a leakage-proof manner, dispatching it only to specific actors when and where it is necessary. In this sense, blockchain seems very suitable to match the needs of each actor constituting a specific supply chain. Indeed, early stages actors would like to limit the amount of shared data to the minimum necessary for gaining the next actor's trust. Conversely, end actors would like to have full transparency about products coming from the early stages of the supply chain.

Another interesting example of technology applied to the food sector and specifically artificial intelligence is that of Wasteless.[5] This start-up, founded in Israel in 2018, aims at reducing the big problem of food waste. Indeed, through its proprietary machine-learning pricing engine, Wasteless can price products in real-time based on a series of dynamic variables that include the expiration date, shelf capacity, regional

---

[4]https://ambrosus.com

[5]https://www.wasteless.co

factors, brand strength, on-shelf competition, and more. Prices are displayed on electronic shelf labels or online checkouts, where consumers can see the product's regular price as well as a discounted price for a specific expiration date. In this way, food levels on the shelf and in stock are continuously monitored and costs related to both wastes or out-of-stock situations are reduced.

7.7.2 Agri-Tech

Agriculture is an activity that, since its origins, has been linked to technology improvements in order to be performed more efficiently. Moreover, it has always requested to deal with managing knowledge and information. Taking note of climate or seasonal changes and how to deal with them, understanding the differences between each acreage, thinking about how to improve one crop's production and quality level are just a few examples. Digital transformation has been slow in touching the agricultural world, but nowadays also this sector is living a revolution in key 4.0. As a consequence, Smart Agrifood, Smart Agri-business, Agri-tech are all terms that mean nothing more than the use of the latest technologies in the agricultural sector (Garba, 2019), from IoT or robotics in the field to the use of blockchain or big data. For example, through detailed photographs of the field, taken with satellite technologies or drones, it is possible to verify the state of the vigor of each area composing it. In this way, specific fertilization or harvest plans can be prepared and productions characterized by homogeneous quality levels obtained. The same result can be achieved through sensors and algorithms capable of identifying which is the most suitable harvest day based on different biological or chemical properties of the crops. Further automation can be found in those cases in which autonomously guided agricultural machines are used, capable of interpreting the aforesaid cartographic maps and operating within them through GPS systems and sensors. All those technologies represent an ally of the modern farmer in realizing the so-called "precision farming", a series of techniques aimed at increasing and stabilizing the quality of the yield and contributing to conduct agricultural activities in a more sustainably, also incurring lower costs (Ivanov, Bhargava, & Donnelly, 2015).

The Italian start-up Agricolus,[6] for instance, offers several services mainly related to optimizing agronomic processes for supporting farmers and other agricultural operators and enabling them to make data-driven decisions. This activity can be performed through modern data collection and analysis technologies aimed at enhancing precision farming. In this sense, the start-up has developed a cloud ecosystem able to support decisions that fit with the specific needs of each crop and can be integrated with agricultural machines. Moreover, satellite imagery's analysis can provide vigor and water stress indices or alert for pests and diseases

---

[6]https://www.agricolus.com

that could affect crops. As a consequence, the overall quality of the yield and product's traceability can be improved, and the economic and environmental impact of the agricultural activity constrained. Since using those advanced technologies requires specific expertise and know-how, the company has also launched an Academy for professionals and students that want to use innovative tools in their daily work activity and understand how to manage vast amounts of data and information.

Conversely, for what regards the use of blockchain in the Agri-tech sector, the example of the start-up EzLab[7] is provided. The company, founded in 2014 in Padua (Italy), has begun using smart contracts and big-data technologies, based on the paradigm of the blockchain, in order to vehicle wine information to consumers. Notably, this information, linked to the traceability and sustainability of raw materials, the composition of wines, and the processes that have affected them throughout the production and distribution chains cannot be counterfeited. In this way, traditional models based on web protocols or RFID technologies have been overcome and the company expects to apply blockchain and big-data analytics also to other Agri-tech sectors in the future.

7.7.3 Food Digital Platform

The increasing attention towards sustainability aspects has led to the enhancement of novel forms of food production, distribution, and consumption aimed at shortening the food supply chain (De Bernardi, Bertello, & Venuti, 2020; Murdoch, Marsden, & Banks, 2000; Renting, Marsden, & Banks, 2003). Moreover, pursuing sustainable development has required companies to adopt a systemic approach, starting to cooperate with various subjects throughout their value chain, from suppliers to final consumers (De Bernardi, Bertello, & Venuti, 2019). In this regard, the traditional food system, characterized by a centralized, dependent, competitive, and dominating nature, has been challenged by food systems based on decentralized, independent, community-focused, and sustainable business models (Blay-Palmer et al., 2018). Social embeddedness, trust, transparency, and sense of togetherness have become core concepts along the food value chain (Hendrickson & Heffernan, 2002; Kirwan, 2004). An emergent food digital platform which is based on the concept of the short food supply chain is the Food Assembly (De Bernardi, Bertello, & Venuti, 2019). The Food Assembly's platform was first created in France in 2010 and spread across Europe, reaching almost 1300 entities in 2018.[8] It facilitates direct exchanges between local producers and consumer communities that find themselves creating small temporary local markets. Farmers sell directly to Food Assembly's members and pay a 20% tax-free fee. There are no intermediaries: it is a direct sale.

---

[7]https://www.ezlab.it

[8]https://laruchequiditoui.fr

Every producer fixes price freely because only they can know how much the product is worth. The Food Assembly model allows obtaining transparency and trust maintaining service costs moderate. Another example of digital food platform is Forward Fooding,[9] a company headquartered in London but active on a global level. Forward Fooding represents the first platform for enhancing collaboration among entrepreneurs of food and beverage sectors with their relevant partners that has been ever created. Spurring them to share data with other actors of the network, Forward Fooding aims at helping those companies to implement more sustainable business models, adopting technologically innovative solutions, and addressing some of the issues that currently affect actual food systems through collective data intelligence activities.

7.7.4 Urban Food

A recent report published by the Ellen MacArthur Foundation (2019) estimated that for every dollar spent on the current wasteful and polluting food production system, two further dollars need to be spent in terms of health and environmental costs. The transition towards a more sustainable system started since the introduction of the United Nations Global Compact in 1999, which also cities had the opportunity to join from a few years later in order to contribute addressing the so-called urban food challenge. In fact, the United Nations estimates that from the 21 megacities existing in 2015, by 2030 there will be at least 43 worldwide and by 2050 more than two-thirds of the human beings will populate cities (United Nations, 2018). Mega-cities represent urban areas in which live more than ten million people and this phenomenon will leverage cities' food demand to 80% out of the total. Conse-quently, huge amounts of food and waste will have to be managed. A company that has made the fight against food waste its mission is Too Good To Go.[10] The business model of this company, founded in the UK in 2016, is simple but effective at the same time: restaurants, supermarkets, and hotels have to throw away a lot of fresh and edible food at the end of the day. Thus, instead of wasting it, they use it to prepare some mystery bags. Consumers can thus find the restaurants or the other shops via the geolocation feature on the app and buy that food at lower prices. Payment is made through the app, through which the customer receives a proof of purchase that they must show upon pick-up of the meal. Too Good To Go offers a win-win situation between people and businesses who otherwise would not interact, reducing the serious problem of food waste.

For what concerns cities, in recent years they have increasingly started to develop urban food strategies mainly aimed at achieving three objectives (European Commission, 2017; Olsson et al., 2016). First, enhancing food security and nutrition.

---

[9]https://www.forwardfooding.com

[10]https://toogoodtogo.com

Second, promoting the economic development of urban and peri-urban areas, which can be defined as cities' extents that also involve peripheries and lands with discontinuous buildings and a minimum density of 40 people/ha (Loibl, Piorr, & Revetz, 2011). Third, protecting and restoring local ecosystems, as well as reducing their impact on climatic changes. However, a lot can be done in this direction since actual economic systems are often still based on long food chains. Conversely, shortening them could help reducing regional food provision's vulnerability and the necessity to rely on the global food system (Morgan, 2015). In addition to this, urban strategies have great power in educating people towards sustainability issues, connected with both ecological and social dimensions of the food processes and cultural aspects linked to food's place of origin. Providing as an example an Italian city, the Municipality of Milan had developed a new way of thinking about the food system starting from 2006. As a consequence, together with Fondazione Cariplo, it first launched a public consultation that involved city departments, universities, businesses, and other organizations. Secondly, it established a food policy office and its strategic and comprehensive approach to managing local food challenges, which has led the city to host the Universal Exposition in 2015 and embrace the circularity paradigm. Indeed, through the initiative, called Milan Food Policy, the Municipality has, for example: (i) launched, together with other partners, a food waste hub for collecting and distributing unused food from private canteens and supermarkets; (ii) implemented systems for giving value to organic waste; (iii) improved the logistics for collecting surplus food from private and commercial properties and generate biogas from organic waste; (iv) introduced fiscal measures to encourage food donations to food banks and charities; (v) promoted initiatives in school and through media for raise people awareness about food waste and distributed doggy bags to let students take over left food from schools' canteens.

7.7.5 Food on Demand

The different business models which have been emerging in the food sector result from the combination of opportunities that have been enabled not just by technological evolution. Indeed, also consumers' needs have changed over time and market players have tried to occupy the spaces created by those emerging changes (The European House – Ambrosetti, 2019). The first emergent kind of business model is the so-called *Just-in-Time Online Delivery*, also called *Food on Demand*. Food on Demand is characterized by two big differences from the classic home delivery service: (i) the contact channel between the service provider and the consumer is a web portal or, much more often, a smartphone app; (ii) the provider of the service is, in almost all cases, a third party who divide the meal producer from the end consumer. There are two main typologies of business models based on the concept of Food on Demand. The first one is based on an actor who simply makes available its platform, usually a food delivery app, aggregating restaurants and intermediating between them and end customers (e.g., Just Eat, Delivery Hero, Foodpanda, GrubHub). The second possible business model is the one in which the dispenser simultaneously performs the activities of collecting orders via an app and delivering food to customers at home through its fleet of riders (e.g., Deliveroo, Uber Eats, Glovo). Moreover, in the Food on Demand model, the dispenser can also take care of the food preparation part, thus covering the entire value chain. One company that has recently implemented this kind of activity is the American restaurant chain Domino's Pizza. Indeed, alongside its several physical worldwide stores, the company has launched a website and a smartphone app through which customized orders can be made and the food delivery state tracked.

Another innovative business model that characterizes this new era for food is the *Food Subscription Delivery*. Therefore, some companies offer the customer the opportunity to sign up for their service, establishing the frequency of the delivery and what products receiving according to each one's needs. These services are oriented to those customers who prefer home-made solutions and research the genuineness of raw materials so that having the possibility to cook their meals independently but using high-quality ingredients (e.g., My Cooking Box) or having ready-to-eat meals (e.g., Freshly, Nestor, MealPro). However, these features can also be complemented by the desire to minimize the effort and time required for routine activities such as choosing and purchasing ingredients or providing healthy meals to people that cannot perform those activities autonomously, such as elders or invalid people.

7.8 Conclusion

The ferment characterizing the food sector nowadays is leading to the creation of start-ups exploiting market opportunities by developing new products, new processes, and new business models. Usually, these start-ups adopt disruptive technologies allowing to change the logic of running a business: from the product design to make it smarter, from managing its entire life cycle, to supply and sub-supply relationships for ensuring real-time processing; from production processes that are managed as cyber-physical spaces, to logistics and storage systems (Bagnoli et al., 2018). An increasing number of start-ups, for instance, is focusing on food traceability, healthiness and safety, and customer satisfaction through customized products and services which are technology-centered.

The enormous creativity and innovation of those start-ups are changing the pre-existing business models, leading incumbent companies to question their established models. Internal research and development conducted by large companies may no longer be sufficient in the years to come. The most suitable solutions are oriented to cooperation and networking, involving large companies and small and dynamic start-ups within innovation ecosystems that are based on multiple partnerships with external research institutions, consulting companies, and universities. A virtuous example of this trend is that of the Italian company Barilla, which has created an incubator that allows them to exploit the innovative ideas that are developed by external actors. The recent explosion of incubators leads to two possible future scenarios: a scenario of continuous struggle that would benefit no one or a collaborative scenario in which different actors are inserted in cross-fertilization contexts that would favor the creation of synergies. This last solution would also help the food sector to leave behind the concept of slow-growing that has characterized it for decades and to encourage, at the same time, social and environmental development.

References

Abdelkafi, N., & Täuscher, K. (2016). Business models for sustainability from a system dynamics perspective. *Organization & Environment, 29*(1), 74–96. https://doi.org/10.1177/1086026615592930

Aguilera, R. V., Rupp, D. E., Williams, C. A., & Ganapathi, J. (2007). Putting the S back in corporate social responsibility: A multilevel theory of social change in organizations. *Academy of Management Review, 32*(3), 836–863. https://doi.org/10.5465/AMR.2007.25275678

Allwood, J. M. (2014). Squaring the circular economy: The role of recycling within a hierarchy of material management strategies. In *Handbook of recycling* (pp. 445–477). Amsterdam: Elsevier. https://doi.org/10.1016/B978-0-12-396459-5.00030-1

Amit, R., & Zott, C. (2012). Creating value through business model innovation. *MIT Sloan Management Review, 53*(3), 36–44.

Andersen, M. S. (2007). An introductory note on the environmental economics of the circular economy. *Sustainability Science, 2*(1), 133–140. https://doi.org/10.1007/s11625-006-0013-6

Bagnoli, C., Massaro, M., Bravin, A., & Vignotto, A. (2018). *Business Model 4.0 I modelli di business vincenti per le imprese italiane nella quarta rivoluzione industriale.* Venezia: Edizioni Ca' Foscari. Retrieved from http://edizionicafoscari.unive.it/it/edizioni/collane/studi-e-ricerche

Baldassarre, B., Calabretta, G., Bocken, N. M. P., & Jaskiewicz, T. (2017). Bridging sustainable business model innovation and user-driven innovation: A process for sustainable value proposition design. *Journal of Cleaner Production, 147*, 175–186. https://doi.org/10.1016/j.jclepro.2017.01.081

Björkdahl, J., & Holmén, M. (2013). Editorial: Business model innovation – the challenges ahead. *International Journal of Product Development, 18*(3/4), 213–225.

Blay-Palmer, A., Santini, G., Dubbeling, M., Renting, H., Taguchi, M., & Giordano, T. (2018). Validating the City Region Food System approach: Enacting inclusive, transformational City Region Food Systems. *Sustainability (Switzerland), 10*(5), 1–23. https://doi.org/10.3390/su10051680

Bocken, N., Short, S., Rana, P., & Evans, S. (2013). A value mapping tool for sustainable business modelling. *Corporate Governance, 13*(5), 482–497. https://doi.org/10.1108/CG-06-2013-0078

Bocken, N. M. P., Short, S. W., Rana, P., & Evans, S. (2014). A literature and practice review to develop sustainable business model archetypes. *Journal of Cleaner Production, 65*, 42–56. https://doi.org/10.1016/j.jclepro.2013.11.039

Boons, F., & Lüdeke-Freund, F. (2013). Business models for sustainable innovation: State-of-the-art and steps towards a research agenda. *Journal of Cleaner Production, 45*, 9–19. https://doi.org/10.1016/j.jclepro.2012.07.007

Boons, F., Montalvo, C., Quist, J., & Wagner, M. (2013). Sustainable innovation, business models and economic performance: An overview. *Journal of Cleaner Production, 45*, 1–8. https://doi.org/10.1016/j.jclepro.2012.08.013

Bouwman, H., de Reuver, M., & Nikou, S. (2017). The impact of digitalization on business models: How IT artefacts, social media, and big data force firms to innovate their business model. In *14th International Telecommunications Society (ITS) Asia-Pacific Regional Conference: "Mapping ICT into Transformation for the Next Information Society."* Kyoto, Japan.

Bresciani, S., Ferraris, A., & Del Giudice, M. (2018). The management of organizational ambidexterity through alliances in a new context of analysis: Internet of Things (IoT) smart city projects. *Technological Forecasting and Social Change, 136*, 331–338. https://doi.org/10.1016/j.techfore.2017.03.002

Bunn, M. D., Savage, G. T., & Holloway, B. B. (2002). Stakeholder analysis for multi-sector innovations. *Journal of Business & Industrial Marketing, 17*(2/3), 181–203. https://doi.org/10.1108/08858620210419808

Casadesus-Masanell, R., & Zhu, F. (2013). Business model innovation and competitive imitation: The case of sponsor-based business models. *Strategic Management Journal, 34*(4), 464–482. https://doi.org/10.1002/smj.2022

Chesbrough, H. W. (2006). Open innovation: A new paradigm for understanding industrial innovation. In H. Chesbrough, W. Vanhaverbeke, & W. Joel (Eds.), *Open innovation: Researching a new paradigm* (pp. 1–19). New York: Oxford University Press.

Chesbrough, H. W. (2007). Business model innovation: It's not just about technology anymore. *Strategy and Leadership, 35*(6), 12–17. https://doi.org/10.1108/10878570710833714

Chesbrough, H. W. (2010). Business model innovation: Opportunities and barriers. *Long Range Planning, 43*(2–3), 354–363. https://doi.org/10.1016/j.lrp.2009.07.010

Chesbrough, H. W., & Rosenbloom, R. S. (2002). The role of the business model in capturing value from innovation: Evidence from Xerox Corporation's technology spin-off companies. *Industrial and Corporate Change, 11*(3), 529–555. https://doi.org/10.1093/icc/11.3.529

Choi, J., & Wang, H. (2009). Stakeholder relations and the persistence of corporate financial performance. *Strategic Management Journal, 30*(8), 895–907. https://doi.org/10.1002/smj.759

De Bernardi, P., Bertello, A., & Shams, S. M. R. (2019). Logics hindering digital transformation in cultural heritage strategic management: Evidence from Turin museums. *Tourism Analysis, 24*(3), 315–327. https://doi.org/10.3727/108354219X15511864843876

De Bernardi, P., Bertello, A., & Venuti, F. (2019). Online and on-site interactions within alternative food networks: Sustainability impact of knowledge-sharing practices. *Sustainability, 11*(5), 1457. https://doi.org/10.3390/su11051457

De Bernardi, P., Bertello, A., & Venuti, F. (2020). Community-oriented motivations and knowledge sharing as drivers of success within food assemblies. In A. Lazazzara, F. Ricciardi, & S. Za (Eds.), *Exploring digital ecosystems: Organizational and human challenges. Lecture notes in information systems and organisation.* Cham: Springer.

De Bernardi, P., Bertello, A., Venuti, F., & Zardini, A. (2019). Knowledge transfer driving community-based business models towards sustainable food-related behaviours: A commons perspective. *Knowledge Management Research & Practice*, 1–8. https://doi.org/10.1080/14778238.2019.1664271

De Bernardi, P., & Tirabeni, L. (2018). Alternative food networks: Sustainable business models for anti-consumption food cultures. *British Food Journal, 120*(8), 1776–1791. https://doi.org/10.1108/BFJ-12-2017-0731

De Bernardi, P., Forliano, C., Rotti, R., & Franco, M. (2019). Innovazione e sostenibilità nei nuovi modelli di business del settore vitivinicolo. Analisi del caso Fontanafredda. In F. Moreschi (Ed.), *Il paesaggio vitivinicolo come patrimonio europeo: Aspetti gius-economici, geografici, ambientali, contrattuali, enoturistici, di marketing* (pp. 27–41). Torino: Giappichelli.

De Bernardi, P., Venuti, F., & Bertello, A. (2019). The relevance of climate change related risks on corporate financial and non-financial disclosure in Italian listed companies. In P. De vincentiis, F. Culasso, & S. A. Cerrato (Eds.), *The future of risk management* (Vol. I, pp. 77–107). Cham: Palgrave Macmillan.

de Reuver, M., Bouwman, H., & Haaker, T. (2013). Business model roadmapping: A practical approach to come from an existing to a desired business model. *International Journal of Innovation Management, 17*(1), 1–18. https://doi.org/10.1142/s1363919613400069

Demil, B., & Lecocq, X. (2010). Business model evolution: In search of dynamic consistency. *Long Range Planning, 43*(2–3), 227–246. https://doi.org/10.1016/j.lrp.2010.02.004

Drucker, P. (1994). The theory of the business. *Harvard Business Review*, 95–104.

References

Ellen MacArthur Foundation. (2014). *A new dynamic – Effective business in a circular economy.* Cowes: Ellen MacArthur Foundation Publishing.

Ellen MacArthur Foundation. (2015). *Growth within: A circular economy vision for a competitive Europe.* Cowes: Ellen MacArthur Foundation.

Ellen MacArthur Foundation. (2019). *Cities and circular economy for food.* Retrieved from https://www.ellenmacarthurfoundation.org/publications/cities-and-circular-economy-for-food

European Commission. (2017). *Food in cities: Study on innovation for a sustainable and healthy production, delivery, and consumption of food in cities.* Retrieved from https://ec.europa.eu/research/openvision/pdf/rise/food_in_cities.pdf

European Commission. (2018). *Recipe for change: An agenda for a climate-smart and sustainable food system for a healthy Europe.* Retrieved from https://ec.europa.eu/research/bioeconomy/pdf/publications/ES_recipe_for_change.pdf

Evans, S., Vladimirova, D., Holgado, M., Van Fossen, K., Yang, M., Silva, E. A., & Barlow, C. Y. (2017). Business model innovation for sustainability: Towards a unified perspective for creation of sustainable business models. *Business Strategy and the Environment, 26*(5), 597–608. https://doi.org/10.1002/bse.1939

Foss, N. J., & Saebi, T. (2017). Fifteen years of research on business model innovation: How far have we come, and where should we go? *Journal of Management, 43*(1), 200–227. https://doi.org/10.1177/0149206316675927

Foss, N. J., & Saebi, T. (2018). Business models and business model innovation: Between wicked and paradigmatic problems. *Long Range Planning, 51*(1), 9–21. https://doi.org/10.1016/j.lrp.2017.07.006

Garba, A. M. (2019). Agri-tech opportunities at the bottom of the pyramid: How big is the opportunity and how little has been exploited? Some selected cases in Nigeria. In *Digital entrepreneurship in Sub-Saharan Africa* (pp. 199–220). Cham: Palgrave Macmillan. https://doi.org/10.1007/978-3-030-04924-9_9

Garetti, M., & Taisch, M. (2012). Sustainable manufacturing: Trends and research challenges. *Production Planning and Control, 23*(2–3), 83–104. https://doi.org/10.1080/09537287.2011.591619

Geissdoerfer, M., Bocken, N. M. P., & Hultink, E. J. (2016). Design thinking to enhance the sustainable business modelling process – A workshop based on a value mapping process. *Journal of Cleaner Production, 135*, 1218–1232. https://doi.org/10.1016/j.jclepro.2016.07.020

Geissdoerfer, M., Vladimirova, D., & Evans, S. (2018). Sustainable business model innovation: A review. *Journal of Cleaner Production, 198*, 401–416. https://doi.org/10.1016/j.jclepro.2018.06.240

Girotra, K., & Netessine, S. (2013). OM forum – Business model innovation for sustainability. *Manufacturing & Service Operations Management, 15*(4), 537–544. https://doi.org/10.2139/ssrn.2289291

Gnizy, I. (2019). Big data and its strategic path to value in international firms. *International Marketing Review, 36*(3), 318–341. https://doi.org/10.1108/IMR-09-2018-0249

Godfray, H. C. J., Beddington, J. R., Crute, I. R., Haddad, L., Lawrence, D., Muir, J. F., … Toulmin, C. (2010). Food security: The challenge of feeding 9 billion people. *Science, 327*(5967), 812–818. https://doi.org/10.1126/science.1185383

Hart, S. L., & Dowell, G. (2011). A natural-resource-based view of the firm: Fifteen years after. *Journal of Management, 37*(5), 1464–1479. https://doi.org/10.1177/0149206310390219

Hendrickson, M. K., & Heffernan, W. D. (2002). Opening spaces through relocalization: Locating potential resistance in the weaknesses of the global food system. *Sociologia Ruralis, 42*(4), 347–369. https://doi.org/10.1111/1467-9523.00221

Heyes, G., Sharmina, M., Mendoza, J. M. F., Gallego-Schmid, A., & Azapagic, A. (2018). Developing and implementing circular economy business models in service-oriented technology companies. *Journal of Cleaner Production, 177*, 621–632. https://doi.org/10.1016/J.JCLEPRO.2017.12.168

Inigo, E. A., Albareda, L., & Ritala, P. (2017). Business model innovation for sustainability: Exploring evolutionary and radical approaches through dynamic capabilities. *Industry and Innovation, 24*(5), 515–542. https://doi.org/10.1080/13662716.2017.1310034

Ivanov, S., Bhargava, K., & Donnelly, W. (2015). Precision farming: Sensor analytics. *IEEE Intelligent Systems, 30*(4), 76–80. https://doi.org/10.1109/MIS.2015.67

Johnson, M. W. (2010). *Seizing the white space: Business model innovation for growth and renewal.* Boston, MA: Harvard Business Press.

Joyce, A., & Paquin, R. L. (2016). The triple layered business model canvas: A tool to design more sustainable business models. *Journal of Cleaner Production, 135*, 1–13. https://doi.org/10.1016/j.jclepro.2016.06.067

Khanagha, S., Volberda, H., & Oshri, I. (2014). Business model renewal and ambidexterity: Structural alteration and strategy formation process during transition to a cloud business model. *R&D Management, 44*(3), 322–340. https://doi.org/10.1111/radm.12070

Kirwan, J. (2004). Alternative strategies in the UK agro-food system: Interrogating the alterity of farmers' markets. *Sociologia Ruralis, 44*(4), 395–415. https://doi.org/10.1111/j.1467-9523.2004.00283.x

Lambert, S. C. (2015). The importance of classification to business model research. *Journal of Business Models, 3*(1), 49–61. https://doi.org/10.5278/ojs.jbm.v3i1.1045

Lewandowski, M. (2016). Designing the business models for circular economy-towards the conceptual framework. *Sustainability (Switzerland), 8*(1), 43. https://doi.org/10.3390/su8010043

Linder, M., & Williander, M. (2017). Circular business model innovation: Inherent uncertainties. *Business Strategy and the Environment, 26*(2), 182–196. https://doi.org/10.1002/bse.1906

Lindgardt, Z., Reeves, M., Stalk, G., Jr., & Deimler, M. (2012). Business model innovation: When the game gets tough, change the game. In M. Deimler, R. Lesser, D. Rhodes, & J. Sina (Eds.), *Own the future: 50 ways to win from the Boston consulting group* (pp. 291–298). Hoboken, NJ: John Wiley & Sons. https://doi.org/10.1002/9781119204084.ch40

Loibl, W., Piorr, A., & Revetz, J. (2011). Concepts and methods. In A. Piorr, J. Ravetz, & I. Tosics (Eds.), *Peri-urbanisation in Europe: Towards a European policy to sustain urban-rural futures* (pp. 24–29). Frederiksberg: University of Copenhagen, Academic Books Life Sciences.

Loorbach, D., & Wijsman, K. (2013). Business transition management: Exploring a new role for business in sustainability transitions. *Journal of Cleaner Production, 45*, 20–28. https://doi.org/10.1016/j.jclepro.2012.11.002

Lüdeke-Freund, F. (2010). Towards a conceptual framework of "Business models for sustainability". In R. Wever, J. Quist, A. Tukker, J. Woudstra, F. Boons, & N. Beute (Eds.), *ERSCP-EMSU conference: "Knowledge collaboration & learning for sustainable innovation".* Delft, The Netherlands.

Lüdeke-Freund, F., Massa, L., Bocken, N., Brent, A., & Musango, J. (2016). *Business models for shared value.* Cape Town: Network for Business Sustainability South Africa.

Magretta, J. (2002). Why business models matter. *Harvard Business Review, 80*(5), 86–92133.

Mahadevan, B. (2000). Business models for internet-based e-commerce: An anatomy. *California Management Review, 42*(4), 55–69. https://doi.org/10.2307/41166053

Massa, L., Tucci, C. L., & Afuah, A. (2017). A critical assessment of business model research. *Academy of Management Annals, 11*(1), 73–104. https://doi.org/10.5465/annals.2014.0072

Maurya, A. (2012). *Running lean: Iterate from plan A to a plan that works* (2nd ed.). Sebastopol, CA: O'Reilly Media.

Mayo, M. C., & Brown, G. S. (1999). Building a competitive business model. *Ivey Business Journal, 63*(3), 18–23.

Mitchell, D. W., & Bruckner Coles, C. (2004). Business model innovation breakthrough moves. *Journal of Business Strategy, 25*(1), 16–26. https://doi.org/10.1108/02756660410515976

Morgan, K. (2015). Nourishing the city: The rise of the urban food question in the Global North. *Urban Studies, 52*(8), 1379–1394. https://doi.org/10.1177/0042098014534902

Müller, J. M., Buliga, O., & Voigt, K. I. (2018). Fortune favors the prepared: How SMEs approach business model innovations in Industry 4.0. *Technological Forecasting and Social Change, 132*, 2–17. https://doi.org/10.1016/j.techfore.2017.12.019

References 219

Murdoch, J., Marsden, T., & Banks, J. (2000). Quality, nature, and embeddedness: Some theoretical considerations in the context of the food sector. *Economic Geography, 76*(2), 107–125. https://doi.org/10.1111/j.1944-8287.2000.tb00136.x

Murray, A., Skene, K., & Haynes, K. (2017). The circular economy: An interdisciplinary exploration of the concept and application in a global context. *Journal of Business Ethics, 140*, 369–380. https://doi.org/10.1007/s10551-015-2693-2

Nidumolu, R., Prahalad, C. K., & Rangaswami, M. R. (2009). Why sustainability is now the key driver of innovation. *Harvard Business Review, 87*(9), 56–64.

Nielsen, C., & Lund, M. (2018). Building scalable business models. *MIT Sloan Management Review, 59*(2), 65–69.

Nielsen, C., Lund, M., Montemari, M., Paolone, F., Massaro, M., & Dumay, J. (2018). *Business models: A research overview*. London: Routledge.

Olsson, E. G. A., Kerselaers, E., Kristensen, L. S., Primdahl, J., Rogge, E., & Wästfelt, A. (2016). Peri-urban food production and its relation to urban resilience. *Sustainability (Switzerland), 8*(12), 1–21. https://doi.org/10.3390/su8121340

Onetti, A., Zucchella, A., Jones, M. V., & McDougall-Covin, P. P. (2012). Internationalization, innovation and entrepreneurship: Business models for new technology-based firms. *Journal of Management and Governance, 16*(3), 337–368. https://doi.org/10.1007/s10997-010-9154-1

Osterwalder, A. (2004). *The business model ontology – A proposition in a design science approach*. Lausanne: Université de Lausanne.

Osterwalder, A., & Pigneur, Y. (2002). An e-business model ontology for modeling e-business. In *BLED 2002 proceedings, 2*. AIS Electronic Library (AISeL).

Osterwalder, A., & Pigneur, Y. (2010). *Business model generation: A handbook for visionaries, game changers, and challangers*. Hoboken, NJ: John Wiley & Sons.

Perboli, G., Musso, S., & Rosano, M. (2018). Blockchain in logistics and supply chain: A lean approach for designing real-world use cases. *Institute of Electrical and Electronics Engineers Access, 6*, 62018–62028. https://doi.org/10.1109/ACCESS.2018.2875782

Petrovic, O., Kittl, C., & Teksten, R. D. (2001). Developing business models for eBusiness. *SSRN Electronic Journal*. https://doi.org/10.2139/ssrn.1658505

Pieroni, M. P. P., McAloone, T. C., & Pigosso, D. A. C. (2019). Business model innovation for circular economy and sustainability: A review of approaches. *Journal of Cleaner Production, 215*, 198–216. https://doi.org/10.1016/j.jclepro.2019.01.036

Planing, P. (2015, March). Business model innovation in a circular economy reasons for non-acceptance business model innovation in a circular economy reasons for non-acceptance of circular business models. *Open Journal of Business Model Innovation, 1*(11).

Porter, M. E. (2001). Strategy and the internet. *Harvard Business Review, 79*(3), 62–78. Retrieved from http://www.ncbi.nlm.nih.gov/pubmed/11246925

Porter, M. E., & Kramer, M. R. (2011). Creating shared value. *Harvard Business Review, 89*(1/2), 62–77.

Rachinger, M., Rauter, R., Müller, C., Vorraber, W., & Schirgi, E. (2018). Digitalization and its influence on business model innovation. *Journal of Manufacturing Technology Management*. https://doi.org/10.1108/JMTM-01-2018-0020

Rashid, A., Asif, F. M. A., Krajnik, P., & Nicolescu, C. M. (2013). Resource conservative manufacturing: An essential change in business and technology paradigm for sustainable manufacturing. *Journal of Cleaner Production, 57*, 166–177. https://doi.org/10.1016/J.JCLEPRO.2013.06.012

Rasmussen, B. (2007). *Business models and the theory of the firm. Pharmaceutical industry project working paper series* (Vol. 13). Victoria University of Technology.

Reid, E. M., & Toffel, M. W. (2009). Responding to public and private politics: Corporate disclosure of climate change strategies. *Strategic Management Journal, 30*(11), 1157–1178. https://doi.org/10.1002/smj.796

Reim, W., Parida, V., & Örtqvist, D. (2015). Product–Service Systems (PSS) business models and tactics – A systematic literature review. *Journal of Cleaner Production, 97*, 61–75. https://doi.org/10.1016/j.jclepro.2014.07.003

Renting, H., Marsden, T. K., & Banks, J. (2003). Understanding alternative food networks: Exploring the role of short food supply chains in rural development. *Environment and Planning A, 35*(3), 393–411. https://doi.org/10.1068/a3510

Richardson, J. E. (2008). The business model: An integrative framework for strategy execution. *Strategic Change, 17*(5–6), 133–144. https://doi.org/10.2139/ssrn.932998

Ritala, P., Huotari, P., Bocken, N., Albareda, L., & Puumalainen, K. (2018). Sustainable business model adoption among S&P 500 firms: A longitudinal content analysis study. *Journal of Cleaner Production, 170*, 216–226. https://doi.org/10.1016/j.jclepro.2017.09.159

Romero, D., & Molina, A. (2009). VO breeding environments & virtual organizations integral business process management framework. *Information Systems Frontiers, 11*(5), 569–597. https://doi.org/10.1007/s10796-009-9195-7

Roome, N., & Louche, C. (2016). Journeying toward business models for sustainability: A conceptual model found inside the black box of organisational transformation. *Organization & Environment, 29*(1), 11–35. https://doi.org/10.1177/1086026615595084

Santos, J., Spector, B., & Van der Heyden, L. (2009). *Toward a theory of business model innovation within incumbent firms. SSRN Electronic Journal.* Fontainebleau, France. https://doi.org/10.2139/ssrn.1362515

Schallmo, D. R. A., & Brecht, L. (2010). Business model innovation in business-to-business markets-procedure and examples. In *Proceedings of the 3rd ISPIM innovation symposium: "Managing the art of innovation: Turning concepts into reality"* (Vol. 12, pp. 1–23). Quebec City: The International Society for Professional Innovation Management (ISPIM).

Schaltegger, S., Lüdeke-Freund, F., & Hansen, E. (2012). Business cases for sustainability: The role of business model innovation for corporate sustainability. *International Journal of Innovation and Sustainable Development, 6*(2), 95–119. https://doi.org/10.1504/IJISD.2012.046944

Schaltegger, S., Lüdeke-Freund, F., & Hansen, E. G. (2016). Business models for sustainability: A co-evolutionary analysis of sustainable entrepreneurship, innovation, and transformation. *Organization & Environment, 29*(3), 264–289. https://doi.org/10.1177/1086026616633272

Schweizer, L. (2005). Concept and evolution of business models. *Journal of General Management, 31*(2), 37–56. https://doi.org/10.1177/030630700503100203

Scott, J. (2013). *The sustainable business: A practitioner's guide to achieving long-term profitability and competitiveness: Taking the first steps toward understanding, implementing and managing sustainability from a cost/profit perspective.* Yorkshire: Greenleaf Publishing Ltd.

Sempels, C., & Hoffmann, J. (2013). Circular economy: Transforming a "Waste" into a productive resource. In C. Sempels & J. Hoffmann (Eds.), *Sustainable innovation strategy* (pp. 103–138). London: Palgrave Macmillan. https://doi.org/10.1057/9781137352613_5

Seuring, S., & Müller, M. (2008). From a literature review to a conceptual framework for sustainable supply chain management. *Journal of Cleaner Production, 16*(15), 1699–1710. https://doi.org/10.1016/j.jclepro.2008.04.020

Skarzynski, P., & Gibson, R. (2008). *Innovation to the core: A blueprint for transforming the way your company innovates.* Boston, MA: Harvard Business School Press.

Slywotzky, A. J. (1996). *Value migration: How to think several moves ahead of the competition.* Boston, MA: Harvard Business School Press. https://doi.org/10.5465/ame.1996.19198672

Stahel, W. R. (2013). The business angle of a circular economy – Higher competitiveness, higher resource security and material efficiency. In *A new dynamic: Effective business in a circular economy* (Vol. 1). Ellen MacArthur Foundation Publishing.

Stahel, W. R. (2016). The circular economy. *Nature, 531*(7595), 435–438. https://doi.org/10.1038/531435a

Stahel, W., & Reday-Mulvey, G. (1981). *Jobs for tomorrow: The potential for substituting manpower for energy.* New York: Vantage Press.

Stewart, D. W., & Zhao, Q. (2000). Internet marketing, business models, and public policy. *Journal of Public Policy & Marketing, 19*(2), 287–296. https://doi.org/10.1509/jppm.19.2.287.17125

Stubbs, W., & Cocklin, C. (2008). Conceptualizing a "Sustainability business model". *Organization & Environment, 21*(2), 103–127. https://doi.org/10.1177/1086026608318042

References

Stubbs, W., & Higgins, C. (2018). Stakeholders' perspectives on the role of regulatory reform in integrated reporting. *Journal of Business Ethics, 147*(3), 489–508. https://doi.org/10.1007/s10551-015-2954-0

Teece, D. J. (2008). Managers, markets, and dynamic capabilities. In D. J. Teece (Ed.), *Technological know-how, organizational capabilities, and strategic management* (pp. 87–97). Singapore: World Scientific Publishing. https://doi.org/10.1142/9789812834478_0005

Teece, D. J. (2010). Business models, business strategy and innovation. *Long Range Planning, 43*(2–3), 172–194. https://doi.org/10.1016/j.lrp.2009.07.003

The European House – Ambrosetti. (2019). *La Roadmap del futuro per il Food & Beverage: quali evoluzioni e quali sfide per i prossimi anni.* Retrieved from https://www.ambrosetti.eu/wp-content/uploads/rapporto-Food-2019.pdf

Timmers, P. (1998). Business models for electronic markets. *Electronic Markets, 8*(2), 3–8. https://doi.org/10.1080/10196789800000016

Tirabeni, L., De Bernardi, P., Forliano, C., & Franco, M. (2019). How can organisations and business models lead to a more sustainable society? A framework from a systematic review of the industry 4.0. *Sustainability, 11*(22), 6363. https://doi.org/10.3390/su11226363

Todeschini, B. V., Cortimiglia, M. N., Callegaro-de-Menezes, D., & Ghezzi, A. (2017). Innovative and sustainable business models in the fashion industry: Entrepreneurial drivers, opportunities, and challenges. *Business Horizons, 60*(6), 759–770. https://doi.org/10.1016/j.bushor.2017.07.003

Tukker, A., & Tischner, U. (2006). Product-services as a research field: Past, present and future. Reflections from a decade of research. *Journal of Cleaner Production, 14*(17), 1552–1556. https://doi.org/10.1016/j.jclepro.2006.01.022

Tunn, V. S. C., Bocken, N. M. P., van den Hende, E. A., & Schoormans, J. P. L. (2019). Business models for sustainable consumption in the circular economy: An expert study. *Journal of Cleaner Production, 212*, 324–333. https://doi.org/10.1016/j.jclepro.2018.11.290

United Nations, Department of Economic and Social Affairs, P. D. (2018). *World urbanization prospects: The 2018 revision.*

Upward, A., & Jones, P. (2016). An ontology for strongly sustainable business models: Defining an enterprise framework compatible with natural and social science. *Organization & Environment, 29*(1), 97–123. https://doi.org/10.1177/1086026615592933

Vrontis, D., Bresciani, S., & Giacosa, E. (2016). Tradition and innovation in Italian wine family businesses. *British Food Journal, 118*(8), 1883–1897.

Weill, P., & Vitale, M. (2001). *Place to space: Migrating to eBusiness models.* Boston, MA: Harvard Business Press. https://doi.org/10.1080/1097198x.2001.10856309

Wells, P. E. (2013). *Business models for sustainability.* Cheltenham: Edward Elgar Publishing.

Wirtz, B. W., Pistoia, A., Ullrich, S., & Göttel, V. (2016). Business models: Origin, development and future research perspectives. *Long Range Planning, 49*(1), 36–54. https://doi.org/10.1016/j.lrp.2015.04.001

Yang, M., Evans, S., Vladimirova, D., & Rana, P. (2016). *Value uncaptured perspective for sustainable business model innovation.* https://doi.org/10.17863/CAM.4227

Yang, M., Evans, S., Vladimirova, D., & Rana, P. (2017). Value uncaptured perspective for sustainable business model innovation. *Journal of Cleaner Production, 140*, 1794–1804. https://doi.org/10.1016/j.jclepro.2016.07.102

Zollo, M., Cennamo, C., & Neumann, K. (2013). Beyond what and why: Understanding organizational evolution towards sustainable enterprise models. *Organization & Environment, 26*(3), 241–259. https://doi.org/10.1177/1086026613496433

Zott, C., & Amit, R. (2010). Business model design: An activity system perspective. *Long Range Planning, 43*(2–3), 216–226. https://doi.org/10.1016/j.lrp.2009.07.004

Chapter 8
Funding Innovation and Entrepreneurship

Abstract Innovation is generally recognized as one of the key drivers, if not the main one, for the economic growth and development of a country. Policy-makers are responsible for creating the conditions in which innovation and technology can develop and make a difference, especially in advanced economies. This chapter addresses the main sources of funding for entrepreneurs and start-ups. We will discuss the financial constraints, or the financing gap, that affects the start-ups and small-medium enterprises (SMEs), with a focus on the early stages. Moreover, the chapter will provide an overview of Venture Capital and Corporate Venture Capital, as they are the organizations, which provide finance to innovative firms that are the most crucial and game-changing in the life of a young company. Finally, we will explain who Venture Capitalists and Corporate Venture Capitalists are, how they operate, how they are structured, and what their main goals are.

Keywords Venture capital · Corporate venture capital · Open innovation · Startups · Investment cycle

8.1 Introduction

Investments in innovation drive the technological change of a country and therefore affect the country's ability to foster a positive environment for innovation and its long-term growth. In a more connected, knowledge-based, and global world, where the access to sourcing of services and technologies is virtually open and borderless, the most developed economies are more and more dependent on the need to secure the necessary practical skill levels and knowledge for maintaining a technological advantage and prevailing against other economies (Battisti, Miglietta, Nirino, & Villasalero Diaz, 2019; Ferraris, Santoro, & Bresciani, 2017; Gualandri & Venturelli, 2008; Vrgovic, Vidicki, Glassman, & Walton, 2012).

Co-authored by Luca Morandi—Indaco Venture Partners, Milano, Italy, e-mail: morandi.luca@gmail.com

© Springer Nature Switzerland AG 2020
P. De Bernardi, D. Azucar, *Innovation in Food Ecosystems*, Contributions to Management Science, https://doi.org/10.1007/978-3-030-33502-1_8

This 'attitude was one of the driving forces, for instance, that after the end of World War II caused a massive amount of US public spending poured into the research sector. However, the war was not really over, the Korean War and the Cold War would break out shortly after and the US government could not afford to lose ground on the quest for supremacy.

The trigger event took place on 4 October 1957 when a small 58 cm diameter polished metal sphere with four radio antennas to broadcast radio pulsed was launched from a remote location of southern Kazakhstan into an elliptical low Earth orbit by a country once portrayed as a "third-world backwater with a bellicose foreign policy" (Blank, 2009). That small sphere was the Sputnik, the first man device in space, and it was launched by the Soviet Union from the Baikonur Cosmodrome in Kazakhstan.

Traumatized by the belief that the country was sliding behind the Soviet Union on innovation, the US created a new government agency to spurt innovation by funding new companies. The innovation industry, thus, picked up in 1958, when the Small Business Investment Company (SBIC) Act was approved and, according to Mark Heesen, former President of the National Venture Capital Association "a significant boost was given to the industry with the passage of the Small Business Investment Act." "The SBIC guaranteed that for every dollar a bank or a financial institution invested in a new company, the US government would invest three dollars, so for every dollar that a fund invested, it would have four dollars to invest" (Blank, 2009). The SBIC was a national initiative. However, some big companies such as Bank of America, Firemans Fund, and American Express set up their SBIC fund in Northern California to invest in the emerging microwave and new semiconductor start-ups with premises located south of San Francisco; 60 years down the road, everybody on Earth is aware of the incredible innovation ecosystem, which is now called Silicon Valley.

In the last years, the new venture ecosystem has been radically changed and reshaped by the emergence of alternative sources of early-stage finance opportunities, including incubators, accelerators, science and technology parks, university-affiliated seed funds, corporate seed funds, business angels, and both equity and debt-based crowdfunding platforms. At the same time, large financial institutions that have traditionally invested in late-stage and mature companies have increasingly diversified their investment portfolios to "get into the venture game". In some cases, they made it through the traditional closed-end funds model, while in other cases through direct investments and co-investments alongside the closed-end funds (Bonini & Capizzi, 2019, p. 137).

Financing and supporting innovation and entrepreneurship, as already mentioned, has direct impacts on the long term ability of a country to position itself before the other countries when it comes to technological change, therefore achieving high economical competitive advantage. However, measuring the short to medium term impact of policies adopted by policy makers is not always an easy task to accomplish.

The financing activity of innovation involves a vast number of heterogeneous actors who are dependent on the following main features (Brown, Fazzari, & Petersen, 2009; Hall & Lerner, 2010; Kerr & Nanda, 2015):

8.1 Introduction

(i) **The development stage of the idea that is intended to be financed.** For instance, a research project would rather be more attractive for a Technology Transfer fund or a University linked investment vehicle than to a Growth Capital Fund, which usually deploys its money on more, advanced and developed projects, which are typically post-seed and early-stage phases.

(ii) **The geography where innovation takes place.** In a more developed and vibrant innovation ecosystem, there would be a wider number and type of financers able to cover and provide finance to the broad and long journey that is inherent in the innovation process, such as business angels, venture capital funds, and corporate venture capitals. As opposed to that, a less developed ecosystem would be mostly composed of government-backed investment vehicles, companies, and universities as the main stimulators of innovation processes.

(iii) **The type of innovation that is intended to finance.** Innovation in biotech, for instance, is mostly supported by the investments coming from corporate venture capital arms of big pharma companies and industry-focused investment funds.

Several publications and studies have examined the impact of innovation on the growth of a country by analyzing the impact of venture capital investment on firms' performances. The main conclusions are that venture capital funds provide a boost to the performance of a company not only by the mere supply of finance, but also by the enhancement of professionalism of firms' management which is caused by the expertise, services, and knowledge that venture capital funds bring to the companies (Gualandri & Venturelli, 2008).

This emphasizes the importance of the role of venture capitalists and their possible funding streams in the food sector, which is leaving behind the concept of a slow-growing sector (Hou & Mohnen, 2013; Rama, 2008) by actively engaging in the creation and growth of innovative startups.

The advisory firm PwC conducted a study designed to investigate the performance of a sample of 500 portfolio companies of Venture Capital and Private Equity funds over a 10-year period, i.e., from 2007 to 2017 (PwC, 2019). The outcome of the study shows than when it comes to financials (e.g., revenues, and earnings before interest, text, depreciation, and amortization—namely EBITDA) and employment rate growth, portfolio companies backed by a Venture Capital and Private Equity funds have much higher performances when compared to the national figures (e.g., GDP) and other similar Italian companies.

With regards to revenues, companies backed by Venture Capital funds experienced a 7.1% Compound Annual Growth Rate (CAGR)% growth compared to the national benchmark of a low single-digit 2.0%. When it comes to EBITDA, the same companies grew by 5.6% CAGR% compared to the country average, which was rather negative (0.5%).

The same trend applies to the employment growth, which for venture capital and private equity-backed companies grew by almost 5% (4.8%) CAGR compared to the negative national average of (0.1%).

In this chapter, we discuss the financial constraints, or the financing gap, that affect startups and small-medium enterprises (SMEs), and in general every innovative firm or project which are intended for finance and the different sources of financing for each stage of development of the innovative process.

This chapter will then be focused and provide a complete description of two of the main dimensions that play a leading role in financing innovative firms, Venture Capital funds and Corporate Venture Capital. Moreover, it will provide an overview of who they are, how they operate, how they are structured, and their primary goals.

8.2 The Supply of Finance

As previously discussed, the sources of finance for innovative firms are broad and involve a large number of organizations and parties depending on multiple factors, namely the development stage of the idea, the geography where the innovative firm raises the money, and the type of innovation underlying the innovative firms. Worth remembering here is that given the complexity of the innovation process and the possible type of innovations that may occur at the end of the process, we should use conventions and simplify the type of innovations into three main categories (Abernathy & Clark, 1985; Chesbrough, 2010; Drucker, 2002):

- *innovation of the product*: the development of a new product or service, which encompasses improvements on various features (technical, materials, application, etc.);
- *innovation of the process*: the changes in the way a product or a service is built, including changes in the equipment and the technology used in manufacturing;
- *innovation of the business model*: "enhancing advantage and value creation by making simultaneous—and mutually supportive—changes both to an organization's value proposition to customers and to its underlying operating model." (BCG, 2019). In disruptive and rapidly changing times, this type of innovation could be even more important and lasting than the first two.

Innovative firms are built on the concept of fostering innovation and growth. However most of the time, innovation, growth potential, and the vision behind these ventures may not be easily understood. In fact, by definition, innovation is something that was not present before. So, requires an entrepreneurial attitude and, in general, the ability to discover the potential of a product, a macro trend, or a specific technology. This attempt to foster innovation and disrupt the traditional economics mechanism and business models, was defined by professor Clayton Christensen from the Harvard Business School in the early '90s as one of the key features that differentiate start-ups from established firms, as the latter would have too much to lose from the innovation. This is the reason why, for instance, the traditional book retailing industry was disrupted by a young start-up, Amazon, rather than by other long-competing traditional retailers (Damodaran, 2010).

8.2 The Supply of Finance

The risk associated with innovation processes creates hurdles also for traditional financial institution firms when it comes to evaluating a potential investment in a young venture or startup. Indeed, these companies have no or limited history, small revenues (if any), negative cash flows, and are strictly dependent on equity to survive. Therefore traditional evaluating models such as Discounted Cash Flow (DCF) may not be totally appropriate and should definitely be adopted carefully. So, several adjustments are suggested, as typically *terminal value*, would represent unusual high percentages of the total firm value (e.g., 80%–90%) or even more of *enterprise value.*

The main reason why innovative firms have negative cash flows or, in general, operate in a constant cash constraint environment lies in the fact that most of the time the product or service they are willing to sell is usually not market-ready. Consequently, it does not generate cash and this creates a financing gap that could be covered, in theory, in two ways (Caselli & Negri, 2018; Schwert, 2018):

- borrowed capital;
- equity capital.

In an ideal world, with no market failures such as information asymmetry, moral hazard, and adverse selection, the banking system and other providers of interest-bearing debt would provide the financial resources needed to develop innovative firms. In practice, though, this scenario is not applicable, if not in rare cases of late-stage venture deals, where a venture-debt component is considered. The main reason why the traditional banking system is reluctant to provide financing to innovative firms or startups is related to significant information asymmetry involved, which creates challenges in defining an effective pricing policy of the debt associated. Innovative firms are risky and the degree of uncertainty concerning the return on investment, and the probability of failure are both very high. While equity investors would benefit from the upsides, traditional lenders would set fixed interest rates. Moreover, for the reasons explained before, they would either decide not to grant any loan or to grant a loan with such high interest rates, thus rendering conditions that would be deemed unacceptable by new ventures and startups (Gualandri & Venturelli, 2008).

Innovative firms have a high level of envisaged profitability and an equivalent high level of execution risk; later in this chapter we will see, in fact, that only a handful of <20% of innovative firms survive the startup process and become mature enterprises. This example highlights why equity capital is more suitable for this time of investments, since it is less expensive and better suited for the contextual startup circumstances compared to borrowed capital.

Figure 8.1 illustrates the main sources of finance for innovative firms across their lifecycles, from the outset of the idea throughout the middle stages of development to maturity. As mentioned before, each stage of development of the company involves specific institutions or organizations able to provide finance to the firms.

Every mature company has somehow experienced five phases throughout its lifecycle: (i) idea, (ii) startup, (iii) development, (iv) growth, and (v) maturity (Ndou, Secundo, Schiuma, & Passiante, 2018). There is in fact one additional

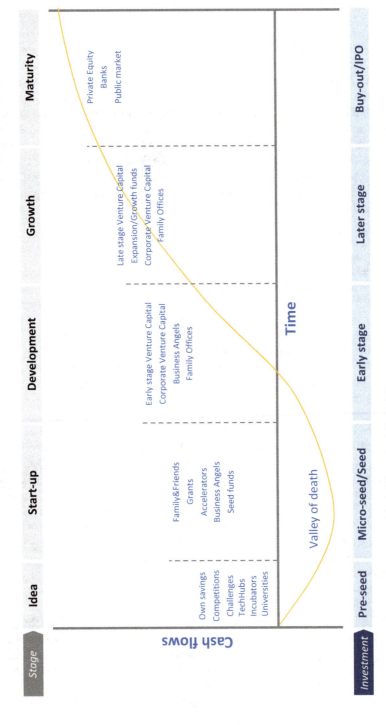

Fig. 8.1 The investment cycle. Source: Adapted from Cardullo (1999)

8.2 The Supply of Finance

phase of the business lifecycle of a company, the decline, which will not be taken into consideration either in this chapter or in the remainder of this book. Indeed, it is focused on the innovative processes and, therefore, on the earlier phases of a company, which lead to its maturity. However, we will provide a high-level description of the last phase of a firm; in this phase, the company approaches its final stage as revenues and margins (and thus cash flows) begin to decline slowly. During the decline phase, a company typically has two to options: (i) shut down, or (ii) adapt to the changing environment and modify its strategy (e.g., business model, market approach, product features).

During their lifecycle, companies encounter several types of external financial support involving many types of organizations and institutions as their lifecycles progress, here are the main ones divided by stage.

- *Idea.* This is the development stage with the highest mortality rate. It is improper here to consider it an innovative firm; most of the time innovation is mostly related to a research project or embryonic ideas of a company. The riskiness associated with these types of projects makes them the perfect candidate to be financed by universities, competitions, and, most likely, own finance. The type of finance provided here is called *pre-seed.*
- *Startup.* Here, the innovative project starts to be defined. Family and friends, as well as business angels, are the ideal sources of finance as they will more likely provide finance to support the entrepreneurs rather than the project. Therefore, personal contacts would play a crucial role. However, also public finance, such as *grants* and institutional money coming from *accelerators* or *seed funds,* would play a relevant role. Public measures will also create indirect support to the start-up since they often provide tax relief and other tax benefits to investors. The type of finance provided here is called *micro seed/seed.*
- *Development.* This might be considered as the most delicate phase, as the company has now been established, people work at the firm, but the product or the service might not be market-ready and thus cash flows are still negative. Venture Capital and Corporate Venture Capital are the ideal source of finance here as they will not only provide smart money but also will bring knowledge, professionality, and network. Moreover, most of all, they will cause the company and the entrepreneurs to switch their mindset towards a more managerial attitude compared to earlier stages. Public measures might also provide some sort of indirect support with the creation of the so defined *matching funds,* investment vehicles backed by the government which basically invest the same amount of money (match) that another qualified investor has invested in the startup in order to generate a leverage effect. Family offices and business angels invest in this stage too. The type of finance provided here is called *early-stage capital.*
- *Growth.* This phase can be considered independent of public intervention as it is likely that the company is already selling its product or service; cash position has reached its equilibrium or, in some cases, the company generates positive cash flows. Venture Capital (especially Late Stage Venture Capital) and Corporate Venture Capital still represent the best option to finance the growth of innovative firms. Alternative funds such as the growth/expansion capital funds, otherwise

defined also early-stage Private Equity funds invest in this stage too. The type of finance provided here is called *later-stage capital.*

- *Maturity.* In this final stage, the company has reached its maturity. Cash flows are positive and the Year Over Year (YoY) revenue growth begins to decelerate as the company has already exploited most of the growth alternatives. In this case, there are two options, IPO (Initial Public Offering) and Buy-out, which in some cases could be explored simultaneously. In fact, in this case, entrepreneurs and, in general, shareholders of the company seek to maximize their return of investment and therefore they test two alternative options in parallel in a process called *dual-track* and decide at the end which of the two suits best in terms of reliability and pricing of the company. The type of finance involved or provided here is both the *IPO* or *Buy-out.*

8.3 Venture Capital

A Venture Capital (VC) fund is an investment vehicle that provides equity financing to companies in their early stages of development. Generally, this is done through a share capital increase, with the objective to support the growth of the company and eventually sell its shares, or the entire company, benefiting from the difference between the amount invested and the amount cashed-in at the exit (Caselli & Negri, 2018; Gladstone & Gladstone, 2004).

VC is part of the broader Private Equity industry and could be divided into two groups which are classified by the type of target company where the VC invests.

- **Early Stage.** Typically, the VC that operates in this segment invests in post-seed and early-stage companies. The type of risk associated with this investment is very high, as the rate of mortality is high. Usually VC funds invest directly in the shareholding capital of the company through a shareholders' capital increase. However, there are alternative options for financing in this stage, such as *convertible notes* and comparable structure, which are essentially loans that investors provide to the company that could be converted into equity in case of a trigger event. Notably, most of the time, this event is the next funding round or a specific commercial milestone, the accomplishment of which would give the investor the right, but not the obligation, to convert its loan into the equity of the firm.
- **Late Stage.** This type of fund invests in companies, which have already overcome the *valley of death.* They have a proper management team leading the company, the product or service (excluding biotech or some med-tech company) is definitely market-ready, and indeed, the company is already making revenues. In this case, funds invest in equity directly as the company as already accomplished the main milestones typical of earlier stages and require finance to provide a boost to the development of the company. Sometimes expansion capital is also considered part of the Late Stage venturing activity. However, this type of financing is mostly seen in more mature companies and does not necessarily need to be invested in innovative firms.

8.3 Venture Capital
231

Table 8.1 Life cycle phases and types of operation

Stage	Type of investment	Shareholding acquired	Leverage	Risk	Rationale	Goal
Startup	Micro-seed/ seed	Minority/ majority	None	Very high	Idea fine tuning	Proof of concept
Development	Early stage			High	Business creation	Industrialization/ first market test
Growth	Later stage	Minority		High/ medium	Scale up	Revenues ramp-up/ internationalization/ M&A

Source: Adapted from Gervasoni and Sattin (2015)

Table 8.1 summarizes some of the main characteristics of the investment in innovative firms sorted by stage of intervention and, thus, type of investment.

It is clear that neither Early Stage funds, which invest in start-up and development stage, nor Later Stage funds make use of financing leverage in order to perform the investment. On the contrary, they invest their finances (i.e., their private equity) directly in the company, or in some cases, to buy residual shares in a secondary transaction from some small shareholder willing to sell. Leverage is, instead, heavily used by Buy-Out funds, which usually borrow money from banks or other financial institutions which lend them the finances (called acquisition financing facility) to buy-out the target company, in addition to their private equity. Most of the time, a typical buy-out deal will be structured with 70% financial resources needed to buy the company provided by the banks, while the remaining 30% will come from the funds; the acquisition financing is then transferred to the acquired company.

The debt gets repaid over time by the company and therefore, without considering any development of the company acquired, i.e. acquired and sold at the same price. This simple and clear structure will be sufficient for the Buy-out fund to make a good return on investment since, at exit, its shareholding capital will have a greater value since the company would have already partially repaid its debt. From this, the resulting equity/debt structure could be, for instance, 50%–50%, which will allow the Buy-out fund to make roughly $1.7\times$ Cash-on-Cash (CoC) multiple on its investment.

This structure could be used in case the company has reached its maturity stage with positive cash flows. Indeed, it will be able to repay the acquisition financing facility and reduce the total amount of debt in the company. Conversely, that is not the case in Early Stage or Later Stage transactions, where companies live in a structural equity gap.

This short example and comparison between Buy-Out funds and VC funds was provided in order to understand the complexity and the difficulty of venture capital. In fact, they need to both make careful choices in identifying the right target companies and pick up the most promising ones that will allow them to make the expected CoC multiple returns.

The activity of a Venture Capital fund is quite broad and difficult to classify. However there are four stages throughout the lifespan of a VC, which are common for every structure (Drover, Busenitz et al., 2017; Drover, Wood, & Zacharakis, 2017; Ruhnka & Young, 1987):

(a) *Fundraising.* It is most commonly used for startups, whereas funds could be somehow defined as a startup too. As we can see from Sect. 8.3.1 of this chapter, the VC funds invest the finance provided by other investors, typically Fund-of-Funds, High Networth Individual Funds (HNWI), Family Office, Pension Funds, and Banks, to name a few. Therefore, before starting their typical activity, they will need to raise money from external parties. This could be a time-consuming activity, which on average, could last approximately 1 year and a half and is divided into a few steps, or *closings*, where the incremental amount of finances are committed to the VC funds. The most important one is the *first closing*, which is the minimum amount of capital needed for the fund activity to start. Example: A VC fund starts its fundraising activity with a target raise of €100 M and the first close of €30 M, this means that before reaching €30 M, the activity of the fund cannot start.

(b) *Deal screening.* This is a crucial phase of any fund, also private equity. However, given what we said before, VC funds must act more carefully in identifying the right target companies. During this activity, the investment team of the fund screen and evaluate a large number of potential candidates (likely, for a medium size fund, around 600–800 per year) for being a portfolio company. On average, out of the total targets evaluated, only a handful of them receive the investment, with an impressive low "success rate" figure of 1–2% of companies that get funded by the VC fund. Part of the evaluation process includes also the *due diligence* phase, where the investment teams, together with external consultants (e.g., business consultants, law firms, financial consultant, etc.) conduct a thorough investigation on multiple aspects of the company such as market potential, product/service distinctiveness, financial strength of the business plan, and any potential issues with the law of fiscal authorities, etc., with the objective to confirm the initial idea of the company, or opposed to that, sufficient elements to pull back from the transaction.

(c) *Investment decision and portfolio management.* Once the due diligence phase is completed, the investment team members will manage deal structuring and will define and negotiate the terms and conditions of the investment with the innovative firms' founders and shareholders. Once the investment is made, the second most crucial activity of a fund begins, the portfolio management; this phase involves the value creation, or destruction, of the portfolio companies. Typically this activity is carried out both through a formal support, since most of the time investment team members sit on the Board of Directors of the portfolio companies, and through informal support, hence a constant backing, support, and teamwork with the management of the companies in order to create an effective strategy for the company, challenge and review the business plans, provide support on business development and people management, lead on subsequent financing rounds. This type of support is called *Hands on Approach*, which is very common in the VC industry, so much so that in some cases, especially with super-early stage companies, this could also be called *company building*.

8.3 Venture Capital

(d) *Exit.* In this phase, the investment team is fully focused on extracting the value from the investment made years earlier. There are essentially three types of exit: (i) Initial Public Offering, (ii) Acquisition (both from a Private Equity and a Company), or (iii) Liquidation. In the first two types of exit, VC funds make a profit or recover the investment made (1.0x CoC multiple), while with the latter it is unlikely that the funds will ever get their investment back. It is rather more common that, in this case, the funds will be required to pour more money into the company. Contrary to popular perception, successful exits play only a minor role out of the total portfolio companies as only ~20% of them create profit for the fund (the *VC Funnel*, reported later); however, that 20% can compensate and outmatch the other 80% failures.

In order to be effective, flexible, and quick, every VC fund is organized following a pre-defined general framework of clear rules, guidelines, and roles within which the different bodies of the fund will act with certain level of freedom. There are four pillars under which every fund is structured:

(a) *structure*: defines how and when capital will be deployed at fund level;
(b) *investment strategy*: defines where, how and how much, the fund will invest;
(c) *corporate governance*: defines the decision process and bodies involved;
(d) *alignment of interest*: defines the type of engagement and incentives of fund bodies.

8.3.1 Structure

The Venture Capital fund is the vehicle through which the investments in the portfolio companies are made. Funds are usually structured as closed-end funds (difference between closed-end fund and other alternative structures will be discussed in coming sections) with a typical maturity of 10 years and is organised with the characteristic GP/LP layout.

(a) *GP* (General Partner): a fund manager, or team of people, that manage an investment. A GP can manage more than one fund at once and also in different asset classes, such as venture capital, private equity, private debt, infrastructure, and so on. GP also invests an amount of money (1–2% of fund capital) acquiring fund units in order to share with the LPs the same risk-reward. The GP charges a management fee every year to the Limited Partners (LPs) in order to support the fund activity (e.g., people, staff functions, rent). Moreover, in order to be encouraged to overperform, it receives a certain percentage (usually 20%) of the surplus above the hurdle rate of the fund, the so called *carried interest* (discussed in further detail in the coming sections).
(b) LP (Limited Partner): the legal status of an investor in an investment fund, which has limited rights and obligations and does not interfere with the management of the investments or portfolio companies. LPs acquire units of the fund by

committing to an investment in the fund until the drawdown. As a return, they will receive the hurdle rate (although not given for granted), which is the minimum cumulative interest rate (5–6% in venture capital, 8–9% in private equity) that the GP envisions the single fund will make. In case overperformances triggered the carried interest, they will receive, on top of the returns gained with the hurdle rate, also the surplus in returns, net of carried interest.

There are also other features which define the structure of a fund:

(a) *Closed-end vs. Open-end.* The closed-end structures envision an initial capital injection or commitment from investors, which is defined in value. Therefore, there is no possibility to increase the amount of money managed and it is unlikely that any change in investor (LPs) composition will occur. An open-end structure, instead, envisions various capital injections over the life span of the vehicle, which may also differ in terms of amount. As opposed to the closed-end structures, in the open-end structure multiple cash injections occur over time and new LPs are allowed to come in.

(b) *Capital usage.* There is a basic difference between funds with *allocated capital* and funds which use a *capital call* in order to draw down the amount needed for the investments. In allocated capital structures, LPs provide the whole amount of money required by the fund at the incorporation date. In capital call structures, investors provide the committed amount of money to the fund upon a call from the fund managers.

(c) *Duration.* There are funds *limited* in time, where at the time of capital commitment from LPs is defined by how long the fund will last and how the lifespan of the fund will be divided. Typically, it is split in three phases: (i) *Investment period* (usually 4–5 years), when the investments in portfolio companies are made; (ii) *Management period* (usually 5–6 years), when the value creation and subsequent exit of portfolio companies happens; and (iii) G*race period* (usually 2–3 years), a potential extension of the fund duration in case there remaining companies in the portfolio of the fund. As opposed to that, in the *unlimited structures,* GP/LP do not define any specific deadline or timeframe that the fund activity should be compliant with. This structure, defined *evergreen funds*, provides more freedom and is less common compared with the first ones. Funds limited in time are, in general, preferred by LPs because they enable them to see the real returns from the investment activity within a pre-defined time (Gualandri & Venturelli, 2008).

8.3.2 Investment Strategy

The investment strategy of a fund defines the perimeter within which the investment team will act with independence.

A clear and well set out investment strategy could increase the effectiveness and flexibility of the decision process, easing the deal origination and execution as well as the management of the portfolio companies (Bernstein, Giroud, & Townsend, 2016; Drover, Wood et al. 2017).

According to best practices, an investment strategy must set out to define few clear elements in order to keep the fund's structure and investment team focused and aware of the mission (Gladstone & Gladstone, 2004; Ruhnka & Young, 1987). Usually, the investment strategy of a fund defines five fundamental characteristics.

(a) *Ticket size*. The amount of money that can be allocated to a single investment, for instance, as the first investment in a portfolio company, as well as the cumulative investments made in the same portfolio company as fund managers (and risk allocation standards) want to avoid risk concentration.

(b) *Type of investment*. It defines the adoptable investment strategy in a company such as investment in equity, shareholder's loan, convertible notes, listed stock, and so on. In fact, investment funds, especially in venture capital, not only invest in equity but also in other types of securities, which allows mitigating the risk and/or increasing the benefit in case of upsides. For instance, it is quite common in seed or early-stage investments to subscribe to a convertible note first, instead of an equity investment. This note, which is basically a convertible loan, allows the fund to convert the loan into equity at the following financing round at a discount compared to a pre-money valuation of the round itself and, thus, receiving shares at a lower implicit valuation.

(c) *Stage*. It defines the stage of the company where the fund is allowed to invest, such as seed, early-stage, or late-stage venture capital investments. An investment fund could also have multiple investment strategies within the same asset class (e.g., private equity vs. venture capital) in order to mitigate and diversify the risk associated with one specific investment strategy. So, for example, a venture capital fund could invest at the same time, and with specific limits, up to 75% in late-stage venture and up to 25% in seed investment.

(d) *Scope*. This characteristic applies both to a geographical and an industrial scope. In fact, a fund could have an investment strategy which is industry agnostic, so that it can make investment in every industry possible. As opposed to that, a fund could also have a focalized investment strategy in a single industrial field, such as life science, food, and agro-tech. This classification also applies to the geographical scope which could be either home country-focused, or could have a broader scope, however, excluding the few global investment funds; it is more common to have an investment strategy with an overhang on the home country with the possibility to make investments also outside the country up to certain limits.

(e) *Role*. Defines basically how the fund will (or would like to) act during the investment round between (i) a leading role and (ii) a follower role. In fact, venture capital deals, as opposed to traditional buy-out private equity deals, mostly take place as a co-investment, or syndication, with other investment funds. Therefore, every deal has a deal leader and a deal follower. For instance, leading the round not only means investing the majority of the round but also getting better deal conditions or specific governance rights.

8.3.3 Corporate Governance

From the organizational point of view, the corporate governance of an investment fund is quite complex and articulate, and many independent funds at international levels adopt a structure composed of four different corporate bodies.

(a) *Board of Directors (BoD)*. This body works at a GP level and should be composed of executive and non-executive members with an appropriate balance of skills, experience, and knowledge. BoD is responsible for setting the strategic goal of the investment company (GP) and provide a strong link with the LPs. Its main responsibility, though, is to take care and be responsible for the approval process of the investment, add-ons, and divestment.

(b) *Investment team.* It is the most important body of an investment fund structure, as it is responsible for creating value or destroying it for the LPs. Composed of operative members with investment experience, complementary skills, and background. It is responsible for the investment activity and portfolio management of the fund, including deal screening, deal structuring, portfolio monitoring, and business development and fundraising.

(c) *Investment committee.* This body cooperates and assists the investment team as it provides guidance on the evaluation of the investments, integrate investment teams with specific skills, and knowledge and provide network opportunities. It is made of external and independent members; however, important LPs, which have made significant investments in the fund, could also nominate some members.

(d) *Advisory board.* This is a discretionary body composed of external members appointed, usually, by the most important LPs or anchor investors. It verifies the coherence between the investments made and the investment strategy of the fund and also assesses any potential conflict of interest.

From the authorization process point of view, the key role, as mentioned earlier, is played by the BoD (or sometimes the executive committee, a body nominated by the BoD standing for it) which also have the legal responsibility of approving or not approving any investment transaction and any transaction on the portfolio.

In this regard, the investment team, in order to minimize the possibility that the BoD rejects an investment proposal, presents the same proposal to the Investment Committee in the first place, which should provide an initial qualitative filter and support in refining the investment proposal.

As showed in Fig. 8.2, which provides an overview of how a typical investment process is structured, the investment team is involved in every single step of the deal process, from deal flow screening until the exit. The BoD and the Investment Committee, instead, are involved only in the review of the process and in the approval of the operations structured and outlined by the Investment Team.

The way decisions are adopted in investment funds represent only the final process of screening and evaluation of several investment opportunities where only a handful of around 1–2% receive their first investment. Going forward, once

8.3 Venture Capital

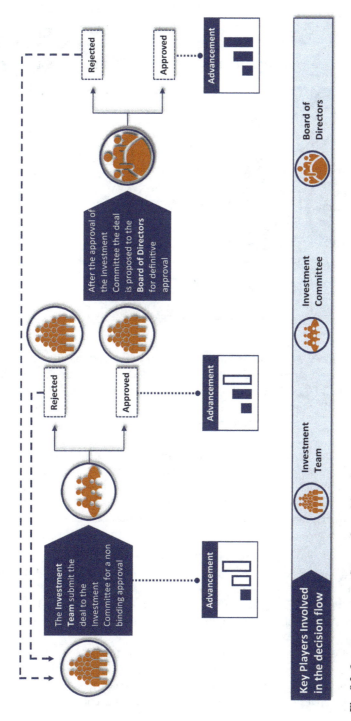

Fig. 8.2 Investment process. Source: Own elaboration

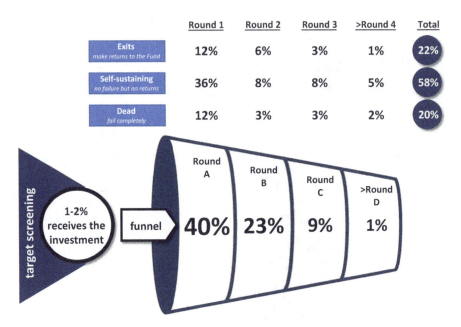

Fig. 8.3 The startup funding cone. Source: Own elaboration

the company receives its first institutional investment round (typically a seed round), the natural selection process of startups gets even tougher with very small numbers. Roughly only 20% of the portfolio companies of venture capital funds managed to raise their third or fourth round, which could correspond to a robust Series C or D round. This is alternatively known as the Startup Funding Cone, as shown in Fig. 8.3.

Before receiving any investment, and this applies not only to the first seed institutional investment but also to later-stage investment, a very disciplined and somehow rigid selection process takes place, that is why only 1–2% of the analyzed companies receive the investment. In this stage, investment teams, supported by external advisors, carry out analysis and audits on multiple aspects, namely the most important ones are:

(a) *Market and business due diligence.* It provides a better understanding of the risk and potential of both the product and service of the company and the specific market in which the company operates and how it is positioned compared to competitors, both current and potential. This analysis will also help perform stress tests and challenges to the original business plans presented by the company.

(b) *Financial and fiscal due diligence.* It assesses the truthfulness of past financial figures and also provides support in assessing the likelihood of future figures. It helps to identify potential financial and fiscal issues regarding actions taken before the investment by the management team of the company.

8.4 Corporate Venture Capital 239

(c) *Legal due diligence.* As well as the financial due diligence, it assesses the potential issues of a legal nature that may affect the company and the business, and therefore, might have an impact also on the valuation of the company.
(d) *Environmental due diligence.* This has the same goal as legal due diligence but takes into consideration environmental regulations and legislation that may have an impact on the company business.

8.3.4 Alignment of Interest: Carried Interest

The alignment of interest between the LPs and the other bodies involved in the management of a fund is a fundamental pillar of the structure of closed-end GP/LP structures as it creates a strong connection and alignment between the interest of the LPs and the GP (for instance the investment team). Wealth creation is primarily derived from an extra performance fee (*carried interest*), which is distributed to the GP only in case of returns to LPs above a certain minimum return rate (*hurdle rate*) to LPs that GP was committed to.

Basically, at the outset of the lifespan of the fund, GP invests a portion of the total size of the fund. In general, 1–2%, which is thus subscribed by both the GP and the LPs acting as investors in the fund. However, the units of the fund acquired by the GP committing to the investment have similarities to the mechanics of the preferred shares in public companies, for instance. In case the total capital gain of the fund reached and outmatched the hurdle rate, the extra gain is shared by GP and LPs disproportionately in favor of the GP. Generally it follows the 80/20 ratio, which means that in this case, although GP has invested in 1% of the fund, in case of an extra return, it receives 20% of the capital gain above the hurdle rate.

In order to align the interest between the LPs, GP, and other relevant bodies of an investment fund, carried interest is also subscribed not only by members of the investment teams but also by members of the investment committee as a further incentive.

8.4 Corporate Venture Capital

Corporate Venture Capital (CVC) is the set of activities aimed at fostering innovation both outside and inside the same company promoting corporate venturing activities. It allows corporations to rapidly adapt and respond to changes in the markets by acquiring a better point of view on the potential opportunities and uncommon understanding of the potential threats (Chesbrough, 2002; Dushnitsky & Lenox, 2005).

In the literature there several definitions of Corporate Venture Capital definitions exist, but since corporations are more complex and heterogeneous compared to investment funds, it is difficult to find one single definition that could be used a true representation of the phenomenon.

However, there are two definitions provided by the British Venture Capital Association and one by Professor Henry Chesbrough that includes most of the possible variations:

- BVCA: *"Corporate Venture Capital is a form of equity investment that has evolved greatly since its emergence around 40 years ago. It is a 'catchall' name used to describe a wide variety of forms of equity investment exercised by corporations. At the most basic level, Corporate Venture Capital describes an equity investment made by a corporation or its investment entity into a high growth potential, privately held business"* (BVCA, 2012).
- Professor Henry Chesbrough: *"Corporate Venture Capital is the term used to describe the investment of corporate funds directly in external start-up companies. Our definition excludes investments made through an external fund managed by a third party, even if the investment vehicle is funded by and specifically designed to meet the objectives of a single investment company. It also excludes investments that fall under the more generic rubric of "corporate venturing", for example, the funding of a new internal venture that, while distinct from a company's core definition and granted some organizational autonomy, remain legally part of the company. Our definition does include, however, investments made in startups that a company has already spun off as independent business"* (Chesbrough, 2002).

Over the last years, the number of corporate venture capitals launched by corporations has increased rapidly. As a consequence, the corporate venture capital funding surged reaching its all-time high in 2018 with global activity of over 2700 deals and approximately \$53Bn funding, corresponding to a 2.6× and 5.3× increase respectively compared to 2013 figures.

Corporations are facing a big challenge to hunt for growth as mature markets are facing slower economic growth, while the middle class in developed geographies is shrinking. In this context, corporate venture capital represents an alternative and effective way to pursue growth compared to traditional ways. Traditionally, in fact, companies pursued growth essentially in the following two ways:

- *Organic growth.* It refers to the expansion of companies' operations and financial figures leveraging internal resources, mostly driven by R&D and business development departments. Except for biotech and pharma companies, it usually produces slow, but solid and constant, growth rates. It has a slow adaptive capabilities and low flexibility.
- *Inorganic growth.* It includes the broader mergers & acquisitions type of activity such as acquisition, divestment, and joint venture. Inorganic growth represents the quickest way to provide an immediate boost to revenues and (at least in the medium-long term) margins. However, it requires a high level of competences and mindsets within the company and requires a high degree of capital in order to be effective. Given the nature of the transaction, it is preferable to handle one

transaction at the time and also consider post-merger integration activities in the plan. In fact, most of the failures in the acquisition are attributable to bad planning vis-à-vis the crucial post-deal phase which, in some cases, fails in creating the synergies (e.g., commercial, cost, scope) which were the basis for the investment rationale before the transaction took place.

In this context, corporate venture capital represents a valuable trade-off between the flexibility required to explore potential external growth opportunities and the adaptability to the core business of the company and its structure. Corporate venture capital allows also reducing the risk of investing in one single business at the time. In fact, the best practice of investment in corporate venture requires the corporation to make multiple investments in start-ups in order to reach an effective risk diversification.

As opposed to the traditional venture capital's objective of reaching an above-market financial return, corporate venture capital typically pursues, through three different models, two main objectives in various shades between the two:

- *Strategic goals.* They allow the company to generate revenue and margins, bring innovation through the development of new products or processes, enter into new markets or consolidate its position within the current ones. A corporate venture capital mainly focused on strategic goals will create effective synergies between the mother company and the invested company providing management skills and other types of expertise.
- *Financial goals.* They achieve financial returns, which put the corporate venture capital closer to the traditional target of venture capital. However, instead of reaching above the market results, in general, corporate venture capital set lower return targets, which are above the company's cost of capital. Worth noticing that the financial returns are, anyway, used as a driver of sustainability of the strategic objectives.

As previously mentioned, based on an analysis provided by the British Venture Capital Association (see Table 8.2), it is possible to identify three different models used by corporate venture capital with various balances between control and risk. The adoption of one model instead of another by a company is influenced by corporate's needs and long-term goals:

- *Model 1—Corporate Direct Investment*: direct investment by the corporate into startups without the incorporation of an ad-hoc investment vehicle; the activity is carried out by a cross-functional internal team.
- *Model 2—Internal Dedicated Fund*: benefits from a greater degree of independence in the decision-making process, although it is a totally captive vehicle. In this case, the activity is carried out by a dedicated team composed of professionals coming from the company and professionals coming from external environments, mostly from venture capital and private equity.
- *Model 3—External Fund*: in this case, the company acts like a Limited Partner; the activity is carried out entirely by the investment team of the venture capital where the corporate has decided to invest. Depending on the type and amount of

Table 8.2 The corporate venture capital models

	Corporate/direct investment *Balance sheet*	Corporate/direct investment *Balance sheet*	Corporate/direct investment *Balance sheet*
Purpose	Gain direct business and technology experience in emerging areas	Emerging business and technology with more autonomy for step out options	Investing with primary financial goal with tight relationship with financing parent company
Structure	Direct investment funding each deal, closely related to business divisions and future opportunities	Corporate acts ad LP in a captive fund. Greater fund autonomy.	GP external firm; LP corporate investor. Potential ad-hoc conditions with corporate
Success measure	Measurements of direct strategic inputs	Primarily financial with a level of strategic exposure	Predominantly ROI
HR	Internal employees	Mixture of external VC professionals and internal corporate talent	Experienced venture capital professionals and secondees from corporate
Managerial effort	High	Medium	Low
Capital intensity	Medium	High	Low
Innovation potential	Low	Medium	High

Source: BVCA (2012)

investment of the company in the venture capital, in some cases companies are granted with a co-investment right. So, it will enable the company to invest alongside the venture capital, when the venture capital decides to invest in a startup. It is also common to establish a deal-flow sharing type of relationship between the venture capital and the corporation.

8.5 Conclusions

When talking about innovation and innovative firms, we usually think about the stereotype of the young entrepreneurs, or 'startupper' if you will, funding a company in the backyard garage, raising an outrageous amount of funding by investors and eventually going public through an IPO.

As opposed to this stereotype, innovation is a long and struggling process, which starts with an idea taking shape inch by inch with effort, sweat, few fancy moments, and a lot of work.

This journey is surrounded by many organizations and persons that support the innovative firms in this journey not only by providing capital, but also especially in the early stages of development, with knowledge, guidance, and access to networks.

Among the major and more effective ways to raise capital, there are two that stand out: Venture Capital and Corporate Venture Capital. Both venture capital and corporate venture capital were born as an answer to two specific threats, the first being the Soviet Union, and the need to adapt quickly to market needs and demands as the second.

References

Abernathy, W. J., & Clark, K. B. (1985). Innovation: Mapping the winds of creative destruction. *Research Policy, 14*(1), 3–22.

Battisti, E., Miglietta, N., Nirino, N., & Villasalero Diaz, M. (2019). Value creation, innovation practice, and competitive advantage: Evidence from the FTSE MIB index. *European Journal of Innovation Management.*

BCG. (2019). *Business model innovation.* Retrieved from https://www.bcg.com/capabilities/strat egy/business-model-innovation.aspx

Bernstein, S., Giroud, X., & Townsend, R. R. (2016). The impact of venture capital monitoring. *The Journal of Finance, 71*(4), 1591–1622.

Blank, S. (2009). *The secret history of silicon valley 12: The rise of "Risk capital" part 2.* Retrieved from https://steveblank.com/2009/10/29/the-secret-history-of-silicon-valley-12-the-rise-of-% E2%80%9Crisk-capital%E2%80%9D-part-2/

Bonini, S., & Capizzi, V. (2019). The role of venture capital in the emerging entrepreneurial finance ecosystem: Future threats and opportunities. *Venture Capital, 21*(2–3), 137–175.

Brown, J. R., Fazzari, S. M., & Petersen, B. C. (2009). Financing innovation and growth: Cash flow, external equity, and the 1990s R&D boom. *The Journal of Finance, 64*(1), 151–185.

BVCA. (2012). *Guide to corporate venture capital.* Retrieved July 21, 2019, from https://www.bvca.co.uk/Portals/0/library/documents/BVCA%20Guide%20to%20Corporate%20Venture%20Capital.pdf

Cardullo, M. W. (1999). *Technological entrepreneurism: Enterprise formation, financing and growth.* Baldock: Research Studies Press Ltd.

Caselli, S., & Negri, G. (2018). *Private equity and venture capital in Europe: Markets, techniques, and deals.* London: Academic Press.

Chesbrough, H. W. (2002). Making sense of corporate venture capital. *Harvard Business Review, 80*(3), 90–99.

Chesbrough, H. (2010). Business model innovation: Opportunities and barriers. *Long Range Planning, 43*(2–3), 354–363.

Damodaran, A. (2010). *The dark side of valuation: Valuing young, distressed, and complex businesses.* Upper Saddle River, NJ: FT Press.

Drover, W., Busenitz, L., Matusik, S., Townsend, D., Anglin, A., & Dushnitsky, G. (2017). A review and road map of entrepreneurial equity financing research: Venture capital, corporate venture capital, angel investment, crowdfunding, and accelerators. *Journal of Management, 43*(6), 1820–1853.

Drover, W., Wood, M. S., & Zacharakis, A. (2017). Attributes of angel and crowdfunded investments as determinants of VC screening decisions. *Entrepreneurship Theory and Practice, 41*(3), 323–347.

Drucker, P. F. (2002). The discipline of innovation. *Harvard Business Review, 80*, 95–104.

Dushnitsky, G., & Lenox, M. J. (2005). When do incumbents learn from entrepreneurial ventures? Corporate venture capital and investing firm innovation rates. *Research Policy, 34*(5), 615–639.

Ferraris, A., Santoro, G., & Bresciani, S. (2017). Open innovation in multinational companies' subsidiaries: The role of internal and external knowledge. *European Journal of International Management, 11*(4), 452–468.

Gervasoni, A., & Sattin, F. L. (2015). Private equity e venture capital. Manuale di investimento nel capitale di rischio. Guerini Next.

Gladstone, D., & Gladstone, L. (2004). *Venture capital investing: The complete handbook for investing in private business for outstanding profits.* Upper Saddle River, NJ: FT Press.

Gualandri, E., & Venturelli, V. (2008). *Bridging the equity gap for innovative SMEs.* London: Palgrave Macmillan.

Hall, B. H., & Lerner, J. (2010). *The financing of R&D and innovation.* In *Handbook of the economics of innovation* (Vol. 1, pp. 609–639). North-Holland: Elsevier.

Hou, J., & Mohnen, P. (2013). Complementarity between in-house R&D and technology purchasing: Evidence from Chinese manufacturing firms. *Oxford Development Studies, 41*(3), 343–371.

Kerr, W. R., & Nanda, R. (2015). Financing innovation. *Annual Review of Financial Economics, 7,* 445–462.

Ndou, V., Secundo, G., Schiuma, G., & Passiante, G. (2018). Insights for shaping entrepreneurship education: Evidence from the European entrepreneurship centers. *Sustainability, 10*(11), 4323.

PwC. (2019). *The economic impact of private equity and venture capital in Italy.* Retrieved from https://www.pwc.com/it/it/publications/assets/docs/economic-impact-2018.pdf

Rama, R. (Ed.). (2008). *Handbook of innovation in the food and drink industry.* New York: CRC Press.

Ruhnka, J. C., & Young, J. E. (1987). A venture capital model of the development process for new ventures. *Journal of Business Venturing, 2*(2), 167–184.

Schwert, M. (2018). Bank capital and lending relationships. *The Journal of Finance, 73*(2), 787–830.

Vrgovic, P., Vidicki, P., Glassman, B., & Walton, A. (2012). Open innovation for SMEs in developing countries – An intermediated communication network model for collaboration beyond obstacles. *Innovations, 14*(3), 290–302.

Chapter 9
A European Food Ecosystem: The EIT Food Case Study

Abstract This chapter aims to present the traits and key success factors of the "European Institute of Innovation and Technology" (EIT), analyzing the "EIT Food" case. To highlight EIT Food's strategic position as orchestrator and catalyzer of innovation, knowledge, and business creation, the case study uses the lens of the "quadruple helix model innovation". EIT Food's mission, vision, strategies, objectives, values, and activities are finalized to foster and drive the challenges of the European food innovation ecosystem. The case study gives evidence on the role that a territorial innovation ecosystem can play to develop a culture of innovation and entrepreneurship, enabling the transition from a knowledge economy to a knowledge society, namely from a triple to a quadruple helix model.

With a social mission and trusted multi-stakeholder independent community that is coming together to solve the challenges of the food system, triggering innovative bottom-up activities, EIT Food drives the shift towards an ecosystem perspective and fosters a sense of "collective stewardship" toward social, environmental, and economic sustainability. The entrepreneurial spirit and participatory approach of all the heterogeneous actors are increasingly being cultivated through open innovation methodologies and open innovation spaces to improve human health, access to quality food, and address the main challenges of the food system. EIT Food innovation ecosystem business model is people-centric and resource-smart based and finalized to stimulate connections and partnerships between consumers, citizens, businesses, startups, research institutions, students, and food supply chain stakeholders throughout Europe. The case study focuses on the key elements that characterize EIT Food, and hence, untangle under what conditions it shapes and influences economic, technological, and societal thinking within its ecosystem.

Keywords Food innovation ecosystem · EIT food · Quadruple Helix · Value network · Knowledge society

---

Co-authored by Andy Zynga—EIT Food, Heverlee, Belgium, e-mail: andy.zynga@eitfood.eu

© Springer Nature Switzerland AG 2020
P. De Bernardi, D. Azucar, *Innovation in Food Ecosystems*, Contributions to Management Science, https://doi.org/10.1007/978-3-030-33502-1_9

9.1 Introduction: The European Institute of Innovation and Technology (EIT)

In the last years, the concept of innovation ecosystem has increasingly gained ground in the literature on strategy, innovation, and entrepreneurship. A set of definitions and concepts have been developed by scholars in different contexts, by using innovation ecosystem with different labels and, in some cases, with different meanings and purposes: digital innovation ecosystem (Rao & Jimenez, 2011), hub ecosystems (Nambisan & Baron, 2013), open innovation ecosystem (Chesbrough et al., 2014), platform-based ecosystem (Gawer, 2014).

Gomes, Facin, Salerno, and Ikenami (2018), performing a systematic analysis of the different concepts of innovation ecosystems, characterized a construct with the following features: an innovation ecosystem, composed of interconnected and interdependent networked actors, which includes the focal entity, customers, suppliers, complementary innovators, and other agents as regulators, is set for the co-creation of value (Gomes et al., 2018). This definition implies that partners and members face cooperation and competition in the innovation ecosystem, which: i) has a lifecycle, ii) follows a co-evolution process, and iii) creates an ecosystem common good which consists in the creation of value for the society.

In an innovation ecosystem, innovation and entrepreneurship are two distinct but intertwined strategic drivers of economic growth in the knowledge economy (Tataj, 2015). Nonetheless, to fruitfully implement innovation processes in the economy it is now indispensable engage the public as a new and relevant contributor to innovation, giving architecture to new ways of dialogue and collaboration to moving the ecosystem to the knowledge society (Carayannis & Campbell, 2012; Owen, Macnaghten, & Stilgoe, 2012; Stilgoe, Lock, & Wilsdon, 2014).

When considering highly innovative environments (e.g., Silicon Valley, Tel Aviv, and Cambridge Massachusetts), innovation and entrepreneurship appear as ever-present and continuous information exchange and knowledge sharing make such innovation ecosystems flourish. An innovation ecosystem consists of a group of different actors and dynamic processes, which together produce solutions to face grand challenges (Oksanen & Hautamäki, 2014). The dynamic process that makes such innovation ecosystems develop, depends on the entities sustaining such a process usually called either animators, facilitators or orchestrators, but also on the strong involvement of greater public since i) it can help resolve major challenges, producing more welcome innovations, and ii) it is ethically fair to give a chance to civil society gain greater access to and influence over the innovation process and its results (Carayannis & Campbell, 2009).

Therefore, the emergence of a certain innovation ecosystem depends on: i) a leading public institution committed to develop a territory and attract the necessary resources; ii) a harmonic business sector where established large companies and new start-ups specialize and cooperate under value chains and clusters, from local markets permeable to product innovations and connected to global networks; and iii) a risk-taking entrepreneurial culture which accepts facing major challenges and is

9.1 Introduction: The European Institute of Innovation and Technology (EIT)

open to change and evolution through the ability of nurturing its human capital. Moreover, other enabling factors include the dynamic interaction and "cross-fertilization" between business and academia, academia and government, government and business, organizations and individuals, as well as services supporting knowledge transfer and developing innovation networks.

In this context, the European Institute of Innovation and Technology (EIT) could be presented as an innovative ecosystem. It has a status of a European Union Agency (EC 294/2008) with a key mission to establish and fund a new type of pan-European innovation network that brings together research, education, and innovation. As highlighted by scholars, the nature of collaborative partnerships and the way partnership networks function have a marked improvement over single actors seeking to create social and economic value in isolation. As stated by Tataj (2015), in order to enable the collective capacity to develop new products and services to the market, it is necessary to understand networked environments that are conducive to innovation.

A main structure for innovation networks is known as the Knowledge Triangle, composed of education, business creation and innovation, and engaging people as active partners of change. Entrepreneurship is viewed as the glue for the Knowledge Triangle since it acts as a catalyst for value creation not only by integrating the network but also by creating synergies between the three remaining components. The Knowledge Triangle can be interpreted as a multidimensional dynamic construct which has marked a shift from: i) intellectual property-based research to open innovation; ii) university to education to learning environments with a strong peer-to-peer learning component; and iii) innovation within homogenous sectors to cross-sector innovation in collaboration with trans-disciplinary social, creative, and process networks (Tataj, 2015). In this vein, due to its properties of driving economic and social innovations, the Knowledge Triangle was used as the conceptual framework for the creation of the European Institute of Innovation and Technology (EIT) and its accompanying Knowledge and Innovation Communities (KICs) (EIT, 2019a).

The European Institute of Innovation and Technology (EIT) is a European collaborative project created by the European Union to strengthen Europe's innovative capabilities and stimulate innovation by integrating businesses, universities, and research institutions. This integration of key innovation partners has been coined "Innovation Communities", and EIT has specifically-designed Innovation Communities that seek to find solutions to specific global challenges including, among others, climate change, sustainable energy, digital advancements, health innovations, smart mobility, and food solutions for a sustainable world.

Since its inception in 2008, EIT has become the EU's largest innovation ecosystem, which through the coordinated initiatives of its many members, the EIT communities, provides a range of support activities designed to ignite entrepreneurship and innovation. The key strategic initiatives are: i) education programs that encompass technical and entrepreneurial training; ii) business creation and startup acceleration services; iii) the ability to participate in, and create, innovation driven research projects, and iv) communication and dissemination of researches and best practices as well as public engagement. Through these initiatives, EIT facilitates the introduction of innovative products and services to viable markets, assists aspiring entrepreneurs and everyday community members in identifying entrepreneurial opportunities, and, most importantly, combines ideas from a collection of industry and academic members to give European markets a competitive advantage.

The EIT mission can be divided into two components (EIT, 2018):

1. to contribute to the competitiveness of Europe, its social, environmental and economical sustainable growth and job creation by promoting and strengthening synergies and cooperation among businesses, education institutions, and research organizations;
2. to create favorable environments for creative thoughts and to enable world-class innovation and entrepreneurship to thrive in Europe.

The EIT model established over 50 innovation hubs and over 640 products across Europe, raised over 890 Million Euros in external capital through supported ventures, created over 6100 jobs in European markets, educated over 1700 Master and PhD students, and supported the creation of over 1250 startups (EIT, 2019b).

Furthermore, EIT activities are guided by a set of six pre-established community values, which describe the philosophy as to how business should be conducted by institutional and individual members. These values reflect EIT's joint vision and mission statements and are meant to serve as a guide for all communications and decision-making processes (EIT, 2019b). The EIT values and a short description are listed below.

1. **Inspiring**: inspire entrepreneurs and innovators to create solutions for pressing challenges by stimulating knowledge and experience sharing.
2. **Passionate**: integrate Europe's innovators to foster a better and more sustainable future—both economically and socially.
3. **Engaging**: display commitment, innovativeness, and result-orientation when engaging with stakeholders, aim to accelerate venture creation processes and work with stakeholders to bring ideas to markets.
4. **Open**: cultivate openness, transparency, and interactions among stakeholders and community members; support the development of future innovation and stimulate knowledge sharing and co-creation among stakeholders.
5. **Dynamic**: assist innovators and entrepreneurs harness their potential by engaging them with enthusiasm, creativity, and energy—presenting the KIC as dynamic and flexible.
6. **Excellent**: willingness to achieve excellence in activities through professional, efficient, and results-oriented approaches.

There is abundant literature highlighting that action is needed to overcome the fragmented European innovation and research landscape, and transform the traditional segmented methods of "business as usual" (Gill et al., 2018). EIT brings together leading members (i.e., businesses, universities, research institutions, and communities) from specific industries or challenge areas (e.g., food, climate, health, manufacturing, and digital) and integrates them to create the knowledge triangle as a

9.1 Introduction: The European Institute of Innovation and Technology (EIT)

means to form dynamic trans-disciplinary partnerships that focus on finding solutions to specific global challenges.

9.1.1 Knowledge and Innovation Communities (KICs)

Innovation Communities are agglomerations that strengthen cooperation among businesses (e.g., large corporations and small and medium enterprises—SMEs), research centers, and university partners who integrate their activities and resources in order to collectively create an environment that is supportive of entrepreneurship and innovation, where a collection of creative thoughts drives successful innovations (De Bernardi, Bertello, & Forliano, 2019). These communities provide access to human capital, intellectual capital, knowledge, financial resources, and new markets in order to (i) train a new generation of entrepreneurs who can later (ii) develop innovative products and services to (iii) drive the change in the main European strategic sectors.

The EIT innovation communities are dynamic and creative partnerships that harness European innovation and entrepreneurship in areas with high innovation potential. The innovation communities carry out activities that are relevant to the entire innovation chain, i.e., training and education programs, fostering transitions from research to market with startup incubators and accelerators, and creating innovation projects (European Commission, 2019).

These activities are set out in individual Framework Partnership Agreements (FPAs) and Specific Grant Agreements (SGA) signed with the Innovation Communities. The FPAs establishes long-term cooperation and sets out its terms and conditions as well as the general terms and conditions, rights and obligations applicable to the specific grants that may be awarded by the EIT for actions under the Framework Partnership Agreement, which is entered into for a period of 7 years (European Commission, 2019).

EIT, as an institution, has the responsibility to guide and orchestrate these activities and establish common strategies, but it is the individual communities that must adopt and apply these processes into practice, in a manner that is culturally relevant, ethically acceptable, and economically viable based on the norms of their specific locations. Sustainable products and services, new entrepreneurs and other forms of human and intellectual capital, company revenue, and increased job availability have emerged as a result of the innovation communities' activities, thus providing concrete evidence of the effectiveness of Europe's largest innovation network.

To date, EIT has successfully established eight innovation communities, formally named "Knowledge Innovation Communities" (KICs) (Fig. 9.1).

Each KIC is set up as a legal entity and appointed a CEO who oversees its operations. KICs are awarded a high degree of autonomy to define their legal status, organizational culture, and modus operandi. They have also been designed for

Fig. 9.1 Knowledge and innovation communities. Source: EIT (2019c)

adaptability, to be able to react in effective and flexible ways to their specific challenges and changing environments.

For the remainder of this chapter, and in line with the objectives of this book, we focus on EIT's Food KIC, and provide insight for three distinct audiences—individuals seeking to engage in entrepreneurial activities in the food system, members (individual or institutional) of the Food KIC, and entities wishing to recreate similar initiatives in their local environment. For individuals, we hope that this analysis will assist them in identifying entrepreneurial opportunities for action as well as for access to engage in innovative and entrepreneurial activities in the food system. Our aim for individual members and institutions is to illustrate best methods and effective practices to engage in trans-disciplinary collaborations, with bottom-up and participatory approaches, to tackle food system challenges. Finally, for entities, we hope that this case study can clearly define the concepts and elements that lead to successful collaborations and holistic involvement of all ecosystem members.

9.2 EIT Food: Pan-European Food Network

EIT Food, one of the KICs of EIT, is Europe's leading food innovation and entrepreneurship initiative, working to make the European food system more sustainable, healthy, and trusted by consumers and communities (Gebruers, 2017). It is a pan-European consortium that seeks to catalyze the global transformation on how food is innovated, produced, and valued by the whole society.

EIT Food has been described as a "people-centric" and "research-smart" vehicle for transforming the European food system and a driver for consumer confidence and for improving global health (EIT Food, 2016). It brings together a strong and complementary group of world-class multinational enterprises, leading SMEs, tier-1 scientific institutions, not-for-profit organizations, and social entrepreneurs covering the complete food value chain as well as neighboring industries. In a perfect quadruple helix innovation dimension, EIT Food could be considered as a "*multi-layered, multi-modal, multi-nodal and multi-lateral system, encompassing mutually complementary and reinforcing innovation networks and knowledge clusters consisting of human and intellectual capital, shaped by social capital and*

9.2 EIT Food: Pan-European Food Network

underpinned by financial capital" (Carayannis & Campbell, 2009, 2010; Leydesdorff & Etzkowitz, 2003; Volpe, Friedl, Cavallini, & Soldi, 2016).

It is composed of world-class members involved in dynamically intertwined processes of co-opetition, co-evolution, and co-specialization within and across regional and sectoral innovation ecosystems (Carayannis, Goletsis, & Grigoroudis, 2017). Seeking collaboration with and leveraging expertise from all relevant stakeholders and partners on local (network partners), regional (associations), European (other European bodies), as well as global level (global network partners), the network is currently composed of over 50 partners from across 13 European countries (Table 9.1 and Fig. 9.2).

EIT Food members comprise food system giants such as Nestlé, PepsiCo, and Givaudan, Puratos, Siemens, John Deere, and Colruyt Group. These industry members are then complemented by a selection of leading universities and scientific partners such as KU Leuven, University of Cambridge, TU Munich, University of Turin, and the University of Warsaw, among others. This consortium also includes the 'Rising Food Stars' Association, which has a history of supporting top-notch European agri-food tech startups (Gebruers, 2017).

The members are orchestrated by EIT Food to transform the current food system, stimulating connections and partnerships between businesses, startups, research institutions, universities, and food supply chain stakeholders throughout Europe, but also with a strong public engagement strategy addressed to the whole civil society. Furthermore, it supports innovation and entrepreneurship to generate common sustainable initiatives to feed future generations by improving human health, access to quality food, and overall ameliorate challenges related to the environment. Together, the members offer a wide range of services to support entrepreneurial approaches such as innovation competitions (e.g., Foodathons), funds for startups during different growth phases, educational activities such as online courses, summer schools and seminars (e.g., Digital Food Supply Chains, and Sustainability for Entrepreneurs), full-immersion entrepreneurship training (e.g., The Global Food Venture Program; Innovator Fellowship), and regional support for areas with unremarkable histories of innovation activities (RIS countries). In its role as a food ecosystem focal entity, EIT does not navigate the innovation and entrepreneurship field in an ad-hoc manner. Instead, it is guided by a common mission to promote shared vision and collaboration amongst its members, focusing on smart co-existence and cross-fertilization of activities within the knowledge triangle, leading to new connectivity with the consumer.

9.2.1 EIT Food Co-location Centers

EIT Food is headquartered in Leuven, Belgium, and is further supported by five Co-Location Centers that are designed to stimulate innovation, develop human capital, and encourage consumer involvement at the regional level. Co-Location Centers (CLCs) function as separate legal entities across Europe, and are located in

Table 9.1 List of member countries and partners by country

Country	Higher education	Research institution	Business industry	Non-governmental (Other)
Belgium	**KU Leuven**—Leuven Food Science and Nutrition Research Centre		**Colruyt Group,** Edingensesteenweg 196, 1500 Halle, Belgium **Puratos NV** Industrialaan 25, B-1702 Groot-Bijgaarden, Belgium **EUFIC** Rue Joseph Stevens 7, 1000 Brussels, Belgium	**Rising Food Stars** HeadquartersCountry: Belgium
Finland	**University of Helsinki** P.O. Box 53 (Fabianinkatu 32), FI-00014 University of Helsinki, Helsinki, Finland	**VTT** P.O. Box 1000, FI-02044, VTT, Finland	**Valio** Meijeritie 4, 00370 Helsinki, FinlandNorth-East	
France			**DANONE Research** Rd 128, Avenue de le Vauve 91767 Palaiseau—France **Eurofins NDSC** Chimie Alimentaire Rue Pierre Adolphe Bobierre 44323 NANTES CEDEX 3 FRANCE **Groupe SEB** 112, chemin du Moulin Carron, 69134 Ecully, France **ROQUETTE** 1 rue de la Haute Loge, 62136 Lestrem, France **SODEXO** 255 quai de la bataille de Stalingrad, 92166 Issy-les-Moulineaux Cedex, France	

Germany	**University of Hohenheim** Hohenheim Research Center for Bioeconomy, Wollgrasweg 43, 70599 Stuttgart, Germany **Technical University of Munich,** Arcisstr. 21, 80333 Munich, Germany	**DIL German Institute of Food Technologies** Office Brussels, Rue du Luxembourg 47-51, B-1050 Brussels, Belgium **Fraunhofer IVV,** Giggenhauser Str. 35, 85354 Freising, Germany	**DOEHLER** Riedstrasse, 64295 Darmstadt, Germany **John Deere GmbH & Co. KG,** European Technology Innovation Center, Strassburger Allee 3, 67657 Kaiserslautern, Germany **HERBSTREITH & FOX KG** Turnstrasse 37, 75305 Neuenbuerg, Germany **SIEMENS** Otto-Hahn-Ring 6, 81739 Munich, Germany **BOSCH** Stuttgarter Str. 130, D 71301 Waiblingen, Germany	
Iceland		**MATIS OHF** Vinlandsleid 12, 113 Reykjavik, Iceland		
Ireland			**ABP Food Group** 14 Castle Street, Ardee, County Louth, IrelandNorth-West	
Israel	**TECHNION, Israel Institute of Technology** Biotechnology & Food Engineering Department, Technion, Israel Institute of Technology, Haifa 3200000, Israel		**ALGATECHNOLOGIES** Kibbutz Ketura, D.N. Hevel Eilot, 88840, Israel **Strauss Group** 49 Hasivim St., POB 194, Petah Tikva 4959504, Israel	

(continued)

Table 9.1 (continued)

Country	Higher education	Research institution	Business industry	Non-governmental (Other)
Italy	**University of Turin** Via Verdi 8, 10124 Torino, ItalySouth		**AIA** Via Tomassetti 9, 00161 Rome, ItalySouth **Barilla** Via Mantova, 166	43122 Parma | Italy	
The Netherlands			**DSM** Alexander Fleminglaan 1, 2613 AX Delft, Netherlands **KOPPERT** P.O. Box 155, 2650 AD Berkel en Rodenrijs, The Netherlands **PLANT LAB** Veemarktkade 8a, 5222 AE 's- Hertogenbosch, The Netherlands	
Poland	**University of Warsaw** Office of University Advancement, Krakowskie Przedmieście 26/28, 00-927 Warsaw, Poland	**IARFR PAS** 10 Tuwima Str., 10-748 Olsztyn, Poland	**MASPEX** Ul. Legionów 37, 34-100 Wadowice, Poland	
Spain	**Universidad Autonoma de Madrid** Einstein 3, E-28049 Madrid, Spain	**AZTI** Parque Tecnológico de Bizkaia, Astondo bidea. Edif. 609, 48160—Derio (Bizkaia), Spain **CSIC** c/Serrano 113, E-28006 Madrid, Spain	**ACESUR** Carretera de la Carolina, Km 29, 23220—Vilches (Jaen), Spain **Angulas Aguinaga** Laskibar 5, 20271 Irura, SpainSouth **Grupo AN S. Coop** Campo de Tajonar s/n, 31192 Tajonar (Navarre), Spain	

| Switzerland | **EPFL (Ecole Polytechnique Federale de Lausanne)** Station 13, 1015 Lausanne, Switzerland **ETH Zürich** Schmelzbergstrasse 9, CH-8092 Zürich, Switzerland | **Nestlé Research** Center Verschez-les- Blanc, Lausanne 26, Switzerland, CH-1000 | **BÜHLER AG** Gupfenstrasse 5, CG-9240 Uzwil, Switzerland **Givaudan Suisse SA** 8310 Kemptthal, Switzerland | |
| United Kingdom | **Queen's University Belfast** Northern Ireland Technology Centre, Queen's University of Belfast, Cloreen Park, Belfast BT9 5HN, United Kingdom **University of Cambridge** Department of Plant Sciences, Downing Street, Cambridge CB2 3EA, UK **University of Reading** Whiteknights, Reading, Berkshire, RG6 6UR, United Kingdom | **Quadram** Norwich Research Park, Colney Lane, Norwich NR4 7UA, United Kingdom | **PepsiCo Inc.** International, Beaumont Park Technical Centre, Leicester, LE4 1ET, UK **Waitrose** Doncastle Road RG12 8YA, Bracknell, United Kingdom | **Agrimetrics** Lawes Open Innovation Centre, Rothamsted Research, Harpenden AL5 2JQ, United Kingdom |

Source: Own elaboration based on https://www.eitfood.eu/partners/

Fig. 9.2 Visual cloud of EIT food members. Source: EIT Food (2018)

Leuven, Madrid, Munich, Reading, and Warsaw (EIT Food, 2018). They are defined by their functional or geographical aspects, in order to best provide the proximity and local context to stimulate sustainable innovations in the food system best. The resulting CLC locations and their partners represent an assortment of the well-balanced and complementary university, research, and industry partners.

These CLCs ensure the local co-financing and knowledge transfer from one region to another, and thus reduce the risk of developing redundant projects, in different locations, levels, or with a different set of partners. The CLCs and the countries they comprise are as follows (Fig. 9.3):

1. **Leuven, Belgium**—includes partners from the Belgium France, and Switzerland.
2. **Madrid, Spain**—includes partners from Spain, Italy, and Israel.
3. **Munich, Germany**—includes partners from Germany and the Netherlands.
4. **Reading, U.K.**—includes partners from the UK, Ireland, and Iceland.
5. **Warsaw, Poland**—includes partners from Eastern Europe and Nordic countries.

EIT Food has developed mid and long-term goals with clear deliverables and expected impact through a total funding volume of more than 1.5 billion Euros in the 7 years (EIT Food, 2018) (Fig. 9.4).

9.3 EIT Food Vision, Mission, Strategy, Values and Goals

"The Food I Value—Attitudes Transformed". The EIT Food vision is to catapult Europe to the center of a global transformation in food system innovation brewing

9.3 EIT Food Vision, Mission, Strategy, Values and Goals

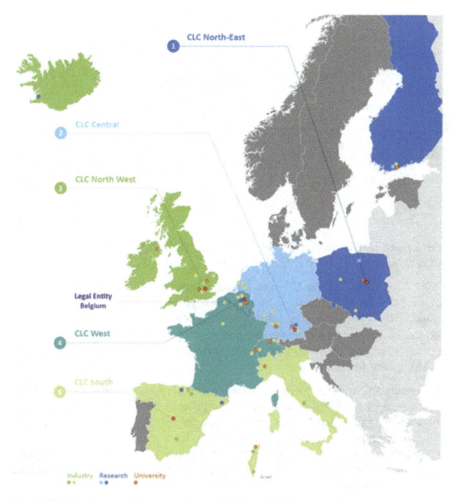

Fig. 9.3 EIT food co-location centers. Source: EIT Food (2018)

values for society (Gebruers, 2017). EIT Food will foster a sense of "collective stewardship" in which industry, government, science and education commit to support individuals in their right to enjoy a sustainable, safe and healthy diet.

Specifically, EIT Food actively engages the society in the food transformation processes to improve nutrition outcomes, increase security, transparency, traceability, and resource efficiency, fostering consumer and community trust in food systems (EIT Food, 2019a).

In order to drive these transformations, EIT Food developed demand-tailored programs that are specifically designed to support its value-based "P E O P L E" approach: Participation of citizens, Education and entrepreneurial support, Openness to the world, Performance through excellence and implementation of the results,

Sources of funding (in €k)	2017	2018	2019	2020	2021 - 2024	TOTAL
EIT funding	4,000	34,091	44,200	57,100	264,609	404,000
NON-EIT funding of which:	3,900	120,382	132,600	171,300	775,543	1,203,725
1) Overall partners' contribution	3,900	119,557	131,235	167,950	751,835	1,174,477
2) Other sources	-	825	1,365	3,350	23,708	29,248
TOTAL	7,900	154,473	176,800	228,400	1,040,152	1,607,725

Fig. 9.4 EIT food estimated budget. Source: EIT Food (2018)

Leveraging SMEs' innovation capability, and Enduring approach to ensure the sustainability of EIT Food (EIT Food, 2018).

"The Food that Connects Us—Food System Transformed". EIT Food mission is to catalyze the transformation of the food sector by building, managing, and empowering a sustainable and trusted multi-stakeholder community, by following an integrated seed-to-fork approach, with the engagement of consumers in the process of change, driven by the development of digital technologies (EIT Food, 2018). It aims to achieve its mission by:

- creating and scaling-up agri-food start-ups, to unlock the potential and competitiveness of small and medium-sized enterprises;
- developing talents and leaders to transform the food system, boosting skills and entrepreneurial mindsets;
- launching new innovative products and ingredients to make the food system resource-efficient, secure, transparent and trustful as well as to deliver healthier and more sustainable food;
- engaging citizens, communities, and civil society so that they can become agents of change.

In order to guide and evaluate its contribution to the food ecosystem challenges, EIT Food has defined six strategic objectives, some of which are further broken down into smaller "SMART" goals:

1. **overcome low consumer trust**: support Europeans in the transition towards a smart food system that is inclusive and trusted, for example through the EIT Food Barometer and the dataset of Trust Tracker that assess consumer's trust in the food system and its products as well as the awareness of, and perceptions towards, healthy and sustainable diets;
2. **create consumer-valued food for healthier nutrition**: enable individuals to make informed and affordable personal nutrition choices, providing long-lasting and cost-effective solutions for public health in relation to genetic predisposition,

age, dietary restrictions, lifestyle, and environmental factors. For example, EIT Food supports consumers in becoming central drivers in a shared food economy through the concept of My Food, My Nutrition, My Health, developing personalized consumer interfaces and support platforms, via novel monitoring devices, narrowing the gap between people's best intentions and actual food intake. Moreover, it promotes educational programs for personalized nutrition coaching, retailer-assisted food shopping, and meal preparation;

3. **build a consumer-centric connected food system**: develop a digital food supply network with consumers and industry to improve safety, real-time traceability, quality and sustainability of ingredients, developing and integrating on-site diagnostic and sensor technologies (e.g., smart labeling and blockchain technology). These technologies allow to identify potential threats and alert stakeholders, especially retailers across the whole food system, and enable auditability as a pan-European surveillance and alert system from food fraud or unintended contamination (De Bernardi, Forliano, Rotti, & Franco, 2019; Tirabeni, De Bernardi, Forliano, & Franco, 2019). An example of some initiatives centered on the consumers are: EIT Food Assistant, Your Fork2Farm, The Web of Food, The Zero Waste Agenda, MyFoodPortal, EIT Food Trust Barometer, and EIT Food Ambassadors;

4. **enhance sustainability through resource stewardship**: develop solutions to transform the traditional "produce-use-dispose" model into a circular bio-economy, targeting reductions in food waste, energy, and water consumption across the supply chain, including logistics, last-mile delivery, and consumption. EIT Food initiatives include the development of new food manufacturing processes with quality standards and guidelines for zero waste by a cascade approach, diversifying the use of raw materials, reducing microbial/chemical contamination risks, and engaging the consumer via new home devices to enhance energy efficiency and recycling and to reduce food miles. Evolving from a linear to a circular food system will encourage consumers to participate in the food system again and create local food communities, mainly since it is expected that in 2050 the 80% of food will be consumed in cities, giving citizens the power to revolutionize the food system;

5. **educate to engage, innovate, and advance**: provide 'food system' skills for students, academics, entrepreneurs and professionals through advanced training programs and open online courses addressing specific skill gaps. This strategic objective is finalized to spark a new generation of European pioneers and business entrepreneurs by fostering entrepreneurial culture and mindset through education and training programs. Summer schools, training workshops, boot camps, etc. are designed with industrial-academic co-mentorship activities for multidisciplinary teams. For example, it has been created EIT-branded certification programs for students and professionals to provide them with key food systems knowledge and new technological competences.

6. **catalyze food entrepreneurship and innovation**: foster innovation at all stages of business creation. For example, EIT Food provides entrepreneurs and start-ups with Food expert networks, infrastructures (pilot plants, equipment, incubation

space, etc.), and finance to catalyze entrepreneurial collaboration and sustainable growth. Furthermore, it provides a KIC breeding ground for start-up creation and cross-disciplinary SME partnerships, offering expertise/mentoring on infrastructure, patenting/licensing, and human resources as well as encouraging R&D activities.

EIT Food is a fundamental player in the European innovation landscape and has positioned itself as an important contributor to forthcoming European initiatives by closing the gap between applied research and its possible market applications. Specifically, it aims to capitalize on the results of previous European projects (e.g., Horizon 2020) and focuses on further developing these results, bringing them to markets as new products or services. EIT envisions the creation of close synergies through its member's cooperation in order to manage more efficiently resources under co-creation, co-sharing, and cross-fertilization approaches. To achieve this and make significant progress on their six strategic objectives, EIT food has established a Policy Council, with specific advisory roles (EIT Food, 2018).

In addition to key players from the food system, Directorate Generals (DGs) such as DG RTD (Research and Innovation), DG EAC (Education and Culture), and DG AGRI (Agricultural and Rural Development) also participate in designing the activities of EIT Food. Currently, EIT Food has developed a powerful collaboration with DG RTD to develop a consistent path from research to go-to-market strategies related to the Food 2030 program, which was launched by the European Commission in 2017 (EIT Food, 2018). To highlight this, EIT is a part of the coordination action of DG RTD to work with the Commission on the implementation of the Food 2030 policy.

EIT Food partnerships venture beyond the knowledge triangle of education, business creation, and innovation, and include consumer engagement for increased effectiveness. Communication serves as the element that connects the dimensions of the knowledge triangle and, thus, establishes activities within EIT Food's four key learning pillars (Fig. 9.5) to tackle the aforementioned challenges of the European food system.

In essence, to improve the entrepreneurial capacity and culture of the entire food system, and unchain the potential of SMEs, EIT Food programs are finalized to accelerate innovation, creating jobs, yielding economic benefits for businesses and environmental benefits for natural resources, thereby increasing Europe's competitiveness (Gebruers, 2017). Specifically, EIT Food purpose over a 7 years span is to:

1. establish 86 startups, and support the development of 533 additional startups, attracting a total of 191.6 million Euros;
2. educate over 400 students from EIT's Master's programs and have 285,000 participants enrolled in their educational programs;
3. bring to market 398 new or improved products, services, and processes by 2024;
4. engage 147,000 participants in the annual Food Trust Tracker.

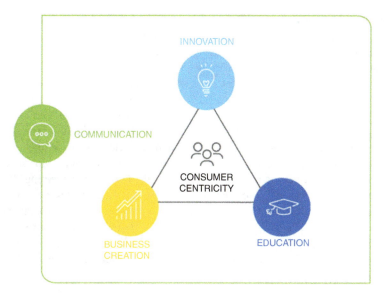

Fig. 9.5 Four pillars of EIT food. Source: EIT Food (2019b)

9.4 EIT Food Strategic Pillars and Business Areas

In order to achieve their strategic objectives and purposes, EIT Food depends on and constructs innovation initiatives based on the four foundational pillars: i) Education, ii) Innovation, iii) Entrepreneurship & Business Creation, and iv) Communication & Public Engagement (Fig. 9.5).

Building on the initial conceptualization of the "knowledge triangle" (i.e., innovation, education, and business creation), EIT Food adds a component of "communication", thus giving it an advantage as a consumer-centered approach that engages everyday European citizens and provides them with the opportunity to become agents of change for their food system.

Many scholars (Powell, Packalen, & Whittington, 2010) analyzing the Critical success factors (CSFs) in developing knowledge ecosystems considered as central, two features and one mechanism: 1) a diversity of organizational forms; 2) the presence of an anchor tenant, and 3) the mechanism of cross-realm transposition. All these CSFs are part of the activities managed by EIT Food. Specifically, the presence of multiple actors such as universities, public research organizations, entrepreneurial firms, established companies, and start-ups, as well as the presence of an activity leader for each project proposal, increases the innovative capacity of the ecosystems (Baptista, 1998). At the same time, a cross-network collaboration by which ideas, new technologies, and business models are transposed from one to another, create the so-called mechanism of cross-realm transposition.

In general, activity proposals are solicited with an annual call in the areas of: i) Grand Challenge, namely strategic objective 1 (overcome low consumer trust &

enhance transparency), ii) Innovation, iii) Education, iv) Business Creation, and v) Communication. Next to this general call for activity proposals, EIT Food also includes a call to "Infrastructure Projects", namely activities that have strategically relevance and/or that build key infrastructure to achieve EIT Food's strategic objectives. Examples are the Accelerator and Incubator Networks, FoodUnfolded, and the Master in Food Systems program. All proposals need to be aligned with EIT Food's overall vision, mission, and set of KPIs, contributing at least to one of the strategic objectives. They must articulate the market need, output and impact, and demonstrate a realistic prospect for market and/or societal success, including the competitive landscape. The proposals, executed by a consortium of partners of EIT Food, from both academia/research institutes and industry, representing different areas of the food system, and including at least three members representing a minimum of two different CLCs, also include a roadmap for implementation of the results, milestones with measurable go/no-go criteria, expected risks and a dissemination plan. All Activities are expected to be led by a partner organization that takes the role of the project "facilitator". The activity leader is responsible for the project management and report on all outputs, deliverables, impact, and financial aspects achieved.

Each proposal requires the collaboration of multiple partners since food challenges cannot be solved in a classical bilateral approach, but with a strong partner commitment and a European dimension involving multiple countries and partners to drive a change in innovation culture. Moreover, EIT Food expects from the project consortium the definition of the added value and business/societal impact traced with quantifiable changes in societal trends and EIT Food KPIs, e.g., creating a new start-up, product or service, achieving specific consumer engagement targets, delivering a number of upskilled students. The projects have to use innovative approaches, demonstrating that methodologies, technologies, and/or processes applied or to be developed go beyond the current state-of-the-art.

Over the next 5 years, EIT Food partners will invest almost 1200 million Euros with a match of up to 400 million Euros financed by EIT Food and will rely on its four focus areas, or pillars, in order to move innovation forward.

9.4.1 Innovation

Currently, EIT Food drives the change through partners' co-creation projects that may provide breakthrough solutions for societal challenges with a focus on developing technology-based products, services, and business models with tangible economic or societal impact (Call for proposal 2020 Guidelines). Annual proposals are assessed and assigned to the best and motivated teams of EIT Food members, who are then tasked with carrying out the activities in an entrepreneurial manner, e.g., always including open innovation practices as central components. Furthermore, these teams are meant to engage consumers in dynamic value creation activities in order to tackle pressing challenges in the food system. EIT Food aims to act as an investor, identifying innovation and entrepreneurial opportunities with a high potential to scale-up, and providing economic and societal impact to face challenges in a sustainable way. Under the innovation pillar, EIT Food aims to pave a development path for the implementation of innovative ideas, fueled by the co-founding of partners, and building on and implementing promising results of successful research projects (EIT Food, 2018).

9.4.2 EIT Food's Innovation Programs

In its role finalized to stimulate and accelerate the innovation processes that will lead to sustainable transformations of a resilient food system EIT Food community is committed to increase consumer trust, creating consumer-valued food for improved nutritional outcomes, and building a consumer-centered and connected food system that naturally enhances sustainability by promoting a circular bio-economy (De Bernardi, Bertello, & Venuti, 2019; De Bernardi, Bertello, Venuti, & Zardini, 2019). By actively involving and empowering consumers to be active members in efforts to engage in 'future-proofing' food systems, EIT Food simultaneously creates the innovators and entrepreneurs of tomorrow and builds and inclusive an innovative community.

The Innovation branch of EIT Food is further developed into four main innovation programs[1]:

1. **Inclusive and Trusted Food System**: innovation activities involve consumers and deem them responsible co-creators. EIT Food is demonstrating how technology and innovation in food systems are positive elements for consumers by bringing together the most novel technologies, which enable greater food safety and transparency.
2. **Healthier Nutrition**: innovation activities are helping to reduce the prevalence and risk of developing metabolic disease through personalized nutrition services. For example, non-invasive tools, online information services, and novel technologies that assist individuals in making healthier, more informed, food choices (Wahlqvist, 2002).
3. **Connected and Transparent System**: EIT Food is increasing the connectivity and transparency of the food system to improve the safety, real-time traceability, and quality and sustainability of ingredients benefitting both consumers and industry.
4. **Circular Bio-economy**: the consortium is developing multidisciplinary approaches to encourage a circular bio-economy culture among consumers. This approach focuses on reusing bi-products and waste, thus increasing the environmental sustainability of our food system.

---

[1]For a full list of EIT Food's recent innovation activities please visit—https://eitfood.eu/innovation

9.4.3 Education

The education pillar follows a multi-targeted, non-classical approach to develop and promote a creative, knowledgeable and out-of-the-box thinking human resource force, which will be the key human and intellectual capital able to transform the food system. The target audiences include firstly top students in academic institutions, but also professionals in the food and adjacent sectors, as well as citizens and consumers in the public space representing various cultures and consumer cohorts. In this vein, EIT Food educational core strategy is to provide EIT-branded Food Systems Master of Science (MSc) that can bridge compartmentalized skills/know-how/expertise overcoming the shortage of talented recruits through the EIT Food Academy. The main programs offered with this pillar are: (i) extracurricular, industry-mentored program Food Solutions for BSc/MSc/PhD students; (ii) the Food Entrepreneur Summer School for students and professionals (SMEs, enterprises) to work jointly on business-relevant case studies; and (iii) the groundbreaking Global Food Venture Programme.

EIT Food also trains students, entrepreneurs, and food system stakeholders, via workshops, summer school programs, and online educational programs such as Massive Open Online Courses (MOOCs) and Specialized Private Online Courses (SPOCs). EIT Food seeks to establish the 'entrepreneur' as a role model in universities and academic settings, thus allocating the same recognition to the 'successful entrepreneur' as one would to the 'successful scientist or professor'. It has also initiated the migration from a classical degree-based education model to one that includes a continuous skills-based human capital development approach.

9.4.4 Business Creation and Entrepreneurship

EIT food provides support for startups, entrepreneurs, and aspiring entrepreneurs through a powerful business creation ecosystem. Support is made available at every phase of venture maturation, or company development, from ideation, to acceleration, to funding. It has developed a successful end-to-end business creation approach (i.e., explore, nurture, scale, and grow sustainably) that begins with support and stimulating for idea generation. Then it moves viable to its accelerator, from then startups are funded for further development by the EIT Food Sparks and the Rising Food Stars community of successful and fast-growing startups.

Through business creation, EIT Food seeks to educate, coach, and guide entrepreneurs on their journey from 'idea to viable product or service' in order to establish European world leaders on the food innovation domain, provide access to unique expertise and technologies through the network of members and access to funding opportunities, thereby accelerating and reducing the risk of operating a new venture (EIT Food, 2018). Specifically, EIT Food offers:

9.4 EIT Food Strategic Pillars and Business Areas 265

- **An unparalleled network**: access to 50+ of Europe's leading food system businesses, universities, and research organizations.
- **European reach**: they have a presence in every country in Europe and other territories, thus helping businesses reach new markets and develop internationally.
- **A powerful brand**: as the designated EU body to transform Europe's food system, EIT members benefit from a powerful brand, making new businesses more attractive to investors and customers.
- **Long-term support**: they provide support from the generation of ideas for as long as new ventures require it.

Furthermore, these services are spread out through three categories of entrepreneurial phases of development—namely:

1. Explore: "I've got a great idea!"—it is for individuals, academics, and aspiring entrepreneurs who are driven to solve the complex challenges facing the food system. These activities are designed to help transform ideas into viable market solutions by providing individuals with the skills, network, and funds needed to validate their business idea and accompanying business models. Three key programs under the explore phase include EIT Food's "Make-It!", "Change Makers", and the "SEEDBED Incubator".
2. Nurture: "I've got a new business"—it is for entrepreneurs and registered startups that are well on their way to transforming the food system and would benefit from EIT Food's support services to bring their new business to markets. Two key programs under nurture that help support existing startups include "Innovation Prizes" and "EIT Food's Accelerator Network".
3. Scale: "I've got a growing business"—scale elevates high-potential, and mature food system startups and early scale-ups to the next phases of becoming international businesses and game-changers. A key program under nurture if the "Rising Food Stars", discussed in greater detail in Sect. 9.9.1.

Finally, EIT Food employs a business creation model named "Smart Entrepreneurial Development", which integrates the most relevant aspects for successful business creation. This approach goes beyond raising funds and garnering profits. Moreover, it is especially targeted at young entrepreneurs, startups, and SMEs by combining access to a network, access to competence and technology, support for scaling prototypes, access to funding sources, and access to markets (Fig. 9.6).

9.4.5 Communication and Public Engagement

EIT Food is the first of the EIT KICs to actively seek to encourage community and citizen participation in entrepreneurial and innovation activities. It seeks to move citizens from being passive recipients, to actively engaged players, to enthusiastic agents of change. This is achieved through multiple tools, including consumer-led

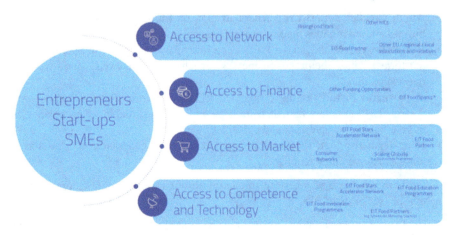

Fig. 9.6 Smart entrepreneurial development model. Source: EIT Food (2018)

innovation campaigns and available digital platforms. Furthermore, EIT places a degree of recognition on everyday consumers and potential entrepreneurs. This effort to collectively support European citizens to become critical change agents in the transition toward a sustainable food system is the first time everyday citizens have been empowered as active agents of change in food systems (EIT Food, 2018).

EIT Food does not only engage citizens through online communication channels and look and feel campaigns, but also considers them important co-creators in idea generation and concept prototyping phases to improve satisfaction with new products and services. Furthermore, through its Citizen Participation Forum, EIT Food provides consumers and everyday citizens with an institutional voice for change, thereby having great influence on the direction of future EIT Food activities.

EIT Food holds the belief that every member is responsible for and connected to the food system. Therefore, it is only through collective efforts that food systems can be improved and prepared for the future. EIT Food is currently building an inclusive community of food system members that involves actors throughout the supply chain, especially consumers, in order to deliver a resilient food system that produces both healthy and sustainable food and is trusted by society. EIT Food's public engagement activities are further grouped into the following three areas:

1. **Dialogue and engagement**: through events and (digital) platforms—e.g., "FoodUnfolded".
2. **Offering guidance**: by providing targeted information—e.g., "SEE & EAT".
3. **School programs**: e.g., "EIT Food School Network".

The entirety of EIT Food activities aims to fully integrate the knowledge triangle of Education, Innovation, and Business Creation. Given the emerging challenges threatening our food ecosystem coupled with the notion of systems thinking, it is clear to see that catalyzing innovation through the Knowledge Triangle Integration (KTI) model is the logical next step to achieving sustainability. This new proposition of the Knowledge Triangle defines communication as the unifying element that leverages the four pillars of EIT Food; especially, to overcome the relevant social and global challenges best and, to integrate food consumers as independent and essential partners within the whole food supply and nutrition chain (EIT Food, 2018). EIT Food's KTI aims to transform new knowledge into tangible innovations that can provide substantial benefits for sustainability efforts. It dedicates a specific focus on entrepreneurship as a possible channel to diffuse the collectively generated knowledge and innovations and thus foster greater societal engagement. The KTI framework also acknowledges the need for institutions and industries to organize innovation activities in-house so that they can better understand and communicate their mission, as well as receive assistance from complementary partners when carrying out their diverse projects.

9.5 EIT Food Growth Strategy

Despite the many successes of EIT Food in creating a world-class complementary network of food system stakeholders, one must realize that this is not a single action, or a static undertaking but a continuous and dynamic process. To continuously expand their partnerships and networks, and to tackle the challenges in integrating the knowledge triangle with their fourth communication pillar, EIT Food has designed a thorough growth strategy. This policy applies to both EIT Food Core Partners and Network Partners and functions as a balance keeper between industry and non-industry, and geographical balance. Furthermore, a partnership of representatives from the CLCs and the EIT Food management is tasked with making sure this policy is implemented and continuously developed to meet the ever-evolving grand challenges.

EIT Food wants to be an open consortium that actively seeks to engage new partners. However, interested parties must demonstrate that they meet the same 'admissions' standard and criteria as existing consortium partners. The core principles that guide member acceptance are as follows (EIT Food, 2019c):

- **Excellence and Complementarity**: Applicants must demonstrate that they bring and added value to the existing partner network and to the food value chain, or are able to introduce new and emerging technology competencies, and commit to fully supporting and contributing to EIT Food's strategic ambitions.
- **Resource Commitment**: Candidates must demonstrate their ability and commitment to providing the required financial contributions to achieve EIT Food's objectives.
- **Regional Coverage**: Determined by an EIT Food working group that continuously identifies regions of interest, or priority regions, and countries where they may find new partners, and ensure that specific attention is given to the EIT RIS areas.

9.6 EIT Food Organizational Structure

EIT Food has designed its organizational structure to govern the KIC as efficiently as possible in order to achieve the highest impact with its strategy. This structure can be defined as a results-driven model that is founded by transparency, innovation, ability to adapt quickly, and connectivity. EIT Food's overarching organizational principles are as follows:

- partnerships guided by solid leadership and coupled with project ownership and execution by partners;
- well-defined and transparent decision-making mechanism and reporting processes;
- prioritization of outcomes over processes to generate commercial output and value to society;
- innovation by responsible partnerships with consumers that foster creativity;
- commitment to a flexible, scalable, and self-learning framework, striving for continuous improvement;
- promotion of growth and planning for future diverse income sources.

In essence, the EIT Food organizational structure is designed to promote value creation and capture, as well as to establish norms that safeguard compliance with the objectives and values of EIT Food.

9.6.1 EIT Food Organizational Governance Structure

EIT Food is characterized by a strong central government that provides strategic advice and leadership, while allowing regional autonomy and entrepreneurship to maximize partner engagement. This central government further allocates decision-making power strategically to represent all dimensions of the food system, thereby creating the perfect conditions for cohesion and co-ownership throughout its network. EIT Food consists of several legal entities and legally binding agreements, which are as follows:

- the KIC Legal Entity EIT Food;
- the five CLC Legal Entities (discussed in the following sections);
- Rising Food Stars, a startup association;
- EIT Food Sparks, an investment vehicle.

EIT Food is presented as a not-for-profit association with limited liability under Belgian Law. All EIT Food partners constitute the entirety of the association and govern as members of both EIT Food and the CLC legal entities. EIT Food's overall organizational structure is characterized by a clear separation of operations, supervision, and partnerships. The KIC is managed by an expert executive team that is adept at quickly reacting and interacting in response to dynamic external conditions.

9.7 Multi-Annual Business Models

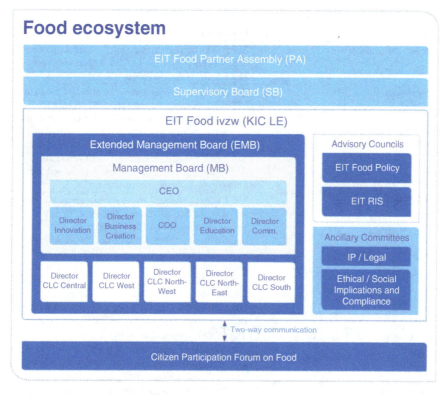

Fig. 9.7 EIT food organizational structure. Source: EIT Food (2018)

For an illustration of the main governance bodies of the EIT Food, as well as a short description, see Fig. 9.7 and Table 9.2, respectively.

The activities outlined in Table 9.2 are conducted and made possible by five core processes of EIT Food—(i) strategic planning, (ii) business planning, (iii) Area Portfolio Planning, (iv) Activity Management and Reporting Process, and (v) the continuous improvement process (EIT Food, 2018). For a more detailed description of these five core processes, see Table 9.3.

9.7 Multi-Annual Business Models

With its "future-focused" vision, EIT food plans ahead and creates multi-annual business models, that guide the sustainable development of its products and services, human and intellectual capital, and innovative solutions in order to manage itself in way that fosters a connected European food system which focus special attention to consumers and civil society.

Table 9.2 Governance, management, and executive positions of EIT food

Position	Description
Partner Assembly (PA)	EIT Food's highest decision body; decides on strategic issues and approves the EIT Food Strategic Agenda. The PA elects the supervisory board members
Supervisory Board (SB)	Consists of one representative from each CLC. The EIT Food partner assembly elects these individuals from a list presented by each CLC that consists of a list of candidates with a maximum of three external members. The SB appoints its chairmans, the CEO, and the COO, and it is the chairman's responsibility to sustain the strategic position of EIT Food and secure long-term consortium sustainability
Chief Executive Officer (CEO)	The CEO is appointed by and works under the supervision of the SB. S/he helms EIT Food's daily operations and focuses on achieving the goals and objectives according to established business plans. The CEO is tasked with liaising with EU, national, and international programs, coordinating their activities with EIT Food. The CEO also works in close collaboration with the functional directors to prepare the Strategic Agenda as part of annually drafted business plans
Chief Operating Officer (COO)	The COO is responsible for the administrative assignments reading the redaction of the Business Plan. S/he is also responsible for the allocation of EIT funds to the CLCs and KIC partners
Education, innovation, business creation, and communication directors	EIT Food's functional directors are responsible for developing pillar's strategies and their implementation in the respective key business area
Management Board (MB)	The MB is chaired by the CEO, and consists of the COO and the functional directors. MB serves as a support system for the CEO in executing the KIC's daily operations and implements a range of activities designed to support the integration of the knowledge triangle
Extended Management Board (EMB)	Chaired by the CEO, is comprised of the MB members, and the CLC directors who coordinate the CLC activities and ensure that KIC-level objectives are met, and promote inter CLC-collaborations
Citizen participation forum on trust	Provides everyday consumers with the possibility to express their opinions and beliefs, and to evolve from passive to active relationship with consumers and citizens. The Forum works on policy recommendations to strengthen EIT Food's consumer centered approach. The Director of Communication chairs the Citizen Participation Forum
Advisory councils	
Food policy council	Focuses on vision and development for European food systems and sets a framework future endeavours

(continued)

9.7 Multi-Annual Business Models

Table 9.2 (continued)

Position	Description
EIT RIS council	Contains representatives from science, industry, government, and non-governmental organizations from EIT RIS countries that advice the development and implementation activities specific to RIS countries
Ancillary committees	
IP and legal committee	Composed of IP experts that represent each CLC, and one person representing EIT Food, and one representative of the Rising Food Stars. This community handles any arising issues regarding consumer rights and processes
Ethical, social implications, and compliance committee	Composed of one representative from each CLC, appointed by the PA, and serves to advice the MB with regard to ethical and social issues, including compliance with privacy and compliance with applicable regulations

Source: EIT Food (2018)

Table 9.3 EIT food core processes

Core process	Responsible member	Description
1. Strategic planning	CEO	Guides the work of the entire KIC by developing and maintaining a long-term vision for the development of European Food Systems
2. Business planning	COO	Translates the vision to the annual Business Plan (BP) through a call for proposals (CfP) scoped and guided by the SB
3. Area Portfolio planning	Functional directors	Transforms (BP) into an executable plan. This involves the creation of detailed Activity Plans per activity and the Partner Agreements, which summarize the responsibilities of each partner
4. Activity management and reporting	COO	Tracks implementation of BP through regular reporting, quality control, KPI tracking, and ecosystem wide communications. These activities result in the annual Cost and Performance Report and the related KPI and impact reports
5. Continuous improvement	COO	Regularly collects lessons learned and best practices throughout the ecosystem in order to identify elements that improve efficiency

Source: EIT Food (2018)

With this business model approach, EIT Food aims to continuously expand its activities, incorporating emerging knowledge and adapting to the changing environmental conditions in efforts to raise EIT Food into a high-impact and sustainable innovation and educational entity.

9.7.1 Financial Sustainability

EIT Food's main funding streams come from the EIT and the KIC's partners' contributions. However, the business model approach discussed above aims at ensuring financial sustainability once the annual EIT contributions decrease. EIT Food has focused on developing a diversified income stream and therefore ensuring a sustainable future and the progression of the consortium. This sustainability-based model is guided by the EIT Governing Board and prepares EIT Food for the total loss of EIT KAVA funding. This model is holistically inclusive of all parts of the network, and all four pillars are expected to contribute to the projected sustainability income, thereby delivering significant and reliable financial income streams (EIT Food, 2018).

Possible additional income streams are tools to assist EIT Food in breaking even with expenses, and eventually to re-invest in its own services to continue serving as a catalyst for food system transformation. For example, in current calls for proposals, applicants are asked to describe the mechanisms and financial planning for generating a financial backflow to EIT Food upon successful completion of the activity. This novel approach is based on a sustainability contribution that partners are expected to pay once they commercialize the results of activity-funded projects.

Finally, EIT is continuously adapting and developing its sustainability model annually. In essence, the sustainability of EIT Food will be ensured through a joint long-term vision and partner commitment with its innovative business model approach to deliver significant and continuous income streams (Fig. 9.8).

9.8 EIT Community

9.8.1 EIT Food Partnerships

As abundantly stated in this text, the food system is a complex structure, which comprises multiple layers and includes partners from several industries (e.g., electricity, transportation, marketing, etc.). Furthermore, many calls to action have centered on the concept of systems thinking in order to decrease the inter-sectorial and inter-industrial gaps. In efforts to address these challenges within the European food system, EIT Food employs a well-defined and clear partnership growth strategy to deliver impact for all members of the food system.

EIT Food's partners form a remarkable group of world-class multinational enterprises. SMEs, universities, research institutes, and everyday citizens that complement each other's capabilities. Furthermore, the key leaders of partner organizations express a personal and organizational commitment to the EIT Food strategy and its approaches, which the main driver of the sustainable success of EIT Food (EIT Food, 2018). EIT Food strategically selects its partners in efforts to create its network of world-class and well-balanced resources that encompass every phase of

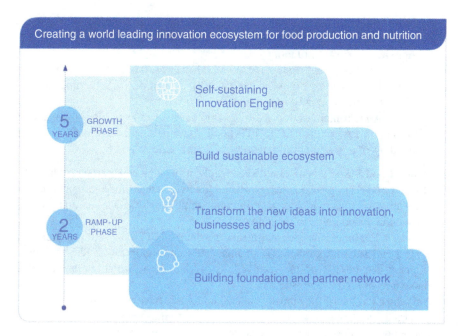

Fig. 9.8 Multi-annual business model. Source: EIT Food (2018)

the food value chain and its complementary areas. The existing partnerships also pave the way for integrating the complex entities of SMEs, startups, and consumers.

Through this multi-disciplinary partner network and to organize the roles and responsibilities of each consortium member, EIT employs a model that consists of different categories that represent different partner rights and responsibilities. For instance, they are: "EIT Food Partners", "Network Partners", "Associate Partners", and the startups of the "Rising Food Stars".

9.8.2 Partner Categories

EIT Food employs a partnership model that consists of three options for becoming a network member, each with a different set of predefined rights and obligations—i.e., Core Partners, Rising Food Stars, Network Partners and Associate partners.

- **Core Partners**: they are formal partners of EIT Food and participate in PA. All EIT Food core partners formally select their desired membership level that is based on their financial contributions (e.g., annual membership fees, and KIC Complementary Activities), which determines their voting rights and access to certain pools of funding.

- Gold: Annual membership fee of 100,000 Euros. These Core Partners are granted five voting rights in the PA and unlimited access to "KIC Added Value Activities" (KAVA) funding.
- Silver: Annual membership fee of 50,000 Euros. These Core Partners are granted two voting rights in the PA and capped KAVA funding at max 500,000 Euros annually.
- SME: Annual membership fee of 25,000 Euros, can attend, speak, and vote (1) in the PA, participate in EIT Food Activities, and have access to EIT Funding of a maximum of amount of 250,000 Euros.

- **Rising Food Stars**: it is an established legal entity and a core partner of the KIC. Rising Food Stars provides serves as an attractive element for a large number of innovative startups, which engage in collaborations with EIT Food and provide substantial added value to the network.
- **Network Partners**: they are not formal partners of EIT Food but participate as project and network partners. Their financial contribution to the KIC is a management fee of 4% of the received KAVA funding, which is capped at a maximum of 60,000 Euros annually.
- **Associate Partners**: they must be a legal entity and have the ability to contribute or participate in one or more of the EIT Food Activities upon invitation of a Core Partner or EIT Food. These partners may participate in EIT activities with no EIT funding when invited to participate by EIT, a Core Partner; Associate partners do not have the right to lead activities. These partners may use the label of "Associate of EIT Food" for the time they participate, and the EIT Food MB may invite these partners to Matchmaking or Innovation marker activities to help them expand their network. Associate partners are not required to pay a membership fee and do not participate in the Food Partner Assembly.

EIT Food Core Partners, as members of the consortium, commit to pay the partnership fee and to support and facilitate the active participation of their organizations in the array of EIT Food Programs. Rising Food Stars is an association of high-potential startups tackling issues in the food system, and functions to enable networks and open collaboration among a large pool of innovative startups. These startups benefit from EIT Food's extended networks and its access to technology, financial resources, and human capital. These startups, however, not only cultivate outputs from the Rising Food Stars but also provide valuable input to the EIT Food ecosystem by driving EIT Food activities as linked third parties. Moreover, they do that through their breakthrough and innovative technologies and disruptive business models. Finally, network partners are legal entities that have demonstrated their capability to contribute to the KAVA. They function to extend to complement and extend the reach of EIT Food, especially to SMEs and consumers throughout Europe.

9.9 Start-Up Support

9.9.1 Rising Food Stars

Rising Food Stars is a unique association that functions as a supportive entity for startups by providing them with access to knowledge, networks, and the entrepreneurial opportunities to engage in EIT Food's diverse range of activities.

Importantly, it is important to note the distinction that Rising Food Stars is a subsidiary of EIT Food central and functions as a not-for-profit entity, and is itself a Core Partner of EIT. This provides an interesting outcome since it means that all of the startups currently being housed by the Rising Food Stars are also core partners in the network, but with slightly higher restrictions than the Core Partners discussed in Sect. 9.8.2.

Upon joining Rising Food Stars, startups benefit from access to the expert partner network, programs, technological resources, technical-entrepreneurial support, and access to potential markets and distribution channels. These services, collectively, provide the opportunity to significantly accelerate the development of startups and ensure their growth potential. Specifically, like Core Partners, Rising Food Stars members are viewed as core partners, albeit existing limits regarding access to EIT Funding. These members do not pay a membership fee but are capped at a maximum of 100,000 Euros from KAVA funding. These startups do, however, have the possibility to apply for further funding through EIT Food but will need to justify their requests explicitly.

Furthermore, it is not only the startups that benefit from this partnership. The resulting collaborations between Rising Food Stars and other EIT Food Partners provide and entrepreneurial and fluid innovation culture that brings added human capital from the entire food system to EIT Food. In addition to that, it funnels unprecedented value to emerging innovations in terms of new technologies and innovative business models.

Rising Food Stars elevates startups to viable business ventures, and helps entrepreneurs gain international recognition as game changes for future food systems.

Specifically, the benefits provided by Rising Food Stars are as follow:

- provides access to, and collaboration with, EIT Food's expert network of industrial, academic, and research partners, and provides access and communication and distribution channels to potential markets;
- encourages startups to further develop their innovation in EIT Food projects in an international context;
- increases the visibility of startups by promoting access to the most popular Food System events in Europe and other areas;
- provides guidance on European project opportunities including funding and financial possibilities;
- supports innovations, investments, and business growth;
- facilitates access to necessary laboratories and equipment at partner research institutions and companies to further develop products and technologies.

Finally, in order to become a member of the Rising Food Stars, startups need to respond to an annual call for new members. The call is launched every Spring on the FS6 platform (an application website, that is home to over a million tech founders and startups searching for funding) (FS6, 2019).

9.9.2 EIT Food Sparks

EIT Food Sparks is a unique initiative to provide access to funding. Food Sparks is financed by voluntary EIT Food partners who are granted access to the deal flows, and therefore does not utilize EIT funding. The target group for funding is startups that have graduated from the EIT Food accelerator. The initiative not only funds high-potential startups, but it also provides access to management support, the entirety of existing EIT Food human capital, distribution, and dissemination channels, and opens doors to potential markets. This is a one-of-a-kind program that not only supports, but also accelerates the success of startups.

9.10 EIT Food Impact

EIT Food's strategic objectives, highlighted by the extended educational, innovation, communication, and business creation programs, will lead to significant impacts for people, consumers, and hopefully to the whole food system. Its progress, performance, and impact will be monitored through Key Performance Indicators (KPIs).

9.10.1 EIT Food Impact through Synergies

EIT functions as a powerful bridge between initiatives at the European, national, and regional levels in efforts to improve the overall impact of EIT Food. To achieve this, EIT Food has defined three distinct approaches to harness the potential of these synergies in a structured manner in order to most effectively generate the desired impact and reach essential potential entrepreneurs that are traditionally external to the agri-food system.

1. Specifically, the directors from the three EIT Food pillars relating to the knowledge triangle (i.e., Innovation, Education, Business Creation) are encouraged to actively seek collaborations in the form of co-creation projects with other stakeholders in the food system. Furthermore, based on EIT Foods Strategic Report for 2018–2024, the Food KIC already possesses a list of the most promising partners

and initiatives in order to define concrete and sustainable projects to create maximum impact.

2. Two-way exchanges and consultations with relevant initiatives that are coordinated by the Director of Communication to identify joint opportunities and work together towards common policy goals. The Food Policy Council will be the governing body (when applicable) to maximize the impact of the synergies.

3. Information and communication (i.e., knowledge exchanges and open innovation) will be pursued with other organizations (e.g., with a consumer focus), governmental bodies, and other mutually beneficial programs through the communication team.

EIT Food actively seeks collaborations as far as to call for projects, and in business creation endeavors, especially in promoting startups. With this in mind, EIT Food enables internal synergies by employing the Knowledge Triangle Integration model in order to unite Education, Research and Innovation, Business Creation and Entrepreneurship, and Communication (EIT Food, 2018).

9.10.2 Key Performance Indicators

EIT Food operates based on a results-driven performance management approach, which closely monitors EIT Food's performance (e.g., progress, inputs, and outputs) through well-defined and measurable Key Performance Objectives (KPIs).

EIT as an institution already contained established KPIs; however, these did not account for the specific targets of the food system, so EIT Food developed its own specific set of KPIs that are designed to measure the progress of EIT Food continuously. The specific EIT Food KPIs serve as qualitative indicators that seek to optimize measurements and tracking of the impact EIT Food aims to achieve. Furthermore, each pillar of the KIC has its specified KPIs.

- Innovation & Research KPIs: Measure the extent to which EIT Food brings innovation to the market and the involvement of relevant successors.
- Education KPIs: Measure the progress of the provision of education to students, professionals, and executives (including non-food disciplines) by EIT Food.
- Entrepreneurship & Business Creation KPIs: Measure how EIT Food enables sustainable business creation (e.g., the number of Rising Food Stars)
- Communication & Community Engagement KPIs: Focuses on issues such as awareness of EIT and the KIC brand (EIT Food) and the potential value of cross-KIC activities.

For a projection of the KPIs, see Fig. 9.9.

Finally, EIT Food is also engaged in actively monitoring number of KIC and network partners, as well as their consortium membership satisfaction rate.

	Short-Term (3 years)	Mid Term (7 years)	Long Term (>10 years)
Economic Impact	• Creation of more than 30 new businesses • More than 30 new products and services brought to the market • More than 100 additionally skilled students through industrial mentored food solution projects annually	• Increased supply chain efficiency and effectiveness is enabled by unlocking opportunities of digitalisation and other emerging technologies • New markets such as personalised in the sector • Additional revenues for farmers as partners of shared value chains	• Reduction in the health care costs related to nutrition by enabling healthier nutrition • Sector growth and job creation through higher level of innovation, successful new business creation and efficiency gains
Environmental Impact	• New solutions and products (e.g. new nutrient sources) enhancing resource efficiency and biodiversity are developed	• Significant reduction in waste and a more circular economy are achieved by means of creating collective resource stewardship	• Significant reduction of environmental impacts along the entire food supply chain; measures to mitigate climate change are showing effects
Societal Impact	• More than 1,5 million people make use of the wide array of opportunities for engagement and participation and access EIT Food information sources	• People increasingly have trust in the food value system and its actors • All actors, especially consumers, benefit from an increased transparency and traceability in the food supply chain	• Healthier people: Significant increase of EU citizens achieving recommended intake of levels of sugar, salt and saturated fat • Food security: Food system is able to satisfy the growing global demand

Fig. 9.9 Projected impacts of EIT food. Source: EIT Food (2018)

9.11 Conclusions

EIT Food is on a mission to create a new horizon for food system innovations and entrepreneurship in Europe. By building bridges between consumers, startups, industry partners, innovators and entrepreneurs, SMEs, and universities, EIT Food aims to create immediate actions from trans-disciplinary expert collaborations to achieve a sustainable and future food system.

Many experts and scholars agree that research, innovation, and education should be viewed through a more holistic lens, and research results better put into practice through innovation which transform knowledge into capacity, resulting in new products and services (Tataj, 2015). Regarding food systems, interventions should be more focused on a specific challenge, concrete, detailed, and transparent, while at the same time keeping in mind the possible contributions of different food system actors. Furthermore, to create these synergies that drive the innovations to begin with, access to support services for startups, SMEs, industry, and lower performing actors of the food system should be improved.

EIT Food implements the organizations' objectives to enhance entrepreneurship on the path towards social, economic, and environmental wellbeing, bringing the European Food system at the helm of innovations of the twenty-first century. By eliminating its fragmented structure, lack of consumer trust, limited innovation, and slow adoption of new technologies, EIT Food is steadily achieving its mission to catalyze the transformation of the food system by building, managing, and empowering a sustainable and trusted multi-stakeholder network of food ecosystem agents of change.

References

Baptista, R. (1998). Clusters, innovation, and growth: A survey of the literature. In G. M. P. Swann, M. Prevezer, & D. Stout (Eds.), *The dynamics of industrial clustering* (pp. 13–51). Oxford: Oxford University Press.

Carayannis, E. G., & Campbell, D. F. J. (2009). 'Mode 3' and 'Quadruple Helix': Toward a 21st century fractal innovation ecosystem. *International Journal of Technology Management, 46*(3/4), 201–234.

Carayannis, E. G., & Campbell, D. F. J. (2010). Triple Helix, Quadruple Helix and Quintuple Helix and how do knowledge, innovation, and environment relate to each other? *International Journal of Social Ecology and. Sustainable Development, 1*(1), 41–69.

Carayannis, E. G., & Campbell, D. F. J. (2012). *Mode 3 knowledge production in Quadruple Helix innovation systems – 21st-century democracy, innovation, and entrepreneurship for development.* New York: Springer.

Carayannis, E. G., Goletsis, Y., & Grigoroudis, E. (2017). Composite innovation metrics: MCDA and the quadruple innovation Helix framework. *Technological Forecasting and Social Change, 131*, 4–17.

Chesbrough, H., Sohyeong, K., & Agogino, A. (2014). Chez Panisse: Building an open innovation ecosystem. *California Management Review, 56*(4), 144–171.

De Bernardi, P., Bertello, A., & Forliano, C. (2019). Unpacking Higher Educational Institutions (HEIs) performances through the institutional logics lens. In *IFKAD 14th international forum on knowledge assets dynamics-knowledge ecosystems and growth* (pp. 1537–1555). Matera: Institute of Knowledge Asset Management (IKAM), Arts for Business Institute, University of Basilicata.

De Bernardi, P., Bertello, A., & Venuti, F. (2019). Online and on-site interactions within alternative food networks: Sustainability impact of knowledge-sharing practices. *Sustainability, 11*(5), 1457.

De Bernardi, P., Bertello, A., Venuti, F., & Zardini, A. (2019). Knowledge transfer driving community-based business models towards sustainable food-related behaviours: A commons perspective. *Knowledge Management Research & Practice,* 1–8. https://doi.org/10.1080/14778238.2019.1664271

De Bernardi, P., Forliano, C., Rotti, R., & Franco, M. (2019). Innovazione e sostenibilità nei nuovi modelli di business del settore vitivinicolo. Analisi del caso Fontanafredda. In F. Moreschi (Ed.), *Il paesaggio vitivinicolo come patrimonio europeo: Aspetti gius-economici, geografici, ambientali, contrattuali, enoturistici, di marketing* (pp. 27–41). Torino: Giappichelli.

European Commission. (2019). *Regional innovation scoreboard 2019.* Retrieved from https://ec.europa.eu/growth/sites/growth/files/ris2019.pdf

European Institute of Innovation & Technology. (2018). *EIT – Making innovation happen.* Retrieved from https://eit.europa.eu/sites/default/files/EIT_Making%20innovation%20happen_leaflet_0.pdf

European Institute of Innovation & Technology. (2019a). *Knowledge and innovation communities.* Retrieved from https://eit.europa.eu/our-communities/eit-innovation-communities

European Institute of Innovation & Technology. (2019b). *EIT at a glance.* Retrieved from https://eit.europa.eu/who-we-are/eit-glance

European Institute of Innovation & Technology. (2019c). *EIT fact sheet. Making innovation happen!* Retrieved from https://eit.europa.eu/sites/default/files/europe_day_-_english_factsheet.pdf

European Institute of Innovation & Technology Food. (2016). *Call for KICs factsheet.* Retrieved from https://eit.europa.eu/sites/default/files/eit_food_factsheet_0.pdf

European Institute of Innovation & Technology Food. (2018). *Strategic agenda 2018–2024 EIF food – Making innovation happen.* Retrieved from https://www.eitfood.eu/media/documents/EIT-StrategicAgenda-Booklet-A4-Final_disclaimer.pdf

European Institute of Innovation & Technology Food. (2019a). *About EIT food. Improving food together*. Retrieved from https://www.eitfood.eu/about-eit-food

European Institute of Innovation & Technology Food. (2019b). *Global food venture programme 2019*. Retrieved from https://www.eitfoodacademy.eu/phd-s/programme-2019/

European Institute of Innovation & Technology Food. (2019c). *EIT Regional innovation schemes (EIT RIS)*. Retrieved from https://eitfood.eu/regional-innovation-scheme/

F6S. (2019). *Where startups grow together*. Retrieved from https://www.f6s.com/f6s

Gawer, A. (2014). Bridging differing perspectives on technological platforms: Toward an integrative framework. *Research Policy, 43*(7), 1239–1249.

Gebruers, K. (2017). Introducing EIT food: Connecting businesses, research centers, universities, and consumers in Europe. *Cereal Foods World, 62*(6), 290–291.

Gill, M., Den Boer, A. C. L., Kok, K. P., Cahill, J., Callenius, C., et al. (2018). A systems approach to research and innovation for food system transformation. In *FIT4FOOD2030*.

Gomes, L. A., Facin, A., Salerno, M. G., & Ikenami, R. K. (2018). Unpacking the innovation ecosystem construct: Evolution, gaps and trends. *Technological Forecasting and Social Change, 136*, 30–48.

Leydesdorff, L., & Etzkowitz, H. (2003). Can "the public" be considered as a fourth helix in university–industry–government relations? Report of the fourth Triple Helix conference. *Science and Public Policy, 30*(1), 55–61.

Nambisan, S., & Baron, R. A. (2013). Entrepreneurship in innovation ecosystems: Entrepreneurs' self–regulatory processes and their implications for new venture success. *Entrepreneurship Theory and Practice, 37*(5), 1071–1097.

Oksanen, K., & Hautamäki, A. (2014). Transforming regions into innovation ecosystems: A model for renewing local industrial structures. *Innovation Journal, 19*(2), 2–16.

Owen, R., Macnaghten, P., & Stilgoe, J. (2012). Responsible research and innovation: From science in society to science for society, with society. *Science and Public Policy, 39*(6), 751–760.

Powell, W. W., Packalen, K. A., & Whittington, K. B. (2010). Organizational and institutional genesis: The emergence of high-tech clusters in the life sciences. In J. Padgett & W. W. Powell (Eds.), *The emergence of organization and markets*. Stanford: Stanford University.

Rao, B. U., & Jimenez, B. T. (2011). A comparative analysis of digital innovation ecosystems. In *2011 Proceedings of PICMET '11: Technology Management in the Energy Smart World (PICMET)* (pp. 1–12).

Stilgoe, J., Lock, S. J., & Wilsdon, J. (2014). Why should we promote public engagement with science? *Public Understanding of Science, 23*(1), 4–15.

Tataj, D. (2015). *Innovation and entrepreneurship. A growth model for Europe beyond the crisis*. New York: Tataj Innovation Library.

Tirabeni, L., De Bernardi, P., Forliano, C., & Franco, M. (2019). How can organisations and business models lead to a more sustainable society? A framework from a systematic review of the industry 4.0. *Sustainability, 11*(22), 6363. https://doi.org/10.3390/su11226363

Volpe, M., Friedl, J., Cavallini, Simona, & Soldi, R. (2016). Using the quadruple helix approach to accelerate the transfer of research and innovation results to regional growth. *European Committee of the Regions.*

Wahlqvist, M. L. (2002). Chronic disease prevention: A life-cycle approach which takes account of the environmental impact and opportunities of food, nutrition and public health policies—The rationale for an eco-nutritionaldisease nomenclature. *Asia Pacific Journal of Clinical Nutrition, 11*, 759–762.